Software Reliability
Engineering

Software Reliability Engineering

More Reliable Software
Faster Development and Testing

John D. Musa

McGraw-Hill

New York   San Francisco   Washington, D.C.   Auckland   Bogotá
Caracas   Lisbon   London   Madrid   Mexico City   Milan
Montreal   New Delhi   San Juan   Singapore
Sydney   Tokyo   Toronto

Library of Congress Cataloging-in-Publication Data

Musa, John D.
    Software reliability engineering : John D. Musa.
        p.   cm.
    Includes bibliographical references and index.
    ISBN 0-07-913271-5
    1. Computer software—Reliability. I. Title.
QA76.76.R44M87   1998
005.1—dc21   98-25765
                                              CIP

*Sci
QH
76.76
.R44
M87
1998*

McGraw-Hill

A Division of The **McGraw·Hill** Companies

1 2 3 4 5 6 7 8 9 0   DOC/DOC   9 0 3 2 1 0 9 8

ISBN 0-07-913271-5

The sponsoring editor for this book was Simon Yates, the editing supervisor was Paul R. Sobel, and the production supervisor was Pamela A. Pelton. It was set in Century Schoolbook by Renee Lipton of McGraw-Hill's Professional Book Group composition unit.

Printed and bound by R. R. Donnelley & Sons Company.

McGraw-Hill books are available at special quantity discounts to use as premiums and sales promotions, or for use in corporate training programs. For more information, please write to the Director of Special Sales, McGraw-Hill, 11 West 19th Street, New York, NY 10011. Or contact your local bookstore.

This book is printed on recycled, acid-free paper containing a minimum of 50% recycled, de-inked fiber.

To Marilyn and Holly

Contents

Introduction: How to Use This Book   xi
Acknowledgments   xiv

Chapter 1. Overview of Software Reliability Engineering   1

1.1 What Is Software Reliability Engineering and How Does It
     Help Development and Testing?   2
1.2 The Software Reliability Engineering Process   5
1.3 Fone Follower   7
1.4 Types of Test   8
1.5 Systems to Test   9
1.6 Frequently Asked Questions   11
     1.6.1 Effectiveness and Benefits   11
     1.6.2 Concepts   15
     1.6.3 Relationships with Other Practices   18
     1.6.4 Application   20
1.7 Background   24
     1.7.1 Software Reliability Concepts   25
     1.7.2 Reliability   28
     1.7.3 Software Reliability and Hardware Reliability   35
     1.7.4 Software Reliability Modeling   36
1.8 Problems   39

Chapter 2. Defining Necessary Reliability   41

2.1 Concepts   41
     2.1.1 Failure and Fault   41
     2.1.2 Failure Severity Classes   42
     2.1.3 Failure Intensity   43
2.2 Procedure   44
     2.2.1 Defining *Failure* with Severity Classes for Product   45
     2.2.2 Choosing a Common Measure for All Associated Systems   46
     2.2.3 Setting a System Failure Intensity Objective for Each System
            to be Tested   46

2.2.4 Determining the Developed Software Failure Intensity
       Objective for the Product and Its Variations   51
2.2.5 Engineering Strategies to Meet the Developed Software
       Failure Intensity Objectives   53
2.3 Special Situations   56
2.3.1 Other Failure Groupings   56
2.3.2 Allocation of Failure Intensity Objective to Components 57
2.3.3 Software Safety and Ultrareliability   59
2.4 Frequently Asked Questions   62
2.4.1 Definition of Failure   62
2.4.2 Failure Severity Classes   64
2.4.3 Setting Failure Intensity Objectives   65
2.4.4 Concepts   69
2.4.5 Application   73
2.5 Background   77
2.5.1 Defining Failure with Severity Classes   77
2.5.2 Setting System Failure Intensity Objectives   87
2.5.3 Availability   91
2.5.4 Reliability Combinatorics   92
2.6 Problems   94

Chapter 3. Developing Operational Profiles   97

3.1 Concepts   97
3.2 Procedure   101
3.2.1 Determining Operational Modes   102
3.2.2 Identifying Operation Initiators   103
3.2.3 Choosing Tabular or Graphical Representation   104
3.2.4 Creating an Operations List   105
3.2.5 Determining Occurrence Rates   112
3.2.6 Determining Occurrence Probabilities   115
3.3 Special Situations   116
3.3.1 Handling the Evolution of the Definition of Operation
       during System Development   117
3.3.2 Applying the Module Usage Table   118
3.4 Frequently Asked Questions   119
3.4.1 Uses   120
3.4.2 Concepts   122
3.4.3 Application   124
3.5 Background   129
3.5.1 Determining Operational Modes   129
3.5.2 Operations and Runs   130
3.6 Problems   133

Chapter 4. Preparing for Test   135

4.1 Concepts   136
4.2 Procedure   140
4.2.1 Preparing Test Cases   140
4.2.2 Preparing Test Procedures   146
4.3 Frequently Asked Questions   150
4.4 Background   156

        4.4.1 Test Efficiency   156
        4.4.2 Increasing Test Efficiency by Using Run Categories   157
        4.4.3 A Graphical View of Test Selection   159
    4.5 Problems   161

Chapter 5. Executing Test   163

    5.1 Allocating Test Time   163
    5.2 Invoking Test   164
    5.3 Identifying System Failures   168
        5.3.1 Analyzing Test Output for Deviations   168
        5.3.2 Determining Which Deviations Are Failures   169
        5.3.3 Establishing When Failures Occurred   171
    5.4 Special Situations   174
        5.4.1 Establishing When Failures Occurred for Tests on Multiple
               Configurations   174
        5.4.2 Uncertainties in Establishing When Failures Occurred   175
        5.4.3 Multiple Versions in the Field   178
    5.5 Frequently Asked Questions   178
        5.5.1 Test Process   179
        5.5.2 Counting Failures   182
        5.5.3 Measuring When Failures Occurred   186
    5.6 Background   192
        5.6.1 Allocating Test Time   192
        5.6.2 Invoking Tests   192
        5.6.3 Counting Failures   193
    5.7 Problems   196

Chapter 6. Applying Failure Data to Guide Decisions   197

    6.1 Certification Test   198
    6.2 Reliability Growth Test   201
    6.3 Special Situations   205
        6.3.1 Evolving Programs   205
        6.3.2 Unreported Failures   208
        6.3.3 Certification Test at Different Risk Levels and
               Discrimination Ratios   213
        6.3.4 Operational Profile Variation   217
    6.4 Frequently Asked Questions   221
        6.4.1 Theory   221
        6.4.2 Application   227
        6.4.3 Special Situations   238
    6.5 Problems   239

Chapter 7. Deploying Software Reliability Engineering   241

    7.1 Persuasion   241
    7.2 Executing the Deployment   243
    7.3 Using a Consultant   247
        7.3.1 Consultee   247
        7.3.2 Consultant   248
    7.4 Frequently Asked Questions   249

Chapter 8. Software Reliability Models   259

  8.1 General Characteristics   261
      8.1.1 Random Process   263
      8.1.2 With and Without Fault Removal   265
      8.1.3 Particularization   265
  8.2 Classification   266
  8.3 Comparison   267
      8.3.1 Time Domains   269
      8.3.2 Model Groups   279
  8.4 Recommended Models   290
      8.4.1 Description   292
      8.4.2 Interpretation of Parameters of Logarithmic Poisson
             Execution Time Model   311
      8.4.3 Derivation of Models   315
      8.4.4 Parameter Prediction   320
      8.4.5 Parameter Estimation   334
  8.5 Frequently Asked Questions   338

Appendix A. Software Reliability Engineering Process Step by Step   341

Appendix B. Template for Workshops   343

  B.1 Defining System Workshop (Chap. 1)   344
  B.2 Defining Necessary Reliability Workshop (Chap. 2)   344
  B.3 Developing Operational Profiles Workshop (Chap. 3)   345
  B.4 Preparing for Test Workshop (Chap.4)   346
  B.5 Executing Test Workshop (Chap. 5}   346
  B.6 Applying Failure Data to Guide Decisions Workshop (Chap. 6) 346

Appendix C. Glossary   347

Appendix D. Summary of Useful Formulas   355

**Appendix E. Software Reliability Engineering and Testing
Functions Aided by Software Tools**   357

Appendix F. Using CASRE   359

  F.1 Installation   360
  F.2 Creating the Failure Data File for CASRE   361
  F.3 Executing CASRE   362
  F.4 Interpreting CASRE Results   365
  F.5 Problems   366

Appendix G. Problem Solutions   367

Appendix H. References to Users of Software Reliability Engineering   371

Bibliography   375
Index   381

Introduction: How to Use This Book

I designed this book with the goal of most efficiently teaching you what software reliability engineering is and how to apply it in software development and testing and software development. My object is to concretely help you deal with the conflicting and very stressful pressures that are probably impinging on you (If they aren't, where do you work and do they have any job openings?!). Software reliability engineering is a skill that can make you more competitive, whether you develop or use software-based systems or are a university student learning to become a software developer or user. The book focuses on practice, presenting methods that have been successfully used in many applications, and avoiding ideas that have not yet been sufficiently proved in actual use.

As you will see, I pay particular attention to testing, but with a very broad perspective. For example, I expect that testers will participate on the system engineering team and will directly interface with users of the software-based product. Also, I envision that many other software development personnel will be involved with testing and must therefore have a broad understanding of it.

I expect that the book will be of special value to you if you are a software tester, software developer, system engineer, system architect, quality assurance engineer, reliability engineer, or development manager of a project that contains software; or, of course, a student preparing for one or more of these roles. It is intended to help you as a text in learning the subject, a deskside companion as you start to apply software reliability engineering, and a reference in handling special situations you may encounter. Thus you will see particular emphasis on simplifying the material and organizing it for easy learning. The organization and presentation of the material evolved through seven years of experience teaching this subject to several thousand practitioners in many different organizations and a wide variety of software applications, and guiding them in learning it. I pay special attention to describing the software reliability engineering process step by step. The table of contents reinforces this hierarchy and makes it easy to find the detail for any step. Finally, I devoted special effort to preparing an index with multiple terms for recalling a topic.

The core sections (sections other than frequently asked questions, special situations, and background) of Chaps. 1 to 6 include only the material that you need to know for the common situations you will encounter in practice. The software reliability engineering process used in practice is described in Chap. 1. The chapter structure of the book reflects the process, each of Chaps. 2 through 6 covering one of the principal activities. I illustrate the process throughout by a unified simple example, Fone Follower. This example is adapted from a real project, but with proprietary data deleted and the material simplified for learning.

Each chapter includes up to three supplementary sections: special situations, frequently asked questions, and background. The special situations sections present techniques that are usually needed only for certain projects and systems. The frequently asked questions sections provide some 350 of the better questions (and answers) that have been posed to me in my experience teaching several thousand practitioners and consulting for various organizations. They represent the backgrounds, ways of learning, and perspectives of different people working on different projects. You may find that some of them correspond with yours. Thus they may help you better understand the topics. Professors should find many of these useful to assign as exercises, in addition to the problems provided at the end of many chapters. The background sections contain supplementary information that can enrich your understanding of the chapter but is not essential to exercising the practice. For example, it may present theory or explanation that justifies or supports various activities of the practice. The order of the supplementary sections is a natural one; you progress from material that occurs sometimes in practice to an elucidation of practice to material that describes the rationale behind the practice but doesn't have to be understood to perform the practice.

Both the frequently asked questions and the background sections may cover topics already treated in the core sections. However, they do so from different perspectives or greater depth. I considered the possibility of integrating this material with the corresponding material in the core sections but deliberately decided not to do so. Most practitioners told me that the core sections should be as simple and short as possible, so that they could learn the essential basics quickly, and that all supplementary material should be separated from them.

Chapter 7 discusses how to deploy software reliability engineering in your organization. The background material needed to enrich your understanding of software reliability models is quite extensive, hence it is covered in a separate chapter (Chap. 8).

Appendix A provides a step-by-step outline of the software reliability engineering process; I recommend you keep it by your desk as a guide and checkoff list the first time you use software reliability engineering. In my classes for practitioners, we learn by doing through workshops. Each workshop has teams of participants organized on project lines. After we cover each chapter, each work group discusses the material related to that chapter and tries to apply it to their project. If university students are working on a sample software engineering project as part of their total course work, the workshops can integrate very nicely with it. I have provided the template that we use to guide the workshops in App. B. This will help guide project teams that are deploying software reliability engineering, particularly if they are using a self-study approach.

Appendix C contains a glossary of terms used in this book and App. D a summary of the few formulas you may need. Appendix E lists the software reliability engineering and testing functions that can be helped with software tools.

Appendix F describes how to use CASRE, the Computer-Aided Software Reliability Estimation tool (Nikora 1994). Although not the only software reliability estimation tool, I chose it because of its convenient graphical user interface and its wide availability through the CD ROM included in the *Handbook of Software Reliability Engineering* (Lyu 1996). CASRE consists of a graphical interface and the SMERFS (Statistical Modeling and Estimation of Reliability Function for Software) software reliability estimation program (Farr and Smith 1992). CASRE developers plan a new version with an improved user interface. We can also expect a new version of SMERFS called SMERFS Cubed (SMERFS 3), with a graphical interface of its own. Both new programs will hopefully be distributed on the Internet (see Software Reliability Engineering web site below).

Some chapters include problems designed to reinforce the material presented; I have provided the answers to these problems in App. G. Appendix H is a sampling of references to papers and articles that have been published by users of software reliability engineering. These papers may be useful to you as models of applications, particularly when the application is similar to yours.

University students, researchers, and others who wish to explore the theory of software reliability engineering in depth will find Musa, Iannnino, and Okumoto (1987) an excellent reference. The *IEEE Transactions on Software Engineering* and the *IEEE Transactions on Reliability* frequently publish papers in this area.

The IEEE Technical Committee on Software Reliability Engineering, a branch of the Software Engineering Technical Council of the IEEE Computer Society, is generally considered the leading professional organization in this field (web site http://www.tcse.org). Among other activities, it publishes a newsletter and it sponsors the annual International Symposium on Software Reliability Engineering. Other relevant professional organizations include the IEEE Reliability Society, the American Society for Quality Control and The European organization ENCRESS (web site http://www.csr.ncl.ac.uk/clubs/encress.html). There is an electronic bulletin board on the Internet (subscribe at vishwa@hac2arpa.hac.com,post to sw-rel@igate1.hac com).

I personally maintain a regularly updated Software Reliability Engineering web site (http://members.aol.com/JohnDMusa/). It provides information on a course I teach based on this book. In the course, you apply software reliability engineering to your own job and receive guidance and feedback. The site also includes a general overview, a section for managers, a list of published articles by those who have applied this practice, a Question of the Month (with answer), information on software reliability estimation programs, links to other sites, and other resources.

Acknowledgments

I am grateful to the many colleagues who have read and commented on part or all of this book, including James Cusick, Willa Ehrlich, Susie Hill, Steve Meyer, Steve Peirce, and Ray Sandfoss of AT&T; Prof. Mary Helanger, Linköping University, Sweden; James Widmaier, National Security Agency; Prof. Mladen Vouk, North Carolina State University; and Prof. Carol Smidts, University of Maryland. I am indebted to Adrian Dolinsky for providing some of the questions in Chap. 7. Particular thanks go to Kathy Yale for the enormous and demanding work of word processing that has made the book a reality.

Feedback from managers and practitioners in my classes has been invaluable; they include such organizations as ATT&T, Cisco Systems, Computing Devices Canada, Eastman Kodak, Hewlett-Packard, Lucent Technologies, Microsoft, Motorola, National Security Agency, Nokia, Tandem Computers, Texas Instruments, and many more too numerous to list.

Some material from Musa, J. D., A. Iannino, and K. Okumoto, *Software Reliability: Measurement, Prediction, Application,* New York: McGraw-Hill, 1987 has been incorporated, generally in modified and updated form, with permission.

John D. Musa

Software Reliability Engineering

Overview of
Software Reliability Engineering

Be sure to read the Introduction to the book before starting this chapter; it explains the organization of all the chapters.

Software development is plagued with one or more high risks:

1. Unreliability of the released product

2. Missed schedules

3. Cost overruns

These situations can lead to loss of market share and/or loss of profitability. Hence the pressure we developers and testers feel is often overwhelming.

In response to this problem, much attention has been given to the mechanics of development and testing, and many tools have been built to support the process. Researchers have addressed the theory of software development and testing and the many difficult questions it entails. However, we have paid too little attention to the *engineering* of reliability in software-based products. *Engineering* software reliability means developing a product in such a way that the product reaches the "market" at the right time, at an acceptable cost, and with satisfactory reliability. You will note that *market* is in quotes; this is to convey a broad meaning beyond the world of commercial products. Even products built for the military and for governments have a market in the sense that product users have alternatives that they can and will choose if a product is too late, too costly, or too unreliable.

The traditional view of development and testing does not provide us with enough power to achieve this engineering goal. Software reliability engineering takes a much broader, more proactive view. Software reliability engineering, for example, has shown that the most efficient testing involves activities that occur throughout the product life cycle and that interface with system engineering and system design tasks. Software reliability engineering therefore empowers testers to take leadership positions in meeting user needs. It involves system engineers, system architects, potential users, managers (Musa, 1996c), and developers as collaborators (Musa, 1996a, 1996b, 1997c, 1997d, 1997g; Musa and Widmaier, 1996).

The standard definition of *reliability* for software (Musa, Iannino, and Okumoto, 1987) is the probability of execution without failure for some specified interval of natural units or time. Thus we use a definition that is compatible with that used for hardware reliability, although the mechanisms of failure may be different. The compatibility enables us to work with systems that are composed of both software and hardware components.

The product characteristics described—reliability, development time, and cost—are attributes of a more general characteristic—product quality. Product quality is the right balance among these characteristics. Getting a good balance means you must pick quantitative objectives for the three characteristics and measure the characteristics as development proceeds.

Projects, of course, have for some time been able to set objectives for delivery date and cost of products and measure progress toward these objectives. What has been lacking until recently has been the ability to do the same thing for reliability for software-based systems. Since the 1940s, we have been able to set reliability objectives and measure reliability for pure hardware systems. However, the proportion of such systems is now rapidly diminishing to near nonexistence, hence the need for and the development of software reliability engineering.

1.1 What Is Software Reliability Engineering and How Does It Help Development and Testing?

Software reliability engineering is the only standard, proven best practice that empowers testers and developers to simultaneously

1. Ensure that product reliability meets user needs

2. Speed the product to market faster

3. Reduce product cost

4. Improve customer satisfaction and reduce the risk of angry users

5. Increase their productivity

You can use software reliability engineering for any release of any software-based product, beginning at the start of any release cycle. Hence you can easily handle legacy products. We use the term *software-based* to emphasize that there are no pure software systems; therefore, hardware must always be addressed in your analysis. Before applying software reliability engineering to the testing of any product, you must first test (or verify in some other manner) and then integrate the units or modules into complete functions that you can execute.

Software reliability engineering works by applying two fundamental ideas. First, it delivers the desired functionality for the product under development much more efficiently by quantitatively characterizing the expected use of the product and using this information to

1. Precisely focus resources on the most used and/or most critical functions

2. Make testing realistically represent field conditions

Critical means having great extra value when successful or great extra impact when failing. This value or impact can be with respect to human life, cost, or system capability.

Second, software reliability engineering balances customer needs for reliability, development time, and cost precisely and hence more effectively. To do so, it sets quantitative reliability as well as schedule and cost objectives. It engineers strategies to meet these objectives. Finally, software reliability engineering tracks reliability in test and uses it as a release criterion. With software reliability engineering you deliver "just enough" reliability and avoid both the excessive costs and development time involved in "playing it safe" and the risk of angry users and product disaster resulting from an unreliable product.

Software reliability engineering is based on a solid body of theory (Musa, Iannino, and Okumoto, 1987) that includes operational profiles, random process software reliability models, statistical estimation, and sequential sampling theory. Software personnel have practiced software reliability engineering extensively over a period dating back to 1973 (Musa and Iannino, 1991b). At AT&T it has been a best current practice (BCP) since May 1991 (Donnelly, Everett, Musa, and Wilson, 1996). Selection as an AT&T BCP was significant because very high standards were imposed. First, you had to use the proposed practice on several (typically at least 8 to 10) projects and achieve significant, documented benefit to cost ratios, measured in financial terms. You then developed a detailed description of the practice and how you used it on the projects, along with a business case for adopting it. Committees of experienced third- and fourth-level managers subjected the description and the case to a probing lengthy review. Typically, the review lasted several months, with detailed examinations being delegated to first-level software managers and senior software developers. The review of the software reliability engineering BCP proposal involved more than 70 such people. Comments requiring action before final review of the proposal exceeded 100. Even then, the software reliability engineering BCP was only one of five approved from the set of some 30 proposals made in 1991.

In addition, the American Institute of Aeronautics and Astronautics approved software reliability engineering as a standard in 1993, resulting in significant impact in the aerospace industry (AIAA, 1992). A major handbook publisher issued a *Handbook of Software Reliability Engineering* in 1996, further evidence of the field's importance (Lyu, 1996). The IEEE has also been active in developing standards for software reliability engineering.

Organizations that have used software reliability engineering include Alcatel, AT&T, Bellcore, CNES (France), ENEA (Italy), Ericsson Telecom (Sweden), France Telecom, Hewlett-Packard, Hitachi (Japan) IBM, NASA's Jet Propulsion Laboratory, NASA's Space Shuttle project, Lockheed-Martin, Lucent Technologies, Microsoft, Mitre, Motorola, Nortel, North Carolina State University, Raytheon, Saab Military Aircraft (Sweden), Tandem Computers, the U.S. Air Force, and the U.S. Marine Corps, to name just a few. There is a selection of papers and articles by users of software reliability engineering, describing their experience with it, in App. H.

Tierney (1997) reported the results of a survey taken in late 1997 that showed that Microsoft has applied software reliability engineering in 50 percent of its software development groups, including projects such as Windows NT and Word. The benefits they observed were increased test coverage, improved estimates of amount of test required, useful metrics that helped them establish ship criteria, and improved specification reviews.

AT&T's Operations Technology Center in the Network and Computing Services Division has used software reliability engineering as part of its standard software development process for several years. This process is currently undergoing ISO certification. The Operations Technology Center was a primary software development organization for the AT&T business unit that won the Malcolm Baldrige National Quality Award in 1994. At that time, it had the highest percentage of projects using software reliability engineering in AT&T. Another interesting observation is that four of the first five software winners of the former AT&T Bell Laboratories President's Quality Award used software reliability engineering.

The International Definity project represents one application of software reliability engineering. They applied it along with some related software technologies. In comparison with a previous software release that did not use these technologies, customer-found faults decreased by a factor of 10, resulting in significantly increased customer satisfaction. Consequently, sales increased by a factor of 10. There were reductions by a factor of 2 in system test interval and system test costs, 30 percent in total project development interval, and a factor of 10 in program maintenance costs (Abramson et al., 1992).

As further witness to the value of software reliability engineering, growth of this field is very strong. The IEEE Computer Society's Technical Committee on Software Reliability Engineering grew from around 40 people at its founding in 1990 to over 1000 in mid 1996, an annual growth rate of about 70 percent. Annual growth of software reliability engineering research in the same period was about 35 percent, as judged by the number of papers submitted to the annual International Symposium on Software Reliability Engineering (ISSRE).

Experience with the application of software reliability engineering indicates a cost of implementation of around 0.1 to 0.2 percent of project development costs for most projects. This proportion is smaller for large projects and larger for small projects. For small projects, the total effort is usually no more than 1 staff month. This includes the costs of education, developing operational profiles, and data collection and processing.

1.2   The Software Reliability Engineering Process

The process of applying software reliability engineering first requires that you determine which systems are associated with the product you will test. In doing this you will need to understand the types of software reliability engineering test. Consequently, we will first look at the latter topic and then address the issue of determining which associated systems to test.

The software reliability engineering process proper consists of five activities. They are define "necessary" reliability, develop operational profiles, prepare for test, execute test, and apply failure data to guide decisions. They are illustrated in Fig. 1.1, with the project phases in which you customarily perform them shown at the bottom of the figure. Note that "execute test" and "apply failure data to guide decisions" occur simultaneously and are closely linked, with the relative emphasis on application increasing with time as the amount of failure data available increases. Each of these activities is discussed at length in a chapter of this book (Chaps. 2 to 6).

The process diagram, for simplicity, shows only the *predominant* order of work flow, indicated by the arrows, in the software reliability engineering process. In actuality, the tasks frequently iterate and feed

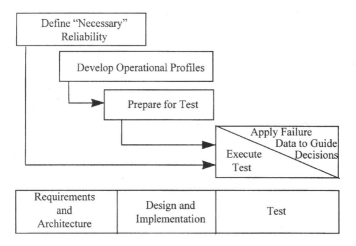

Figure 1.1   Software reliability engineering process diagram.

back to earlier tasks in a manner analogous to the spiral (as contrasted to the waterfall) model of the overall software development process. Just as some requirements and architecture changes may follow test in the software development process, changes in defining "necessary" reliability may follow executing test and applying failure data to guide decisions in the software reliability engineering process.

The Post Delivery and Maintenance life-cycle phase, which follows Test, is not shown in Fig. 1.1. During this phase, you can determine the reliability actually achieved and the operational profile really experienced. This information affects the definition of "necessary" reliability and the development of the operational profile for the next release. It can result in reengineering of the product and the development process.

Testers conduct the first two activities, "define necessary reliability" and "develop operational profiles," in partnership with system engineers. We originally thought that these activities should be assigned solely to system engineers and system architects. However, this did not work well in practice. Testers depend on these activities and are hence more strongly motivated than system engineers and system architects to ensure their successful completion. We resolved the problem when we made testers part of the system engineering and system architecture team.

This approach also had unexpected side benefits. Testers had much more contact with product users, which was very valuable for knowing what system behavior would be unacceptable and how unacceptable it would be and for understanding how users would employ the product.

System engineers and system architects obtained a greater appreciation of testing and of where requirements and design needed to be made less ambiguous and more precise, so that test planning, test case, and test procedure design could proceed. System testers made valuable contributions to architecture reviews, often pointing out important capabilities that were missing.

The architecture phase includes the software reliability engineering activity of selection of the mix of strategies of fault prevention, fault removal, and fault tolerance. Thus it affects both product and process design. Testers may not perform this activity, but they need to understand it, because it will affect them.

1.3   Fone Follower

Let's consider an illustration that we will apply throughout this book to help make the process of applying software reliability engineering more concrete. The illustration is drawn from an actual project, with the details modified for the purposes of simplicity and protecting any proprietary information. This particular example was selected because it deals with telephone service and hence can be understood by almost anyone. Also, it was small (total staff less than 10, extra effort required by software reliability engineering about 1 staff month). It in no way implies that software reliability engineering is limited in application to telecommunications or to small projects. In fact, software reliability engineering has been applied to systems ranging from 5000 to 10,000,000 lines of source code. Applications outside of telecommunications include (at least) medical imaging, knowledge-based systems, a wide area network-based education system, a capital management and accounting system, a compiler, terminal firmware, instrument firmware, military systems, and space systems.

Fone Follower is a system that enables you to forward incoming telephone calls (fax or voice) anywhere in the world, including to cellular or other portable phones. You, as user, call Fone Follower and enter the telephone numbers at which you plan to be as a function of time.

Calls from the telephone network that would normally be routed to your telephone are sent to Fone Follower. It forwards both fax and voice calls in accordance with the program you entered. If there is no response to a voice call, you are paged if you have pager service. If there is still no response or if you don't have pager service, the voice calls are forwarded to your voice mail.

Fone Follower used a vendor-supplied operating system whose reliability was not known at the time. Subscribers view service as the combination of standard telephone service with the call forwarding provided by Fone Follower.

1.4 Types of Test

There are two types of software reliability engineering test, reliability growth test and certification test. These types are not related to phases of test such as unit test, subsystem test, system test, or beta test, but rather to the objectives of test. The main objective of reliability growth test is to find and remove faults. During reliability growth test, you use software reliability engineering to estimate and track reliability. Testers and development managers apply the reliability information to guide development and release. You typically use reliability growth test for the system test phase of software you develop in your own organization. It can also be used in beta test if you are resolving failures (removing the faults causing them) as you test. To obtain "good" (with moderate ranges of uncertainty) estimates of failure intensity, you need a minimum number of failures in your sample, often 10 to 20.

Reliability growth test includes feature, load, and regression test. *Feature test* is a test in which operations are executed separately, with interactions and effects of the field environment minimized. Sometimes interactions are minimized by reinitializing the system between the operations. *Load test* involves executing operations simultaneously, at the same rates and with the same other environmental conditions as those that will occur in the field. Thus the same interactions and impact of environmental conditions will occur as can be expected in the field. Acceptance test and performance test are types of load test. *Regression test* is the execution of some (usually randomly selected) or all feature tests after each system build that has a significant change. You should include all critical operations in the regression test suite.

Load test typically involves competition for system resources with the queueing and timing problems that can result. Also, there is frequently a degradation of data with time. The foregoing factors thus can uncover potential field failures resulting from interaction that would not be stimulated by feature and regression test. Although interaction is somewhat more important for multiuser systems, it is also important for single-user systems such as software executing on personal computers, because there can be different interactions among operations resulting from the sequences in which they execute.

Certification test does not involve debugging. There is no attempt to "resolve" failures you identify by determining the faults that are causing them and removing the faults. The system must be stable. No changes can be occurring, either due to new features or fault removal. With certification test you make a binary decision: accept the software or reject the software and return it to its supplier for rework. In certification test, you require a much smaller sample of failures. In fact, you can make decisions without any failures occurring if the period of execution without failure is sufficiently long. We generally use certification test only for load test (not feature or regression test).

1.5   Systems to Test

You can define "system" in whatever way is convenient for purposes of study or analysis. It can consist of any combination of hardware, software, and personnel elements. In general, you will define a "system" for each entity you will separately test.

We will, of course, want to test the actual product we are developing as a system. We will use reliability growth test as long as we are developing even part of the product. This may be followed by certification test as a rehearsal if our customer will be conducting an acceptance test. If we are simply integrating the product from components, we will conduct only certification test of the integrated product. We will also want to identify major variations of the product as systems to be tested. A different hardware configuration of the product (that accomplishes the same functions) is essentially a different system. You may have substantially different versions because you must be able to execute on different platforms or with different operating systems. International products may have to operate with different interfaces in different countries.

If you have *supersystems* or systems in which the product operates as a component, these should be considered as potential systems to be separately tested. If users judge the product by the reliability of the supersystem and if the interaction of the product with the other systems comprising the supersystem is complex and hence difficult to define, you will probably want to test that supersystem separately. This is because independent testing of the product with an interface driver will be chancy, because you may not characterize the interface correctly. You often test supersystems in the case of packaged software. Other illustrations include printers and personal computers. If you test one or more supersystems that involve the product, you may also want to test the corresponding supersystems for the variations of that product.

Some supersystems can't be practically or economically tested in system test, but they can be in beta test and hence must be scheduled for that phase. Beta test, of course, involves direct execution in the field environment, identifying failures, and applying the failure data. Beta testing does not require that you develop operational profiles, prepare test cases and procedures, or invoke test cases with test procedures.

You will also want to test *acquired software* (not developed by your organization) components as systems in their own right if their reliability is unknown or questionable and if early detection of unreliability can prevent schedule delays or cost overruns. Ordinarily such testing is necessary only for the first release of a product, although it could be necessary for a subsequent release if that release requires a new or substantially changed acquired component. Acquired software includes off-the-shelf or packaged software, software that is reused from another product or a component or object library, and subcontracted software. If you know that a component has sufficient reliability for your product from previous experience, it is not necessary to test it separately. If you are not sure of the component but have a good relationship with the supplier, you may decide to have them perform reliability growth test, under surveillance, and skip the acceptance testing, saving time and cost. Note that size is an important factor in deciding whether to test a component. If the component is a major one, testing it separately can be cost effective. If you have small acquired software components (including objects), separate testing will be cost effective only if they are used in many systems.

There appears to be great potential in the application of software reliability engineering to testing object libraries needed for object-oriented development, because you can expect to use the objects in many systems. In fact, the further growth and use of object-oriented development may depend on this marriage of technologies: Object-oriented concepts have made better modularization possible, but we often are not realizing the promise and benefits of reuse because developers (probably rightly) have enormous resistance to using objects of undetermined reliability.

There is, of course, a limit to how many systems you will select for separate testing. Each separate test involves extra cost. Although you can conduct multiple tests in parallel, at some point limited people and computer resources may cause schedule delays as well. Costs include developing one or more additional operational profile(s), developing test cases and procedures, and executing the tests. You should select an additional system for separate test only when the benefits of separate test outweigh the extra time and costs involved. The benefits are the reductions in risk of customer dissatisfaction or schedule delays (both leading to lost market share) and reduction in risk of extra development costs.

The costs of separately testing an additional system may be reduced if a system has an operational architecture (its components correspond to operations or groups of operations), because it's relatively simple to obtain operational profiles for the components and hence relatively easy to separately test the components.

Although it may not be cost effective to test more than a few systems separately, it is not as expensive and hence it may be practical to determine failure intensities for a larger number of separate components that are tested together. This is because you only have to classify failures by components and measure processing done for those components (either by counting natural or time units expended). However, because of the errors in estimating failure intensity from small failure samples, making multiple failure intensity estimates may not be practical.

In the case of Fone Follower, we tested the operating system acquired component, Fone Follower itself, and the supersystem that includes the telephone network and Fone Follower. We could have used certification test for the product as well, but we did not do so because it would have lengthened time to delivery.

1.6   Frequently Asked Questions

In this section we will first look at questions that have been raised concerning the need for applying software reliability engineering and the benefits that result from using it. The following sets of questions deal with clarifying the concepts of software reliability engineering, its relationships with other practices, and where and when it can be applied.

1.6.1   Effectiveness and benefits

1   Why is software reliability so important in the area of software quality?

ANSWER: Software reliability is a very specific and measurable property in the larger concept of software quality, which can be rather fuzzy. It is probably the most inclusive and important property because it deals with freedom from departures from user-specified behavior during execution. In other words, the software executes in the way the user wants it to. Other aspects of quality not incorporated in reliability (for example, maintainability) will be strictly secondary if the program does not operate satisfactorily.

2   How does software reliability compare in effectiveness with other approaches to quantifying quality?

ANSWER: Software reliability is the most important aspect of quality to the user because it quantifies how well the software product will function with respect to his or her needs. Certain other measures of quality may have some relation to software reliability, but they are much less direct. For example, the number of faults remaining has some connection to reliability, but it is developer-oriented and it does not indicate impact on operation. Further, you cannot measure but only infer faults remaining, and this with rather poor accuracy. The number of faults found has *no* correlation with reliability. If only a few faults are found, this can indicate either reliable software or poorly tested, unreliable software. The number of problems uncovered in design or code inspection has properties similar to faults found as a quality measure. Other measures such as program complexity are even more remote from the user's concept of quality.

3 Doesn't the copying of hardware reliability by software reliability result in an inappropriate technology?

ANSWER: Software reliability was *not* copied from hardware reliability. It was developed with full cognizance of the differences. However, we deliberately defined software reliability to be mathematically compatible so that the reliability of systems with both components could be evaluated. We studied but rejected other approaches such as fault counting because of their incompatibility, among other reasons. An incompatible definition would not be practically useful because real systems always have components of both types.

4 Can software reliability engineering help us with Total Quality Management, as characterized by the Baldrige award?

ANSWER: Software reliability engineering is integrally connected and is in fact a *keystone* to Total Quality Management. It provides a user-oriented metric that is highly correlated with customer satisfaction. It is a keystone in the sense that you cannot manage quality without a user-oriented metric of system reliability, and you cannot determine reliability of software-based systems without a software reliability measure.

Software reliability engineering is associated with most of the major categories in the Baldrige award scoring system.

5 Some people say that software reliability engineering is inadequate because it does not focus sufficient attention on preventing catastrophic failures. Is this true?

ANSWER: No, the statement represents a failure to understand software reliability engineering properly. Catastrophic failures generally represent some fraction of all failures. Hence tracking and reducing all failures will also reduce the proportion of catastrophic failures.

6 We resolve every failure that occurs in test. Why then do we need to estimate software reliability?

ANSWER: Because otherwise, you will have no idea of how much additional testing you should do.

7 Can software reliability concepts contribute to root cause analysis (the determination of the ultimate causes of faults, done with the objective of improving the software engineering process that generated the faults)?

ANSWER: Yes. The operational profile (defined in Chap. 3) highlights those functions that execute frequently. Failure reports related to these functions or to failures with high severity of impact should receive priority in root cause analysis studies. Then quality improvement actions undertaken on the basis of root cause analysis will address those causes first that will have the greatest effect on customer perception of quality.

8 How can we use software reliability engineering to improve the design and test process?

ANSWER: We can use software reliability engineering to improve the design and test process in several ways:

a. We can use knowledge of the operational profile (defined in Chap. 3) to focus design effort on the most frequently used functions.

b. Driving test with the operational profile will activate the most-frequently used functions first, allowing us to find and remove their faults first and thus reducing failure intensity rapidly.

c. The failure intensity objective you establish with the customer suggests the level of design and test effort you need and what range of techniques you should employ.

d. The failure intensity objective provides a release criterion for determining when to stop system test.

e. Measurement of reliability differences resulting from different software engineering techniques, along with the cost and time duration associated with them, will provide the basis for selecting these techniques on future projects.

9 Can you beneficially apply software reliability engineering to "one shot" programs that you rapidly construct in real time from off-the-shelf components and use for just a limited period? Illustrations include user-programmed systems and agents and applets on the Internet.

ANSWER: Yes, although clearly not in the same sense you would apply it for commercial software you expect to have substantial use. A useful analysis would be to determine the reliability level to which you would have to build the components such that systems of acceptable reliability could be constructed.

10   Why do we need to measure software reliability? Wouldn't it be more effective to establish the best software development process we can and apply it vigorously?

ANSWER: The essential question is, What do you mean by "best"? Best must be defined by someone, preferably the users of the ultimate software-based product. A definition without measurement is very imprecise. We need to know the *level* of reliability that users require. And note that highest level may be wrong because the resulting development time and cost may be unacceptable. Finally, we have no satisfactory way of determining the activities that should be incorporated into a process unless we can measure their effectiveness in yielding desired product characteristics such as reliability, development time, and cost.

11   Does the Capability Maturity Model (CMM) sponsored by the Software Engineering Institute require measurement of reliability of software-based systems?

ANSWER: Yes, explicitly at levels 4 and 5 and indirectly at level 3.

12   Where can software reliability engineering make its greatest contributions in improving the software development process?

ANSWER: In speeding up the development of function (and at the same time reducing cost) for a product while maintaining the necessary reliability.

13 My company is evolving from a developer of software to a company that primarily integrates software developed by others. How will this affect the software reliability engineering we do?

ANSWER: You will continue to have a strong need for software reliability engineering because you must continue to ensure the reliability of the final product and achieve the right balance among reliability, development time, and cost. In fact, you probably will have a greater need for software reliability engineering because you will want to certification test many of the components being delivered to you. However, you will find less need for reliability growth testing.

14 Can we use software reliability engineering for ultrareliable systems?

ANSWER: Yes. Some statisticians have argued that you cannot, because the time required for testing would be impractically long. This view is based on a hardware perspective that usually does not hold for software. Usually only a limited number of the software operations must be ultrareliable, and they are usually ones that do not occur frequently. With the use of appropriate software architecture such as firewalls, the operations can be isolated. Because they are usually not invoked very frequently, they can be certified to very high levels of reliability with practically achievable amounts of testing. Finally, because processing is cheap and rapidly becoming cheaper, you can speed up testing by performing it on many processors in parallel.

15 When do you involve users in software reliability engineering?

ANSWER: You involve users in setting product and supersystem failure intensity objectives and in developing operational profiles (including determining operational modes). If users specify acceptance tests, they will be involved in them.

16 Can you apply software reliability engineering to systems with a low production volume?

ANSWER: Yes. The only difference is that the product budget will probably be lower. Hence the resources available for test will be less. As a result, you may feel more pressure to keep the number of systems tested, the number of operational modes, the number of operations, the number of test cases, and the amount of test time low.

17 Sometimes I hear of new software reliability engineering ideas that I do not find in this book. Why?

ANSWER: We have deliberately limited this book to ideas that have been proved in practice, unless noted otherwise. Some of the ideas you have heard about may indeed be promising, and some of these may be proven in practice in the years to come. What you see here is the state of the practice at the beginning of 1998.

1.6.2 Concepts

1 The term *software reliability* is disturbing. Software doesn't wear out like hardware, so how can you apply a hardware concept?

ANSWER: First, the term *software reliability* is in general use, like it or not. However, we have deliberately decided to promote the usage further to emphasize compatibility of software and hardware reliability calculations and their joint use in computing system reliability. It is true that software doesn't wear out in the same sense as hardware, although it tends to degrade with time as its functions evolve and as it is maintained. Software reliability is really a measure of confidence in the design. You could estimate design confidence for hardware systems. You usually don't, because wear-out phenomena tend to swamp out design defects for most hardware systems.

2 Aren't we stretching things when we say that software failure is random? Hardware really does seem to fail randomly, but software is the result of an intellectual process that can be controlled.

ANSWER: The randomness of hardware failure is no more "real" than that of software. The concept of randomness is used to model behavior that is affected by so many factors that a deterministic model is impractical. We may think that we control intellectual processes and hence their products, but this is illusory. Many defects (for example, memory lapses) occur in intellectual processes. These defects are caused by a wide range of factors, so the whole is best modeled by a random process.

3 How can you talk of a reliability for software? It isn't the same situation as we have for hardware. You let me pick the software tests and establish their sequence and I'll give any reliability estimate you want. For example, if you take a run that executes without failure and repeat it endlessly, you will get a reliability that approaches 1.

ANSWER: Manipulation of the reliability estimate is possible. You must know at least one run that fails and one that succeeds. You then select them in the proportions you desire. However, we aren't really interested in the behavior of the program for an artificial set of tests. We are concerned with the typical environment of runs (usually randomly sequenced) that will normally be encountered. Manipulation of tests is also possible for hardware and is just as unreasonable as for software. For example, you can obtain a very low reliability for most automobile tires by running them incessantly over a set of spikes.

4 How can you view the use of a system as being random? If people learn the weaknesses of a system, they will avoid them.

ANSWER: Suppose people do learn the weaknesses of a system and avoid the faulty operations rather than ask the software designer to correct them. This acceptance is equivalent to a redefinition of the system requirements. Incidentally, there is no reason why use of the remaining operations should not be regarded as a random process.

5   How can software reliability vary with time, because it doesn't wear out?

ANSWER: Note that software reliability varies with *execution time*. As failures occur and faults underlying them are uncovered and corrected, reliability will increase. Any variation of software reliability with time occurs solely because time and execution time have some relationship.

6   In our application, my management tells me that our objective is perfection with respect to certain functions that are critical to the success of our overall mission (success of all of these functions is necessary for mission success; none can fail). How can we apply software reliability measures?

ANSWER: Expecting perfection is unrealistic, although admitting that your goal is less than perfection may be difficult from a public relations standpoint. What you really want to do is to determine the degree of "near perfection" needed.

You will be in good company, because developers of "life critical" software such as that used in medical systems, aircraft and air traffic control, and nuclear power plants deal with such questions.

Setting an appropriate objective for the critical functions generally depends on the impact of failure, usually in terms of cost or human life. Although it may be difficult to set precise objectives, it is usually possible to come up with bounds or approximate objectives. An approach that is frequently useful is to look at past experience or similar situations to estimate what is acceptable. For example, in the United States, people are apparently willing to accept the current risk level with respect to automobile use of about one fatal accident per 10^6 h of operation, because this risk does not influence people to stop driving.

An annual failure cost level that represents an appreciable fraction of a company's annual profits would probably be considered unacceptable, as would a failure risk level that would result in serious public demand to stop the operations supported by the system you are considering.

7   Do failure measures at different phases of test (for example, unit test, subsystem test, system test) have equal significance?

ANSWER: Measures taken later in test generally will give a better indication of what to expect in operation. This is because more data is available, and the data that is available is usually based on more of the system being present and on a test operational profile that is closer to the true operational profile.

However, this does not mean that data taken early in development will not give useful approximations of what to expect in operation. You must adjust early data to account for only part of the system being present and for test operational profiles that depart from the actual operational profiles.

8   Is software reliability engineering requirements-based?

ANSWER: Yes. This does not mean that we ignore useful information we may have about the design or the history of the project.

9   What are some of the common misconceptions about software reliability engineering?

ANSWER: The most common misconceptions are that

a. It is primarily concerned with software reliability models and prediction

b. It incorrectly copies hardware reliability theory

c. It deals with faults or bugs

d. It doesn't concern itself with representative testing

e. Testing ultrareliable software is hopeless

10   Are attaining reliability growth and evaluating the reliability that exists conflicting objectives?

ANSWER: Probably not, but if they are, then only to a limited extent. Evaluating existing reliability requires that you represent field conditions accurately when you test (i.e., you select your tests in accordance with the operational profile defined in Chap. 3). Attaining optimal reliability growth implies that you select your tests so that you increase reliability per unit test time as rapidly as possible. To a certain degree, selecting tests in accordance with the operational profile gives the most rapid reliability growth, because you will test frequently executed code early and find and remove any faults that lurk within it. However, you may also repeatedly exercise some frequently executed code before less frequently executed code is exercised for the first time. The repeated execution may result in removal of almost all the faults in that code, so continued execution of the code doesn't result in much further reliability growth. Thus it is possible that an approach other than pure operational-profile-driven selection may improve test efficiency under certain conditions. No well-defined picture of what those conditions are exists at this time, however.

11   Why is software reliability so different from hardware reliability? I know software is quite different from hardware, but why can't software failure data be treated like hardware failure data?

ANSWER: Software and hardware reliability do have the same definition: probability of failure-free operation for a specified time. The principal difference is that software reliability is more likely to change with time than hardware reliability, either as faults are removed during reliability growth test or as new code (which may contain additional faults) is added. Hence the need for models to characterize this change. If software is stable (not evolving and not being debugged), the software failure data can be treated like hardware failure data.

12   You have noted that, in general, the relative order of importance of significant quality attributes is reliability, schedule, cost. Are there any major departures from this order?

ANSWER: Yes. Government and military applications often rank cost ahead of schedule.

13   Which is more appropriate, a run-oriented view of software reliability or a time-oriented one?

ANSWER: Because all runs have a frequency of occurrence and a duration during execution, the two views are equivalent.

14 Do the environmental factors that influence hardware reliability affect software reliability?

ANSWER: In general, no. Hardware reliability is mostly affected by physical variables like temperature and mechanical stress. Software reliability is mostly affected by how the software is used.

15 How will the move to network computing (i.e., applets, Java, client-server networks, etc.) affect software reliability engineering?

ANSWER: It should not affect basic theory and it probably will not affect the basic methods used in practice. However, we can expect to see more emphasis on small software components used in a wide variety of applications within a domain. Hence software reliability engineering will frequently be applied to domains, and certification test within domains will increase in importance. The components may be combined into larger numbers of systems and there may be larger numbers of operational modes (defined in Chap. 3).

16 Why should you have a reliability objective? Shouldn't you strive for zero defects (faults)?

ANSWER: Setting an objective of zero defects (faults) ignores the considerations of product delivery date and product cost. You want a balance among the characteristics of reliability, delivery date, and cost that best meets user needs.

1.6.3   Relationships with other practices

1 Which of the following attributes of quality can be incorporated in and measured by software reliability?

   a. Functionality (presence of features)

   b. Quality of failure messages

   c. Ease of learning

   d. User friendliness in operation

   e. Maintainability

   f. Hardware fault tolerance or recoverability

   g. Performance

   h. Extensibility

   i. Support level (speed of response to support requests)

   j. Software fault tolerance or recoverability

   k. Ease of relating user problem to system capabilities

   l. Tolerance to user faults

ANSWER: Attributes a, b, d, f, g, j, and l. We can relate all of these quality attributes to behavior of the program in execution that users may view as unsatisfactory.

·2 How can you use software reliability to characterize functionality?

ANSWER: Determine what functions your customers want or need and how often they need them. Consider the absence of a function as a failure. For example, suppose customers want a status display function of unsold seats per flight for an airline reservation system on a daily basis for making pricing decisions. You would then consider the absence of the function as a failure. Hence you have 41.7 failures per 1000 h in addition to whatever other failures may exist. Although this possibility of incorporating functionality into a software reliability exists, it usually isn't done. Normally, you establish a fixed set of functions for a product release and measure software reliability with respect to that set.

3 How are software safety and software reliability related?

ANSWER: Software safety is one aspect of software reliability. Reliability implies proper functioning of software, and safety is one of the requirements that must be met for proper functioning. You can categorize failures as safety-impacting or non-safety-impacting. For example, a system might have two safety failures per 1000 h. Note that an unsafe system is also unreliable.

4 What is the survivability of a system?

ANSWER: *Survivability* usually refers to reliability of the system with respect to a specified set of critical functions when the system has been degraded in some way. For example, you might represent survivability of a spacecraft by the reliability of the navigation functions when the spacecraft is subjected to radiation.

5 Can software be unsafe without the possibility of software failures occurring?

ANSWER: Not really, if you interpret "failure" in the broad sense of "behavior that the customer will view as unsatisfactory." Certainly, an unsafe event that occurred would be interpreted as unsatisfactory. Hence unsafe events would constitute a subset of failures.

6 How is risk assessment related to software reliability?

ANSWER: Risk assessment is a study of the probability that certain undesirable events will occur. These events include software failures but can include other events as well, such as cost overruns. Thus risk assessment can be more general than software reliability.

7 How does failure modes and effects analysis (FMEA) relate to software reliability engineering?

ANSWER: Software reliability engineering is a macroscopic approach that takes a global, or "big picture," view of the software product involved. FMEA is a microscopic approach that looks at particular failures, how they can be caused, and how to prevent them. It is more expensive to apply than software reliability engineering due to the detailed analysis effort required. Thus it is most practical for trying to prevent critical failures. You can integrate the two practices as follows. Apply software reliability engineering to reduce the total failure intensity. Perform FMEA on potential severity 1 failures you can identify and implement appropriate failure prevention or fault tolerant features for them.

8 How is software reliability engineering related to cleanroom development?

ANSWER: There are many similarities between software reliability engineering and cleanroom development, but software reliability engineering is the more general practice. Cleanroom development includes hierarchical specification and design and team reviews that apply formal correctness verification. You can use software reliability engineering with cleanroom development, but you can also use it with any other development methodology.

9 We have a very close relationship with our software supplier. As we test their software, we send them trouble reports. They send us fixes, we integrate them, and continue test. What type of test are we performing?

ANSWER: Reliability growth test.

10 Does function point analysis have a role in software reliability engineering?

ANSWER: Not to any extent. Function point analysis was originally developed to support cost estimation and measures of productivity. The number of lines of code can vary widely for the same functionality, depending on a programmer's conception of the problem and his or her style. Hence lines of code is not a good measure to use when estimating cost or measuring productivity. However, the number of faults created (and hence failure intensity) is highly correlated with the number of lines of code written, because the human error rate appears to be relatively constant per line of code. Thus function point analysis is not needed for obtaining good predictions of failure intensity.

1.6.4 Application

1 Does reliability have any particular psychological effects on users of a system that need to be considered?

ANSWER: When users first begin to employ a new system, it is important that the reliability of frequently used functions be high. If they are not, the system will rapidly gain a bad reputation, which may later be difficult to overcome. Users may avoid using parts or all of the system or attempt to work around it. This situation is another powerful argument for determining the expected use for a system and using it to guide testing, with the most frequently used functions tested first.

2 Can you apply software reliability engineering to systems that are designed and tested "top down?"

ANSWER: Yes. When applying software reliability engineering to system test, you will probably have a shorter test period because there will be fewer faults to remove. However, it seems likely that there will always be a substantial system test period before the release of any software product. It will always be necessary to run the code through a number of functional tests.

3 Flight software used on space missions is often "one of a kind." Does this present a problem in software reliability engineering application in that previous experience may not be applicable to the next mission?

ANSWER: No. Estimates of failure intensity during test will be based on failure data, which will depend on this mission and not previous ones.

4 Can reuse of software be helpful from a reliability as well as a cost standpoint?

ANSWER: Yes. Reused software components tend to have a higher reliability, resulting in higher system reliability. But you must verify the reliability of a reused component for the system in which you will employ it and for the use and environment of that system.

5 What are the most common mistakes people make in applying software reliability engineering?

ANSWER: Two of the most common are

a. In constructing the operational profile (defined in Chap. 3), they miss some operations with significant probabilities of occurrence because they neglect to consider special or transient environments (for example, a database in the process of being populated).

b. They do not test in accordance with the operational profile. Reliability estimates obtained then do not reflect actual expected use.

6 Can software reliability engineering be applied to object-oriented development?

ANSWER: Yes

7 Do any special changes have to be made to apply software reliability engineering to an object-oriented program?

ANSWER: No

8 What changes in the "traditional" software development process are necessary to implement software reliability engineering?

ANSWER: The changes are not substantial, and they carry many additional benefits beyond software reliability engineering itself:

a. You need to determine one or more operational profiles (defined in Chap. 3) for the product.

b. System testing must be consistent with the operational profile.

Only the first change involves any appreciable effort. The establishment of an operational profile will let you focus development on those functions that are most frequently used, with a strong net gain in productivity. The change in system test represents a change in order of test rather than magnitude of effort. Software reliability engineering requires that you record test output and examine it for failures, but this is not a new requirement above good conventional system testing practice.

Incidentally, software reliability engineering does not heavily affect the work of system architects and developers, unless perhaps there is a desire to build failure recording and reporting features into the delivered product.

9 Some of our project people are uncomfortable with the idea of suggesting that customers set failure intensity objectives. How do you deal with that?

ANSWER: Point out that it is to the long-term benefit for both them and their customers that they understand customer requirements in specific quantitative terms. Of course, this assumes that both understand the tradeoffs involved among reliability, time of delivery of new features, and cost. Better understanding means that the customer will be more likely to be satisfied and that the development organization will be more likely to predominate vis-à-vis its competitors. Although there may be some initial resistance to letting customers set failure intensity objectives, this should disappear with greater understanding.

10 What differences must you consider in applying software reliability engineering to packaged software (i.e., software that is sold to a large volume of customers)?

ANSWER: Initial sales of packaged software probably depend more on getting a lot of *useful* functionality to market ahead of competitors. Hence rapid testing of the most-used features to some minimum standard of reliability is very important. Meeting some minimum standard is essential because if the product fails too often, it will get a bad reputation from which it may never recover. But you should not test any longer than you have to because otherwise a competitor may deliver a product incorporating the most-used features before you do. Achieving good reliability for the lesser-used features can await later releases. Thus operational development (discussed in Chap. 3) is an excellent approach.

When you set the ultimate failure intensity objective to be achieved, the tradeoff with cost will be particularly important due to the severe competition on price that is common.

With the large numbers of users typical for packaged software, you will need to employ sampling to get operational profile (defined in Chap. 3) data and data on reliability needs. You may have to provide some inducement to users to provide the data. Some software suppliers have included use recording with beta test versions provided free to early users, often distributed over the Internet. Note that you must take care in interpreting data from a special group of users such as this; they may not be representative of the total eventual user population.

11 Our product must operate with a wide variety of interfacing hardware and software. How do we organize testing in this situation?

ANSWER: Each of the configurations of hardware and software that your product must work with forms a supersystem when combined with your product. You need to test each of these supersystems.

You can see that it is quite easy for the number of supersystems to get out of hand. You may wish to develop a *configuration profile* (Juhlin, 1992), which is a list of configurations and their probabilities of occurrence. These probabilities are usually determined as fractions of users associated with a particular configuration. This data is usually a reasonable approximation of the fraction of use and is easier to collect. You can use the configuration profile to allocate your testing effort, even to the extent of not testing rarely occurring configurations.

Another strategy is to define a base configuration plus a set of delta configurations. Each delta configuration represents only the changes that make up a particular variation from the base configuration. Many of the deltas will affect only a limited set of operations. You can often save a great deal of testing time by testing the base configuration for all operations and testing the delta configurations for only those operations associated with them.

12   Why should we set a reliability objective? Why don't we just develop an operational profile (defined in Chap. 3) and use it to allocate our development resources and make our testing realistic?

ANSWER: The operational profile will help you greatly in allocating development resources and conducting realistic tests, but it can't guide you in determining how long you should test or how much effort you should put into reliability improvement strategies. You need an absolute measure such as a failure intensity objective to help you there.

13   Should we consider collaboratively developed software as developed or acquired software?

ANSWER: If your organization is one of the collaborators, you should consider it as developed software and at least do reliability growth test. If not, you would consider it as acquired software and only do certification test.

14   We produce a notebook computer, writing some basic firmware and software that lets a standard commercial operating system run on it. The product must work with various printers. How do we test the computer with them?

ANSWER: Plan a set of supersystem tests, each test comprising the computer and one of the printers.

15   One of the components of our system is no longer supported. Should we perform certification test on it?

ANSWER: Yes, if you have not done so already. You need to know its reliability and how that will affect your system reliability. If the effect is unacceptable, you will have to find an alternative component or some way of increasing the reliability of the existing one.

16 Can we apply software reliability engineering to legacy systems? When?

ANSWER: Yes, beginning at the start of any release cycle.

17 Can we apply software reliability engineering to unit testing of a product?

ANSWER: In theory, yes. But it is generally not practical to do so unless the unit is expected to be used in multiple products, because of the effort and cost required to develop an operational profile for the unit. Using software reliability engineering to certify components expected to be used in multiple products is highly desirable, however.

18 What types of systems are typically deferred to beta test because they can't be economically tested in system test?

ANSWER: Supersystems, because it is often very expensive to reproduce or even simulate the systems that interact with your product. This is particularly true for networks of systems that extend over a substantial geographical area.

19 When we test interfaces, should we use certification or reliability growth test?

ANSWER: When you test an interface, you usually test it in two ways: in each of the interfacing systems that it spans, checking the variables transmitted, and as the system that includes both of the interfacing systems, observing overall behavior. The type of test is the same as the type of test used for the system in question.

20 How does software reliability engineering apply in an organization that uses a layered architecture for all its products: user interface, application, and database?

ANSWER: The activities involved should essentially be the same. Some of the layers, such as the database and the user interface, will probably be products in their own right, where these products become components that are combined with an application to yield a "final" product that is delivered to "final" users. Note that products such as the database and the user interface will work with many other systems. Hence you must consider a number of external systems as initiators of operations when developing operational profiles, and you can expect a need to test a number of supersystems.

1.7 Background

This section provides further general background for the practice of software reliability engineering. It explores in greater depth some of the concepts related to software reliability. It then compares software reliability with hardware reliability and finally discusses software reliability modeling. For further background, see Musa, 1988, 1989b, 1991c, 1995b; Musa and Ackerman, 1989, 1991; Musa, Ackerman, and

Everett, 1994; Musa, Buckley, Keller, Lyu, and Tausworthe, 1995; Musa and Ehrlich, 1996; Musa and Everett, 1991, 1993a, 1993b; Musa and Iannino, 1990; and Musa and Okumoto, 1986.

1.7.1. Software reliability concepts

Understanding software reliability engineering has become a vital skill for both the software manager and software engineer. This knowledge is also important to managers and engineers of products that include software and to users of these products. Fortunately, in the past 25 years a body of knowledge has been developed to help meet this need, and much practical experience has been gained on actual projects. Some problems remain, but further progress in solving them is dependent on confronting them in real project situations and gathering relevant data. The measures are sufficiently accurate and useful that the benefits in using them exceed their costs.

A primary objective of software reliability engineering is to help the engineer, manager, or user of software learn to make more precise decisions. A strong secondary objective is to make everyone more concretely aware of software reliability by focusing attention on it. Better decisions can save money on a project or during the life cycle of a piece of software in many ways. In general, the total savings that we expect are more than 10 times greater than the cost of applying these ideas. Consider the following simple example for illustrative purposes: a 2-year software project with a system test period of about 6 months. The amount of testing is usually highly correlated with the reliability required, although it is not the only factor. Suppose you could establish that you need only 5 months of test to get the reliability that you need for the particular application. Then you might well be able to save 4 percent of the development cost of the project. Compare this with the cost of application of software reliability engineering, which is typically 0.1 to 0.2 percent of project development cost. The cost effectiveness of the methodology is high.

Software reliability engineering is "engineering" in the sense that you design and build to the level of reliability needed for the product, you balance testing with other reliability improvement approaches, and you allocate testing resources in accordance with the use and criticality of the operations.

The principal cost in applying software reliability engineering is that for developing the operational profiles (defined in Chap. 3) required. The cost of developing the operational profiles for a system varies with its size and the accuracy required, but an average effort is 1 to 2 staff months for systems in the range of hundreds of thousands of source instructions. Updating an operational profile for subsequent releases is a much smaller task. Software reliability engineering is expensive to use for unit test at the current state of the art unless the units are used in multiple systems.

Many types of test have been separately named. You can apply software reliability engineering to all types of test that, taken *together* at each point in time (let's say, over a day), follow the operational profile. Thus it can include feature, regression, configuration, load, stress, stability, bang-bang, operational scenario, performance, and security test. It usually excludes installation test.

The three most important quality characteristics of a software-based product are reliability, schedule, and cost. Note that these are primarily user-oriented rather than developer-oriented attributes. Quantitative measures have existed for a long time for the latter two characteristics, but the quantification of reliability has been more recent. It is most important, however, because the absence of a concrete measure for software reliability generally means that reliability will suffer when it competes for attention with schedule and cost. In fact, this absence may be the principal reason for the well-known existence of reliability problems in many software products.

Reliability is probably the most important of the characteristics inherent in the concept "software quality." It is intimately connected with defects, and as Jones (1986) points out, defects represent the largest cost element in programming. Software reliability concerns itself with how well the software functions to meet the requirements of the user. We distinguish "customer" from "user" in the sense that the customer is the person or persons who make the software acquisition decision, whereas the user operates the software. Usually, but not necessarily, communication between user and customer is good, so that user requirements are included in the customer requirements.

Reliability is the probability that the software will work without failure for a specified period of time. "Failure" means the program in its functioning has not met user requirements in some way. "Not functioning to meet user requirements" is really a very broad definition. Thus reliability incorporates all those properties that can be associated with execution of the program. For example, it includes correctness, safety, and the operational aspects of usability and user friendliness. Note that safety is actually a specialized subcategory of software reliability. Reliability does not include portability, modifiability, or understandability of documentation.

Initial (and many present) approaches to measuring software reliability were based on attempting to count the faults or defects found in a program. This approach is developer-oriented. Also, what was often counted were in reality either failures (the occurrences of malfunction) or corrections (for example, maintenance or correction reports), neither of which are equivalent to faults. Even if you correctly count faults found, they are not a good quality indicator (is a large number good or bad?). Faults remaining is a better indicator, but reliability is even richer.

Reliability is user-oriented rather than developer-oriented. It relates to operation rather than design of the program, and hence it is dynamic rather than static (Saunier, 1983). It takes account of the frequency with which problems occur. It relates directly to operational experience and the influence of faults on that experience. Hence, you can easily associate it with costs. It is more suitable for examining the significance of trends, for setting objectives, and for predicting when those objectives will be met. It permits one to analyze in common terms the effect on system reliability of both software and hardware, both of which are present in any real system. Thus, reliability measures are much more useful than fault measures.

This does not mean that some attention to faults is without value. But you should focus the attention on faults as predictors of reliability and on the nature of faults. A better understanding of faults and the causative human error process should lead to strategies to avoid, detect, and remove or compensate for them.

We usually define *software availability* as the expected fraction of operating time during which a software component or system is functioning acceptably. Assume that the program is operational and that we are not modifying it with new features or repairs. Hence, it has a constant failure intensity. We can compute availability for software as we do for hardware. It is the ratio of uptime to the sum of uptime plus downtime, as the time interval over which the measurement is made approaches infinity. The downtime for a given interval is the product of the length of the interval, the failure intensity, and the mean time to repair (MTTR). Usually the failure intensity applied here is a figure computed for serious failures and not those that involve only minor degradation of the system. It is generally not practical to hold up operation of the system while performing fault determination and correction in the field. Therefore, we ordinarily determine MTTR as the average time required to restore the data for a program, reload the program, and resume execution. If we wish to determine the availability of a system containing both hardware and software components, we find the MTTR as the average of the hardware repair and software restoration times.

Note that the term *maintainability* has the same definition for hardware and software, the average staff hours required to resolve a failure. However, the significance is somewhat different. Resolution for hardware occurs on-line and affects downtime. Resolution for software occurs off-line and does not affect downtime.

There are several other terms in common use that are related to reliability. *Integrity* is the probability that a system operates without security penetration for a specified time, given a specified threat profile and rate of arrival of threats. *Recoverability* is the average time to recover from failure, including data cleanup or reinitialization. It is the software analog to MTTR for hardware.

1.7.2 Reliability

We can define reliability quantities with respect to natural units (discussed in Chap. 2) or time units. We are currently concerned with two kinds of time. The *execution time* for a program is the time that is actually spent by a processor executing the instructions of that program. The second kind of time is the familiar garden variety that we normally experience. Execution time is important, because it is now generally accepted that models based on execution time are superior. However, quantities must ultimately be related to ordinary time to be meaningful to many engineers or managers. If computer utilization, which is the fraction of time the program is executing, is constant, ordinary time will be proportional to execution time. As an example of these two types of time, consider a word processing system serving a secretary. In one week, there may be 40 h of time during which the system is running. There might be 2 h of execution time for the word processing program itself.

Weekly average computer utilization, although often relatively constant in the field, tends to increase over a system test period. You can describe the relationship of time to execution time during system test using the calendar time model (Musa, Iannino, and Okumoto, 1987).

There are four general ways of characterizing failure occurrences in time:

1. Time of failure

2. Time interval between failures

3. Cumulative failures experienced up to a given time

4. Failures experienced in a time interval

These are illustrated in Tables 1.1 and 1.2.

Note that the foregoing four quantities are random variables. By *random,* we mean that we do not know the values of the variables with certainty. This frequently happens when there are so many factors (many unknown) affecting the value that it is not practical to predict it. There are many possible values, each associated with a probability of occurrence. For example, we don't really know when the next failure will occur. If we did, we would try to prevent or avoid it. We only know

TABLE 1.1   Time-Based Failure Specification

Failure number	Failure time (s)	Failure interval (s)
1	10	10
2	19	9
3	32	13
4	43	11
5	58	15
6	70	12
7	88	18
8	103	15
9	125	22
10	150	25
11	169	19
12	199	30
13	231	32
14	256	25
15	296	40

TABLE 1.2   Failure-Based Failure Specification

Time (s)	Cumulative failures	Failures in interval
30	2	2
60	5	3
90	7	2
120	8	1
150	10	2
180	11	1
210	12	1
240	13	1
270	14	1

a set of possible times of failure occurrence and the probability of each. The probability of each time of occurrence is the fraction of cases for which it occurs.

Note that *random* does not carry any connotation of true irrationality or unpredictability, as some mistakenly assume. *Random* means *unpredictable* only in the sense that the exact value is not known. However, the average value and some sense of the dispersion *are* known. *Random* does not mean *unaffected by other variables.* Although failure occurrence is random, it is decidedly affected by such factors as test strategy and program use. Nor does *random* imply any specific probability distribution, which some mistakenly assume to be *uniform.*

There are at least two principal reasons for this randomness. First, the commission of errors by programmers, and hence the introduction of faults, is a very complex, unpredictable process. Hence the locations of faults within the program are unknown. Second, the conditions of execution of a program are generally unpredictable. For example, with a telephone switching system, how do you know what type of call will be made next? In addition, the relationship between program function requested and code path executed, although theoretically determinable, may not be so in practice because it is so complex. Because failures are dependent on the presence of a fault in the code *and* its execution in the context of certain machine states, a third complicating element is introduced that argues for the randomness of the failure process.

Table 1.3 illustrates a typical probability distribution of failures that occur within a time period of execution. Each possible value of the random variable of number of failures is given along with its associated probability. The probabilities, of course, add to 1. Note that here the random variable is discrete, because the number of failures must be an integer. We can also have continuous random variables, such as time, that can take on any value. Note that the most probable number of failures is 2 (probability 0.22). The mean or average number of failures can be computed. You multiply each possible value by the probability it can occur and add all the products, as shown in the table. The mean is 3.04 failures.

You can view a random process as a set of random variables, each corresponding to a point in time. We can have a discrete or continuous time random process. One characteristic of a random process is the form of the probability distributions of the random variables. For example, one common form of the distribution is Poisson. The other principal characteristic is the form of the variation of the process in time.

TABLE 1.3   Typical Probability Distribution of Failures

Value of random variable (failures in time period)	Probability	Product of value and probability
0	0.10	0
1	0.18	0.18
2	0.22	0.44
3	0.16	0.48
4	0.11	0.44
5	0.08	0.40
6	0.05	0.30
7	0.04	0.28
8	0.03	0.24
9	0.02	0.18
10	0.01	0.1
Mean failures		3.04

We will look at the time variation from two different viewpoints, the mean value function and the failure intensity function. The *mean value function* represents the average cumulative failures associated with each time point. The *failure intensity function* is the rate of change of the mean value function or the number of failures per unit time. For example, you might say 0.01 failure per hour or 1 failure per 100 h. Strictly speaking, the failure intensity is the derivative of the mean value function with respect to time and is an instantaneous value.

Each alternative form of expressing reliability, failure intensity, or reliability proper has its advantages. The failure intensity statement is more economical because you only have to give one number. However, the reliability statement is sometimes better suited to the combination of reliabilities of components to get system reliability. If the rate of failure at each point in time is of paramount concern, failure intensity may be the more appropriate measure. When you require proper operation of a system for some time duration to accomplish some function, reliability is often best. An example would be a space flight to the moon. Figure 1.2 shows how failure intensity and reliability typically vary during a test period, as faults are removed. The time for the test peri-

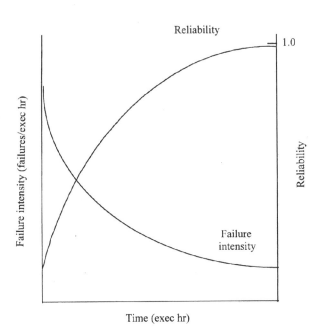

Figure 1.2   Reliability and failure intensity.

od will typically represent hundreds or thousands of runs. Note that we define failure intensity, just like we do reliability, with respect to a specified environment.

As faults are removed (for example, during a reliability growth test phase), failure intensity tends to drop, and reliability tends to increase. When we introduce new features or make design changes, we usually introduce new faults. The result is a step increase in failure intensity and a step decrease in reliability. If we introduce new features and fixes at the same time, there can be a step increase or decrease in failure intensity, depending on whether the faults introduced by new features or the fault removals predominate. There will be a corresponding decrease or increase in reliability. If a system is stable (that is, the code is unchanging), both failure intensity and reliability tend to be constant. This would be the situation for a program that has been released to the field, with no changes in code and no repairs being made.

The term *mean time to failure* (MTTF) is used in the hardware reliability field and to a decreasing extent in software reliability. It is the average value of the next failure interval. The use of MTTF is attractive, in that *larger* indicates *better*. However, there are many cases in software reliability in which MTTF is undefined. Failure intensity is preferred because it always exists. Also, failure intensities are simple to work with because they combine additively. In an approximate nonrigorous sense, the two are inverses of each other. The hardware reliability field uses the term *mean time between failures* (MTBF) when repair or replacement is occurring. It is the sum of MTTF and MTTR.

Table 1.4 illustrates an example of the random process of failures in simplified fashion, showing the mean value function of the cumulative number of failures experienced at two different time points. The time points are $t_A = 1$ h and $t_B = 5$ h. A random process whose probability distribution varies with time is called *nonhomogeneous*. Most failure processes during reliability growth test fit this situation. Figure 1.3 also shows the related failure intensity function at t_A and t_B. Note that the mean failures experienced increases from 3.04 to 7.77 between these two points, whereas the failure intensity decreases.

The two most important factors affecting failure behavior are

1. The number of faults in the software being executed

2. The operational profile

The number of faults in the software is the difference between the number introduced and the number removed during its lifetime.

Programmers introduce faults when they develop code. They may introduce faults during original design or when they are adding new features, making design changes, or repairing faults that have been

TABLE 1.4   Probability Distribution at Times t_A and t_B

Value of random variable (failures in time period)	Probability	
	Elapsed time $t_A = 1$ h	Elapsed time $t_B = 5$ h
0	0.10	0.01
1	0.18	0.02
2	0.22	0.03
3	0.16	0.04
4	0.11	0.05
5	0.08	0.07
6	0.05	0.09
7	0.04	0.12
8	0.03	0.16
9	0.02	0.13
10	0.01	0.10
11	0	0.07
12	0	0.05
13	0	0.03
14	0	0.02
15	0	0.01
Mean failures	3.04	7.77

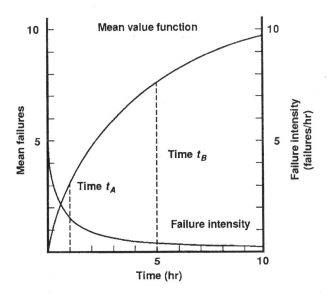

Figure 1.3   Mean value and failure intensity functions.

identified. The term *developed code,* defined as instructions that have been created or modified, is used deliberately. In general, only code that is new or modified results in fault introduction. Code that is *reused* to perform essentially the same functions that it performs in another application does not usually introduce any appreciable number of faults, except possibly in the interfaces. It generally has been thoroughly debugged in the previous application. Note that the process of fault removal often introduces some new faults because it involves modification or writing of new code. It is hoped (if you have a programming staff of reasonable competence) that the new faults entered are fewer than the faults being removed.

Fault removal obviously can't occur unless you have some means of detecting the fault in the first place. Thus fault removal resulting from execution depends on the occurrence of the associated failure. Occurrence depends both on the length of time for which the software has been executing and on the operational profile. When you execute different operations, you encounter different faults, and the failures that are exhibited tend to be different—thus the effect of the operational profile. For example, you can expect that an electronic telephone switching system operating in a business district will have a software reliability different from that in a residential area.

We can often find faults without execution. They may be found through inspection, compiler diagnostics, design or code reviews, or code reading.

Fault removal is also dependent on the efficiency with which faults are found and removed. For example, a failure resolution team may remove 95 faults for every 100 failures reported. The efficiency depends on factors such as how well the circumstances surrounding the failure are documented and the degree of structuring and clarity of the program.

We have seen that the failure process depends on the *system* being built, the nature of the development process for a particular *project,* and the *use* of the system. Because the system and the project are so closely associated, they are often used interchangeably in naming a particular failure process.

The following relationships apply to reliability generally (hardware or software). Reliability, denoted $R(t)$, is related to failure probability $F(t)$ by

$$R(t) = 1 - F(t) \tag{1.1}$$

The failure probability is the probability that the time of failure is less than or equal to t. If $F(t)$ is differentiable, the failure density $f(t)$ is the first derivative of $F(t)$ with respect to time t. The hazard rate $z(t)$ is the conditional failure density, given that no failure has occurred in the interval between 0 and t. It is given by

$$z(t) = \frac{f(t)}{R(t)} \tag{1.2}$$

and it is also related to the reliability by

$$R(t) = \exp\left(-\int_0^t z(x)dx\right) \tag{1.3}$$

In software reliability engineering, the hazard rate in the field is piecewise constant, discontinuities occurring only at new releases. The hazard rate is equal to the failure intensity λ. Hence from Eq. 1.3 you can derive the relationships between reliability and failure intensity given in App. D.

The MTTF Θ is related to the reliability by

$$\Theta = \int_0^\infty R(x)dx \tag{1.4}$$

where the integration is performed with respect to the operating time of the system.

1.7.3 Software reliability and hardware reliability

The field of hardware reliability has been established for some time. Hence, you might ask how software reliability relates to it. In reality, the division between hardware and software reliability is somewhat artificial. Both may be defined in the same way. Therefore, you may combine hardware and software component reliabilities to get system reliability.

Both hardware and software reliability depend on the environment. The source of failures in software is design faults, whereas the principal source in hardware has generally been physical deterioration. However, the concepts and theories developed for software reliability could really be applied to any design activity, including hardware design. Once a software (design) defect is properly fixed, it is in general fixed for all time. Failure usually occurs only when a program (design) is exposed to an environment that it was not developed or tested for. Although manufacturing can affect the quality of physical components, the replication process for software (design) is trivial and can be performed to very high standards of quality.

Engineers have not applied the "design reliability" concept to hardware to any extent. The probability of failure due to wear and other physical causes has usually been much greater than that due to an unrecognized design problem. It was possible to keep hardware design failures low because hardware was generally less complex logically than software. Hardware design failures had to be kept low because retrofitting of manufactured items in the field was very expensive. The emphasis on hardware reliability may be starting to change now, however. Awareness of the work that is going on in software reliability, plus a growing realization of the importance of design faults, may be having an effect. This growing awareness is strengthened by the parallels that people are starting to draw between software engineering and chip design.

Because introduction and removal of design faults occur during software development and test, you can expect software reliability to vary during these periods. Hardware reliability may change during certain periods, such as during initial burn-in or at the end of useful life. However, it has a much greater tendency than software toward a constant value.

Despite the foregoing differences, we have developed a software reliability theory in a way that is compatible with hardware reliability theory. Thus you can compute system reliability figures using standard hardware combinatorial techniques (Lloyd and Lipow, 1977; Shooman, 1986). In summary, hardware and software reliability share many similarities and some differences. One must not err on the side of assuming that software always presents unique problems, but one must also be careful not to carry analogies too far.

1.7.4 Software reliability modeling

To model software reliability one must first consider the principal factors that affect it: fault introduction, fault removal, and the environment. Fault introduction depends primarily on the characteristics of the product and the development process. The most significant product characteristic is program size. Development process characteristics include software engineering technologies and tools used, level of experience of personnel, volatility of requirements, and other factors. Note that you may develop code to add features or remove faults. Fault removal depends on failure discovery and the quality of the repair activity. Failure discovery, in turn, depends on the extent to which the software has been executed and the operational profile. Because some of the foregoing factors are probabilistic in nature and operate over time, software reliability models have generally been formulated in terms of random processes in execution time. The models are distinguished from each other in general terms by the probability distribution of failure times or number of failures experienced and by the nature of the variation of the random process with execution time. Note that you can convert execution time into natural or time units appropriate to the application, and these are often easier to measure.

A software reliability model specifies the general form of the dependence of the failure process on the factors mentioned. The possibilities for different mathematical forms to describe the failure process are almost limitless. We have restricted ourselves to considering well-developed models that have been applied fairly broadly with real data and have given reasonable results. A thorough treatment of models is presented in Chap. 8. You can determine the specific form of a model from the general form by establishing the values of the parameters of the model through one of the following:

1. Estimation—applying statistical inference procedures to failure data taken for the program

2. Prediction—determination from properties of the software product and the development process (this can be done before any execution of the program)

There is always some uncertainty in the determination of the specific form. This is generally expressed in terms of *confidence intervals* for the parameters. A confidence interval represents a range of values within which a parameter is expected to lie with a certain confidence. For example, the 0.75 confidence interval of total failures that will be experienced in infinite time may be 150 to 175.

Once the specific form has been established, you can determine many different characteristics of the failure process. For many models there are analytic expressions for

1. The average number of failures experienced at any point in time

2. The average number of failures in a time interval

3. The failure intensity at any point in time

4. The probability distribution of failure intervals

A good software reliability model has several important characteristics. It

1. Gives good projections of future failure behavior

2. Computes useful quantities

3. Is simple

4. Is widely applicable

5. Is based on sound assumptions

Projection of future failure behavior assumes that the values of model parameters will not change for the period of projection. If the net effect of the opposing influences of fault introduction and fault repair should change substantially, we must either compensate for the change or wait until enough new failures have occurred so that we can reestimate the model parameters. Incorporating such changes into the models themselves has generally been impractical due to the added complexity. In any event, the complexity is not worthwhile, considering the accuracy with which parameters are generally known.

In general, software reliability models are based on (although this is often not stated explicitly) a stable program executing in a constant environment. This means that neither the code nor the operational profile is changing. If the program and environment do change, they often do so, and are usually handled, in a piecewise fashion. Thus, the models focus mainly on fault removal. Most models can account for the effects of slow fault introduction, however. Some assume that the average net long-term effect must be a decrease in failure intensity. If neither fault introduction, fault removal, or operational profile changes are occurring, the failure intensity will be constant and the model should simplify to accommodate this fact. We assume that the behavior of the program is compared with the requirements with enough thoroughness that all failures are detected. It is possible to compensate for programs or environments that are changing (see Secs. 6.3.1 and 6.3.4).

For a program that has been released and is operational, it is common to defer installation of both new features and repairs to the next release. Assuming a constant operational profile, the program will exhibit a constant failure intensity.

In general terms, a good model enhances communication on a project and provides a common framework for understanding the software development process. It also enhances visibility to management and other interested parties. These advantages are valuable, even if the projections made with the model in a specific case are less accurate than desired.

Developing a practically useful software reliability model involves substantial theoretical work, tool building, and the accumulation of a body of lore from practical experience. This effort generally requires several person years. In contrast, the application of a model that is well established in practice requires a very small fraction of project resources. Consequently, the use of well-established models is strongly recommended.

It has sometimes been suggested that a large range of models be applied to each project. The ones that perform best (or some weighted combination of them) would be used. This approach may be suitable for research investigations. However, the use of more than one or two models is conceptually and economically impractical for real projects.

1.8 Problems

1. We have a text processing software product, developed totally within our software house. It must work with operating systems 1 and 2 and printer systems (hardware and software) A, B, C, and D. What systems should we test?

2. We have an object library of five objects that are used, respectively, in 20, 12, 4, 2, and 1 systems. Which objects would you select for separate test?

3. Our product uses a database that will be delivered 2 weeks before the start of system test. Should we certification test it?

2

Defining *Necessary* Reliability

Defining what we mean by necessary reliability for a product in quantitative terms is one of the key steps in achieving the benefits of software reliability engineering. The quantitative definition of reliability makes it possible for us to balance customer needs for reliability, delivery date, and cost precisely and to develop and test the product more efficiently. Before we discuss the procedure for defining necessary reliability, we need to make sure we have a common level of understanding of the relevant concepts.

2.1 Concepts

We will discuss failures, faults, and the distinction between them; failure severity classes; and failure intensity.

2.1.1 Failure and fault

A *failure* is a departure of system behavior in execution from user requirements; it is a user-oriented concept. A *fault* is the defect that causes or can potentially cause the failure when executed; it is a developer-oriented concept (Musa, 1989a). For example, suppose that a particular dialog box should appear on your screen when you click on a specific menu item, but it does not. This behavior constitutes a failure. The fault that is causing the failure might be missing code. The distinction between these two concepts is important; it has often been confused in the literature. The definitions presented here are Institute of Electrical and Electronics Engineers (IEEE) and American Standards Association (ASA) standards. We designate failures and faults by the system component in which they arise: commonly, hardware, software, or human. The discussions in this book can generally apply to all designations of failures and faults unless otherwise noted.

Note that *failure* implies operation of the system. A software failure must occur during execution of a program. Potential failures found by programmers as the result of design inspections, code reading, and other methods do not count. Some projects have included documentation faults in the count of software faults. This is generally *incorrect,* because documentation does not directly affect the execution of the program. Documentation faults may well lead to human user failures because the users will receive incorrect information on the use of the program. However, users are not software components; you should consider them as a separate system component with regard to failures and reliability.

A software fault is a defect in code. It is caused by an *error,* which is an incorrect or missing action by a person or persons. For example, a systems engineer may make an error in defining the requirements, resulting in a fault in the code, which in turn results in a failure when executed under certain conditions.

2.1.2   Failure severity classes

A *failure severity class* is a set of failures that have the same per-failure impact on users. We assign severity classes to failures primarily for use with failure frequencies to prioritize failures for resolution.

Common classification criteria include human life, cost, and system capability impacts. Each of these criteria can include many subcriteria, some of which may be important for a particular application. For example, cost impact may include extra operational cost, repair and recovery cost, and loss of present or potential business. System capability impact may include such subcriteria as loss of critical data, recoverability, and downtime. For systems where availability is important, failures that result in greater downtime will often be placed in a higher failure severity class. Also note that severity can change with the time of a failure. For example, a failure of a banking system during the lunch hour when many customers are waiting for service is more severe than at other times. When you are defining the failure severity classes you will use, experience indicates that the best approach is to brainstorm all the possible factors you may want to consider and then narrow those down to the most significant ones. Some factors are real but difficult to measure, such as impact on company reputation and its influence on market share.

In general, failure severity classes are widely separated in impact because it isn't possible to estimate impact with high accuracy. For example, failure severity classes based on cost may be separated by factors of 10. There usually aren't more than four failure severity classes;

TABLE 2.1   Failure Severity Classes
Based on Cost

Severity class	Definition ($)
1	>100,000
2	10,000–100,000
3	1000–10,000
4	<1000

these represent a range in effect of about 1000. A greater range of effect isn't useful; the effect of the lowest class would be so negligible that these failures would be essentially insignificant.

Table 2.1 shows an example of failure severity classes based on cost (per failure). Failure severity classes based on system capability impact are frequently used in telecommunications, as shown in Table 2.2.

2.1.3   Failure intensity

Failure intensity is an alternative way of expressing reliability (you may recall that reliability is the probability that a system will operate without failure for a specified number of natural units or a specified time— known as the mission time). We commonly use failure intensity in software reliability engineering because of its simplicity and intuitive appeal. It was originally defined only as failures per unit time. Thus you will see it expressed most often with respect to time in formulas and derivations. For example, you might have 1 failure per 1000 h.

The type of time used for hardware is usually ordinary time (age or operating time) because it represents the principal failure-inducing stress placed on hardware. Musa (1975) first recognized that execution time (the time the program is executing) is the essential metric for software because it represents the failure-inducing stress placed on programs. Note that a program in a period of nonexecution cannot fail. Musa recognized that the number of instructions executed was even more basic than execution time. However, execution time had the advantages of more manageable numbers and closer relationship with

TABLE 2.2   Failure Severity Classes Based on System Capability Impact

Failure severity class	Definition
1	Unavailability to users of one or more key operations
2	Unavailability to users of one or more important operations
3	Unavailability to users of one or more operations but workarounds available
4	Minor deficiencies in one or more operations

the metrics used in hardware reliability. A close relationship was desirable because the ultimate objective was to look at system reliability. Most software reliability theory has been developed in terms of execution time.

Extensive experience with software-based products has shown that it is often more convenient to express failure intensity as failures per natural unit. A *natural unit* is a unit that is related to the output of a software-based product and hence the amount of processing done. Some illustrations are pages of output (one failure per 1000 pages printed), transactions such as reservations, sales, or deposits (one failure per 1000 transactions), and telephone calls (one failure per 1000 calls). Users prefer natural units because they express reliability in terms that are oriented toward and important to their business. The measurement of natural units is often easier to implement than that of execution time, especially for distributed systems, because otherwise we must deal with a complex of execution times. This is true even though for some distributed systems, the execution times of the programs running on the various processing elements will be proportional to each other. Because natural units are related to the amount of processing done, they also represent the amount of failure-inducing stress placed on the software. Thus you can expect the number of failures experienced to be related to the number of natural units that have occurred. Note that natural units readily form a common measure across hardware and software.

We have been talking about failure intensity as an alternative way of expressing reliability. Thus the units we choose for expressing failure intensity are used for expressing reliability as well. For example, if we speak of a failure intensity of five failures per 1000 printed pages, the reliability will be expressed in terms of some specified number of printed pages.

Although there are many possible ways in which components can interact to affect the reliability of a system, there is only one "combination" of components that is easily and hence widely applied in practice: If the successful operation of the system requires successful operation of all the components, the system failure intensity will be the sum of all the component failure intensities.

2.2 Procedure

In order to define what we mean by the necessary reliability for each system we are analyzing for our product development, we must

1. Define *failure* with severity classes for the product
2. Choose a common measure for all associated systems
3. Set a failure intensity objective for each system to be tested

If you are developing any software for the product or its variations, for that software, you must

1. Find the developed software failure intensity objective
2. Engineer strategies to meet the developed software failure intensity objective

If you are simply integrating components to create the product, the foregoing two tasks are not necessary. Although all the foregoing activities were traditionally done just by system engineers and system architects, including testers in these activities provides a strong basis for a better testing effort. Similarly, you should involve users in failure definition and in setting system failure intensity objectives.

2.2.1 Defining *failure* with severity classes for the product

Defining failures implies establishing negative requirements on program behavior, as desired by users. This sharpens the definition of the function of the system by providing the perspective of what the system should not be doing. The definition process consists of outlining these requirements in a project-specific, consistent fashion for each severity class.

For Fone Follower, we will use system capability impact as the severity class classification criterion. Defining failure specifically for this product in terms of different severities, we obtain the classification shown in Table 2.3.

TABLE 2.3   Failure Severity Classes For Fone Follower

Failure severity class	Failure definition
1	Failure that prevents calls from being forwarded.
2	Failure that prevents entry of phone numbers to which calls will be forwarded.
3	Failure that makes system administration more difficult although possible through alternate means: For example, the system administrator (a telephone company employee that controls Fone Follower) can't add or delete users from the convenient graphical user interface provided with the system but can use a less convenient text interface that is provided.
4	Failure that causes minor inconvenience: For example, system administrator's screen doesn't display current date.

2.2.2 Choosing a common measure for all associated systems

As previously noted, the measure of choice is natural units. The natural unit should have an average constant amount of processing (which can be viewed as the number of instructions executed, summed over all machines in the case of distributed processing), where the average is taken over the interval between failures. In some cases, a product may have multiple natural units, each related to an important (from the viewpoint of use and criticality) set of functions of the product. In this case, select time as the basis for failure intensity. It will usually be easiest to measure ordinary time, and it will provide a common measure across hardware and software, although execution time is preferable when measuring the software parts of systems. Time is an acceptable approximation of execution time if average (over the interval between failures) computer utilization (the ratio of execution time to time) does not vary much from one such interval to another. This situation often holds, so time is proportional to execution time and may be used in place of it. If the situation does not hold, we will measure actual execution time and convert to an adjusted time by dividing by computer utilization averaged over the life of the system in question, as described in Sec. 5.3.3.

2.2.3 Setting a system failure intensity objective for each system to be tested

Setting system failure intensity objectives for the systems to be tested involves setting these objectives for supersystems, the product and its variations, and acquired components. Normally we will set the same failure intensity objective for the variations of the product as for the basic product.

We will set the system failure intensity objectives for the supersystems directly. If a product and its variations stand alone (they are not part of any supersystems), we will also set the system failure intensity objective for them (the same objective for all variations) directly.

If a product is part of one or more supersystems, we proceed as follows to set the system failure intensity objective for it and its variations. Determine the system failure intensity objective required of the product by each supersystem by subtracting the total of the expected failure intensities of the other component systems from the system failure intensity objective of the supersystem. Then take the minimum of these system failure intensity objective requirements as the system failure intensity objective for the product.

Set the system failure intensity objective for each acquired component as the expected failure intensity for that component.

Set the system failure intensity objective for a supersystem or the stand-alone product based on an analysis of the specific needs and expectations of users and users' customers in relation to the product characteristics. You should measure the present major quality characteristics (failure intensity, development time, and development cost) and determine the degree of satisfaction with them. This should be done in the context of the capabilities of competing products and the failure intensities of connecting systems. Competing systems may represent competing companies or simply alternative technologies or alternative implementations. Then change the characteristics as needed, noting that there is a tradeoff among them.

For a given release, the product of the following factors tends to be roughly constant and related to the amount of new functionality added and the current level of software development technology (the number decreases as the technology advances):

1. Failure intensity

2. Development time

3. Development cost

Increasing development time or cost, or both, makes it feasible to set a lower failure intensity objective. Similarly, attaining a shorter development time will increase cost or failure intensity or both. Achieving a lower cost will increase development time or failure intensity or both. Reducing the functionality (number of operations) to be added allows you to decrease some combination of failure intensity, development time, and development cost. However, greater new functionality and/or a lower failure intensity may result in a lower operational cost so that the total cost of buying and operating the product for your customers may be less. Hence each product must be studied separately and sometimes for several different customer types. Section 2.5.2 discusses life-cycle cost optimization.

It would be helpful if we knew the precise relationships among failure intensity, development time, cost, functionality, and technology. Then we could make accurate tradeoffs. Many of the variables that affect failure intensity are known (see Sec. 8.4.4), as is whether increasing the values of the variables increases or decreases failure intensity. However, the exact relationships and the values of the constants generally are not known. Determining these relationships awaits the collection and intelligent analysis of data from large numbers of projects.

If you cannot obtain *any* information that would let you follow the foregoing procedures, the guidelines of Table 2.4 may help you. Please note that these are experiential to a large degree, although there is some logic to support them. The guideline with respect to the risk to

TABLE 2.4   System Failure Intensity Objective Guidelines

Failure impact	Typical failure intensity objective (failure per hour)	Time between failures
Hundreds of deaths, more than 10^9 cost	10^{-9}	114,000 years
One or two deaths, around 10^6 cost	10^{-6}	114 years
Around $1000 cost	10^{-3}	6 weeks
Around $100 cost	10^{-2}	100 h
Around $10 cost	10^{-1}	10 h
Around $1 cost	1	1 h

human life is based on the fact that the risk of death in an automobile accident in the United States is in the vicinity of one per million hours of travel. Because we generally accept this level of risk, as witnessed by our general use of automobiles, it seems appropriate to apply it more generally. Consequently, guidelines for failure intensity objectives for aircraft control systems and aircraft traffic control systems are commonly in the area of one failure per billion hours of travel (assuming aircraft capacities of 100 to 400 passengers and acting conservatively). It is interesting to note that the aircraft fatal accident rate in the United States from all causes (hardware, software, operations) was about 250 per billion hours in 1997, with a government goal to reduce this to 50.

The cost criteria, which are entirely independent of the human life criteria, are based on the assumption that a "cost of failure" of around $1 per operating hour is generally acceptable. Such a cost is generally small in comparison with most operating costs (for example, wage costs).

We often state reliability figures in terms of individual users because this is a particularly convenient way for marketing experts to relate user needs and perceptions to quantitative specifications.

Let us now illustrate the process using Fone Follower. Fone Follower was a new product with no existing competitors. Market studies showed that a subscriber demanded no more than one failure per 10,000 calls on the standard telephone network and would tolerate no more than two failures per 10,000 calls when calls were forwarded. Fone Follower processes an average of 100,000 calls per hour. Thus we set the system failure intensity objective for the supersystem of the telephone network and Fone Follower at two failures per 10,000 calls. We set the system failure intensity objective for Fone Follower at one failure per 10,000 calls.

If user needs are expressed in terms of the most severe (severity 1) failures, convert any failure intensity objective expressed in these terms to a failure intensity objective for total failures from all severity classes by dividing by the expected ratio of severity 1 to total failures. As an illustration, if the severity 1 failure intensity objective is one failure per 1000 h and 10 percent of all failures are severity 1 failures, you should convert to a failure intensity objective for total failures of 10 failures per 1000 h. It is generally undesirable to set failure intensity objectives for classes of failures (by severity or any other category). When you estimate failure intensity by classes of failures, you reduce the sample size available, decreasing the accuracy of the estimate. The validity of the conversion from a severity 1 failure intensity objective to a total failure intensity objective depends on the ratio of severity 1 to total failures remaining constant over time. It appears that most projects have this experience. For example, on the Space Shuttle Ground System, ratios were taken of critical and major failures to total failures (Misra, 1983). The ratios were 0.33, 0.36, 0.38, and 0.36 at the four "quarter" points of the system test period.

You should set the failure intensity objective as an average over all operations (tasks, defined in Chap. 3) rather than try to meet the stringent requirements of a few critical but rarely occurring operations. You will see in Sec. 4.2.2 that we accelerate the testing of such operations over the frequency that would normally occur in the field, while maintaining a common failure intensity objective. This in effect divides the failure intensity objective for such operations by the acceleration factor.

In the process of setting objectives, you may need to convert reliability to failure intensity and vice versa. To convert from reliability to failure intensity, use

$$\lambda = \frac{-\ln R}{t} \tag{2.1}$$

where R = reliability, λ = failure intensity, and t = number of natural or time units. If R is larger than 0.95,

$$\lambda \approx \frac{(1 - R)}{t} \tag{2.2}$$

with less than 2.5 percent error.

To convert from failure intensity to reliability, use

$$R = \exp{(-\lambda t)} \tag{2.3}$$

If λt is less than 0.05,

$$R \approx 1 - \lambda t \tag{2.4}$$

with less than 2.5 percent error.

If reliability is 0.992 for 8 h, the failure intensity is one failure per 1000 h. Failure intensities of one failure per 1000 pages printed or one failure per 1000 transactions would convert to reliabilities of 0.992 for eight pages printed or 0.992 for eight transactions, respectively.

Equation 2.3, which relates reliability to failure intensity, is based on systems with a constant (for the period of the mission time) failure rate, which is the case for software systems that are stable (no changes are being made to them). Systems with varying failure rates (for example, systems in test) may have different expressions for reliability during test but will have the foregoing expression for reliability when testing stops and a system is released to the field.

The two conversion Eqs. 2.3 and 2.1 are related as follows:

$$R = \exp(-\lambda t)$$

$$-\lambda t = \ln R$$

$$\lambda = -\frac{\ln R}{t}$$

Table 2.5 shows some equivalents of reliability and failure intensity figures of general interest.

For many products, availability is the most important consideration in setting a failure intensity objective. *Availability A* is the fraction of time during which a system is functioning acceptably. It is given by

$$A = \frac{t_U}{t_U + t_D} \tag{2.5}$$

where t_U is the uptime, and t_D is the downtime. We may express the downtime as

$$t_D = t_m \lambda t_U \tag{2.6}$$

where t_m is the downtime per failure and λ is the failure intensity.

TABLE 2.5   Reliability and Failure Intensity
Equivalents

Reliability for 1-h mission time	Failure intensity
0.368	1 failure/h
0.9	105 failures/1000 h
0.959	1 failure/day
0.99	10 failures/1000 h
0.994	1 failure/week
0.9986	1 failure/month
0.999	1 failure/1000 h
0.99989	1 failure/year

For software, we usually take the downtime per failure as the time to recover from the failure, not the time required to find and remove the fault that is causing the failure. From Eqs. 2.5 and 2.6 we obtain

$$A = \frac{1}{1 + t_m \lambda} \qquad (2.7)$$

If the availability is specified for a product, the downtime per failure will determine what the failure intensity objective must be:

$$\lambda = \frac{1-A}{At_m} \qquad (2.8)$$

For example, if a product must be available 99 percent of the time and downtime is 6 min (0.1 h), the failure intensity objective will be approximately 0.1 failure per hour or 100 failures per 1000 h.

Because understanding user needs is so important, it is highly desirable to involve users in the planning of failure intensity objectives (and in developing operational profiles, as we shall see in Chap. 3). The perceived quality of a product to a user is ordinarily higher if that user has participated in the development in some way. In any case, the user is likely to gain a better appreciation of the realities of development and be more reasonable in his or her requests. Further, extending participation to users generally creates strong reservoirs of good will and is an important factor in developing long-term customer satisfaction.

If your product has a few major customers, the choice of which users to involve is relatively simple. Most such customers will not view the time such users spend in working with you as an excessive demand. However, if you have a large base of small customers, as is the case for packaged software or applications downloaded from the Internet, you may need to resort to random sampling of users, and you may need to limit the amount of effort you request from each of them. You may also need to offer incentives for their participation (money, a free product, etc.). Here you must be careful that the need to get volunteers and the incentives do not skew the sample of users you are obtaining, or you must compensate for this in interpreting the user needs that this sample of users expresses.

2.2.4 Determining the developed software failure intensity objective for the product and its variations

If you are developing any software for the product or its variations, in each case you will need to set the developed software failure intensity objective. Note that suppliers who simply integrate software components will not need developed software failure intensity objectives, unless the control program that links the components is sufficiently large that we should consider it in itself as developed software.

First you must find the expected acquired failure intensity for each system (product or variation). To do this, estimate the expected failure intensities for the hardware and the acquired software components in the system. The estimates should be based (in order of preference) on

1. Operational data

2. Vendor warranty

3. Experience of experts

A component failure is a behavior that would cause system failure. Add all of the expected component failure intensities to get the system expected acquired failure intensity.

You can now obtain the developed software failure intensity objective for each system by subtracting the expected acquired failure intensity from the corresponding system failure intensity objective.

In the case of Fone Follower, we obtained operational data from vendors that indicated that the total failure intensity for all hardware components was 0.1 failure per hour and that the operating system failure intensity at a load of 100,000 calls per hour, on the chosen computer, was 0.4 failure per hour. Because there are 100,000 calls per hour, the hardware failure intensity converts to one failure per million calls and the operating system failure intensity converts to four failures per million calls. Adding the hardware and operating system failure intensities, we obtain an expected acquired failure intensity of five failures per million calls.

Subtracting the expected acquired failure intensity of five failures per million calls from the system failure intensity objective of 100 failures per million calls yields a developed software failure intensity objective of 95 failures per million calls.

In most cases, the acquired software components will be the same for the product and all its variations. Hence, because the system failure intensity objective is usually the same for the product and all its variations, the developed software failure intensity objective will also be the same.

If the developed software failure intensity objective for the product is greatly different from the failure intensities of the acquired components, consider a rebalancing of the developed software failure intensity objective with the failure intensities of the components if other choices of components are available. If you expect the developed software failure intensity objective to be difficult to meet, increase it by either increasing the system failure intensity objective (this may require renegotiation with customers) or decreasing the expected hardware and acquired software failure intensity objectives, which will require either finding new suppliers or components or renegotiating with existing suppliers.

Simple addition of the failure intensities of acquired components to obtain acquired failure intensity is based on assuming that all components must function for the system to function and that they are independent of each other. Note that this is an approximation; every operation may not require all components to function for the operation to function. Then adding the failure intensities of all acquired components may overestimate the failure intensity that must be allocated to acquired components and underestimate the failure intensity that can be tolerated for the developed system. The underestimate is acceptable because you will be conservative and "playing it safe." If the components are not independent of each other, a failure in one may cause a failure in another. But the first failure will already have caused the system to fail; hence our simplified approach also works in this case from a practical standpoint.

2.2.5 Engineering strategies to meet the developed software failure intensity objectives

Once you have set the developed software failure intensity objectives for the product and its variations, it is necessary in each case to engineer the right balance among reliability strategies and determine where to focus them to maximize the likelihood of meeting the objectives in as timely and economical a fashion as possible. Because the objectives for the product and its variations are often the same, the strategies will often be the same. Note that suppliers who are just integrating software components will generally not have to concern themselves with engineering reliability strategies, although they will have to select and probably certification test the components in such a way that the system failure intensity is met for the product and each of its variations. Although this engineering has in the past primarily been the province of system engineers and system architects, the impact on testing is substantial. Hence it is at least necessary for testers to understand it. It is better to go further by including testers in the system engineering and system architecture teams.

There are three principal strategies, fault prevention, fault removal, and fault tolerance. As we will see shortly, testing is part of the fault removal strategy. Recall that faults refer to defects in code; defects in requirements and design are described as errors.

You prevent faults through such activities as applying requirements methodologies, holding requirements reviews, implementing design methodologies, conducting design reviews, establishing and enforcing standards, and using requirements and design tools that prevent errors from occurring that cause faults. The effectiveness of fault prevention can be measured in theory by the proportion of faults remaining after prevention activities. Of course, you can only approximate the measure because faults don't actually exist until coding occurs. However, it appears likely that in the future you will be able to relate fault prevention effectiveness to measures of errors removed and estimates of errors remaining prior to coding, using analogs of the software reliability models used in testing. The proportion by which you reduce errors is expected to result in similar proportionate reductions in faults and in failure intensity, but studies will be needed to determine the precise relationships.

We remove faults primarily through code reviews and test. You can measure the effectiveness of code review by the proportion of faults left after code review. You estimate the total number of faults as the total number of faults found since the start of coding plus the number of faults remaining. We probably will be able to estimate the latter by using analogs of the software reliability models used in testing, but this has not yet been demonstrated. Again, there will be a corresponding reduction in failure intensity, as long as you conduct the code reviews for all the code that is executed by the operations that make up most of the occurrence probability experienced in the field. We can measure the effectiveness of test by the ratio of failure intensity after test to the failure intensity at the start of test. It should be possible to run experiments with different testing approaches such as test selection methods and use software reliability measurement to evaluate their relative effectiveness. We discuss a way of measuring test efficiency (relative effectiveness with respect to execution time of test) and a possible approach to improving it in Secs. 4.4.1 and 4.4.2. Note that the effectiveness measures defined for test assume that the faults that are causing the failures that are identified are, in turn, identified and removed.

You must achieve fault tolerance by design. Determine what deviations are likely to occur that are also likely to lead to failures and implement software to counteract them. We can measure the effectiveness of fault tolerance by the reduction in failure intensity that results.

One way of describing the balance of strategies to apply to a development project is by the effectiveness factors to be achieved by fault prevention (actually measured as an error reduction factor), fault removal (code review effectiveness and test effectiveness), and fault tolerance. It would be very helpful if practitioners could collect data on failure intensity reduction obtained for specific strategies such as requirements reviews and even for parameters of these strategies such as failure intensity reduction obtained as a function of staff hours expended per thousand source lines of developed code.

It should be possible to gain insight into the best set of strategies for different developed software failure intensity objectives by collecting and analyzing project data. "Best" would involve considering the effect of the strategy on development time and cost. For example, fault tolerant strategies increase development time and cost. They may increase operational costs in the field, although this factor is diminishing with the rapid increases occurring in computing power per cost unit. Requirements and design reviews are usually in the critical path of a project; extra time devoted to them directly delays the delivery date.

Because these studies have not currently been done, we will simply present some approximate guidelines drawn from experience and discussions with software developers.

First, you can expect fault reduction through test to be essential on every project, regardless of the amounts of fault prevention or fault tolerance implemented. Software that has a failure intensity objective of less than 0.1 failure per 1000 execution hours will probably require the use of at least some fault tolerance. We have divided systems into about four categories and suggested strategy guidelines for each, as indicated in Table 2.6. Remember that these figures refer to execution hours. Although the possibility of commercial software failing every half hour of execution time may seem high, computer utilizations are often sufficiently low that this is only once per day.

Let's now consider where to focus the reliability strategies. The most valuable tool is the operational profile (described in Chap. 3) and the knowledge of which operations are critical. This information will suggest which operations should receive the most attention and how the

TABLE 2.6 System Failure Intensity Objective Categories with Strategy Guidelines

Reliability level	Failure intensity range (failures per 1000 execution hours)	Strategy guidelines
Ultrareliable	<0.1	Fault tolerance, extensive requirements and design reviews essential.
High reliability	0.1–10	Fairly extensive requirements and design reviews desirable; some fault tolerance may be desirable.
Commercial	10–2000	Guide any requirements or design reviews with operational profile and criticality.
Prototype	>2000	Testing usually more practical than fault tolerance or requirements or design reviews.

attention should be divided. You can use the operational profile to allocate resources among the operations. The information can be particularly useful in regard to reviews, whose time duration must be limited due to their presence on the critical path. Allocate the time available for the reviews in accordance with the operational profile and the criticality information.

If you have defined major components of your product as systems to be tested, knowledge of how the actual failure intensities in the field of these components at the last release compared with their objectives can suggest which need the most attention.

Finally, you will probably want to devote some effort to improving your development process. This is really an activity that partly transcends project boundaries, even though a product must have the process tuned to its particular needs. The general procedure here is to prioritize the failures you experience in the field by impact, which can be measured as the "product" in some sense of failure intensity and severity. Analyze the failures in order of their impact. Determine where and why the fault causing the failure was introduced and how the introduction could have been prevented through development process changes. Could the fault have been detected earlier? Is there an improvement in the development process that would have made this happen? Establish which process changes would be cost effective and proceed to implement them in the order of their benefit/cost ratios.

2.3   Special Situations

On some projects you may sometimes wish to set failure intensity objectives for special groups of failures for various purposes. In doing this for components, you may wish to allocate a system failure intensity among various components. Or you may wish to set objectives for and track some quantity other than failure intensity. Finally, many projects are concerned with safety, a subset of reliability, or with systems that must be ultrareliable. These special situations are discussed here.

2.3.1   Other failure groupings

Most projects limit characterization of failures to "severity class." However, it is possible to characterize failure into groups in many other ways for special purposes, such as

1. *Component* (part of a system, for example, a software module)

2. *Operation group* (set of associated operations—defined in Chap. 3— such as data entry operations, report generation operations)

3. *Failure category* (set of failures that have the same kind of impact on users, such as safety)

4. *Job role,* such as data entry or customer service

Components represent a *physical* division of a system, whereas operation groups represent a *functional* division. For example, you might characterize failures by component to identify problem components. You can use (at least in theory) operation groups to differentiate reliabilities of different activities such as data entry or report generation. Failure categories are useful for making, for example, safety estimates. Grouping by job roles lets you evaluate reliabilities associated with these roles. However, dividing the failure sample will reduce the accuracy of failure intensity estimates due to small sample problems, so this is not a good idea in most cases. In practice, the number of groups you can define is limited by small sample problems and by errors resulting from estimating the group/total failure ratios.

If you wish to use one of these characterizations, the procedure will be analogous to that for setting a failure intensity objective for a specific severity class such as severity class 1. You will estimate the expected group/total failure ratio. The total failure intensity objective will be determined by dividing the group failure intensity objective by the group/total failure ratio.

2.3.2   Allocation of failure intensity objective to components

We generally determine the failure intensities of hardware and acquired software components from existing experience with these components. It is a simple matter of combining their actual failure intensities and then finding out what the failure intensity objective for the developed software must be to yield the failure intensity objective for the product. We don't generally consider tradeoffs, because we do not usually have the freedom to select among different versions of acquired components at different failure intensity levels for a product we are building. We usually can't negotiate failure intensities with suppliers either, because off-the-shelf components will generally be used because of limitations on development time. However, tradeoffs can be possible when multiple versions of the components exist or when we can have them developed to order.

Here is an approach for allocating or budgeting failure intensity to multiple components for the situation in which tradeoffs are feasible. There are two steps:

1. Divide the system into appropriate components

2. Determine what the component failure objectives must be

The principal criteria for dividing the system into components are the nature of the system configuration, project management issues, and the greater effort and cost of managing reliability for a larger number of components.

System configuration suggests the appropriate division when there are common components that exist across different operational modes, when the project integration is phased by component, when certain components are critical, or where there are components with known failure intensities. Project management considerations suggest the appropriate division when different components are developed by different organizations or where certain components have high development risk.

Note that dividing the system into components that correspond as much as possible with existing components that we can reuse is extremely desirable. Clearly there will be much less development time and cost for using an existing component than for developing a new one. We can expect the reused components to have lower initial failure intensities than the corresponding newly developed components. Hence we can build the remaining components to less stringent reliability standards than would otherwise be the case. Consequently, they will cost less and require less time to develop. Remember that database management systems, graphical user interfaces, etc., are actually reusable components.

Let's show the process by considering a variation of our familiar Fone Follower illustration that we will call Fone Follower Fast. The objective of Fone Follower Fast is to quickly provide a basic subset of Fone Follower capabilities before any competitors can get to market. Fone Follower Fast uses hardware and an operating system provided by different divisions of the same external supplier. The application program is developed in-house. The failure intensity of the hardware is accurately known. The operating system is being custom-built for Fone Follower Fast, and the supplier is willing to negotiate different levels of failure intensity with different delivery dates.

There is no "correct" solution for dividing the system into components. One possible solution would be to divide the system into two components: hardware with operating system and application. This solution is achieved for less effort and cost than dividing into three components. However, because we are dealing with two divisions of the supplier, it will probably be best to work with three components.

Now we will determine the component failure intensity objectives. Let us sketch out an overview of the process before plunging into the details:

1. Establish known component values

2. Pick a trial allocation of component failure intensity objectives to minimize system development time, development risk, or development cost

3. Compute a trial system failure intensity figure from trial component failure intensities and compare this to the requirement

4. Modify the allocation and recompute the trial system failure intensity until it matches the requirement

Recall that the system objective is 100 failures per million calls. The hardware chosen for Fone Follower Fast has a failure intensity of one failure per million calls. Then the operating system and application together can have a failure intensity of no more than 99 failures per million calls.

Project managers for the operating system and the application estimate, based on experience and all the data available to them, the development durations for different failure intensity objectives given in Table 2.7. Although there is certainly some uncertainty in these figures, we will not complicate our illustration by conducting a sensitivity analysis here.

For our first trial, let us try to complete both software components in 39 weeks. The trial failure intensity objectives are 6 failures per million calls for the operating system and 100 failures per million calls for the application. Unfortunately, the sum of the two failure intensity objectives, 106, exceeds the required amount of 99. Try a second allocation based on 42 weeks development time. The component failure intensity objectives are 4 failures per million calls for the operating system and 95 failures per million calls for the application. The sum of the failure intensities, 99, meets the requirement.

2.3.3. Software safety and ultrareliability

There is a fairly widely held opinion that software safety and software reliability are such different concepts that they don't have much to con-

TABLE 2.7   Fone Follower: Development
Durations for Different Failure Intensity Objectives

Failure intensity (failures per million calls)	Development time (weeks)
Operating System	
2	45
4	42
6	39
Application	
90	45
95	42
100	39

tribute to each other. This is unfortunate, because we may not be approaching some of the difficult problems we are facing with all the tools that are available to us. This may have come about because the cultures in which these concepts were developed have been somewhat different.

We usually define *software safety* as freedom from *mishaps,* where a mishap is an event that causes loss of human life, injury, or property damage. *Software reliability* is the probability that a system will run without failure for a specified period of time. A *failure* is any behavior in operation that will cause user dissatisfaction. Although the fact has not been widely recognized, note how mishaps form a subset of failures, because clearly a mishap would result in user dissatisfaction. Consequently, software safety is really a subset of software reliability. Once one recognizes this fact, it is evident that all the theory, models, and statistics of software reliability apply to software safety as well. Further, you can generally apply techniques that have been refined in the software safety world, such as fault-tree analysis, to the software reliability world.

Demonstrable software safety is very dependent on realistic testing. The concept of operational profiles, developed in the software reliability area, can be very helpful in focusing testing on those software functions that will be encountered most in the field.

The strategies of fault tolerance, fault avoidance, and fault removal that we use to improve software reliability can also be used to improve software safety. In the fault-avoidance area, we can use the rich heritage of requirements reviews, design reviews, and code inspections for software reliability and software safety simultaneously.

Software safety requirements often are very demanding in that frequency of mishaps must be very low, but we may require this same low frequency of failures as well. Thus software safety is usually closely linked to ultrareliability requirements. There has been a great deal of pessimism about testing and measuring reliability for ultrareliable software. Although the problem is challenging, there are techniques that you can apply.

There is no clear dividing line between high reliability and ultrareliability (Musa, 1994d), but the term *ultrareliability* is often used to refer to failure intensities of less than 10^{-4} failures per execution hour (one failure per 10,000 execution hours).

It is important to realize that the need for ultrareliability refers to *operations* (tasks, as defined in Chap. 3) rather than systems. For example, the operation that shuts down a nuclear power plant in an emergency must be ultrareliable. This does not imply that the entire system must be ultrareliable; there are many routine operating and data logging operations that do not require it. In many cases it is much easier to separate software by operation than it is for hardware and to focus reliability-enhancing efforts just on the critical operations.

There is an important distinction you should make in regard to reliability of hardware and software components. Reliability of hardware components is affected by factors such as aging and wear. Consequently, reliability is related to ordinary time. In contrast, only the execution time of the program affects reliability. The execution time of a software function is often only a small fraction of the ordinary time taken by the entire system for its operation.

For example, planetary probes commonly involve flights of several years. Although the hardware must be ultrareliable for this time period, the critical software functions may not have the same requirements. Critical navigation and maneuver software, for example, may execute only about 10 times in a 5-year flight, with each execution lasting 3 to 5 s. Thus such software requires reliability over a total execution time of about 0.01 h, a duration that is shorter than the flight by a factor of about 4×10^6.

The expense, development time, and difficulties involved in building ultrareliable functions are such that we need to take a very realistic attitude in setting failure intensity objectives. Some designers have argued that relating failure intensities to the existing "average" human death rate of about 10^{-6}/h is reasonable, on the basis that we generally "accept" that rate. The argument assumes that death is the most catastrophic event possible to a person. Thus, the acceptable intensities for other failures of lesser impact can scale up from there. Failures that would entail effects on many people would result in scaling down the failure intensity objective by the number of people involved.

It is also important that we separate operations by criticality and apply ultrahigh reliability objectives only to those operations that require them. This implies that the software architecture must be modular by operation and that special care be taken to prevent interactions between modules.

You should carefully establish the duration for which the software must function. The failure intensity acceptable for the software is the system failure intensity divided by the *duty cycle,* or proportion of time that the software is executing. Thus to obtain a system failure intensity of, say, 10^{-9} failures per hour for a planetary probe, where the duty cycle of the navigation and maneuver module might be 0.25×10^{-6}, we would need a module failure intensity of 4×10^{-3} failures per execution hour.

Testing of ultrareliable functions requires a test duration that is several times the reciprocal of the failure intensity objective (Miller, 1989). The multiplier increases with the level of confidence required. Many have concluded that we therefore cannot certify ultrareliable software through testing. This is overly pessimistic. It is based entirely on statistical reasoning, not taking into account a number of software engineering considerations that ease the problem. In the planetary probe case we have taken as an example a full system test necessary to demonstrate a level of 10^{-9} failures per hour would require some multiple of 10^9 h (about 114,000 years). However, the test of the navigation and maneuver module requires only a multiple of 250 h, which is readily achievable.

There are at least two other factors that can mitigate the testing problem. Many ultrareliable applications are implemented on relatively inexpensive embedded computers. It is feasible to test software on N machines, reducing the time duration by a factor of N. It is also possible to test software on a set of faster machines, as long as the instruction set is a superset of that of the target machine for the application. It is quite conceivable to obtain an overall speedup by a factor of 10,000 (perhaps 1000 machines running 10 times as fast) by these methods.

Alternatives to the application of software reliability engineering appear worse. They all involve relying on trying to make the process of software engineering sufficiently rigorous such that the products can be counted on to be reliable. But there is no standard software development process in place at present and there is no evidence to indicate that there ever will be. In fact, the discipline of software process engineering virtually guarantees that there will not be. Any process is replete with opportunities for human error and hence failure. But as noted, there is no standard for the intensive scrutiny required to ensure an ultrareliable process. Even if there were, process attributes are less concrete, visible, and measurable and hence much harder to check than the product attributes software reliability engineering uses.

2.4   Frequently Asked Questions

In this section we will first consider questions about the definition of failures. Then we will look at questions about severity classes and setting objectives. After answering many conceptual questions that have arisen, we will end by responding to practical questions that came up in applying the methods of this chapter.

2.4.1   Definition of failure

1 Would you define *failure* differently in a very competitive environment?

ANSWER: Possibly. You might define failure in a competitive environment as any departure of program operation from customer *expectations* rather than requirements. There is a danger, however. If you are too free in labeling behaviors as failures, you may end up overemphasizing reliability at the expense of other customer values such as cost and delivery date. One possibility would be to define failure as any departure of program operation from behavior that one might expect of your principal competitors' products.

2   How should you view incorrect or inconsistent requirements in relation to defining failures?

ANSWER: Incorrect or inconsistent requirements differ from the requirements that were intended. Hence they contain errors, which may result in faults that can cause failures.

3   Our programmers implemented exactly what the written requirements specified. Is it still possible for a failure to occur?

ANSWER: Yes, your system engineers may have made an error by inadequately understanding user requirements. The system's behavior will not meet user requirements; hence there will be a failure.

4   Many operating systems can recover from certain kinds of software malfunctions and continue to process work. Are these malfunctions failures?

ANSWER: If the only system requirement is to process work, the answer is No. Failures relate only to external behavior of the system, not internal malfunctions.

5   Can a deficiency in performance of a software component (for example, excessive response time at a given traffic level) be a failure?

ANSWER: Yes, as long as it is a requirement for that software component. Note that in this case the fault may be complex and distributed throughout the software component, because it relates to insufficient speed of execution. Poor response time can also result from system overload. This can be a hardware failure resulting from inadequate design or capacity or a "human subsystem" failure resulting from a violation of operating procedures. Although it is possible for a performance deficiency to be a failure, you may prefer to separate performance requirements from functional requirements to prevent such a deficiency from being counted as a failure. You would do this to avoid failures that depend on hardware capacity.

6   Are there situations where you might want to simultaneously give broad and narrow definitions to failures? For example, you might broadly define a failure as "any program operational behavior that is unsatisfactory to the customer." The simultaneous narrow definition would be "any departure of program operation from written program requirements."

ANSWER: Yes. Failure intensity calculated on the basis of the narrow definition would indicate reliability based on the developer's understanding of what the customer wanted (or possibly developer-customer agreement on what was needed if the customer thoroughly understood and reviewed the requirements document). It would thus describe reliability with respect to what could be achieved for the current version of the program. It may not be reasonable to expect a system to satisfy more than the explicit requirements in the current version.

Failure intensity calculated on the basis of the broad definition indicates reliability based on customer satisfaction. The difference between the two failure intensities is an indicator of the joint effects of three major factors, the quality of the customer-developer communication, the rate of change of functionality needed by the customer, and the rate of change of program environment.

7 If a nonfunctional requirement is not met, does that indicate a failure?

ANSWER: No, because there is no departure of system *behavior* in execution from user requirements.

2.4.2 Failure severity classes

1 To what extent can we associate severity of failures with criticality of operations?

ANSWER: In general, we can associate severity of failures with criticality of operations very well when the failures prevent the operations from working at all. Then the impact of the failure is the impact of the operation not working. Usually anyone who understands the overall set of operations being performed and how the particular operation relates to them can clearly establish this.

When the failures only degrade the execution of the operations, the severity of the failures depends on the degree of the degradation as well as the criticality of the operation. Evaluation of impact here is more complex.

2 How do we handle the fact that different users may assign different severities to a failure? For example, in a telecommunications system, connection time greater than a certain value may be represented by degraded basic service to a telemarketer and hence be a class 2 failure. It may be only an annoyance to a residential customer and hence a class 3 or 4 failure.

ANSWER: The most practical approach is to apply the user profile (list of user types with their associated probabilities of occurrence) to each failure. Determine the severity of that failure for each user type. Take the weighted (by user probability) sum of failure severities as the severity of that failure, and use it for all occurrences of the failure.

3 It is the practice on our system to select failure severity classifications based at least partly on whether a workaround exists to circumvent the problem. Does this make sense?

ANSWER: Yes. When a workaround does not exist, the cost or other impact of the failure will be greater.

4 Does the severity classification of a failure remain the same from release to release?

ANSWER: Usually but not always.

5 Most reliability strategies are directed at reducing failure intensity. Is it possible to also focus on reducing the severity of a failure?

ANSWER: Yes. This will be a fault-tolerant technique that reduces the severity of a failure rather than eliminating it. For example, when a failure is detected, the program may keep it from propagating and causing greater damage.

6 Is there such a thing as fault severity?

ANSWER: This is not a term that is in general use, because the cost of finding and removing a fault is usually very small compared to the impact of a failure. Hence there is little need to differentiate among faults.

Some researchers have used this term to signify the total impact of all failures associated with a fault, taking account of both the different failures caused by the fault and the frequency of occurrence of these failures. This results in a concept that is dependent on the operational profile and is hence quite complex. We strongly advise against this definition of the term.

2.4.3 Setting failure intensity objectives

1 How do you discuss reliability needs with the user?

ANSWER: Usually you talk about reliability needs in terms of the *product*, because the user is not normally interested in the reliability of the software per se. It is generally the developer's responsibility to determine what the reliabilities of the various associated systems of the product and the various hardware and software components of each system should be. Further, you would normally discuss reliability along with other system attributes that it affects, such as cost and delivery date, so that the user is forced to recognize the reality of the tradeoff.

2 Why don't we establish a developed software release criterion based on the number of failures remaining rather than failure intensity?

ANSWER: First, the software user can more readily interpret failure intensity in terms of impact on operations and cost. Second, you can combine the developed software failure intensity with the failure intensities of acquired components to yield a system reliability figure. You can't do either of these things with number of failures remaining. Note that failures remaining indicates remaining failures that would occur in infinite test time, not remaining failures that would occur in the field.

3 I am developing a contractual specification for software that will be delivered to a user by my company. How should I incorporate a failure intensity specification?

ANSWER: Assuming that the operations to be performed by the software are well specified, you should determine the expected operational profile. The contract should specify that there will be an acceptance test with input states picked randomly to verify performance of the operations, the probability of selection of each operation being determined by the operational profile. State the desired failure intensity objective. The contract would require that failure intensity be demonstrated by means of certification test.

4 If software is developed in several versions, with some but not all shared code, what are the factors that influence the cost of achieving a specified level of software failure intensity?

ANSWER: If all versions have the same failure intensity objective and operational profile and if common faults are corrected for all versions (all the foregoing usually hold), the amount and cost of system test and debugging required will depend on the number of versions and the total number of faults. To a first approximation, the total number of inherent faults for all versions will be proportional to the total number of source lines that are developed (source lines inherited by one version from another are not counted).

You can minimize the cost of reliability by reducing the number of versions and by designing the different versions so they use as much common developed code as possible.

5 Why not just specify the availability of a software system? Why is reliability of so much interest?

ANSWER: Although the user is affected by lack of availability of software to function acceptably, interruptions in acceptable functioning (characterized by reliability) are often even more important. It is often possible to "work around" a system that is unavailable by delaying tasks or using other systems. Interruptions occur unpredictably and cause disruption, which is usually much more expensive. However, if disruption is not significant and your customer wants to state requirements in terms of availability, you can easily do so. See the answer to Question 11 in this section.

6 We have found that both availability and reliability are important to our users in the following sense. An interruption in service requires substantial recovery time for the user in returning to his or her work. Can both availability and reliability be incorporated in the same metric?

ANSWER: Yes. Suppose there is a failure every 10 h with a downtime of 6 min and a recovery time for the user of 18 min. The conventional availability is then 0.99. You can compute an "effective availability" based on effective downtime. In this case, effective downtime is 24 min and effective availability is 0.96. Effective downtime includes actual system downtime plus the recovery times caused by interruptions. Effective availability will always be the same or less than classical availability.

7 Is there some way to combine customer requirements for reliability and rapid response to problems into a single metric?

ANSWER: Yes. If we generalize the concept of downtime to be the time interval between failure (system behavior during operation that does not meet the customer's requirements) and the point where the system has been restored to operation that is satisfactory to the customer (this does not necessarily mean that the underlying fault has been removed), we can combine failure intensity and downtime into a generalized availability.

8 How do we relate a "probability of failure on demand" requirement to a failure intensity requirement?

ANSWER: Note that the probability of failure is given by $\lambda\tau$ for small $\lambda\tau$, where λ = failure intensity and τ = execution time. Thus, dividing the failure probability by the time of execution of the program will give a failure intensity requirement (assuming $\lambda\tau$ is small). When τ is small, the failure intensity requirement for the program becomes much easier to meet.

9   How can you say that there is a tradeoff between reliability and cost when building a more reliable product saves money?

ANSWER: Improving reliability generally does increase development costs. However, it reduces operational costs and the net result may be a reduction in total costs.

10   Can you have different failure intensity objectives for different users and their uses (hence different parts of the operational profile)?

ANSWER: Yes. You typically handle this by assigning failure intensity objectives to operational modes, which are sets of operations and which can generally be related to users. However, we don't generally recommend this because the accuracy of failure estimates for the different users will suffer because of small sample problems.

11   Availability is often the prime criterion for performance of systems that support people in doing their work. How do we relate this to reliability?

ANSWER: Determine the allowable unavailability by subtracting availability from 1. Dividing unavailability by the product of mean time to restore the system and availability will yield allowable failure intensity.

12   Our users define our reliability requirement in terms of failures per thousand transactions. We want to convert this requirement into a requirement in execution time, but the execution times of the individual transactions vary widely. What should we do?

ANSWER: Use the average execution time per transaction.

13   Should the frequency of a failure be taken into account in assigning its severity?

ANSWER: No, severity relates to per-failure impact.

14   Can we set a separate failure intensity objective for a particular operational mode?

ANSWER: It is theoretically possible but not practical. In most cases the number of failures that we will experience in a particular operational mode will be small. Hence the error associated with an estimate of failure intensity for the particular operational mode will be large. Thus setting an objective and tracking failures across all operational modes is more practical and will give more usable results.

You may occasionally make an exception to this single failure intensity objective approach. If an operational mode is expected to experience more than 20 failures (and sometimes even as low as 10) and tracking its failure intensity separately is very important, it may be feasible to set a separate objective for it.

15 In setting a failure intensity objective for a product, should you take into account the customers of the product's users?

ANSWER: Yes. Such an analysis usually indicates a deep understanding of your users' needs. However, you must verify this understanding by explicitly presenting your analysis to the users.

16 Can we set different developed software failure intensity objectives within the same system (for example, for different failure severity classes or different operational modes)?

ANSWER: In theory, yes. However they will not be useful. You will have to divide your failure sample into multiple sets. Each will usually be small, resulting in large uncertainties in either estimating failure intensity or reaching a certification decision.

17 Can we set different failure intensity objectives for variations of our product (for example, different versions developed for different platforms or different countries)?

ANSWER: This is possible but undesirable because it complicates your record keeping. However, because the testing of the versions will be separate and the versions will usually be sufficiently different such that failure data from one cannot be applied to the other, you will not have the problem of increased uncertainty in failure estimation due to division of the failure data sample into small sets.

18 We have determined the developed software failure intensity objective for the product we are designing. It is much lower than the failure intensities of the acquired components for the product. Should we do anything?

ANSWER: You should at least investigate alternatives. The design for the product may be out of balance, in that the developed software failure intensity objective may be much more difficult to meet than the failure intensities specified for the acquired components. An out-of-balance condition is likely to result in longer development durations and higher costs than would otherwise be the case. You should investigate various alternatives of requiring lower failure intensities for the acquired components and the resultant schedule and cost impacts.

19 Software reliability engineering has always specified software failure intensity objectives in terms of execution time. Why are you specifying them in ordinary time or natural units related to ordinary time?

ANSWER: Because ordinary time is better understood by most users. It is true that the failure-inducing stress in software is best measured in execution time. However, it is relatively easy to convert from ordinary time to execution time by measuring computer utilization (you multiply by it).

2.4.4 Concepts

1 Aren't software failures due primarily to changes in the environment?

ANSWER: Yes and No. A change in the environment is likely to result in more failures if the program has not been tested in the changed environment. However, failures can also occur in a familiar environment. Hardware failures are also likely to increase when the environment changes. The increase may be less noticeable because of the failures that are constantly occurring due to wear-out.

2 Are there conditions under which the number of failures is equal to the number of faults?

ANSWER: Yes. If each failure results in the reduction to zero of the fail set of the associated fault, or the set of runs that will cause that fault to generate the failure, there will be no repeated failures and the numbers of failures and faults will be equal. If you only count the first occurrences of failures, as is commonly the case during test, *and* in each case the fail set of the associated fault is reduced to zero, the number of counted failures will equal the number of faults.

3 How can software continue to operate with a backlog of failures whose faults have not yet been removed?

ANSWER: Most failures affect only one or a limited set of program operations; the others can continue to operate. Many even affect only some runs of one operation. Further, most software failures only impair the operation and do not disable it.

4 What is failure modes and effects analysis (FMEA)? When might I want to use it for software?

ANSWER: FMEA looks at component failures and determines what kind of system failures can result. FMEA based on specific failures is probably not practical for software; if you knew what specific failure would occur, you would fix it during the coding phase. However, conducting FMEA at the module level can help you identify which modules are most critical to the proper systems operation. This can help you focus design review, code review, and unit test efforts. Note that a given module can have a range of system failure severities that result from its failures; hence you will be identifying criticality in an average sense.

Because FMEA can involve considerable effort and cost, you will probably want to limit employing it to highly used and/or most critical operations. The operational profile can be a valuable aid in helping you identify these.

5 Why can't we just count faults per thousand lines of delivered executable source code instead of implementing software reliability engineering?

ANSWER: The fault measure is a useful tool for the *developer,* and it may point up components or routines that need attention. However, software reliability engineering has additional advantages. It is *customer*-oriented, because failures per thousand hours of execution relates directly to the customer's operations and costs. And software reliability can be combined with hardware component reliabilities to obtain overall system reliability.

6 If you want a customer-oriented quality measure, why don't you just use "faults found by customers" instead of failure intensity or reliability?

ANSWER: Faults found by customers is only minimally useful to the customer. It does not indicate how frequently trouble will be experienced in operation, and hence it is not possible to estimate the impact or costs of failure. Most important, it only tells you what the quality is of software that has been in the field for some time, not the quality of the new release you are just getting or about to get.

7 Because the failure intensity is proportional to the number of faults remaining, why can't we just use faults for a software quality metric instead of failure intensity?

ANSWER: Because the faults you count are the faults *removed,* and this is very different from the faults *remaining.* You might conceivably estimate the faults remaining as a result of estimating the inherent faults. However, the accuracy of the resultant measure is much worse than that of failure intensity.

8 It seems to me that counting faults is much easier than counting failures, because data collection takes place just within the development team. When you count failures, you must collect data from testers or customers in the field. Don't you agree that it's better to take the easier approach?

ANSWER: First, it isn't true that counting faults is easier. Failures must be reported before the development team can work on the faults. They must be sorted and compared so that repetitions are eliminated before fault correction is initiated. The failure count is available *first,* and you can only determine the fault count after the extra processing occurs. And finally, even if counting faults were easier, the strong advantage of having a customer-oriented quality measure would outweigh any extra data collection effort.

9 Isn't it true that a fault can cause multiple different failures?

ANSWER: Yes.

10 Can different faults cause the same failure?

ANSWER: No. This answer confuses many people, but it is correct. We define a *fault* as the defect that causes a failure. Thus, for the same failure, you must have the same fault. Sometimes two failures appear to be superficially the same. For example, they may both exhibit the same warning message. However, examination of the complete output states will often show them to be different. In that case, you may have two different faults or you may have one fault causing two different failures.

11 If a fault is never detected, is it still a fault?

ANSWER: Yes.

12 Does the number of faults detected in a program vary with the environment in which the program is used or tested?

ANSWER: Yes. If the environment is limited (few possible input states), it is possible that the program may execute without failure forever. In that case, no faults will be found. However, with a more extensive set of input states, there are likely to be failures and hence some faults will be detected.

13 Why does fault removal depend on the operational profile?

ANSWER: The failures that the faults cause must occur so that you can identify the faults for removal. The occurrence of the failures depends on the operational profile. In fact, it also depends on the particular sequence of runs selected.

14 Which is more closely related to the number of inherent faults, the number of unique failures (i.e., number of failure types) or the total number of failures (with repeated failures being counted)?

ANSWER: The number of unique failures.

15 How would you characterize a worm or a virus in software reliability terms?

ANSWER: Worms and viruses are categories of deliberately induced faults. They clearly will adversely affect the failure intensity of the program containing them. In general, because only one or a few are typically induced, statistically based models such as software reliability are not especially useful in viewing their effects.

16 Is a program virus a single fault?

ANSWER: Usually, because it ordinarily causes a single related set of behaviors (such as file erasures and perhaps a crash) that the user finds undesirable.

17 Can requirements have faults, because it is sometimes evident that they are of poor quality?

ANSWER: Faults are by definition defects in *code*. The errors that cause the faults may be ambiguous or incorrect specification of requirements. Sometimes the existence of these errors is evident. For example, the requirements may be so ambiguous that it is difficult to construct tests. In the latter case, one can go to the customer and determine what functions are wanted. Tests can be based on these functions. If the program experiences failures, the faults that cause them can be traced back to errors of poor specification.

18 Some faults result in more frequently occurring failures than others. Is this due to their virulence?

ANSWER: No, because frequent failures is not a characteristic of a fault but depends on how often the fault is activated. Hence, it depends on the operational profile and the code exercised by each function.

19 Suppose you include a faulty code sequence in several modules. How many faults have you introduced?

ANSWER: Probably as many faults as there are repeated faulty code sequences. Faults are defined by the failures they make occur, and the differently located code sequences will probably cause different failures.

20 What is the meaning of mean time to repair (MTTR) for software?

ANSWER: Often, where recovery consists of a system reload plus perhaps a database recovery, the time for the reload (and recovery, where applicable) is the MTTR. This is analogous to a hardware system where units are replaced by spares and later repaired. The actual software debugging and correction time doesn't normally apply, because the system would not shut down while this activity was in process.

21 Suppose that a software failure causes only a temporary interruption or deterioration in performance of some aspect of a system. This might happen for systems that are designed to automatically recover from certain kinds of software failures. Can we characterize the nature of these interruptions in some useful way?

ANSWER: Yes. In addition to calculating the reliability, you can also compute the availability. The latter will account for the length of the periods of reduced performance.

22 How can you say that higher software reliability costs more? Quality theorists say that higher quality costs less.

ANSWER: The quality theorists are referring to the reduction of defectives in manufactured products through higher quality of the manufacturing process. This reduces costs because of the reduction in rework needed to give the same delivered quality to customers. The analog in software development is that prevention of faults costs less than removal to get the same level of reliability. But a higher level of reliability does cost more.

23 Does fault tolerance necessarily imply that the fault will not cause a failure?

ANSWER: Usually it does. However, some people make the broader interpretation: the fault will not cause an intolerable failure. This can mean that the fault must not cause a failure of a certain severity or greater. Some people say, "the system degrades gracefully." The role of fault-tolerant methodology in this situation is to lower the severity classification of the failure to an acceptable level.

24 What is the difference between hardware fault tolerance and software fault tolerance?

ANSWER: A system or component is *fault tolerant* if it operates satisfactorily in the presence of faults (defects that would cause failures, that is, unsatisfactory operation, if not counteracted). Hardware and software fault tolerance refer to the source of the faults. Software components may be hardware fault tolerant or software fault tolerant or both. Hardware components are often hardware fault tolerant but usually not software fault tolerant.

25   What does maintainability mean for software?

ANSWER: Maintainability is the speed and ease with which a program can be corrected. It is analogous to hardware maintainability, except that we usually consider the repair time for hardware as downtime, affecting availability. Software correction is generally performed off-line, such that software maintainability does not affect software availability.

2.4.5   Application

1   Are there cases where it is difficult to determine whether a failure is due to hardware or software?

ANSWER: Yes, but this usually occurs less than 5 percent of the time. If in doubt, be consistent. Classify the failure as nonsoftware if it doesn't reappear on a rerun with all software and with known nonsoftware inputs exactly the same.

2   Use of failure-oriented rather than fault-oriented quality measurements is fine in theory, but it depends on taking field measurements. How can we get them, because we can't put the reporting burden on customers?

ANSWER: It might be a problem if we required customers to record failures manually. But we can automate the process, with most failures of higher severities being recognized by appropriate verification or auditing software. Reporting to a central data collection point can also be automatic. The principal problems that can occur are excessive overhead from the recording software and the inability to recognize all failures. The first problem is diminishing in importance as computer throughput increases. One can compensate for the second problem if the proportion of failures missed remains approximately constant with time.

3   When we test an early release of our software, some failures may have catastrophic effects because software fault-tolerant features may be absent that will be present in future releases. Do we classify such failures as catastrophic?

ANSWER: No. Remember that we are primarily interested in the operational reliability of the software, not its reliability during test. Hence you should classify failures by the severity of impact that would result if the entire system were present. If the fault-tolerant feature does not work properly after it has been installed, you have a failure at that point.

4   We have observed clusters of failures that seem to follow in the wake of severe failures, but we never experience this problem for failures of lesser impact. Is there any explanation for this?

ANSWER: Failures with systemwide consequences may corrupt system control tables much more than less severe failures. This can result in a rapid succession of repeated failures until the system is reinitialized.

5   Some faults seem to be uncovered and removed earlier than others. Is it because they are easier to find?

ANSWER: There is no evidence to indicate that the average effort required to find a fault increases as test proceeds. Nor has any correlation between complexity or subtlety of fault and phase of test period been observed. Some runs occur more frequently than others and hence are likely to occur earlier; if they contain faults, those faults are found and removed earlier.

6   In system test, what is the effect of correcting a fault that unblocks a path that could not previously be executed past the fault?

ANSWER: There is some small probability that the previously unexecuted end of the path will contain one or more additional faults and thus cause one or more failures. The decrease in failure intensity normally resulting from the original fault removal will be slightly less than expected. Model estimation procedures will pick this up automatically and adjust parameters accordingly. However, the overall effect will be small because

a. Blocking occurs rarely in system test (although it can be frequent in unit test).

b. Even if it does, the unexecuted part of the path will not often contain a fault.

7   During test we find a number of faults (and hence implied failures) by code reading. How can we reflect these in our software reliability estimates?

ANSWER: You don't have to and should not do anything. By finding more faults through code reading, you will reduce the failure intensity more rapidly than would normally be the case. Failures will occur less frequently and the estimation process will automatically take care of this.

8   Do we count a fault found by a programmer on his or her own without test?

ANSWER: No. There may be faults found and fixed indirectly as the result of correcting failures found during test. We may subtract the average number of such faults from the number of new faults spawned. The new remainder is used in computing the fault reduction factor B. But you don't have to worry about correcting failure intensity estimates. The removal of the additional faults will cause failures to occur less frequently and the estimation process will yield lower failure intensities.

9   Should customers be totally uninterested in the estimated number of faults that remain in a system that is delivered to them?

ANSWER: No, this is as extreme as *only* being interested in the number of faults. The number of faults remaining indicates the effort and cost involved in elevating the software to a higher level of reliability and has some relationship to how long this should take. *They should have little interest in how many faults the developer has removed to date, however.* Their prime interest should be in the failure intensity, because that will indicate the level of their operational problems and costs.

10   Should we try to balance failure intensities between different components of a system so that they are *equal?*

ANSWER: Not necessarily. You must take account of different cost impacts, perhaps due to different repair costs for the components.

11   How would you handle "fail-safe" systems with software reliability engineering?

ANSWER: Fail-safe systems are those that respond to all malfunctions that might affect safety with action that prevents a safety failure from occurring. Thus a fail-safe system is really a fault-tolerant system in which the fault-tolerant response is limited to those faults that could cause safety failures. The application of software reliability engineering to fault-tolerant systems is discussed in Musa, Iannino, and Okumoto (1987), Chap. 4.

12   How do you measure software reliability for systems where the set of functions performed during installation is different from those during operation of the system?

ANSWER: Define installation and operation as separate operational modes.

13   How should you handle a system with an operation that is critical during a certain time period or periods and routine the rest of the time?

ANSWER: Be conservative and consider the operation as critical.

14   Can operational modes overlap?

ANSWER: They should not overlap in the sense of having two operational modes occurring at the same time. However, they can overlap in the sense of having the one or more identical operations in their operational profiles.

15   Can we use analysis of deviations rather than failures to improve reliability?

ANSWER: Yes. Identification of deviations is often more suited to automation than identification of failures; hence it is often cheaper. However, analysis may be more costly because you may analyze many deviations that won't lead to failures. It may increase the rate of reliability improvement by discovering potential failures before they become real ones. It may be possible to certify high-reliability systems faster with deviation intensity rather than failure intensity because deviation samples are usually larger than failure samples.

16 Availability is more important for our system than reliability; we can tolerate a moderate frequency of interruption of service as long as the downtime at each interruption is short. What should our reliability strategy be?

ANSWER: You will still want to keep failure intensity from being too large, because, of course, that can adversely affect availability. However, you will stop short of employing expensive strategies to obtain very high reliability. Instead, you will focus your efforts on implementing checkpoints. Checkpointing is the technique of periodically saving intermediate process states in long term storage. The more frequently you checkpoint, the more you reduce the downtime necessary for the process to recover and hence increase availability. More frequent checkpointing increases overhead and reduces the load capacity and/or response time of the system, so there is a tradeoff for you to make.

17 How can we convert failure intensities expressed in execution time to failure intensity expressed in ordinary time?

ANSWER: To convert failure intensities expressed in execution time to failure intensities expressed in ordinary time, multiply by the computer utilization. Computer utilization of a software component or system is the ratio of the execution time for that software component or system to ordinary time. The ratio used is the long-term average. Remember also that in determining computer utilization the count of execution time of "filler" operations is limited to the necessary minimums. A *filler operation* is a low-priority operation (usually an audit or housekeeping operation) that should be executed at some minimum frequency but that is allowed to "fill" unused capacity of the processor on which it is executing.

For example, Fone Follower must occasionally conduct a database audit to find and correct (if possible) phone numbers that have become corrupted with time. The average computer utilization over all operations, including the minimum required database audit frequency, is 0.05. The computer utilization is high during the day but very low at night and on weekends. During these times, the filler operation of database audit is allowed to use the spare capacity available, because extra database audits cost nothing and confer a slight added benefit.

If we counted the execution time during which the fill were occurring, we would get a computer utilization of 1. Hence if there are fill operations that are allowed to take up any extra capacity of a processor on which they are executing, the execution time in the extra occurrences of execution over the minimum needed for proper functioning of the system is not counted.

18 We find it useful to describe software reliability in different units for different operational modes of our telecommunications switching system. For example, we use failures per thousand calls for our user mode but failures per thousand transactions for our system administration mode. Is there any problem in doing this?

ANSWER: Not a serious one. However, you must establish a common unit (perhaps hours) to be used for the system failure intensity objective. You must determine the proportionality constants that enable you to convert among the different units.

2.5   Background

This section will provide more background on failures, the faults that cause them, and the errors that lead to faults. We will revisit failure severity classes and discuss failure intensity objectives. We will discuss the topic of availability in more detail. Finally, we will present the basic principles involved in determining system reliability from component reliabilities. We will be discussing the concepts from the viewpoint of software, but they are sufficiently general that they can apply to hardware or human systems (or combinations of them with software systems) as well.

2.5.1   Defining failure with severity classes

In this section, we will first discuss failures, then the faults that cause them, and finally the errors that cause the faults. Although this is the reverse of the order in which they occur, this approach emphasizes that the failure is what is most important in the eyes of the user. Faults and errors are subordinate; they may exist but not cause a failure: In that case, they are not important.

What precisely do we mean by the term *failure?* It is the departure of the external results of system operation from user needs. So our failure is something dynamic. A system has to be operating for a failure to occur. The term *failure* relates to the behavior of the system. Note that a failure is not the same thing as a "bug" or, more properly, a "fault." The very general definition of failure is deliberate. It can include such things as deficiency in performance attributes and excessive response time when desired, although there can be disadvantages in defining failure too generally.

A *fault* in software is the defect in the program that, when executed under particular conditions, causes a failure. There can be different sets of conditions that cause failures. Hence a fault can be the source of more than one failure. A fault is a property of the program rather than a property of its execution or behavior. It is what we are really referring to in general when we use the terms *defect* or *bug*. It's *very* important to make the failure-fault distinction. This may not be apparent to you now, but it should be after you have delved more deeply into the field. There has been, and frequently remains, much confusion because these terms were once mixed up and erroneously used interchangeably. If you get them clear in your mind, you will avoid much trouble that has bedeviled others trying to learn software reliability engineering.

Consider this simple example. A user requests a display at system start-up. It does not appear. That departure from how the program should behave is a failure. The fault associated with the failure might be that an initialization instruction for a variable was not provided. Note, however, that a fault does not have to be localized in nature. The fault could be an inefficient routine that has to be rewritten.

Reference to Fig. 2.1 may be helpful as we explain the important concepts relating to software failures and faults. The set of bars at the left represents the runs (U, V, W, X) for a program. The length of the bar represents the execution time for that run.

One recognizes a *software failure* by noting a discrepancy between the actual value of an output variable resulting from a run and the value of that variable required by users. You can view a run as a transformation of an input state to an output state. Thus a failure represents a transformation that does not meet user requirements. A *deviation* involves a discrepancy of the actual value of a variable with respect to the value we expect. The discrepancy can be in an intermediate variable in the processing done by the run or in an output variable. All failures are deviations, but deviations are failures only if they violate user requirements.

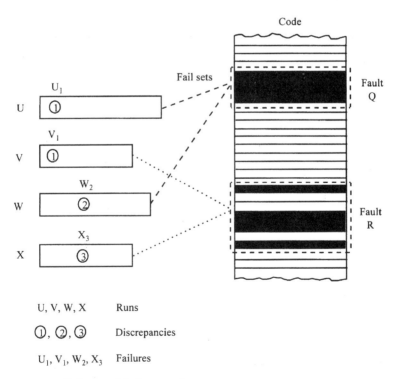

Figure 2.1 Failure and fault concepts.

Note that the requirements frequently do not specify the values of all output variables because some may not be significant. The time of a software failure is the time at which the discrepancy occurs. Discrepancies are noted in Fig. 2.1 as circled numbers. Note that a failure is the conjunction of a run or input state and a discrepancy. Thus when the same discrepancy occurs on different runs, you have two different failures. In Fig. 2.1, discrepancy 1 occurs on different runs U and V and you have failures U_1 and V_1. The same failure can repeat only if the same run is repeated. Run W has discrepancy 2 and failure W_2, and run X has discrepancy 3 and failure X_3.

The definition of failure is really project-specific and must be established in consultation with users. For example, you may define failure as a program crash requiring interruption of processing and program reload. On the other hand, you may consider a very small variation in system behavior (for example, an incorrect title on a report) as a failure. If your product has substantial competition, your competitors may try to emphasize behavior of your software that they consider weaknesses. In that case, you may want to designate occurrences of such behavior as failures if they are likely to substantially influence potential users.

Requirements, in hardware as well as software systems, are usually somewhat subject to interpretation. You may view them as restricted to being written and hence explicit, or they may involve implicit needs as well. For legal purposes, requirements should be explicit. Also, explicit requirements generally result in lower development costs. They reduce the number of failures due to misunderstanding of user requirements. However, the explicit requirements never include all the requirements important to the user because neither the user's nor designer's understanding of user needs is perfect. Hence, you will probably increase customer satisfaction if you allow for implicit requirements to some degree. In effect these are errors of omission in the explicit requirements. Whether explicit or implicit, requirements must reflect a considered consensus of expectations of users and their managers who are funding the product. Thus, we will not interpret the sometimes extreme and unreasonable desires of a few users as requirements.

You will further delimit and interpret the exact nature of requirements by considering what variations in system behavior are tolerable. In establishing requirements, you provide *positive* specification of a system. In defining failures, you supply a *negative* specification. You describe what the system must not do. Engineers using software reliability concepts have found that this negative specification is an extremely valuable system engineering technique. It adds another dimension of communication with the user.

Note that in all cases we focus on operational requirements rather than on requirements for maintainability, documentation, etc.

Sometimes the determination of who the user is may be vague. This is particularly true for a new product whose market may be somewhat uncertain. You must complete identification of the user or range of users you expect before you can define all failures. Don't forget that users can be both internal and external to a customer's organization.

Systems engineers often currently find themselves involved in establishing the definition of failure for their project, although this task may shift to system testers as software reliability engineering spreads and system testers take more of a lead role. System engineers may also be the final arbiters in interpreting the definition during test. This fact makes it desirable for the systems engineers to work closely with the system test team, perhaps even as members. They are likely to receive some direct questions from the test team about whether a certain behavior is a failure or not. Does it violate system requirements? Members of the test team can't currently always resolve exactly what the requirements are, hence the necessary reference to the systems engineers. Again, this situation may change as the spread of software reliability engineering encourages testers to broaden their roles. However, for now, systems engineers should review at least some fraction, if not all, of the trouble reports. They need to determine if the test teams are interpreting requirements correctly. If testers are members of the system engineering team, the foregoing necessary communication becomes much easier.

The process of establishing the requirements for a system involves a consideration of the environments the system will operate in and, hence, the operational profiles. This information should be used in test planning so that testing represents expected operational use. In establishing the requirements, the systems engineer should consider the possibility of unexpected input states occurring due to failure in some other system. It is necessary to provide an appropriate response that minimizes performance degradation, data corruption, or undesirable outputs. Systems that respond rationally to unexpected input states are said to be *robust*.

When comparing the output state that results from a particular run with the required output state, note that extraneous output variables can occur. Some of these may be significant in that they cause data corruption that ultimately leads to failure. Variables that are members of the input states of future runs can be unintentionally changed, resulting in unexpected input states for which the program was not designed. Hence there can be a tendency for the program failure intensity to increase as it executes. There is a particular danger of missing unwanted extraneous output variables and hence missing failures when test is automated. Normally in automated test, checks are run for only a fixed set of output variables. If extraneous output variables cause data corruption during test, the tester may lose some control over input state selection unless the system data is reinitialized before each run. Such loss of control is not necessarily a bad thing; it in fact occurs during load testing and realistically represents the field environment.

There are at least two techniques for dealing with data corruption. First you may make a system data corruption tolerant. To do this, you design the system to behave rationally for the additional input states that can result from data corruption. Second, you can employ data correction. Simple data correction schemes employ reinitialization of all or part of the data. Reinitialization can be periodic or generated in response to detection of a problem by an auditing program. Reinitialization can result in a failure or some loss of capability over the short term. However, the total set of reinitializations that occur in a consistent approach to countering data corruption has a positive average effect on reliability over the long haul. You automatically incorporate the results when you estimate reliability based on failure data. Sophisticated data correction involves techniques of redundancy (error correcting codes, checksums, etc.). Such corrections are expensive, but they can prevent failure and loss of capability.

2.5.1.1 Faults. Software reliability depends heavily on the defects in a software product and the correction activity undertaken to correct them. Consequently, we want an entity to characterize these defects. Generally we have used the software fault to do this. You execute the program and count the software faults by observing the repair actions taken in response to failures. However, there are several complex issues related to the definition and practical use of the concept of the software fault. Software developers have not generally discussed or appreciated these complexities. The result is that the concept of a software fault is less precise and more variable than that of a software failure.

In considering possible approaches to defining the term *software fault,* it is instructive to view two widely differing concepts—the absolute and the operational. The absolute concept views the software fault as an independent entity that you can define without reference to software failures. The operational concept views the software fault as an entity that exists only with reference to actual or potential software failures. "Potential" refers to the fact that the failure will occur for an input state if that state is executed. In the operational view, we define the software fault as the defect that is the cause for a particular failure. Both of these concepts represent polarizations that do not fully represent the intuitive notions of practitioners and that are not fully useful in some sense.

The absolute concept makes it necessary to postulate a "perfect" program to which an actual program can be compared. Then the software fault is a defective, missing, or extra instruction or set of instructions. It may be an instruction (set) in the perfect program that is not matched in the proper sequence in the actual program. Alternatively, it may be an extra instruction (set) in the actual program.

Unfortunately, there are many possible "perfect" programs or programs that could meet the program requirements. In theory, you might select the perfect program that the designer was intending to produce and compare the actual program to that. However, this is not possible in practice because this program is not completely defined and known until it has been achieved through repair activity. If the perfect program were known from the start, we would use it and have zero software faults.

The operational concept conflicts with the sense of software engineering practitioners that a software fault has *some* reality on its own. It is an implementation defect and the implementation has physical reality. Furthermore, a number of failures (not just one) may stem from the same implementation defect.

We will take a middle road in defining software faults. We will assume that there is a perfect program that the designer is intending to produce. The full definition of this program comes about only after we have discovered and corrected its imperfections. Thus software faults have an independent reality, but it is one that we do not fully know until we have thoroughly inspected and executed the program. The discovery of software faults usually occurs through observation of potential software failures by code inspection (and imagined execution) or actual software failures by execution (and output state inspection).

We will thus define a *software fault* as a defective, missing, or extra instruction or set of related instructions that is the cause of one or more actual or potential failures. Note that *by definition* multiple faults cannot be combining to cause failure. The entire set of defective instructions that is causing the failure is considered to be the fault. The requirement that the instructions be "related" is specified so that the count of the number of faults cannot be arbitrarily changed by a regrouping of instructions. The right side of Fig. 2.1 illustrates a section of code with faults Q and R. The instructions comprising the faults are shaded. Note that for fault R, not all instructions are adjacent. The faults are designated by the dashed boxes. The set of runs that produces failures for a fault will be called its *fail set*. The fail set for each fault is designated by the dashed or dotted lines connecting each fault with runs. Fault Q causes failures U_1 and W_2. Hence its fail set is U and W. Fault R causes failures V_1 and X_3. Its fail set is V and X.

How does one determine exactly which instructions should be included in a fault? Some judgment is involved. At first glance, when a failure occurs, you would include in the fault just the instructions that must be modified, added, or removed to prevent the failure from recurring. But remember that a fault can cause multiple failures. Hence, if

TABLE 2.8   Program Specification

I	G
>360	1000
60–360	100
<60	0

also changing a few *related* instructions would prevent additional failures from occurring, these instructions should also be included in the fault. Consider the following simple example. Suppose a segment of code must generate values of G corresponding to values of I as shown in Table 2.8. Assume that the code has been erroneously written as shown in Fig. 2.2. If the program is run with I = 320, it will fail by giving an output of 1000. The output should be 100. The obvious definition of the extent of the fault would be line 10. However, it doesn't take much looking to see that there are several related lines, another of which, line 30, is also defective. It makes sense to define the fault as encompassing lines 10 and 30. Note that the extent defined for a fault depends somewhat on your perspective. It is likely that you will confine faults you find in unit test or unit inspection to that unit. However, you are likely to extend the definition of the fault past module boundaries if you discover it in design review or subsystem test.

Fault removal activity involves changing (preferably reducing) the size of the fail set. You can consider that you have removed a fault when the fail set is null. We have partial repair when the size of the fail set changes but does not reach zero. For example, consider a situation where the branching of control of a program depends on the testing of a variable against a value that we established incorrectly. We might reset the value so that the failure just observed doesn't recur, but the value may still be incorrect. In Fig. 2.1, this might be illustrated by the

Line number	Code
10	IF I > 300
20	THEN G = 1000
30	ELSE IF I ≥ 0
40	THEN G = 100
50	ELSE G = 0

Figure 2.2 Program that illustrates extent of fault.

removal of run X from the fail set of fault R. The average extent to which corrections are partial affects the value of the fault reduction factor B.

The sum of the probabilities of occurrence associated with the runs or input states in a fail set for a fault represents the probability of occurrence of a failure caused by that fault. If it is large, we are more likely to uncover that fault (Ramamoorthy and Bastani, 1982).

Note that it was necessary to define failure in terms of discrepancy *and* run. If it had been defined solely in terms of discrepancy, we could not have defined *fault* to implicitly incorporate the possibility that different faults can cause, for different runs, the same discrepancy. In Figure 2.1, note that faults Q and R both caused discrepancy 1, but the discrepancy occurred on different runs, U and V. The same discrepancy can result when the same desired and actual output states exist for different runs.

There are two software fault detection processes that occur during the development and evolution of software: direct and indirect. We can detect software faults directly as a result of procedures that do not involve actual execution of the program. The approaches that fall in this category are

1. Code reviews

2. Use of compiler diagnostics

Removal of software faults found through direct detection prevents the occurrence of potential failures. We detect software faults indirectly through detection of failures. Failures are detected by executing the program, either in test or regular operation. The symptoms of the failure suggest the areas of code to be searched for the software fault that is causing it. We can *prevent* faults through requirements and design reviews.

Inherent software faults are the faults that are associated with a software product as originally written or modified. They do not include faults that are introduced through fault correction (spawned faults) or design changes.

Often, developers have attempted to count faults by counting each occasion on which a program module was changed, with changes that reflect requirements or design changes excluded. Unfortunately, the number of changes and the number of faults do not usually correspond. The difference between the two counts is due to changes that remove multiple faults, changes that constitute only partial removal of faults, and faults that span multiple modules. The two counts do generally become proportional to each other but only when execution time becomes very large. The proportions of changes that remove multiple faults and faults that span multiple modules do not appear to change with time. When partial removals occur, the number of changes per fault increases with time. However, this figure approaches a stable value after you have completed most removals. Because of the variation in the constant of proportionality between changes made and faults removed, it is not feasible to approximate a current count of faults removed by counting changes.

2.5.1.2 Errors. We have been talking about fault detection and correction. We should also give attention to fault *prevention*. This is best approached by looking at the errors that produce faults. An *error* is an incorrect or missing action by a person or persons that causes a fault in a program. Errors can arise from many causes, but most of them can be grouped in one of four categories:

1. Communication

2. Knowledge

3. Incomplete analysis

4. Transcription

Communication errors probably form the largest group, and the proportion can be expected to increase with the size of the project. They are generally of one of three types:

1. Interrole. Between customer and designer, designer and coder, designer and tester

2. Intrarole. Among designers, coders, testers

3. Temporal. Between different times for the same person

The principal factors in improving communication are comprehensive, continually updated documentation, accuracy, and clarity. Clarity is principally a matter of matching information organization to human information processing capabilities. Because of the limitations of human short-term memory, you must limit the number of entities and relationships between entities that must be considered simultaneously. This points to the virtues of object-oriented design, hierarchical organization, structured design, modularity and locality, abstraction (exclusion of anything irrelevant), and clustering. Clustering of entities or relationships with common information richness increases the level of abstraction and efficiency of information communication. An example of clustering is the use of abstract data types. Note that it is also important for clarity to use, as much as possible, entities and relationships whose meanings are standardized and well known.

Defective knowledge results in another category of errors. These errors are particularly prevalent when project personnel are inexperienced. They include errors arising from defective knowledge of the application area, the design methodology, and the programming language.

Errors can result from incomplete analysis. For example, one often does not recognize all the possible conditions that can occur at a given point in the program. Finally, one has the transcription errors that occur between mind and paper or machine.

Errors are sometimes visible in precoding documentation such as requirements and design specifications. Thus reviews or inspections of these documents may turn up errors that will lead to preventing some number of faults.

A fault can be caused by one or more errors. An error can generate several different faults (for example, poor interface specification can result in several faults).

2.5.1.3 Failure severity classes. Failures usually differ in their impact on the operations of an organization. Therefore, you will usually classify them by severity. This will be particularly true for critical systems such as nuclear power plants, where serious failures may be rare but have an enormous impact. You must be careful not to confuse failure severity with the complexity or subtlety of the fault and the difficulty and effort required to identify and correct it. The cost of repairing a fault is usually small with relation to the operational cost impact of the failure. Making failure severity classifications results in a slight increase in data collection effort because you must determine and note the classification.

At least three classification criteria are in common use: cost impact, human life impact, and system capability impact. Cost impact is particularly applicable to any system that is operating in the business world. What does this failure cost in terms of repair, recovery, lost business, and disruption? You need also to consider effects such as lost business or damaged good will. These are difficult to quantify and hence approximate. Human life impact is appropriate for nuclear power plants, air traffic control systems, military systems, or any kind of a system where safety or defense is paramount. System capability impact might be appropriate for an interactive data processing service or a telephone switching system. It might be preferable to use the criterion of cost impact for systems such as this, but you may have situations where the cost impact is difficult to quantify. Also, system capability impact may be more relevant to the user. An example of system capability impact classification is given in Table 2.9 (Bardsley, 1984). The most severe or class 1 failure is one with interruption of basic service. An example of this would be the inability of a telephone switching system to process calls. Class 2 failures involve degradation of basic service. In the same system, you would consider an excessive wait for dial tone as a class 2 failure. Class 3 failures cause inconve-

TABLE 2.9   Failure Severity Classification—System
Capability Impact Example

Class	System capability impact
1	Basic service interruption
2	Basic service degradation
3	Inconvenience, correction not deferrable
4	Minor tolerable effects, correction deferrable

nience but not degradation of basic service. An example is an enhanced
service such as call forwarding that malfunctions. Class 4 failures are
those that have effects that are minor and tolerable, such that you can
defer fault removal. An example is slightly mistimed ringing.

Sometimes the impact on human life of a failure is not immediately
observable. For example, interruption of telecommunications service
among air traffic control centers may not immediately cause an accident and threat to life, but it does represent increased risk. An important question that you must answer with regard to any type of impact,
but particularly cost impact, is, Impact to whom? A developer who delivers a product but has little continuing responsibility for it will have one
viewpoint. A developer who will use the product to provide a service will
have a different view.

Experience indicates that it is generally best to establish your failure
severity classes on the basis of orders of magnitude of the criterion
being measured because the measurement usually can't be that precise. In practice, severity classifications of failures are often made by
more than one person. Consequently, to avoid variability in results, you
should have objective (quantitative, if possible) rather than subjective
classification criteria. Even if the judgment of the quantitative criteria
is prone to error, their existence enhances the likelihood of understanding and reducing differences.

2.5.2   Setting system failure intensity objectives

The first question one must ask in setting a failure intensity objective
is, Who are the users? The second is, What do they want? And third,
Which objective is best for users, in the broadest sense, in their particular competitive environment? Consider a delivered product with a
rapid rate of technological obsolescence. You are likely to take a different approach from that for a stable product delivered internally
within a company and used to provide external service. For example,
when computing costs in a cost-based approach to setting the objective, it is necessary to know, Costs to whom? Legal requirements or

precedents may influence the values of system failure intensity objectives chosen.

System balance is an important consideration for your system in relation to interfacing systems. It is particularly applicable to situations in which development is especially challenging. This could be because one of the systems uses state-of-the-art technology or because the reliability requirements are severe ones. Hence we often use it for military systems. The basic principle you should follow is to *balance* the difficulty of development work on different systems. Assign less-stringent reliability requirements to the systems that have the most severe functional requirements or are most advanced technologically. In the case of software, functions never implemented before or based on untried algorithms might fall in this category. Assign more stringent reliability requirements to systems that are relatively standard and that are used in common practice. For software, this might include previously tested systems that will be reused. This approach generally leads to the least costly development effort in the minimum time.

In setting a failure intensity objective, it is desirable to have some sense of how failure intensity trades off with release date. First, we determine how failure intensity trades off with execution time. The failure intensity at the start of system test is primarily established by the nature of the project and the development process. The relationship between the ratio for failure intensity change in system test λ_0/λ_F and execution time τ for the basic execution time model is (Musa, Iannino, and Okumoto, 1987, Eq. 2.11)

$$\tau = \frac{\nu_0}{\lambda_0} \ln \frac{\lambda_0}{\lambda_F} \tag{2.9}$$

where ν_0 is total failures in infinite time, and λ_0 is initial failure intensity at the start of test. For the logarithmic Poisson execution time model, it is obtained from Eq. 2.12 of the same reference as

$$\tau = \frac{1}{\theta\lambda_0} \left(\frac{\lambda_0}{\lambda_F} - 1 \right) \tag{2.10}$$

where θ is the failure intensity decay parameter. Because the quantities ν_0, λ_0, and θ are fixed in any given case, the comparative variations of execution time τ with failure intensity ratio λ_0/λ_F will be as shown in Fig. 2.3. Note that the increase in execution time with larger ratios of failure intensity is greater for the logarithmic Poisson model (linear rather than logarithmic). You must now use a test schedule to convert execution time to calendar dates.

In many cases, you can trade off development and operational costs of a software-based system and find an optimum failure intensity objective. The basis for optimization is the assumption that you obtain reli-

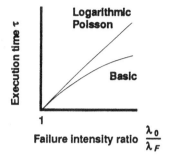

Figure 2.3 Comparative variation of execution time with failure intensity ratio—basic and logarithmic Poisson models.

ability improvement by more extensive testing, which of course affects costs and schedules. We assume that costs and schedules for other phases are constant. This assumption is reasonable because we commonly implement reliability improvement techniques such as structured programming and design reviews on a yes-no basis dependent on their cost effectiveness. You do not ordinarily trade off the degree to which you employ structured programming with reliability. Development cost due to testing decreases with higher failure intensity objectives, whereas operational cost increases (Fig. 2.4). Thus total cost has a minimum. In the packaged software world (for personal computers), support cost (the cost of answering questions and solving problems for users) is closely related to field failure intensity. It is generally the most important consideration in selecting the failure intensity objective. You may view support cost as an operational cost that trades off with development cost.

Figure 2.4 Life-cycle cost optimization.

To find the optimum failure intensity objective, you must first compute the system test cost (Mittermeir, 1982). This should include the cost of profits lost or expenses incurred because you must delay the release date of a program for additional testing. Then you can compute the operational cost. We can now add system test cost and operational cost of failures to obtain the *reliability-dependent component* of total system life-cycle costs. Note that there will also be development and operational costs that are independent of reliability but that add to total system life-cycle costs. Suppose that you can express the reliability-related component of total system life-cycle costs analytically as a function of failure intensity objective λ_F. Then we can use calculus to find the value of λ_F that minimizes the expression. Otherwise, you use a computerized search algorithm to find the value.

Developers sometimes ask if data is available on typical failure intensity objectives for different types of software-based systems. At present, little has been published. However, some more general data is provided in Table 2.10 as a means of assessing risk. For example, note that the probability of a fatal auto accident occurring for a particular car in New Jersey in an hour is about 0.67×10^{-6}. Because this risk causes few people to stop driving, this level of risk might be deemed acceptable for software-based systems that have failures that can endanger human life.

In balancing failure intensity, time to market, and cost, note that time to market is very important when no one has yet entered it. When you are not the market leader, either cost, failure intensity, or functionality can be important, depending on where the market leader is most vulnerable. Product managers tend to be biased toward greater functionality and earlier delivery dates. Field support and operations managers tend to be biased toward lower failure intensity.

We don't usually specify failure intensity objectives for a specific user or customer directly. We can specify objectives for important operation groups, which may well have relationships with particular users or customers. Operation groups often represent types of work such as transaction processing or report generation. For example, a private branch exchange (PBX) may have different objectives for the operation groups for call processing and for system administration. The project may even state these objectives in different units. The objective for call processing may be in terms of failures per thousand calls. The objective for system administration may be in terms of failures per thousand work hours or failures per thousand work tasks. As always, we must strictly limit the number of groups we define to prevent small sample problems. We test operation groups in the context of complete operational mode tests so that interactions between operations are fully explored. We will simply be assigning failures to these operation

TABLE 2.10   Typical Failure Intensities (per 10^6 h)

Event	Failure intensity
Space shuttle catastrophic failures during launch[a]	38,000
Potentially significant safety incidents, U.S. nuclear power plants, 1984–1987[b]	3,400
Horseback riding injuries	2,860
Electric light bulb	1000
Automatic safety shutdowns (scrams) of U.S. nuclear power plants, 1984–1987[b]	500
New York City subway car failures[c]	478
Motorcycling injuries	143
Fires in a specified household (U.S. average)[d]	4.11
Burglaries in a specified household (U.S. average)[d]	2.40
Disabling injuries at home (U.S. per person)[d]	2.12
Thefts of a specified car (U.S. average)[d]	1.08
Deaths at age 35 (per person)[e]	1.02
Fatal auto accidents (New Jersey, 1988) per auto[f]	0.668
Commercial airline (U.S.) fatal accidents	0.5
Deaths by fire (U.S. per person)[d]	2.3×10^{-3}
Deaths by electrocution (U.S. per person)	5.63×10^{-4}

[a]*New York Times,* April 9, 1989, p. 1.

[b]Nuclear Regulatory Commission report, *USA Today,* March 21, 1989, p. 5A.

[c]*New York Times,* November 10, 1989, p. D24.

[d]*New York Times,* October 13, 1989, p. B1.

[e]Burington, R. S. 1950. *Handbook of mathematical tables and formulas,* p. 270. Sandusky, Ohio: Handbook Publishers.

[f]*New York Times,* October 13, 1989, p. B4.

SOURCE: Adapted from Musa, J. D., 1994. Ultrareliability. In John Marciniak (ed.), *Encyclopedia of Software Engineering.* Copyright © 1994 by John Wiley & Sons, Inc. Reprinted by permission of John Wiley & Sons, Inc.

groups so that we can track the separate failure intensities. When different users or customers have different objectives for the same operation group, we will usually take the minimum failure intensity objective.

2.5.3   Availability

When software fails during execution without crashing, it may continue to run and appear available, so you may need a real-time detection mechanism to identify that the failure condition exists. We can also detect failures later by manual or automatic inspection for unacceptable output states. If we detect a failure in real time, the usual response is to correct the data that are likely to have been corrupted by the failure. It is possible to correct the data using checkpoint data that you have recorded at regular intervals during execution of the software or to reinitialize the data. In some cases, execution may have stopped and the correction of data is necessary if it is to continue.

In most cases, you know or can easily determine at least the operation and perhaps even the input state associated with the failure soon after the failure occurs and before you can find and remove the fault. In this situation, it may be desirable to restrict the operational profile while the software developer is addressing the fix so as to exclude the operation or perhaps just the input state (if known) at risk, especially if the particular input state associated with the failure is likely to occur frequently. Downtime will be decreased in this situation. If you have restricted the operational profile, the availability figure is a "degraded capability" rather than a full capability one.

Note that although downtime as defined for software is somewhat different as to cause than that defined for hardware, the resulting system effect is the same. Thus hardware and software downtimes can be combined to get system downtime. Consequently, availability has the same meaning for hardware and software, but the mechanisms that influence it are different.

2.5.4 Reliability combinatorics

Reliability combinatorics are the methods and formulas used to determine system reliability from component reliabilities. We will consider only the basic simple approaches.

In order to compute *system reliability* from *component reliabilities,* where the components fail independently of each other, construct a success logic expression that shows how system success is related to component success. Expressions constructed of AND (system succeeds only if all Q_P components succeed) and OR (system succeeds if any component succeeds) relationships can be handled easily. For AND relationships the system reliability R is

$$R = \prod_{k=1}^{Q_P} R_k \qquad (2.11)$$

where $\prod$ indicates "product of" and the R_k are the component reliabilities. We must express all reliabilities with respect to a common interval of either natural or time units.

We can also express the AND relationship in terms of failure intensities by using the transformation

$$R = \exp(-\lambda t) \qquad (2.12)$$

Taking the logarithms of both sides of Eq. 2.11, noting that the logarithm of a product is the sum of the logarithms of the factors, and using $\ln R_k = -\lambda_k \tau$, we obtain the system failure intensity λ as

$$\lambda = \sum_{k=1}^{Q_P} \lambda_k \qquad (2.13)$$

where Σ indicates "sum of" and λ_k are the component failure intensities. This simplified approach is often appropriate because many systems have pure AND success logic expressions.

In the case of OR and AND-OR expressions, you must conduct your analysis in terms of reliabilities. For OR relationships we have

$$R = 1 - \prod_{k=1}^{Q_P} (1 - R_k) \qquad (2.14)$$

Again, we must express all reliabilities with respect to a common interval of either time or natural units.

Software differs from hardware in that copies of the same program fail identically (these are called *common mode failures*). Such copies configured in an OR relationship do not follow the OR formula above; the system reliability is equal to the common component reliability. Thus redundancy does not improve software reliability as it does hardware reliability.

There have been attempts to improve software reliability by using OR configurations of components that are identical in function but developed by different organizations. This is called N-version development. Generally the failures introduced by the different teams are somewhat different, although they are still correlated. The correlation is due to a common software development culture that results in similar causes for software faults and hence failures. Because we do not currently know this correlation or have any way of readily measuring it, we can only determine the system reliability in this case as a range of reliabilities:

1. The higher reliability is the reliability obtained by assuming the components are independent.

2. The lower reliability is the reliability of a single component (this is equivalent to assuming that the failures in the components are completely correlated or identical).

A convenient shortcut approximation for multiplying reliabilities close to 1 is to add the corresponding failure probabilities (obtained by subtracting reliabilities from 1) and subtract the total from 1. An example is shown in Table 2.11.

TABLE 2.11   Shortcut Approximation to Combining
Reliabilities and Failure Probabilities

	Reliabilities	Failure probabilities
Component	0.999	0.001
Component	0.997	0.003
Component	0.998	0.002
System	0.994	0.006

Note that this approximation works fairly well for reliabilities greater than 0.9 (for example, with reliabilities of 0.9 for two components, you would underestimate the true system reliability of 0.81 as 0.8, a 1.25 percent error). Because the approximation underestimates reliability, we err on the safe side.

2.6   Problems

2.1   We are setting certification standards for an object library that will be used to develop software products in a particular domain. The products must meet a failure intensity objective for severity 1 failures of 10 failures per 1000 execution hours. Previous experience indicates that 10 percent of total failures will be severity 1. We expect that 50 percent of the failures that will occur in the field will be due to incorrect integration of the objects and 50 percent due to faulty objects. Each will consist of 100 objects. Fifty percent of each product will consist of reused objects from the object library. The new objects that are written for a product must meet the same reliability standards as the object library. All objects must work correctly for the product to work. The objects are independent of each other with respect to failure behavior. What total failure intensity objective should we set for each object in the object library?

2.2   What might be a good natural unit for the following products?

a. Color copier
b. Telephone switching system
c. Internet server
d. Laser printer
e. Point of sale terminal
f. Hotel booking system
g. Automatic teller
h. Automobile routing system
i. On-line timetable

2.3   The last release of our product had a failure intensity of 100 failures per 1000 h. It took 1 year to develop and cost $2 million. There were 10 principal functions. The next release will add 10 new principal functions of similar size. We must deliver it in 1 year and reduce the average failure intensity to 90 failures per 1000 h. What can we expect the approximate cost of the next release to be?

2.4   Our new copier must not fail more than once a week. Average daily use during the 5-day work week is 2000 copies per day. Field data indicate that we can expect one mechanical failure every 25,000 copies. What must we set as the failure intensity objective for the copier software we are developing?

3

Developing Operational Profiles

Developing operational profiles will give us information about how users will employ the product we are building so that we can focus our development and test resources. With this information we can substantially improve the efficiency of both development and test. In addition we can make test more realistic. We will first discuss the concepts associated with operational profiles and then we will step through the procedure for developing them (Musa, 1992, 1993, 1995a).

3.1 Concepts

The three principal terms that we need to understand are the operation, the operational profile, and the operational mode.

An *operation* is a major system logical task of short duration, which returns control to the system when complete and whose processing is substantially different from other operations. *Major* implies that an operation should be related to a functional requirement or feature of a product (often enumerated), not a subtask in the design. The operation is a logical concept, in the sense that it can span a set of software, hardware, and human components. It can exist as a series of segments, with a server executing each segment as a process. You can implement the servers on the same or different machines. An operation can be executed in noncontiguous time segments. *Short duration* implies that there are at least hundreds and usually thousands of operations executing per hour under normal load conditions. For example, do not define an aircraft flight trajectory as a single operation. When an operation returns control to the system, it frees resources for a new operation to be invoked.

Substantially different processing implies that there is a high probability that an operation is an entity that will contain a fault not found in any other operation. As a rough guideline, we can consider processing as being substantially different if the processing differs from every other operation by at least 100 deliverable executable lines of source code. The guideline is derived as follows. Extensive data collected by Musa, Iannino, and Okumoto (1987) on a large number of projects indicates a mean density of faults remaining at the start of system test of six faults per thousand source lines. Hence, on the average, 100 different source lines will have 0.6 fault, or a good chance of a fault not found anywhere else. Thus we need to be able to test each operation at least once. You will see in Sec. 4.2.1.3 that we make this possible by allocating at least one test case to each operation, subject to the possibility that rarely occurring noncritical operations may be trimmed from test as long as their failure can't cause per run reliability to fall below its objective.

Whenever possible, you should define an operation so that it involves processing approximately equal to that required for a natural unit. An operation can be initiated by a user, another system, or the system's own controller. For object-oriented systems, an operation often corresponds to a use case, although sometimes you find use cases specified at a lower level such as a run or set of runs.

Some examples of operations are

1. Command executed by a user (for example, in Fone Follower, phone number entry), sometimes characterized by an input screen that is used to specify the parameters of the command.
2. Response to an input from an external system, such as
   a. Processing of a transaction (for example, a purchase, sale, service delivery, or reservation)
   b. Processing of an event (for example, an alarm, mechanical movement, or change in state; in the case of Fone Follower, processing a fax call)
3. Routine housekeeping (for example, a security audit, file backup, database audit, or database cleanup) activated by your own system; in the case of Fone Follower, an audit of a section of the phone number database.

The *operational profile* is simply the set of operations and their probabilities of occurrence. For example, the system operational profile for Fone Follower is shown (only in part for reasons of space) in Table 3.1. The terms *pager* and *no pager* indicate that the processing operation is substantially different depending on whether the subscriber has paging service. Similarly, *answer* and *no answer* refer to whether the forwardee (destination to which you forward the call) answers; processing is substantially different in these two cases.

A *tabular representation* of an operational profile has a name for each operation, and that name has a probability associated with it. The term

TABLE 3.1   System Operational Profile for Fone Follower
(Tabular Representation)

Operation	Operations per hour	Probability
Process voice call, no pager, answer	18,000	0.18
Process voice call, no pager, no answer	17,000	0.17
Process voice call, pager, answer	17,000	0.17
Process fax call	15,000	0.15
...		
...		
...		
Total	100,000	1

comes from the fact that the list of operations and associated probabilities form a table.

A *graphical representation* presents each operation as a path through a graph, hence the term. The graph consists of a set of nodes, which represent attributes of operations, and branches, which represent different values of the attributes. Each attribute value has an associated occurrence probability. These occurrence probabilities can be conditional on previous branches in the path. Note that each attribute in effect has a subprofile for its attribute values. Thus the probabilities for the branches leaving a node must sum to 1. To find the occurrence probability for an operation, multiply the probabilities associated with the branches in the path that represents the operation.

Figure 3.1 presents part of a graphical representation for a private branch exchange (PBX), which is a telecommunications switching system, commonly dedicated to a particular company or institution. In the PBX world, the graphical representation of operations is known as a *call tree*.

The "dialing type" attribute characterizes the use of standard versus abbreviated dialing. Abbreviated dialing is the feature that lets you substitute two-digit codes for commonly called numbers, storing the correspondences in a file associated with your phone. Note that in this illustration, 20 percent of the calls use abbreviated dialing. The "call destination" attribute indicates whether the calls are being made to locations external or internal to the company or institution. Note that the occurrence probabilities here are conditional on the value of the dialing type attribute. Abbreviated dialing is mostly used for internal calls; 90 percent of those calls are internal and 10 percent are external. On the other hand, for standard dialing 30 percent of the calls are internal and 70 percent are external. One of the operations for this PBX is indicated by the thick line.

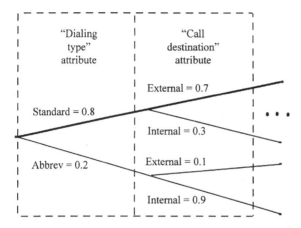

Figure 3.1 Operational profile for PBX (graphical representation).

Note that you can generate a tabular representation of an operational profile from a graphical representation of an operational profile by examining all possible paths and multiplying probabilities. In fact, you will actually do this as one of the steps in generating test cases.

We commonly measure occurrence rates of operations in clock hours. Note that the set of operations with occurrence rates is not itself an operational profile. However, you can easily convert it to one by dividing occurrence rates by total occurrence rate. The occurrence rate form can be convenient for recreating actual traffic levels in test.

An *operational mode* is a distinct pattern of system use and/or set of environmental conditions needing separate testing because it is likely to stimulate different failures. Load test will be divided into operational modes. We will need an operational profile for each operational mode. The same operation may occur in different operational modes, but the occurrence probabilities will be different.

We will also need a *system operational profile,* which consists of the complete set of operations for the system with probabilities of occurrence based on all operational modes.

All testers need to know how to develop an operational profile, because they may encounter situations where it has not been done and will have to do it themselves. In many cases, systems engineers (and perhaps marketing and product management personnel) will be responsible for working with expected users to develop the operational profiles. However, system testers often participate or even lead; this is advantageous because they can ensure that the operational profiles are developed in such a way that testing needs are met. Sometimes systems engineers develop the first drafts of operational profiles and then system architects and developers refine them.

Although you may refine the operational mode operational profiles further with time, you will need initial versions during the requirements phase if you use them for performance analysis. Also, we need the system operational profile early to allocate resources and priorities and to support system engineers in planning for operational development and reduced operation software (ROS). *Operational development* is development that we schedule operation by operation in such a fashion that we implement the most used and/or most critical operations in the first release, and we delay the less used and/or critical, the net result being faster time to market for the most important capabilities. *ROS* is the software analog of reduced instruction set computing for hardware (RISC). By directly implementing only frequently used or critical operations and constructing less frequently used operations in terms of them (or not implementing such operations at all), we can save substantial development time and cost. To allocate testing effort, select tests, and determine the order in which tests should be run, a version of the operational profile that is close to final must be available when you start test planning.

3.2   Procedure

For each system to be tested, you must first determine the operational modes. These are often the same for the product and its variations and sometimes the supersystems. Then you determine the operational profile for the system (across all operational modes) and one for each operational mode. You will use the system operational profile to select test cases to be constructed during the prepare for test activity and to select test cases for execution during all test except load test in the execute test activity (for example, feature test and regression test). You will use each operational mode operational profile to invoke test cases for execution during load test of that particular operational mode.

To develop an operational profile, you

1. Identify the initiators of operations

2. Choose between tabular or graphical representation

3. Create an operations "list" for each (operations) initiator and consolidate the results

4. Determine the occurrence rates (per hour) of the individual operations or attribute values

5. Determine the occurrence probabilities by dividing the individual occurrence rates by the total occurrence rates, of either operations or attribute values, as appropriate

We start all five steps in the requirements phase. We refine them iteratively during the architecture, design, and implementation phases. The first three steps often yield the same results across operational modes and for the system itself and also among the product, its variations, and sometimes supersystems. A new release often requires only slight changes from the previous release for all five steps.

It may not be necessary to identify the initiators of operations if you have extensive experience with the use of the system. You can go directly to the enumeration of operations. However, it is usually a good idea to identify the operation initiators first, because considering them often suggests experts that you should consult in enumerating the operations, and it often suggests including operations that you would otherwise miss.

3.2.1 Determining operational modes

We base the number of operational modes we use and the exact way in which system operation is divided into these operational modes on engineering judgment: More operational modes can increase the realism of test, but they also increase the effort and cost of preparing for and performing system test. The best approach is to first consider all the possible combinations of factors that might cause you to determine separate operational modes. Then limit the resulting operational modes to the most frequently occurring or most critical ones so that you keep the time and cost for developing operational profiles and preparing and executing tests within reasonable bounds.

Some of the factors that may yield different operational modes are

1. Day of week or time of day (prime hours versus off hours)
2. Time of year (year end accounting for financial systems)
3. Traffic levels
4. Different user types (sets of users who are expected to employ the system in the same way)
5. User experience (experts and novices use the system differently; novices tend to use a smaller and simpler set of commands whereas experts may use more of the sophisticated features)
6. System maturity (degree of database population)
7. Reduced system capability (for all or for just certain operations)

We will select three operational modes for Fone Follower:

1. Peak hours—heavy calls and entries traffic, no administration or audit operations executed

2. Prime hours—average calls and entries traffic, administration but no audit operations executed

3. Off hours—low calls and entries traffic, low administration, extensive execution of audit operations

Administration refers to functions performed by telephone company employees such as addition and removal of customers. Audit represents routine periodic checking of the database for corrupted data. The patterns of use shift with time because the system invokes tasks in accordance with the priority order of calls, entries, administration, and audit.

During load test, you test each operational mode in each system. Separating load test by operational modes ensures simultaneous testing of operations that might interact differently under different use patterns, with the different interactions possibly causing different failures.

3.2.2   Identifying operation initiators

The initiators of operations include users of the systems, external systems, and the system's own controller. To identify the users, you usually first determine the expected customer types of the system, based on such information as the system business case and marketing data for related systems. A *customer type* is a set of customers (organizations or individuals who purchase but may not directly employ your product) who have similar businesses and hence tend to have the same user types. Customer types do not necessarily correspond to market segments, which are defined more for sales purposes. Customers are not necessarily paying customers; they may be internal to your organization.

A *user type* is a set of users (individuals who directly employ your product) who tend to employ the product in the same way. You analyze the customer types to determine the expected user types. User types are often highly correlated with job roles. The term *expected* means exactly what it says. It includes current users who can be expected to use the new system. It *excludes* current users who will not be using it because the information they furnish may be irrelevant and misleading, being more reflective of the present work process than the future one. Finally, because different customer types can have the same user types, you consolidate the list of user types across customer types.

The concept of user refers to anyone who may initiate operations on a system. This includes not only those for whom the system was built but also those who maintain and administer the system. But a manager reading a report generated by a system is not a user. On the other hand, a manager accessing the same data on-line *is*.

Next, you determine all the systems that are external to the system under study and that are likely to initiate operations in that system.

TABLE 3.2   Operation
Initiators for Fone Follower

Subscriber

System administrator

Telephone network

System controller

Event-driven systems often have many external systems that can initiate operations in them. Finally, you review the system under study for operations it may initiate itself. These are typically administrative and maintenance functions such as audits and backups.

Consider Fone Follower. It will have customer types that include hospitals and sales organizations. Hospitals will have doctors among their user types, and sales organizations have salespersons. These two user types will probably employ the system in similar ways. Hence, we will characterize both of them as "subscribers." The telephone company that operates Fone Follower will have "system administrators" as a user type.

The principal system that Fone Follower will interface with is the telephone network. We can also expect Fone Follower to initiate operations itself. Thus, we obtain the list of initiators in Table 3.2.

Customer- and user-type lists are sufficient for identifying the operation initiators. You don't need their profiles because you estimate the occurrence probabilities of operations directly. However, if you estimate occurrence probabilities in the context of particular users, you may need a user-type profile to provide weights when combining them together.

3.2.3   Choosing tabular or graphical representation

The choice between the two representations is not a black-and-white one. We tend to pick the tabular representation if most operations can be described by a very small number (typically one or two) of attributes. Often we simply name an operation in a tabular representation by its function, such as the "connect call" for Fone Follower. On the other hand, if most operations are described by multiple attributes, it is easier to consider them attribute by attribute, and in that case, you should select the graphical representation.

Functions or operations that we can characterize by sequences of relatively independent processing decisions are particularly well suited for graphical representation. Note the awkwardness of describing an operation by tabular representation in the case of telecommunications switching: Call processing for call using abbreviated dialing, going out to external network, answered, placed on hold, and then taken off hold to talk.

It is possible to represent some operations in tabular form and some in graphical form. For example, although we have expressed the operations of Fone Follower primarily in tabular form, some of them can be broken down into graphs. You can place nodes in Process voice call that break it down by pager versus no pager action. Similarly, in a graphical representation, you may decide to express a path with few nodes in tabular form.

In actual practice to date, most applications have used the tabular representation.

3.2.4 Creating an operations list

When creating operations lists, it is often convenient to divide this task by operation initiators, because the expertise on the needs of a particular operation initiator is likely to reside in particular persons. Thus we create a list for each initiator, and then we consolidate the lists.

To create the operations list, you should assign a different operation or attribute value to each situation of substantially different processing, unless it occurs with very low probability and performs a noncritical function. *Substantially* means likely to have different failure behavior. As you will see in Sec. 4.2.1.3, we will allocate at least one test case to each operation. We will also execute each operation in test with at least one run, unless it has a very low occurrence probability. Thus we will test every situation of substantially different processing unless it is both noncritical and occurs very infrequently. In the latter case, we might miss a particular failure that could occur and hence not remove a fault that is causing it. However, leaving a fault in the system that only causes very infrequent noncritical failures is not important.

In order to list the operations, you should primarily consult the system requirements. However, multiple sources are important because system requirements are often incomplete. Other useful sources include work process flow diagrams for various job roles, draft user manuals, prototypes, and previous versions of the system. Discussions with system engineers may bring out operations that they missed in the system requirements or that are outdated. Direct discussions with "typical" expected users are usually highly enlightening, often turning up needs for operations that were missed by the system engineers. If you have chosen tabular representation, you will be listing the operations directly. If you have chosen graphical representation, you will be listing the operations indirectly by graphing attributes and attribute values.

If the software system you are developing represents the total or partial automation of some work process, it may be helpful to chart the process, based on the work flow and including hardware, software, and people elements. The work process shows the context in which the software will operate and suggests operations. Note the different tasks the process requires and their probabilities of occurrence. You can often relate these tasks to operations. A useful way to help you define the process is to ask the question How would I explain to a new employee what must be done? User input is vital in creating the chart of the work process. Only those who have practical experience with the existing work process can uncover problems with a proposed process.

You can use a prototype as a second verifying source to system requirements, but you must use it with care, because often a prototype implements only some operations. The most recent version of the product can also serve as a valuable check, but of course it lacks the new operations planned for the next version. Sometimes there is a draft user manual, written to enhance communication with users, that you can check, but it will probably emphasize operations activated by commands, not operations activated by events or data.

One good way to generate an operation list for menu-driven programs is to "walk the tree" of menus for the previous release. However, this may generate too many operations, so you must be alert to the possibility of combining some of them.

It is important to maintain traceability between the operational profile and the requirements as a check on ensuring that you have a complete set of requirements and that all of them are reflected in the operational profile. Traceability becomes particularly important when requirements change, when you combine or divide operations, and when you develop new releases of a product.

If you have trouble identifying the operations, it is often because the requirements are incomplete or fuzzy and need clarification.

Let's construct a list of operations for Fone Follower, starting with the operation initiators of Table 3.2. The list of operations is presented in Table 3.3. The principal activity of the subscriber is to enter the phone numbers of where he or she expects to be at various times. System administrators may perform a number of operations, but adding and deleting subscribers to the service are certainly major ones. An external system, the telephone network, is perhaps the principal initiator of operations, because each call comes from it. One operation is devoted to processing fax calls. There are five operations devoted to processing voice calls, three for subscribers with pagers and two without. The processing differs depending on whether the subscriber answers the originally forwarded call or not or answers it after being paged. The system controller regularly initiates audits of the phone

TABLE 3.3   Operations List for Fone Follower

Operation initiator	Operation
Subscriber	Phone number entry
System administrator	Add subscriber
	Delete subscriber
Telephone network	Process voice call, no pager, answer
	Process voice call, no pager, no answer
	Process voice call, pager, answer
	Process voice call, pager, answer on page
	Process voice call, pager, no answer on page
	Process fax call
System controller	Audit section of phone number database
	Recover from hardware failure

number database during low-traffic hours. Finally, when the system controller detects a hardware failure, it invokes a recovery operation.

The amount of processing required for a phone number entry or for adding or deleting a subscriber is expected to be approximately the same as that for a call. Audits of the phone number database will be done in sections, with the size of the section chosen such that the amount of processing is about the same as that for a call. Recovery from hardware failure is expected to have about the same amount of processing as a call, because the processing only has to determine where the failure occurred and which previous checkpoint must be reloaded. The reloading takes time but doesn't involve processing. Thus the operations should be sufficiently similar in size so that any given run should represent about one natural unit.

For the graphical representation, we also start from each initiator, but we create part of a graph rather than part of a list. Consider a PBX with a call originator as an initiator (another might be a system administrator). We determine the sequence of attributes relevant to a call originator and the possible attribute values of each, generating the graph in Fig. 3.2.

Because the development of the operational profiles is the principal cost in software reliability engineering, and this cost is heavily affected by the total number of operations for the product or domain (for components or objects), it is important that you control this number. The number should relate to the product or domain budget. The number of operations for each operational profile within the product or domain should relate to the relative use and criticality of the system and the operational mode involved. An operational profile does not have a set number of operations, but it typically involves between 50 and several hundred. Larger products can have longer lists; they often extend into

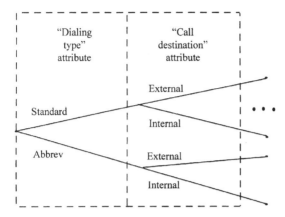

Figure 3.2   Segment of "operations list" for graphical representation of a PBX.

the hundreds but very rarely the thousands. Because the development budget is often related to the expected sales of a product, longer operations lists become feasible for high-volume products. Alternatively, it becomes more feasible to separately test more variations of the product or to define more operational modes. When components are shared across many products (for example, objects), these components can be tested as systems in themselves. Many factors affect the cost of developing an operational profile, but a *very* rough estimate might be half a staff hour per operation.

You may find that the number of operations you need to cover all the situations of substantially different processing is larger than the number of operations for which you want to collect use data, considering the cost. You can solve this problem by defining enough operations to cover all the situations of substantially different processing, ensuring that you will have at least one test case available to cover each situation. However, you limit determining occurrence probabilities to the higher use operations, keeping the effort and cost for developing operational profiles within acceptable bounds.

As a system develops, the set of operations defined for the system may evolve. Such evolution results in a need to adjust the operational profile. Often this comes about because of new information that you uncover as you detail the requirements or as the architecture develops. The most common direct causes are changes in operational architecture (the structure of and relations between operations as you invoke them in the field to accomplish work), the needed granularity of control of resource allocation or test realism, or knowledge of processing differences.

A change in operational architecture may result because you decide to separate an operation into two operations that you initiate independently so that you can reduce response time for a particular operation by deferring some of its deferrable tasks. Note that simply separating the two tasks in time doesn't divide the operation into two operations. There is often some correlation, but it is rarely complete, between the operational architecture and the system architecture that determines how modules and subsystems combine into the system.

The criterion for deciding whether to modify the list is whether the benefit of changing the granularity of operations substantially outweighs the cost (in your engineering judgment). Each change in granularity entails some (usually small) cost and delay in delivery date, because when an operations list changes, you must recompute the operational profile associated with it. Section 3.3.1 explains how to update the occurrence probabilities.

If you have too many operations, you may wish to group some of them. The operations you group should share the same input variables so that you can set up a common and efficient test approach for the domain. But you don't necessarily group all the operations that share the same input variables. If one or more input variables have values or value ranges with easily determined and substantially different occurrence probabilities, you will probably define corresponding multiple operations so that you can differentiate the amount of testing applied.

The degree of operation differentiation you choose to specify is a balance between the greater flexibility in allocating resources and setting priorities that the more detailed profile gives you and the higher cost of gathering and analyzing more detailed data—and managing on that basis. In practice, because you complete an operational profile early in the design phase, the information available limits how refined the operation list can be at that time.

Consider some different ways of defining operations for command X with parameters A and B. Parameter A can have values $A1$ or $A2$ and parameter B can have values $B1, B2,$ or $B3.$ Suppose that setting parameter A has much more effect on the difference in code executed than setting parameter B. Two possibilities are likely:

1. One operation, X, which includes all sets of parameter values.

2. Two operations $X A1 B$ and $X A2 B$; this considers only A's different parameter values as separate operations.

You would probably not define six operations, $X A1 B1, X A1 B2, X A1 B3, X A2 B1, X A2 B2,$ and $X A2 B3,$ with each set of parameter values as a separate operation, because the value of B doesn't have a major effect on the code executed. In all three cases there are six ways to execute X; the only difference is how they are grouped.

We have initially made the conservative assumption that all initiators and all operations they initiate can potentially appear in the operations list. We will eventually find that occurrence rates for some administrative operations are zero for operational modes with peak traffic because of the priority given customer operations over administrative operations.

Differentiation of operations is independent of the task of ensuring that the operations list is reasonably complete. A good way to check the operations list for completeness is to examine the input space to ensure that it is well covered. A program's input space is the set of input states or set of values of input variables that can occur during its operation. This set is not infinite, but it is astronomically large for any program of practical use. Many programs are expected to take some rational action for erroneous inputs, expanding the *required* input space that a program must respond to and be tested for from the design input space established by the program features. The areas of the required input space that do not fall in the *design* input space will contain input states with a higher likelihood of failure, unless appropriate action is taken. Although you can consider environmental variables as you define the operations list, you usually handle them by testing over time. This simplified approach seems to work reasonably well, perhaps because environmental variables vary over time.

In defining the input space, the most important thing is to develop a practically complete list of input variables. Such a list identifies all input variables except those that take on one value with very high probability. In this case, you ignore and thus don't test the alternate values, unless one or more of the alternate values defines, with the other input variables set at some value, a critical run. Ignoring the alternate values is acceptable because they occur so rarely that they have little effect on reliability even if they fail. The degree to which you can do this decreases for systems requiring higher reliability.

If you miss input variables that appreciably affect the program's operation, you cannot clearly identify runs and hence faulty input states. This makes it impossible to reproduce either failures or successful behavior unambiguously. For example, you may not consider some variables as inputs because it is not obvious that they influence a run until they interact with other runs. Rather than wait for such interactions, you should make a conscious effort to identify "indirect" input variables. Examples of such variables will be discussed in Chap. 4.

The required input space may be difficult and time-consuming to delineate, especially if input states have nonzero occurrence probabilities only for certain values of input variables. Instead, define a *speci-*

fied input space by simply listing the set of input variables involved. You assume that each input variable can take on any possible value (a finite number, based on the range and granularity of the machine representation) and ignore the test resources wasted because some input states will have zero-occurrence probabilities. The specified input space will more than cover the required input space and will be much easier to define and select tests for.

In covering input space by defining operations, the amount of input space you can leave uncovered depends on the system reliability objective. If the reliability objective for one run is R_F, the coverage (sum of the occurrence probabilities of the operations that have been defined) must be at least R_F. For example, a per run reliability objective of 0.99 requires that the coverage be at least 0.99. Note how this gives you an opportunity to reduce the number of operations by eliminating rare noncritical ones. Unfortunately, you can't do this until after expending the effort to obtain the occurrence probabilities, unless you already have information that indicates how rarely the operations occur. However, post facto trimming of the number of operations is still valuable because you can avoid allocating test cases to them, saving test case resources for other purposes. In theory, you can trim noncritical operations whose occurrence probabilities total 1 minus the reliability objective for one run. However, you may wish to allow for a margin of error and limit the total to, say, half that value. Thus, a per run reliability objective of 0.99 would allow you to eliminate noncritical operations with occurrence probabilities totaling 0.005.

The set of operations you define should include all operations of high criticality, even if they have low use. To increase the likelihood that you include all high-criticality operations, you should focus on tasks whose unsatisfactory completion would have a severe effect and carefully consider all the environmental conditions in which they may be executed. Postmortems of serious failures in previous or related systems often suggest some of these situations. You will see in Sec. 4.2.1.3 that you will allocate every critical operation at least one test case, ensuring that it will get tested. Thus it is unlikely (although nothing is ever certain) that failures of a critical nature will be missed.

If you are using the tabular representation, and you have multiple operational modes, you may find a spreadsheet useful for organizing your operations lists and the occurrence frequencies and probabilities that will follow.

It is vitally important that you include housekeeping operations that reinitialize or clean up databases (which can become more and more corrupted as execution of user-oriented functions proceeds) in the operations list. Otherwise, the data environment in which these functions execute will not be representative of reality.

3.2.5 Determining occurrence rates

Many first-time users of software reliability engineering expect that determining occurrence rates for operations will be very difficult; our experience generally indicates much less difficulty than expected (Musa, 1997a, 1997b, 1997e; Musa, Fioco, Irving, Kropfl, and Juhlin, 1996). It is best to use actual field data. Use measurements are often available from system logs, which are usually machine-readable. Frequently, such data already exists for the same or similar systems, perhaps previous versions or for the manual system that is being automated. If not, you can often collect it, although this should be the second choice because it will, of course, involve some cost. If the operations are event-driven, you can often simulate the environment that determines event frequency. Finally, even if there is no direct data, you usually have some related information that lets you make reasonable estimates. If you have absolutely no information to estimate relative occurrence rates of operations, make them equal.

If you have selected the tabular representation, you will need to determine the occurrence rates of operations. If you have chosen the graphical representation, you will need to determine the occurrence rates of attribute values. Occurrence rates of operations or operation attribute values are commonly measured with respect to time.

In order to illustrate occurrence rate data for operations, we present system (average over all operational modes) occurrence rates for Fone Follower in Table 3.4. Occurrence rate data for attribute values in the graphical representation of a PBX is presented in Fig. 3.3.

TABLE 3.4 System Occurrence Rates for Tabular
Representation of Fone Follower

Operation	Occurrence rate (operations per hour)
Phone number entry	10,000
Add subscriber	50
Delete subscriber	50
Process voice call, no pager, answer	18,000
Process voice call, no pager, no answer	17,000
Process voice call, pager, answer	17,000
Process voice call, pager, answer on page	12,000
Process voice call, pager, no answer on page	10,000
Process fax call	15,000
Audit section of phone number database	900
Recover from hardware failure	0.1
Total	100,000

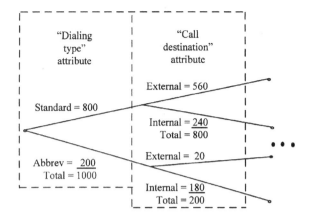

Figure 3.3 Occurrence rates for attribute values in graphical representation of a PBX.

When you count occurrence rates, do not count filler occurrences. A *filler occurrence* is an instance of execution of an operation above the minimum required for proper system operation. Many systems are designed so that they execute certain operations such as audit and maintenance functions (called *filler operations*) when they have not been assigned anything else to do. This makes sense because this may result in some small improvement in system operation, using resources that would otherwise be wasted. However, counting these filler occurrences could yield a distortion in operational profiles and hence a distortion of testing.

For example, for Fone Follower, we allowed the database audit operation to use up any spare capacity of the system. Because there is a great deal of spare capacity on nights and weekends, the audit operation naturally has an occurrence probability of 0.95. However, it only need execute with an occurrence probability of 0.009. If the former occurrence probability were used in specifying the system operational profile, we would develop about 95 percent of the test cases for the database audit operation, and we would devote about 95 percent of our test time to it. This would be totally inappropriate.

If you are measuring field data, take some extra care to ensure that your measurement effort is cost-effective and that you haven't ignored easier alternatives, especially if you are faced with building special recording and measurement tools. For example, you might use a simple operational profile with a moderate number of elements and moderate accuracy for the first version of a software product, refining it for later versions only if you discover in the field that the reliability projections from test are in error.

It may take some effort to develop recording software for operations, but you may be able to develop a generic recording routine that requires only an interface to each application. The recording software for the system must extract sufficient data about input variables to identify the operations being executed. Then it is simply a matter of counting the executions of each operation. You can record an operational profile in either the tabular or graphical representation. Recording just the use of operations is much easier than recording the complete input state because it involves much less data.

The recording process usually does not add much overhead to the application. Because of the importance of field data for developing operational profiles and the relatively low overhead for recording it, it is a good idea to build utilities for recording operations into all software-based systems that you develop. In many cases, it is feasible to collect data from the entire user community. If not, you may have to take just a sample of users. In sampling users, the same guidelines and statistical theory used for polling and market surveys apply; a sample of 30 or even fewer users may suffice to generate an operational profile with acceptable accuracy.

For new systems or new operations you are adding to existing systems, you derive the operational profile from estimated occurrence probabilities, with the aid of data recorded on the use of operations already deployed. Estimation of occurrence rates is usually best done by an experienced systems engineer who has a thorough understanding of the businesses and the needs of the expected users and how they are likely to take advantage of the new operations. It is vital that experienced users review these estimates. Often new operations implement procedures that had been performed manually or by other systems, so there may be some data available to improve the accuracy of the estimates. It is often useful to involve users directly in making occurrence rate estimates. This can be done through questionnaires, but applying Delphi techniques (individual estimates of experts communicated to and revised by the expert group) in a group setting is often superior. When use must be estimated, it is often helpful to create and review the overall work process diagram that the system being built supports.

When a system's operational profile depends on the frequencies of events that occur in an associated system, it may help to simulate the second system to establish event frequencies. For example, if the operational profile of a surveillance system depends on the frequencies of certain conditions arising in the systems being monitored, the operation of these systems can be simulated.

Occurrence rates computed with previous data must be adjusted to account for new operations and environments and expected changes due to other factors. Most systems are a mixture of previously released and new operations, for which you must estimate use. Although estimates are less accurate than measures, the total proportion of new operations is usually small, perhaps 5 to 20 percent, so the operational profile's overall accuracy should be good.

Generally you should determine average occurrence rates for a particular operation over the life of the software release in question. If you want to account for changes in an operational profile over time, it is usually best to define additional operational modes as needed and find occurrence rates for each.

Occurrence rates usually differ with operational modes, especially when the load/capacity ratios differ and operations are assigned selection priorities. For example, if operations awaiting execution queue for processors, and order in the queue depends on the type of operation (a maintenance operation might be lower in priority than an alarm), the total load will affect the relative mix of operations, a heavier load causing a smaller proportion of maintenance operations to occur.

You do not have to be excessively accurate in determining operational profiles; thus you can often save on the data collection effort. A given percentage error in occurrence probability causes the same percentage error in allocating resources. Measurement of failure intensity is generally very robust with respect to errors or variations in occurrence probabilities. A given error in occurrence probability causes a much lower percentage error in failure intensity in most cases. Failure intensity error is largest for the operations with the largest occurrence probabilities, for large positive relative errors, and for operational profiles that tend to be more nonuniform. Musa (1994a) indicates that on the average the percentage error in failure intensity is about 20 percent of the percentage error in occurrence probability. A study by Crespo, Matrella, and Pasquini (1996) also shows that errors in the operational profile do not substantially affect reliability estimates.

In the rare event that a system is completely new and the operations have never been executed before, even by a similar system or manually, the operational profile could be very inaccurate. However, it is still the best picture of customer use you have and so is valuable.

The process of predicting use alone, perhaps as part of a market study, is extremely important because the interaction with the customer that it requires highlights the operations' relative values. It may be that you should drop some operations and emphasize others, resulting in a more competitive product. The approach of reducing the number of little-used operations, reduced operations software (ROS), increases reliability, speeds delivery, and lowers costs (Musa, 1991b).

3.2.6 Determining occurrence probabilities

To determine occurrence probabilities of operations in the tabular representation, divide the occurrence rate for each operation by the total

TABLE 3.5   System Occurrence Probabilities for Fone Follower

Operation	Occurrence probability
Process voice call, no pager, answer	0.18
Process voice call, no pager, no answer	0.17
Process voice call, pager, answer	0.17
Process fax call	0.15
Process voice call, pager, answer on page	0.12
Process voice call, pager, no answer on page	0.10
Phone number entry	0.10
Audit section of phone number database	0.009
Add subscriber	0.0005
Delete subscriber	0.0005
Recover from hardware failure	0.000001
Total	1.0

occurrence rate. To determine occurrence probabilities for attribute values in the graphical representation, divide the occurrence rate for each attribute value by the total occurrence rate for the attribute.

Occurrence probabilities of operations or operation attribute values typically do vary with operational mode, although the attributes and attribute values themselves do not. We express probabilities for the graphical representation as conditional rather than joint probabilities because conditional probabilities relate more easily to engineers' judgment when they must estimate probabilities.

The system occurrence probabilities for the operations in the tabular representation of Fone Follower are shown in Table 3.5. We have sorted the operations in order of descending probabilities. This is customary; it puts the operational profile in a form that is particularly convenient for engineers and managers to use.

You will recall from Sec. 2.2.4 that the developed software intensity objective for Fone Follower was 95 failures per million calls. Hence the reliability per call objective for this software was 0.999905. Therefore we can safely eliminate noncritical operations whose occurrence probabilities total 0.00005. No set of noncritical operations meet this criterion.

The occurrence probabilities for the attribute values in the graphical representation of the PBX are shown in Fig. 3.4.

3.3   Special Situations

Sometimes the definition of an operation can change as a system is developed. The following discusses how the operational profile must be

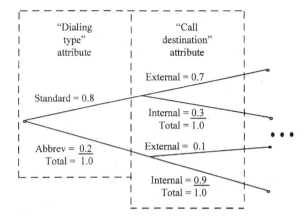

Figure 3.4 Occurrence probabilities for attribute values in graphical representation of a PBX.

adjusted as a result. It also presents the module usage table, which can be useful when allocating design, coding, code inspection, unit test, and other resources among modules.

3.3.1 Handling the evolution of the definition of operation during system development

In Sec. 3.2.4 we identified the occasional need to convert an operational profile developed for one set of operations or network of attribute values to an operational profile for a second set of operations or network that evolves from the first. For simplicity we will use the term *operation* to denote either an operation or an attribute value that is evolving to other operations or attribute values.

Consider the example of a system with operations A, B, and C that will evolve to a system with operations W, X, Y, and Z. The original operational profile is given in Table 3.6.

Suppose that operation A has been replaced by operation W all the time and by operation Y 20 percent of the time in the evolved system.

TABLE 3.6   Original Operational Profile

Operation	Occurrence probability
A	0.54
B	0.36
C	0.1

TABLE 3.7   Mapping of Operation List

	Preoperation		
	A	B	C
Occurrence probability	0.54	0.36	0.1
Postoperation			
W	1	1	
X		0.2	
Y	0.2	0.1	
Z			1

Similarly, operation B has been replaced by W all the time, X, 20 percent of the time, and Y, 10 percent of the time. Operation C is replaced by Z all the time. The mapping is illustrated in Table 3.7. This format, incidentally, is useful for handling other problems of this sort.

In order to determine the occurrence probabilities for the new operational profile, first weight the occurrence probabilities of the old operational profile by the proportion of the time each operation maps to a new operation and add all of them as shown in Table 3.8. You now have initial occurrence "probabilities" for the new operations. However, the total initial occurrence probability is greater than 1, so you must correct all initial occurrence probabilities by dividing by that total.

3.3.2 Applying the module usage table

You can employ module usage tables to indicate the relative usage of program modules. A module usage table is a list of all the program modules along with the probabilities that each is used for any given

TABLE 3.8   New Operational Profile

	Preoperation				
	A	B	C		
Occurrence probability	0.54	0.36	0.1		
Postoperation				Initial occurrence probability	Final occurrence probability
W	0.54	0.36		0.9	0.740
X		0.072		0.072	0.059
Y	0.108	0.036		0.144	0.119
Z			0.1	0.1	0.082
Total				1.216	1

TABLE 3.9   Sample Operation-Module Matrix

Operation	Module			
	1	2	3	4
W	1	0	1	0
X	0	1	1	1
Y	1	1	0	0
Z	0	0	1	1

operation of the program. The module usage table can be the basis for allocating resources and assigning priorities among work activities related to modules. The module usage table is not a profile in the sense that module usage is not disjoint; occurrence probabilities do not necessarily add up to one.

You can construct the module usage table from the operational profile and the operation-usage matrix. The operation-module matrix indicates which operations use which modules. Table 3.9 shows an example of an operation-module matrix, based on the system whose operational profile is given in Table 3.8. Note that operation W uses modules 1 and 3; X uses 2, 3, and 4; etc.

Let q_j be the module occurrence probability and p_i be the operation occurrence probability. Then

$$q_j = \sum_i a_{ij} p_i \qquad (3.1)$$

where a_{ij} is 1 if module j is employed by operation i. The module usage table corresponding to the system defined by Tables 3.8 and 3.9 is shown in Table 3.10.

3.4   Frequently Asked Questions

We will now look at questions that have been asked concerning the uses of operational profiles, concepts relating to them, and the activity of developing and applying them.

TABLE 3.10   Module Usage Table

Module	Occurrence probability
1	0.859
2	0.178
3	0.881
4	0.141

3.4.1 Uses

1 Does the operational profile have applications outside of software reliability engineering?

ANSWER: Yes, you can apply it wherever you need a quantitative description of how a system is or will be used. For example, you can use it in performance evaluation. It can provide guidance about where to focus development resources. It can be the basis for software cost reduction or delivery date speedup based on a software analog to reduced instruction set computing (RISC). The analog is reduced operation software (ROS). The operational profile can be the guiding principle for human interface design: You should make frequently used operations the easiest to learn and simplest to use. It can be the guide for organizing user manuals, with the most frequently used operations placed up front. Because the operational profile highlights the operations of the system, it tends to discourage "feature creep," the undesirable tendency to continually add operations (many infrequently used), by making it highly visible.

2 Can we apply the operational profile concept to hardware?

ANSWER: Yes. In fact, there is a possibility that it may prove to be a very useful approach for certain kinds of hardware failures. Hardware contains many defects (faults) that cause failures only for certain uses (operations or runs). The operational profile and software reliability theory may give insight into such failures.

3 Is the operational profile concept useful for regression test?

ANSWER: Absolutely. Regression test will be most cost-effective in maintaining a high level of reliability if the functions you include are those that are used most frequently in operation.

4 If we apply the reduced operation software (ROS) concept in engineering a product, can we save software development money?

ANSWER: Yes, because the amount of development and system test effort you will require is related to the number of functions that you implement.

5 Does the form of the operational profile have any relationship to our capability to use it to increase productivity?

ANSWER: Yes, a high degree of nonuniformity offers greater opportunity to focus development resources on the most frequently used functions.

6 What is the effect on reliability measures of errors in specifying the operational profile?

ANSWER: Failure intensity (reliability) is generally robust and not greatly affected by errors in specifying the operational profile (Musa, 1994b).

7 How can you say that the cost of developing the operational profile is the principal cost in software reliability engineering? What about the cost of preparing test cases?

ANSWER: You must prepare test cases no matter what testing you do. It is reasonable to charge to software reliability engineering only those activities that differentiate it from other approaches to testing.

8   How can the application of software reliability engineering uncover missing requirements? I don't see the connection.

ANSWER: This has more to do with software development culture than with logic. Some software system engineers, architects, and designers start development from the mindset of How can we apply new technology X? rather than What do our users need? Software reliability engineering includes the development of operational profiles as an integral part of its process. In order to develop an operational profile properly, you must communicate with users in a disciplined way that tends to bring out all the operations they need and their probabilities of occurrence. Thus, needed operations that would otherwise be overlooked tend to be uncovered.

9   Can the development of the operational profile improve product definition? How?

ANSWER: Yes. Developing an operational profile focuses attention on how users will employ your product and the relative importance of the different uses. This will guide you in intelligently allocating your development resources. That will help you do a better job of defining and designing a product to fit user needs at a price they will be willing to pay.

10   Instead of developing an operational profile and test cases to test the next release, why can't we just record the input states of the runs we experience in the field and play them back?

ANSWER: This is usually not a practical approach. The next release will almost always have new features (except in the rare case of "fault removal only" releases) and hence new operations, and you will have to construct test cases for them. Further, your chances of recording rare critical runs are small so you will have to construct test cases for them. The operational profile will be different for the next release, so you will have to develop it anyway.

Finally, it is difficult to avoid bias in recording field runs. For example, if you record on a particular day at a particular site, you may be biasing your test cases to particular environmental conditions such as soak time. The only way to avoid bias is to select the runs to record randomly from a large number of sites over a long period of time. The cost of doing this may well exceed the cost of developing the test cases in the first place.

11   How do operational profiles apply to domain engineering?

ANSWER: We generally practice domain engineering for the development of components that will be used in a number of different systems. The process for developing operational profiles for such components is the same as that used for other systems. The only difference is that you need greater breadth of analysis to understand all the different ways that such components may be used.

3.4.2 Concepts

1 How does obtaining reliabilities of different missions relate to the operational profile?

ANSWER: You may view a *mission* as a subset of the operations that make up the operational profile. You can obtain reliability for each mission by measurement based on testing that subset of operations in accordance with their relative probabilities of occurrence. If missions overlap across the set of operations, you will need to *allocate* the occurrence probabilities of operations belonging to two or more missions among the missions. You can determine the overall reliability for all missions by taking the weighted average of mission reliabilities, the weights being the mission occurrence probabilities. Remember, however, that the accuracy of the reliabilities you measure will be reduced by the fact that you will have a smaller failure sample for each mission than for the total system. Hence the foregoing approach may not be advisable.

2 How does the way in which customers start using new features affect the operational profile?

ANSWER: There may be a transient in the operational profile before it settles down to steady-state operation. For command-driven systems, that is, those systems where the functions selected depend primarily on human input, there is a tendency to use the most basic, easily learned functions first and then progress to the more sophisticated ones. Also, users tend to exercise later the new functions that have just been added to the system. The transient can cause inaccuracies in reliability measurement early in operation, especially for command-driven systems. Hence, for such systems, one should take care to measure during the steady-state period or to compensate for the transient.

3 Does functionality have any relationship to the input space?

ANSWER: Yes. Functionality relates to the size of the input space. Software with greater functionality will have an input space of greater size.

4 Does the concept of input space really capture all the different environments a program can operate in?

ANSWER: Yes, but the input variables can be either direct (assuming that the program has been designed to operate in all those environments) or indirect (if it has not).

5 Do we group runs into operations so that we only have to execute one test case for each operation?

ANSWER: Grouping of runs into operations does not imply that you select only one test per operation; it simply provides the framework for sampling nonuniformly across the input space. If you select operations randomly in accordance with the operational profile and then select runs (input states) randomly within the operation, you will have selected nonuniform random tests that match the operational profile. When an important input variable is known to be nonuniformly distributed with respect to its values, it may be desirable to pick ranges of values and use these to define operations, using the foregoing criteria.

6 Is there such a thing as a "run profile?"

ANSWER: You could in theory develop a run profile consisting of the set of runs and their associated probabilities. Executing all runs would achieve the ideal of exhaustive testing. This is, of course, impractical, but the concept may be helpful in considering the cost-effectiveness of different strategies for sampling from the set of runs.

7 Can an environmental condition be an initiator of an operation?

ANSWER: Only indirectly, through a system that can sense the condition and initiate an operation.

8 How can it be practical to develop an operational profile? There are an astronomical number of ways that a program can be exercised. Who could determine the occurrence probabilities for all of them?

ANSWER: The operational profile is based on a manageable number of operations, which do not usually exceed a few hundred. Operations differ substantially from each other as to the processing they perform. Within an operation, many different input states are possible, each of which may result in slightly different processing. We do not determine occurrence probabilities within an operation but select different runs with uniform probability.

9 Can two different operations execute some modules that are identical?

ANSWER: Yes.

10 What, if any, is the effect on the operational profile of a functional requirement being enumerated?

ANSWER: Enumeration of functional requirements generally implies that we will associate them with the code that implements them and the test cases that verify that they have been met. Enumeration promotes traceability. Hence enumerated requirements are likely to be sufficiently important that they suggest that corresponding operations be listed.

11 Can a nonfunctional requirement suggest an operation?

ANSWER: No. Nonfunctional requirements suggest such things as reliability, schedule, cost objectives, documentation content and formats, and change control procedures.

12 Can we mix the tabular and graphical representations? We basically have a system where we describe some operations by multiple attributes and some by single attributes.

ANSWER: Yes. We can incorporate the operations that have single attributes into the graphical representation as single-branch paths with no nodes. Similarly, we can incorporate paths with only single-branch nodes in the graphical representation into the tabular representation as operations. The latter is particularly convenient for critical operations, which we can handle more conveniently with the tabular representation.

3.4.3 Application

1 Does regression test prevent you from testing in accordance with the operational profile?

ANSWER: No. In fact, your regression test will be more efficient if you do.

2 How can I handle an operational profile that varies continually with time?

ANSWER: Express the operational profile as the weighted sum of two component operational profiles. Express the weight for one component as a function of time (the other weight will be 1 minus the first weight). Determine failure intensities λ_1 and λ_2 for the two different component operational profiles. Then the overall failure intensity will be given by

$$\lambda = \rho(t)\lambda_1 + (1 - \rho(t))\lambda_2 \tag{3.2}$$

where $\rho(t)$ is the weight for the first component and t is time. An operational profile like this would be used only to invoke test cases. To select test cases, you would need to use the average over time.

3 We have a database-oriented system where an important effect of failures can be degradation of the database. It would seem that this would increase the likelihood of other failures. Doesn't this interaction cause problems in defining an operational profile and hence measuring software reliability?

ANSWER: We don't generally take data degradation into account in developing the operational profile. We handle it in load testing by reproducing as accurately as possible the same data cleanup procedure that we use in the field, which may be periodic (for example, a daily reboot) or continuous.

4 What methods can you use for grouping runs into operations?

ANSWER: In general, you look for runs with closely related functions or runs for which the code is executed along the same or similar paths. For example, in an airline reservation system, you might group together all "single leg" journeys (Boston-New York, Chicago-Denver, San Francisco-Los Angeles). This approach is probably best for independent test teams. Otherwise, the team must obtain knowledge of program structure through study of the program and it must map runs to structure.

5 How can you estimate the part of the operational profile that is not covered by test?

ANSWER: If all or almost all failures found during test are resolved, the failures found afterward during operation are indicative of the part of the operational profile that was missed. Assume that the failure intensity during operation is 2 percent of that which occurred at the start of system test. Then, assuming that the operational profile remained unchanged, the probabilities of occurrence of the runs that were missed must have totaled at least 0.02.

6   We can define the operational profile fairly easily for commands being entered as they should be, but how do we define it for erroneous entries?

ANSWER: You probably will not define separate operations to handle erroneous entries but will include them as possible test cases associated with an operation. The best approach is to view the system from a human factors viewpoint, using studies of the nature and frequency of human mistakes to help you come up with the proportion of test cases that have erroneous inputs. When you select test cases for an operation, select the appropriate proportion with erroneous inputs.

7   We are developing a system that will be used for a series of one-of-a-kind missions. In our case, it is an operations control center that will be used for different deep space flights. How should we determine the operational profile?

ANSWER: You could establish a different operational profile for each mission. However, this may be time consuming and unnecessary. You may be able to determine functions that are generic to most or all missions and develop an overall operational profile, saving considerable effort.

8   Do you need to do anything special about the operational profile if the operations have widely differing time durations?

ANSWER: Maybe not, because the operational profile still reflects the probabilities that the different operations are initiated; hence it reproduces the true field environment. However, you may have defined some operations to be too long.

9   We want to collect field data on how our product is being used so we can determine operational profiles for the various operational modes. However, it would be too expensive to collect this data for the many installations at which our product is in use. What can we do?

ANSWER: Select a random sample of installations and collect data for them.

10   Can field failure data be of any help to us in obtaining occurrence probabilities for the operational profile? We typically obtain this data anyway from user reports, but it is much more difficult to get users to collect use data.

ANSWER: Yes, although it is usually less accurate than getting use data directly. Note that if faults are distributed uniformly through the code and runs are approximately equal in length, the fraction of failures experienced by each operation will be equal to its probability of occurrence and may be used as an estimate of that probability. The uniform distribution assumption is reasonably valid for most systems. Uniform run length may not be, but you may be able to adjust the failure data to compensate for this. User reports are generally correlated with failures, but there may be extraneous factors at work here as well. Hence the estimates you get of occurrence probabilities can only be approximate.

11   Should we pick operations to represent *segments* of work initiated by users or complete *sequences?*

ANSWER: If users almost always initiate standard sequences of work and very seldom initiate the individual segments, define the sequences as operations. If users almost always initiate segments of work, pretty much independent of each other, define the segments as operations. If users initiate segments of work but there are many dependencies among them, consider defining operations as sequences and use the graphical representation of the operational profile, with the work segments indicated as branches in the network.

12   We are developing packaged software that must work with hardware and software components from a number of different vendors. It would be impractical to test every possible combination. Is there some rational way to reduce the number of combinations we test?

ANSWER: Yes. Determine the fraction of users that are associated with each option for each component. Multiply the fractions to determine the fraction of users that employ each configuration. Then test only the configurations with the highest fraction of use. For example, suppose the software has the interfacing component options noted in Table 3.11, with the fractions of users noted.

There are 45 possible configurations, but 20 percent of them (9) represent 84 percent of the users, as shown in Table 3.12. You can sharply reduce the amount of testing by only testing these nine configurations. Another possibility is to also test some of the less-used configurations but only do so for limited operational profiles involving the most-used operations.

13   Why are occurrence rates of operations measured in clock hours rather than execution hours?

ANSWER: Occurrence rates of operations are measured in clock hours because you will be invoking runs in test at rates with respect to clock hours.

TABLE 3.11   Components and Component Options with Fractions of Users

| | Option | | | | |
Component	1	2	3	4	5
Personal computer (hardware)	0.30	0.25	0.25	0.15	0.05
Operating system	0.90	0.08	0.02		
Database	0.70	0.25	0.05		

TABLE 3.12   Most Frequently Used
Configurations

Configuration*			
PC	OS	DB	Fraction of use
1	1	1	0.189
2	1	1	0.1575
3	1	1	0.1575
4	1	1	0.0945
1	1	2	0.0675
2	1	2	0.05625
3	1	2	0.05625
4	1	2	0.03375
5	1	1	0.0315

*PC: personal computer (hardware); OS: operating
systems; DB: database.

14   Many of the operations in our system are restricted so that they can only
be initiated by specified user types. Will this affect the way in which we develop the operational profile?

ANSWER: No. There will be fewer cases in which an operation will be listed
under multiple initiators, but this will have no effect on the procedure for
developing the operational profiles.

15   Are there situations in which we should definitely not try to combine two
operational modes into one?

ANSWER: Yes. If the operations of one mode are practically all different from
those of another, combining the modes may produce a number of interactions
and possible failures that will never occur in the field, resulting in a waste of
valuable test and debugging time and money.

16   We have several products that perform very similar functions. The main
difference among them is speed, with the faster products being more costly. Is
there any way we can save effort and expense in applying software reliability
engineering to them?

ANSWER: Yes. Develop the operational profiles for these products side by side.
Many of the operations will be duplicated. You can often collect occurrence rate
information on a common basis. You can perform much test planning jointly;
the products can share many test cases. If the software for the products is
developed in common, it is likely that you can also execute a lot of the testing
in common.

17   Can you construct hierarchies of operational profiles?

ANSWER: Yes. If you have an operation that you want to characterize in more
detail, you can create an operational profile for it. You can also expand the
operation into multiple operations in the original operational profile. For

TABLE 3.13   Example Operational Profile

Operation	Occurrence probability
A	0.6
B	0.3
C	0.1

TABLE 3.14   Suboperational Profile for Operation B

Operation	Occurrence probability
B_1	0.5
B_2	0.4
B_3	0.1

example, suppose you have the operational profile shown in Table 3.13. You can decide to create a suboperational profile to refine operation B, as shown in Table 3.14. You can also expand B directly in the original operational profile, as shown in Table 3.15.

18   How do we deal with the fact that the occurrences of many operations in the field are not independent of each other but tend to form sequences? In other words, after a user of the product initiates operation A, there is a high probability that he or she will next initiate operation D. Random selection of these operations according to their occurrence probabilities might not represent true field conditions.

ANSWER: If a set of operations truly forms a sequence that occurs most of the time, the operations should probably be redefined as a single operation. If the sequence occurs only occasionally, leaving the operations as separate entities to be randomly selected is probably a better approximation to reality.

19   Most users attach greater importance to avoiding failures in existing operations than in new operations, because their work has greater dependency on

TABLE 3.15   Expanded Operational Profile

Operation	Occurrence probability
A	0.6
B_1	0.15
B_2	0.12
B_3	0.03
C	0.1

existing operations and the failure severity impact is greater. Besides using failure severity classification, what else can we do to adjust to this situation?

ANSWER: You can divide input space into the parts that relate to existing operations and those that relate to new operations. Give the corresponding parts of the operational profile relative weights that express the relative importance of the operations. Then use the resulting adjusted operational profile for focusing development effort, prioritizing tests, and other purposes with the greater importance of existing operations accounted for.

3.5   Background

The following will first present some background on determining operational modes and will then delve into the concepts of operations and runs more deeply.

3.5.1   Determining operational modes

A different pattern of system use tends to cause different interactions among operations (major tasks performed by a system) and also among their runs (specific instances of the operation), typically resulting from such things as different contentions for resources and different data passed among or shared by the operations and runs. In effect, this changes the runs that are executed by changing their input states (sets of variables that exist external to the system and influence its execution), although it is not generally practical to explicitly determine what the input state changes are. But you do need to test the system under these different patterns of use, hence the need for defining operational modes.

Different environmental conditions also effectively change the runs that are executed by changing their input states, although again it is not generally practical to explicitly determine what the input state changes are. Examples of environmental conditions are data degradation (characterized by *soak time*) and degree of population of the database.

We don't usually use state of database corruption as a factor in defining operational mode. Rather, we try to represent the same database cleanup procedure in test that exists in the field (for example, daily database reinitialization). Then we let database corruption range naturally over its possible values as each operational mode executes over time.

Many systems that have operators will have substantially different use patterns on nights and weekends when few or no operators are present. Hence it is common to have prime time and off hours operational modes.

The pattern of failures that can occur is significantly different between normal load and overload conditions, because insufficient resources cause memory overflows and queueing delays. Hence there is a need to test under both these conditions. The variation is much smaller with load within the normal or overload ranges; hence it usually isn't worth planning tests at different load levels within the normal or overload ranges.

When a system has different priorities for its operations, it is particularly important that operational modes be defined for both normal traffic and heavy traffic conditions, because the patterns of use will differ. For example, when you have a normal load, some low-priority tasks such as audits and housekeeping operations will execute. Under heavy traffic conditions, they may not run at all.

Similarly, some systems control the operations they will accept, based on system-capability status, in order to reject poorly functioning operations and dedicate capacity to more effective ones. In this case, consider establishing each important system-capability status as an operational mode and testing it separately.

3.5.2 Operations and runs

We can view the execution of a program as a single entity, lasting for months or even years for real-time systems. However, it is easier to characterize the environment if you divide the execution into a set of *operations.* Then the environment is specified by the *operational profile,* as previously defined. In turn, there are many possible instances of operations, each called a *run.* During execution, the factors that cause a particular operation and a particular run within that operation to occur are very numerous and complex. Hence we can view the operations required of the program by the environment as being selected randomly in accordance with the probabilities just mentioned and then the runs within those operations being selected with equal probability.

A run is specified by its *input state* or set of values for the input variables that it receives. The input state is not the same thing as the *machine state,* which is the much larger set of all variable values accessible to the computer. Recurrent runs have the same input state. We judge the reliability of a program by the output states (sets of values of output variables created) of its runs. Note that a run represents a transformation between an input and an output state. Multiple input states may map to the same output state, but a given input state can have only one output state. The input state uniquely determines the particular instructions that will be executed and the values of their operands. Thus it establishes the *path* of control taken through the program. It also uniquely establishes the values of all intermediate variables. Whether a particular fault will cause a failure for a specific run type is predictable in theory. However, the analysis required to determine this might be impractical to pursue.

The input state is of more than just theoretical interest. It is important to understand exactly what the input variables to a run are and to record them for diagnostic purposes. Many failures that are difficult to diagnose result from indirect or "hidden" input variables. These may be data items in a database that were corrupted by a previous run. The program may not function properly for the particular values.

An *input variable* for a program run is any data item that is external to the run and is *used* by it. There doesn't have to be a physical input process. The input variable may simply be located in memory, waiting to be accessed. Correspondingly, an *output variable* for a program run is any data item that is external to the run and is *set* by it. It is not necessary that the output variable actually be used, printed out, or physically moved. An output variable can be a control signal, command, printout, display, or item of transmitted data, among other possibilities. An input variable cannot also be an output variable, but the two can occupy the same memory location at different times. A data item consists of an associated set of one or more data elements. It may be a scalar, array, or structure. The "value" of a data item is the set of values of its elements. A data element is a scalar such as a numerical quantity, logical variable, character string, or even abstract data type. "Association" is determined by the functional use of the data elements. Multiple data elements that relate to a single external condition would be considered associated. An example would be the elements of a vector that locates an aircraft in an air traffic control system.

A data element can have only one value with respect to a run. Therefore, you must consider each use or setting of a quantity that is varying as a separate data element. Suppose the time relative to the start of the run at which a quantity is used or set can change and is therefore significant. Then the data item that describes the quantity should include the time as an element. Consequently, each activation of an interrupt of a given type is a separate data item. Because the number of interrupts occurring during a run can vary, different input states may have different numbers of input variables and hence dimensions. Note that a data element is not a physical or symbolic memory location. You can associate the same physical or symbolic location with multiple data elements by "time sharing" them through dynamic storage allocation.

Externally initiated interrupts such as interrupts generated by the system clock, by operator actions, and by other components of the system outside the program are considered as input variables. Intermediate data items computed by the program during a run and not existing external to the program are considered neither input nor output variables. Hence, interrupts generated directly by a run or interrupts that are determined from other input variables (for example, overflow and underflow) are not input variables.

All runs will terminate sooner or later as a consequence of the input state selected. "Termination" may mean that the program completes a task and searches a task queue for a new one. Some terminations may be premature in the sense that no useful function is completed. If a run is terminated early by operator action, the termination action represents an interrupt that signifies a different input state from a run with a normal termination.

The *input space* for a program is the set of input states that can occur during the operation of the program. An input space is discrete (it is assumed that interrupt times can be stated only to some quantization level). Thus we can identify a given input state by an index number. The number of dimensions of the input space is equal to the sum of the dimensions of the input variables. The input space may change if the program changes.

If the operations are independent, it is relatively easy to determine their probabilities of occurrence. However, an operation may be dependent on a previous operation. For example, this may be true of a control system for which we define an operation as one cyclic operation. In this case, one may ignore the dependencies and use the probabilities of occurrence of each operation computed over a long period of time. This procedure is acceptable because one can set input states by manual intervention. A particular operation in a dependent sequence can be executed in test without actually executing the operation that normally precedes it in the field.

The validity of the foregoing approach may be explained in statistical terms. You can view the sequence of successive operations as a Markov chain, with the relationships between the states being expressed in terms of transition probabilities. A transition probability is the conditional probability that a system in a given state will transfer to some specified state. We will assume a homogeneous environment. Then the transition probabilities will be stationary. It is reasonable to assume that every operation is reachable from every other operation. Consequently, the probabilities of the various states of the Markov chain occurring will approach a steady state, given enough time. Thus you can use the steady-state probabilities to characterize the environment.

There is an alternative approach to the operational profile for characterizing the environment (Cheung, 1980). You may specify the sequence of program modules executed. There is a many-to-one mapping between operations and module sequences. The analog of the operational profile is the set of all possible module sequences and their associated probabilities of occurrence. Instead of these probabilities, however, it is more convenient to use the transition probabilities between modules. If the transition probabilities are dependent only on the two modules involved and are homogeneous, in time the system will reach a steady state. Each module will have a probability of being executed. We can obtain the overall program reliability from the reliabilities of the modules and the transition probabilities. The foregoing approach emphasizes the structural characteristics of the program. You develop sensitivity coefficients to indicate which modules are most critical in affecting system reliability. Identification of critical modules could be useful in suggesting the most efficient testing and evolution strategies. In the former case, one would test to cover modules in descending order of criticality. In the latter, one would try to avoid changes in critical modules when adding new features.

In reality, the foregoing approach is much less practical than the operational profile approach. Probabilities of occurrence of operations are the natural and original information related to program use. They are independent of program structure and can be determined prior to design, whereas module transition probabilities cannot. You would have to determine transition probabilities between modules through program instrumentation and extensive execution. The latter would be essentially equivalent to doing operation-based testing. Estimation of component reliabilities would usually be difficult because the failure samples associated with modules would be small. Hence the module sequence approach is mainly of conceptual value.

3.6 Problems

3.1 Assume that a product has a base development cost C_0 and a cost per operation of C_p. There are P operations. Each operation k has a probability of occurrence p_k. If we had no operational profile information, we would devote the same development resources to each operation. However, we will use the operational profile to adjust the development resources assigned to the less frequently used operations and reduce the overall cost. Let $k = 1$ represent the most used operation. Each other operation will have its cost reduced to a per-operation base component C_{P0} plus a variable component $(p_k/p_1)(C_p - C_{P0})$.

    a. What will the total development cost now be?

    b. What is the percentage cost saving?

    c. If the project base development cost is 10 percent of the total cost before resource reduction, there are 45 operations, the per-operation base cost is half the per-operation cost (again, before resource reduction), and $p_1 = 0.2$, what is the percentage cost saving?

d. What is the percentage cost saving for $p_1 = 0.5$? $p_1 = 0.1$?

e. What is the percentage cost saving if there are 18 operations? 90 operations?

3.2 Assume you are the product manager for Fone Follower. You want to apply the concept of operational development in planning two releases for the product. What capabilities would you put in each release? Refer to Table 3.5.

3.3 You have scheduled a 5-h review of voice call requirements for Fone Follower. How should you divide the time between review of the processing with and without paging? Refer to Table 3.5.

3.4 You are developing an armored amphibious vehicle that will be used by both trainees and battle veterans. What operational modes would you establish?

4

Preparing for Test

In preparing for test, we apply the operational profile information we have developed to planning for efficient test. Preparing for test from a software reliability engineering perspective includes preparing test cases and test procedures. We must prepare for each system of the product that we are testing. However, we can often take advantage of commonalities that may exist. Beta test does not require much preparation, except for any work needed to record results, because you expose your product directly to the field environment.

Software reliability engineering helps guide feature, load, and regression test. As you will recall, feature test occurs first. It consists of single executions of operations, with interactions between the operations minimized. The focus is on whether the operation executes properly. It is followed by load test, which attempts to represent the field use and environment as accurately as possible, with operations executing simultaneously and interacting. Interactions can occur directly, through the slowly corrupting database, or as a result of conflicts for resources. Regression test consists of feature test that is conducted after every build involving significant change. It is often periodic. A week is a common period, although intervals can be as short as a day or as long as a month. The period chosen typically depends on factors such as system size and volatility and the degree to which a system must be ready for rapid release when market conditions change. The focus is to reveal faults that may have been spawned in the process of change.

Some testers say regression test should focus on operations that contain the changed code. This view makes sense if you are sure the possible effects of the changes are isolated to those operations or if system reliability requirements are low, so that cross-effects to other operations do not matter. However, in most cases you cannot rely on isolation, and potential cross-effects can cause unacceptable deterioration in system reliability. So normally you should consider all operations when planning a regression test. However, a change generally results in a smaller probability of failure than a new program, so it isn't really necessary to retest every operation after every change. It is inefficient to cover operations of unequal occurrence probability with equal regression test; hence operations in regression test should be selected in accordance with the operational profile.

In load test, it is necessary to test each operational mode separately so that we will be sampling from the possible interactions among operations that can occur and ignoring the ones that can't. Thus we will be sampling from and only from the failures that can occur due to the interactions.

It is particularly efficient to plan to conduct performance test at the same time as load test. Performance test is also most realistic if driven by the operational profile. The only additional effort required is that you must plan for collection and recording of performance data such as response times and queue lengths.

4.1 Concepts

Before we describe the procedure of preparing for test, we need to discuss some definitions and concepts. When we execute the tests, we will be executing a set of runs. A *run* is a specific instance of an operation. Thus, like an operation, it can be executed in a series of noncontiguous time segments on different machines. A run is characterized by the operation and its *input state* or complete set of *input variables* (variables that are external to the run and affect its execution) and their values. The *input space* is the complete set of possible input states. For a detailed discussion of input variables, see Sec. 3.5.2. An input variable can be *direct* in that it controls the operation directly, such as arguments, menu selections, or entered or accessed data. It results from a deliberate design decision. Or it can be *indirect* in that it only influences the operation. An indirect input variable usually involves an environmental influence such as traffic load, soak time, or an interacting system or process. Soak time is the time a program has executed since the last data reinitialization. Environmental variables affect the program by changing specific variables but through means too complex to specify in detail (for example, heavy traffic may cause a control table to overflow into other variables). Indirect input variables often work through their effects on shared memory through resource conflicts or through the effects of changing system state.

In the Fone Follower illustration, you might characterize a run for the "Process fax call" operation by the direct and indirect variables with their values of Table 4.1. Screening is a feature that allows the

TABLE 4.1   Direct and Indirect Input Variables for Process Fax
Call Operation of Fone Follower

Direct	Indirect
Originator = 201 908 5577	Operational mode = prime hours
Forwardee = 908 555 1212	Database state: signified by time
Billing type = per call	Resource state: signified by time
Dialing type = standard	
Screening = yes	

subscriber to restrict the forwarding of calls to a list of originating numbers that the subscriber enters. "Yes" means that the feature is enabled, and "No" means it is not. The Originator input variable will be set to a specific phone number such as 201 908 5577. The Forwardee, or number to which the call is forwarded, will be set similarly.

The concept of *operation* relates to substantially differing functionality, with failure behavior therefore likely to differ. The concept of *run* recognizes any difference in functionality. Two runs within the same operation may differ in failure behavior, but this is less likely.

A run involves the execution of a test case. A *test case* is the partial specification of a run through the naming of its direct input variables and their values. For example, the run we have just described uses one of the test cases prepared for the operation "Process fax call." We specify it by the direct input variables with their values as shown in Table 4.2. A test case is independent of operational mode. The same test case can execute in different operational modes and hence different environments. Thus a test case can generate multiple runs, each with different potential failure behavior.

Specification of the indirect input variables gives a test case the necessary context so it can become a run. We do this by selecting an appropriate set of operational modes and by the passage of execution time (some indirect input variables such as interaction and data degradation vary with execution time). We control the indirect input variables carefully during feature and regression test so that they have little influence. This is necessary to limit the possible causes of failure until

TABLE 4.2   Fone Follower Test
Case with Its Direct Input
Variables

Originator = 201 908 5577
Forwardee = 908 555 1212
Billing type = per call
Dialing type = standard
Screening = yes

we know that the operation itself is performing reliably. Otherwise, debugging would be unnecessarily complex. For example, in the case of feature or regression test for Fone Follower, reinitialization would give us the same database state for each run. The operational mode would be irrelevant because testing would be confined to just one operation at a time. The same would be true of the resource state because there would be no conflicts or queues for resources.

In load test, the full influence of the indirect input variables is brought to bear. We divide load test into the different operational modes. Each is driven by a test procedure. A *test procedure* is a controller that sets up environmental conditions and that invokes randomly selected test cases at random times. Selection is based on the appropriate operational mode test operational profile and invocation times are based on the operational mode run occurrence rate. The example in Table 4.3 illustrates the specification of occurrence rates for the test procedure for the peak hours operational mode of Fone Follower.

The relationships among operational modes, operations, runs, and test cases are shown in Fig. 4.1. The area represents all possible runs for the system. We represent each run by a point, each operational mode by a region, and each operation by a subregion within the larger region of the operational mode. Both operational modes include the same test case X_A, one that is part of operation X. However, the runs X_{A1} and X_{A2} are different because the operational modes are different, resulting in different environments.

If the operational profile has a graphical representation, we define the operation by a sequence of attributes and the general attribute value choices that are made. The test case involves a more detailed selection among the general attribute value choices. As an illustration, consider the switching system with the graphical representation of the operational profile shown in Fig. 3.1. The operation defined by the Dialing type attribute with general attribute value "Standard" and the

TABLE 4.3   Test Procedure Specification for Peak Hours
Operational Mode of Fone Follower

Operation	Occurrence rate (per clock hour)
Phone number entry	30,000
Process voice call, no pager, answer	110,000
Process voice call, no pager, no answer	90,000
Process voice call, pager, answer	90,000
Process voice call, pager, answer on page	60,000
Process voice call, pager, no answer	50,000
Process fax call, pager	70,000

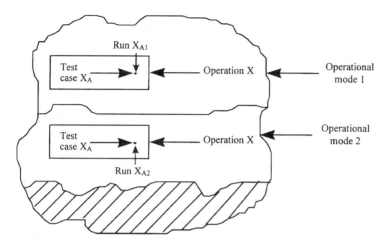

Figure 4.1   Run space showing operational modes, operations, test cases, and runs.

Call destination attribute with general attribute value "External" has been expanded into test cases in Fig. 4.2. The heavy line indicates a specific test case. The Dialing type attribute has only general attribute values, "Standard" and "Abbreviated," and you cannot specify it in greater detail. However, you can specify the Call destination attribute in more detail after selecting the general attribute value "External," which is necessary to specify the operation. You also choose the specific attribute value "777-234-8989," which specifies a particular line being called. Thus we can specify a run.

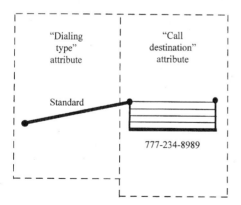

Figure 4.2   Test cases for graphical representation of operational profile.

4.2   Procedure

We will now discuss the procedure for preparing for test, including preparing test cases and preparing test procedures.

In addition to these two tasks, we must provide for the recording of the number of natural or time units at frequent intervals so that we can establish when failures occurred.

4.2.1   Preparing test cases

In theory, one could prepare test cases by simply recording in the field all the input variables (user and other interface interactions and environmental variables) needed to initiate the runs that make up the field execution of the software. This might result in less effort and cost than developing the operational profile and preparing the test cases. However, the recording would necessarily be of a previous version, so it would not adequately represent the load expected for the new system with its new features. Also, you may miss some rarely occurring but critical runs not experienced in the recording period. Finally, one might be able to improve test efficiency through careful test selection, using run categories (see Sec. 4.5.2); this option is not possible when using record and playback.

The process for preparing test cases involves

1. Estimating the number of new test cases needed for the current release

2. Allocating the number of new test cases among the systems to be tested

3. Allocating the number of new test cases for each system among its new operations

4. Specifying the new test cases

5. Adding the new test cases to the test cases from previous releases

4.2.1.1   Estimating the number of new test cases needed for the current release.   You need to account for two factors in estimating the number of new test cases you should prepare for the current release: time and cost. To account for both factors, compute the number of test cases you have time to prepare and also the number you can afford to prepare. Take the minimum of these two numbers as the number of test cases you will plan to prepare.

To obtain the first number, multiply the available time by the available staff and divide by the average work required to prepare a test case. The available time is the time between reasonable stabilization of requirements and the start of test.

To obtain the second number, establish a budget for test case preparation and divide by the average preparation cost per test case. Apparently, there are no studies that would indicate the optimum proportion of the development budget to devote to test case preparation. In the absence of such data, 5 to 10 percent appears to be reasonable. The relative importance of the quality attributes of reliability, development time, and development cost should affect the proportion chosen. If a highly reliable system is required, the proportion of resources you devote to test cases should be larger. If development time and/or development cost are more important, the proportion should be smaller.

Let's illustrate the foregoing calculation for Fone Follower. The available time was 15 weeks (600 h), the available staff was 3.5, and the average work per test case was 3 h. Hence the available resource of 2100 staff hours divided by the work per test case gives a number of 700 test cases.

The product development budget was $2 million. It was decided to devote 10 percent of this budget to preparing test cases. The average preparation cost per test case was $250. The test case budget of $200,000 divided by $250 yields a number of 800 test cases. Consequently, taking the minimum number of test cases, 700 were planned.

You now need to run a sanity check on the number of new test cases you are planning for this release. You have based the number on the time and funds available to you, which is perhaps the best approach for the present state of the practice. But you also need to determine if this number is reasonable for your failure intensity objective. The number of new test cases must usually be greater than the number of new operations you have defined because you ordinarily assign at least one test case to each operation. In fact, you will probably need at least 50 to 100 more new test cases than new operations if you are to test frequently occurring new operations adequately. You should also apply any experience you may have with developing similar systems to similar failure intensity objectives. It is hoped that in the future this art will develop into more of a science. Probably the metric that is most widely used to compare present test case plans with previous experience is the number of test cases per thousand lines of developed (newly written or modified) code. However, if you have a metric you consider better for your application, use it. If you are developing the second or later release of a product, metrics from previous releases that have been validated against field experience will be particularly relevant.

Over the long term, we need to increase our capability to prepare more test cases for a given time and cost, most likely through developing ways to automate test case generation. We typically execute many more runs in test than we generate test cases. The most efficient testing probably occurs when runs are relatively evenly spaced out through an operation (in the sense of Fig. 4.1). That is, in covering the space of runs of an operation, they are relatively equidistant from each other in the sense of being different. By equalizing and maximizing the difference while covering the entire range of possibilities, you probably maximize the likelihood of finding failures for a given number of runs. To take an analogy, a given number of people searching a field for hidden objects that have been randomly distributed across the field will probably find the most objects if they space themselves equidistantly for searching.

Currently, we generate runs in load test by repeating test cases many times under randomly selected sets of indirect variable values that can occur in the field. The random selection of the indirect variables comes about through random invocation in time and essentially random interaction among test cases resulting from random sequencing. The limitation of test to sets of indirect variable values that can occur in the field comes about as the result of realistic representation of patterns of invocation and through definition of operational modes. Thus, we can currently distribute our runs throughout the run space on the basis of indirect variables to a greater extent than on the basis of direct variables, principally because it is cheaper to do so. Lowering the cost of test cases may change this situation.

4.2.1.2 Allocating the number of new test cases among the systems to be tested.
You should allocate the bulk of the test cases to the product itself. Base the number of test cases you allocate to a product variation on the amount of expected use in the field of the variation relative to the product and on the number of operations of the variation that do not occur for the product. Give particular weight to the differing operations that have high occurrence probabilities. For the supersystems, you can use the same test cases you employ for the corresponding product or product variation. Allocate test cases to acquired components based on their size relative to the product and the estimated risk. Usually you will not allocate test cases to acquired components after the first release. However, you may do this if new acquired components are substituted for previous ones or if the acquired components are substantially modified. In the case of Fone Follower, the operating system represented a substantial part of the product and its reliability was unknown. Hence 500 test cases were allocated to the product and 200 to the operating system.

4.2.1.3 Allocating the number of new test cases for each system among its new operations.
We must now take the number of new test cases for each system of the new release and allocate them among the new operations of that system. We proceed in five steps:

1. If you are using the graphical representation of the operational profile, first convert it to the tabular representation by walking through all the paths, obtaining an occurrence probability for each operation (path) by multiplying all the branch probabilities together. You will probably find it desirable to automate this activity.

2. Identify the rarely occurring critical new operations and determine how many test cases to preassign to each.

3. Determine the allocation probabilities for the other new operations.

4. Preassign one test case to each infrequent other new operation.

5. Assign the remaining test cases to the remaining other new operations in accordance with the allocation probabilities.

A *critical* operation is one for which successful execution adds a great deal of extra value and failure causes a great deal of impact with respect to human life, cost, or system capability. An example of a critical operation is the SCRAM operation in nuclear power plants that shuts down a reactor when it starts to overheat and is in danger of a meltdown. The operation that handles this condition is very rarely used, but it is extremely critical. We identify only the rarely occurring critical operations because we expect that we will allocate sufficient test cases to the frequently occurring critical operations by virtue of their substantial occurrence probabilities.

In the case of a new release, we will set the allocation probabilities for the other new operations equal to the occurrence probabilities of the system operational profile. This is a satisfactory approximation; the sum of the occurrence probabilities for the other new operations will be very close to 1. For subsequent releases, divide the system occurrence probabilities for the other new operations by the total of the system occurrence probabilities for the other new operations.

Infrequent operations are those that would not normally be assigned test cases by virtue of their occurrence probabilities. However, we wish to ensure that we assign each operation at least one test case. If we don't do this, we rule out the possibility that the operation can be invoked during test execution. The occurrence probability of an operation is often such that, because of the fact that runs usually substantially outnumber test cases, the operation might well invoke a run even though the occurrence probability might not normally result in test case selection. Thus we determine the threshold occurrence probability below which we would not normally assign a test case to an operation. This is 0.5 divided by the number of new test cases. We then preassign one test case to each other new operation whose occurrence probability falls below the threshold.

This does not mean that rarely occurring noncritical operations will all be allocated test cases, however. Recall that in developing operational profiles, rarely occurring operations are likely to be combined with others or trimmed from the list (see Sec. 3.2.4).

Let's now illustrate allocation of test cases to operations with Fone Follower. We will initially consider the original Fone Follower, which is a first release. We will then describe a second release, Fone Follower 2, so that we can illustrate this situation.

For the initial Fone Follower, all operations were new. We identified the Recover from hardware failure operation as critical, and we preassigned two test cases to it. Because Fone Follower was an initial release, the allocation probabilities for the other new operations were the occurrence probabilities of the system operational profile (Table 3.5). The threshold for infrequent operations was 0.5 divided by the 500 new test cases allocated (all test cases were new), which is 0.001. Note from Table 3.5 that the operations Add subscriber and Delete subscriber both fall below this threshold. Hence we assigned one test case to each. We then assigned the remaining 496 test cases to the remaining new operations in accordance with the allocation probabilities. Thus, for example, because the Process fax call operation had allocation probability 0.15, we allocated 74 test cases to it. The allocation of test cases to operations is thus as shown in Table 4.4.

Now consider Fone Follower 2, which adds two new operations (A and B) to Fone Follower. Operations A and B have system occurrence probabilities of 0.1 each. The system occurrence probabilities of the reused operations from Fone Follower total 0.8. We have allocated 200 new test cases to the Fone Follower 2 product.

Note that there are no critical or infrequent new operations for this release. Now, the sum of the system occurrence probabilities for the

TABLE 4.4 Allocation of Test Cases to Operations of Fone Follower

Operation	Number of test cases
Process voice call, no pager, answer	89
Process voice call, no pager, no answer	84
Process voice call, pager, answer	84
Process fax call	74
Process voice call, pager, answer on page	59
Process voice call, pager, no answer	50
Phone number entry	50
Audit phone number database	4
Add subscriber	1
Delete subscriber	1
Recover from hardware failure	2

other new operations is 0.2. Dividing the system occurrence probabilities for the other new operations by this total, we obtained allocation probabilities for A and B of 0.5 each. Consequently, 100 test cases were allocated to A and 100 to B.

4.2.1.4 Specifying test cases. Select each test case for an operation with equal probability of selection from among all the choices defined by the possible combinations of levels of the direct input variables for that operation. A *level* is a set of values of an input variable that you expect to yield the same failure behavior for the operation because of processing similarities. In the case of the Process fax call operation of Fone Follower, the value of the input variable Forwardee would be a specific phone number. All Forwardees within the local calling area would probably have the same behavior (execute successfully or fail) and hence would form a level. However, because Fone Follower may process destinations within the area code but outside the local calling area differently from those within the local calling area, the former constitutes a different level. The direct input variables and their levels for the Process fax call operation of Fone Follower are given in Table 4.5.

Once you have selected a combination of levels, you then select the values of the input variables randomly with equal probability from the members of the sets that comprise the levels.

If you are using a graphical representation of the operational profile, you will define a run by the specific attribute values of the sequence of attributes that defines the operation it belongs to. These specific attribute values will be input variables. Hence they can have levels. Consequently, you will select a test case for the graphical representation in the same fashion as one for the tabular representation. In the illustration of the switching system given in Figs. 3.1 and 4.2, the Call destination attribute has a general attribute value of "External" (which helps identify the operation) and a specific attribute value of "777-234-8989" (which helps identify the run). One of the possible levels would be "Local," because all Local destinations would be expected to be

TABLE 4.5 Direct Input Variables with Levels for Process Fax Call Operation of Fone Follower

Originator	Forwardee	Billing type	Dialing type	Screening
On screenlist	Local calling area	Flat rate	Standard	Yes
Not on screenlist	Within area code	Per call	Abbreviated	No
	Outside area code	Discount		
	International	Per minute		
	800 number			
	Other carrier			
	Wireless			

processed in a very similar fashion and hence have very similar failure behavior.

You would select the levels of the specific attribute values corresponding to the general attribute values that define the operation, based on equal occurrence probability. Finally, you would select the specific attribute values within the levels, again based on equal occurrence probability. For example, one test case that you may choose will be "standard-local." You will select a specific value for the level of "local," so the test case is actually specified as "standard - 7772348989."

You select test cases within operations with equal probability because it is not practical to collect use data down to the test case level so that you would have a basis for assigning different probabilities. If an operation occurs with high probability and it appears that some runs within that operation occur much more frequently than others, you may want to partition the operation into multiple operations.

Once the test cases are selected, you must prepare the test scripts for them, unless test cases already exist that you can use. The test cases must, when invoked, convey the operation they belong to and their direct input variables to the system under test. They do this through various interfaces. There are many software support tools, generally classified by type of interface, that can help with this task.

Finally, we add the new test cases we develop for each associated system of a release to the sets of existing test cases for the systems from previous releases.

4.2.2 Preparing test procedures

You will need to prepare one test procedure for each operational mode. You must specify the test operational profile and the operation occurrence rate. You need to implement the database cleanup procedure used in the field. There are many possible cleanup procedures, including periodic reinitialization at various standard intervals or continuing database audit and cleanup at various rates. Finally, you must reproduce any other significant environmental conditions necessary to make load test represent field use.

To specify the test operational profile for an operational mode, you start with the

1. Operational mode operational profile, in the case of the first release

2. Test operational profile for the same operational mode of the previous release, in the case of subsequent releases

You then modify the occurrence probabilities to account for rarely occurring critical new operations. For releases after the first, you then again modify the occurrence probabilities to account for reused operations.

To account for rarely occurring critical new operations, we give the same relative importance to that operation in allocating the scarce resource of test time as we do in allocating the scarce resource of test cases. Hence, we set the test occurrence probability for each rarely occurring critical new operation to the proportion of new test cases for this release allocated to that operation. Then we add the initially adjusted probabilities (which usually will sum to other than 1). We divide each initially adjusted probability by the sum to obtain final probabilities.

Let us illustrate this with Fone Follower, operating in the peak hours operational mode, whose operational profile is given by Table 4.6. Note that this operational profile is, of course, not the same as the system operational profile (Table 3.5). The operation occurrence rate for the peak hours operational mode is 500,000 operations per hour.

Because 2 of 500 test cases are allocated to the Recover from hardware failure operation, we will set the occurrence probability of that critical operation to 0.004. The initial and final adjusted operational profiles are shown in Table 4.7. The latter operational profile is the test operational profile for the first release.

Note that we are executing the critical operation with 4000 times the occurrence probability that it would normally have. This number is known as the *acceleration factor*. When we achieve the failure intensity objective of 100 failures per million calls for the product, we are in effect achieving a failure intensity objective of 25 failures per *billion* Recover from hardware failure operations.

One might think that accelerating an operation this much would substantially distort the failure intensity you are estimating, but this is not generally the case because the operation is still occurring relatively infrequently. Suppose the noncritical operations have failure intensity λ_1 and the critical operations have failure intensity λ_2. Then in the Fone Follower example, the actual failure intensity will be

TABLE 4.6 Unadjusted Operational Profile for Fone Follower, Peak Hours Operational Mode

Operation	Occurrence rate probability
Process voice call, no pager, answer	0.22
Process voice call, no pager, no answer	0.18
Process voice call, pager, answer	0.18
Process fax call	0.14
Process voice call, pager, answer on page	0.12
Process voice call, pager, no answer on page	0.10
Phone number entry	0.06
Recover from hardware failure	0.000001

TABLE 4.7   Test Operational Profile for Fone Follower, Peak Hours
Operational Mode

Operation	Initial operational profile	Final operational profile
Process voice call, no pager, answer	0.22	0.219
Process voice call, no pager, no answer	0.18	0.179
Process voice call, pager, answer	0.18	0.179
Process fax call	0.14	0.139
Process voice call, pager, answer on page	0.12	0.120
Process voice call, pager, no answer on page	0.10	0.100
Phone number entry	0.06	0.060
Recover from hardware failure	0.004	0.004
Total	1.004	1.000

0.999999 $\lambda_1 + 0.000001$ λ_2, whereas the estimated failure intensity will
be 0.996 $\lambda_1 + 0.004$ λ_2. The estimation error is then 0.003999 $(\lambda_1 - \lambda_2)$.
Failure intensities among operations are not likely to differ greatly, but
suppose $\lambda_2 = 2\lambda_1$. Then the absolute value of the error is 0.003999 λ_1,
which is less than 1 percent of the failure intensity.

We will now consider the second modification to the operational profile that must be made. Recall that we only need this modification for
releases after the first. It accounts for the fact that we do not need to
test operations from previous releases as thoroughly as new operations
in the current release because they were tested in previous releases.
However, we can't ignore reused operations entirely because the new
operations usually do have some interaction with them that may cause
new failures to appear. Hence, we reduce but do not eliminate testing
the reused operations by weighting them with an *operation interaction
factor,* which indicates the degree to which a new operation causes a
failure in a reused operation, as compared to causing one in a new operation. We don't have much experience with this factor at present, but
initial indications are that values between 0.1 and 0.25 may be reasonable, with larger values indicating greater interaction. We add the
weighted test occurrence probabilities (new operations are weighted 1)
and then we divide the individual values by the total.

Let us now apply this modification to Fone Follower 2. We start with
the previous release test operational profile for the operational mode
we are concerned with. We have placed this operational profile in the
column of Table 4.8 labeled "Previous operational profile." There are no
critical new operations we need to adjust for, only reused operations.
We have placed the occurrence probabilities for the new operations A
and B in the "Initial operational profile" column. We selected an oper-

TABLE 4.8   Test Operational Profile for Fone Follower 2, Peak Hours Operational
Mode

Operation	Previous operational profile	Initial operational profile	Final operational profile
A (new)		0.1	0.25
B (new)		0.1	0.25
Process voice call, no pager, answer	0.219	0.0438	0.1095
Process voice call, no pager, no answer	0.179	0.0358	0.0895
Process voice call, pager, answer	0.179	0.0358	0.0895
Process fax call	0.139	0.0278	0.0695
Process voice call, pager, answer on page	0.120	0.0240	0.06
Process voice call, pager, no answer on page	0.100	0.0200	0.05
Phone number entry	0.060	0.0120	0.03
Recover from hardware failure	0.004	0.0008	0.002
Total	1.000	0.4	1.000

ation interaction factor of 0.2. The "Initial operational profile" column
shows the *weighted* occurrence probabilities of the operations from the
previous operational profile. The total of the initial operational profile
occurrence probabilities is 0.4. The "final operational profile" shows
these occurrence probabilities divided by 0.4, giving the final test operational profile.

We provide for test case invocation to occur at random times to
ensure that the occurrence probabilities are stationary (unchanging
with time). It will also virtually assure that all runs are different. We
do not want to duplicate runs because a duplicate run provides no new
information about failure behavior of the system. Thus duplication
wastes testing resources. Of course, duplication is occasionally necessary. For example, you may need to obtain more information about a
failure that occurred on a run, you may need to verify that debuggers
have properly removed a fault so that a previous failure no longer
occurs, or you may need to ensure that a system change didn't spawn
any additional faults. Invoking test cases at random times will cause
them to execute with different indirect input variables, resulting in the
runs being different.

Software reliability engineering is a practice that is completely separate from test automation from a technical viewpoint. However, the two
can be synergistic. Software reliability engineering provides the brains
required to direct automated test. Test automation provides a faster
pair of hands to carry out software reliability engineering. Hence you
should consider the possibility of test automation if you haven't already
done so. You should use automation wherever it is cost effective.

There are two principal areas of automation to consider, test management and failure identification. Test management includes setting up and invoking runs, recording the runs you have executed (operation, test case, values of indirect input variables) and the outputs of these runs, and cleaning up after the completion of each run.

It would be nice if automated failure identification could be coupled with test automation. At present, this is practical only to a partial degree. Manual analysis is still required to identify some failures, to recognize repeated failures, and to classify some failures by severity. It may be possible to determine failure severity automatically in some cases if the classification criteria are behaviors that are readily observable. For example, if a severity class 1 failure is defined as complete interruption of program execution, you can distinguish this class automatically from the other severity classes. In any case, you will need to associate natural or time units with failures, so you should provide for recording such a measure at frequent intervals. It is a good idea to record the measure every second or its equivalent.

4.3   Frequently Asked Questions

1   Won't testing all operations result in zero defects and perfect reliability?

ANSWER: This is very unlikely, except possibly for extremely small programs. Operations of programs in practical use nearly always have an enormous number of runs (input states). Although some of these runs have similar failure behavior, so that testing one tests many, there is always some risk that you may not uncover some of the faults.

2   My management tracks performance of system testers on the basis of the number of faults they discover. This seems to be in conflict with the software reliability approach. What's wrong with finding the most faults possible?

ANSWER: Rewarding system testers on the basis of faults discovered (fault yield) will distort testing and make it inefficient because the testers will use test cases that are easiest to generate and have the greatest promise of revealing faults. These often are "extreme value" or "boundary" input states that do not occur very frequently in operation. A reward system *should* be based on reducing the cost of failure in operation most rapidly (usually correlated with reducing failure intensity most rapidly, the software reliability approach).

3   Expert debuggers often counsel you to test programs at boundary values or under other conditions that experience has shown to be highly likely to be associated with faults. Why do you advise using the operational profile first in guiding system test?

ANSWER: Use of boundary values and pathological conditions first to direct the range of testing is not cost efficient because some of them occur very infrequently. The operational profile should be used first to guide system test. Then look at runs (input states) within that operation that are likely to be associated with faults.

4 Why is just executing each of the test cases for a system inadequate?

ANSWER: The input states of a system include not only the direct input variables specified for the test cases but also indirect input variables that come from the environment. Thus you do not cover a substantial part of the input space when you simply execute each of the test cases. It is also necessary to execute the test cases in the context of various environmental conditions that realistically represent use expected in the field.

5 Wouldn't it be more efficient to test input states at the extremes, that is, at such situations as overloads, unlikely combinations of inputs, etc.? We seem to find more faults that way.

ANSWER: There is no clear evidence to indicate that extreme states are associated with more faults. If this pattern does occur, the most likely cause would be that developers are not devoting much effort to considering these extreme states.

In any event, the principal objective in test is to reduce the operational cost of failure as rapidly and inexpensively as possible. This means that you should first test those input states for which the cost of failure is highest. This cost depends on probability of occurrence of the input state, severity of the failure, and probability that a fault is associated with the input state. In most cases, we have no evidence to assume that one input state is more likely to be associated with a fault than another, so only the first two (especially the first) factors should be considered. Believing that we can pick the input states most likely to be associated with a fault is an occupational disease we software people share that is akin to that of a broker picking the "hot" stocks.

6 Isn't it more efficient to locate faults by executing every branch in the program instead of testing by operation? If you execute every branch, you will find every fault.

ANSWER: You will *not* find every fault by executing every branch. Failures occur only for certain input states. At the very least, you must execute every *path* to find all the faults. For most systems, the time required would be prohibitive. It is much more efficient to test by operation, using the operational profile for guidance.

7 Software reliability engineering assumes that tests are selected randomly in accordance with the operational profile. We select the tests in an order that corresponds to our estimate of the likelihood they will occur during use. This removes faults rapidly and economically. Are we doing something wrong?

ANSWER: You aren't doing anything too bad; your method is approximately equivalent to software reliability engineering. But applying software reliability engineering is more systematic and methodical and less likely to lead to serious trouble. Also, applying software reliability engineering results in better representation of field conditions; hence failures that may occur in the field are more likely to be uncovered.

8 Are software reliability figures more use dependent than hardware reliability figures?

ANSWER: Both are use dependent. When we speak of hardware reliability, we usually mean *physical* reliability or the probability that a system will survive physical failure mechanisms, which are generally related to the total amount of use. Software reliability refers to design reliability or the probability that the system has no undesired behavior under all the conditions for which we expect to use it. Thus design reliability is dependent on the detailed uses of the system and their probabilities of occurrence.

9 If in test we continually repeat the same runs, will the accuracy of software reliability projections be affected?

ANSWER: Yes, because test will not be representative of use in the field.

10 What do you say to a project that only does feature test and no load test?

ANSWER: If project personnel note that they don't do load test, the best response is to ask whether they have analyzed their situation and determined that load test is unnecessary for achieving the failure intensity objective their users require. Very few projects that aren't performing load test have undertaken such an analysis. Your question may start them thinking about doing one. Many failures result from interactions among operations. Hence projects that don't have load test don't find these failures. It is unlikely that software can be delivered to users and meet reliability objectives without this type of test.

11 Can you divide input space by failure severity class?

ANSWER: Only partially. The run associated with a particular input state may experience zero, one, or multiple failures. If there is one failure, you clearly have a corresponding severity class. However, if there are multiple failures, you may not be able to assign a unique failure severity class.

12 How much test coverage do I need to have 90 percent confidence that my program won't fail in the field?

ANSWER: We assume you mean branch coverage, because instruction coverage is not a very significant predictor of reliability, and path coverage is difficult in practice to measure. We also assume that you have some *period* of failure-free time in mind; otherwise, the reliability level you want to specify is not defined.

Unfortunately, a definitive quantitative answer to your question does not exist at this time. Some useful insight into the problem has been gained by Del Frate, Garg, Mathur, and Pasquini (1995). In a study of five programs, they observed a general positive correlation between branch coverage and reliability, but there was considerable variation in the correlation coefficients. We await further research.

13 Should we allocate test cases among operations on the basis of how likely the test team thinks they will fail as well as on the basis of use?

ANSWER: This answer is debatable. It is analogous to the question, "Should I spread the stocks I buy across the market or should I try to pick them?" If you have very solid information about an operation (operation is very complex, developers of operation had little experience, requirements for operation changed many times, etc.), it probably makes sense to use it. However, be aware that others have had access to this information and have probably acted on it, just as others may have bid up the price of the stock you picked. For example, a development team may have devoted more time and effort to requirements and design reviews for a complex operation, thus tending to neutralize the tendency of more failures to occur for it. We software developers unfortunately do not have a stellar record for identifying which operations are failure-prone. Hence trying to allocate test cases on the basis of such predictions should be approached with great caution.

14 Can a run category exist for a distributed system?

ANSWER: Yes, because a run can exist over multiple machines, and a run category is a group of runs.

15 We are testing a compiler. The possible number of input strings is astronomical, and it would be totally impractical to characterize how frequently they occur. How can we select appropriate test cases?

ANSWER: Define your operations at a higher level than compiling particular input strings. For example, you might define one operation as compiling a logical expression. The occurrence probability of logical expressions would determine how many test cases you select that are logical expressions.

16 We are developing a new release of a product that adds some new operations to the operations of the current release that is in the field. Do we have to test the old operations as well?

ANSWER: Yes, because of the possibility that the implementation of the new operations may have affected the functioning of the old operations. But, substantially less testing is probably necessary. In feature test you execute the regression test cases from the previous release and all the test cases for the current one, which tends to shift the emphasis to the new release. The regression tests for the current release will be a random sample from the test cases used for feature test, maintaining the emphasis. You modify the test operational profile in load test to account for reused operations.

17 How does the setup procedure differ among feature tests, regression tests, and load tests?

ANSWER: Usually setup is done separately for each run in feature test and regression test. In load test, setup is usually done once each day for each operational mode.

18 Does keeping the probabilities of executing operations stationary have advantages beyond that of assuring representative testing?

ANSWER: Yes. It tends to equalize failure resolution workload across developers.

19 When you specify test cases within an operation, do you select levels of direct input variables with or without replacement?

ANSWER: You select them with replacement. However, if you should select a test case that is the exact equal of an existing test case, repeat the selection process one more time.

20 Is software reliability engineering sufficient for system test? Shouldn't we be doing coverage testing of the system as well? Should we lean toward coverage testing for small components?

ANSWER: Software reliability engineering test is inherently more efficient than coverage testing because it focuses testing on the branches that are used the most or are critical. There is no need to have complete coverage; it is quite unnecessary to test branches that are not critical and rarely used.

Software reliability engineering test has an overhead cost, the cost of developing the operational profile. Hence coverage testing costs less for small components such as units or modules unless these components are used in multiple systems. But software reliability engineering test becomes the method of choice as component size increases.

21 Why doesn't regression test include load as well as feature test?

ANSWER: There is no theoretical reason why it does not. It is mainly a question of practicality. We execute regression tests after each build in which there is significant change. Load test typically takes longer than feature test, so repeating it several times can affect delivery date and costs. Regression tests using just feature test should catch the obvious new faults spawned by changes, but they will miss the faults that only cause failures in the context of complex interactions. Thus it may be desirable to include load test in the regression tests of systems where reliability is much more important than delivery date or cost.

22 How can we be sure that we have tested all possible input states?

ANSWER: You can't. Software reliability engineering increases the likelihood that you have tested the most used input states by driving testing with the operational profile. It increases the likelihood that you have tested the critical input states by overrepresenting them among the test cases. By providing for load test in multiple operational modes, software reliability engineering recreates many of the interactions that are likely to occur in the field. Finally, software reliability engineering reproduces the same data degradation conditions that can be expected in the field. Hence, it guides you in testing so that you test the input states that matter.

23 When you select test cases within an operation, shouldn't you depart from random selection to ensure that each level of each input variable gets selected at least once?

ANSWER: Departing from random selection would make implementation more complex and usually wouldn't make much difference. For example, consider the example of Fone Follower we have been using. There are 224 possible combinations of input variables for "Process fax call" and 74 test cases to be selected. The greatest risk of not selecting a particular level of an input variable occurs for "Forwardee." The probability of a particular level not being selected for a test case is about 0.86. The probability of that level not being selected for any test case is $(0.86)^{74}$, or 0.00001422.

24 In testing landing gear software there are input variables we cannot control. What should we do?

ANSWER: It's not clear what you mean by "control" because you can generally set input variables for software to any value you want. Perhaps you are testing the entire system and you do not have access to the interfaces with the software. If that is the case, you may want to consider redefining the system you are testing so that its input variables are accessible and can be controlled by you. Alternatively, you may try to reproduce various environmental conditions in your operational modes, relying on controlling indirect input variables.

25 Do you adjust the test operational profile for infrequent noncritical operations?

ANSWER: No, this adjustment is made only to ensure that each operation is allocated at least one test case.

26 In the context of software reliability engineering, how can we apply our knowledge and experience in developing test cases that are efficient in uncovering potential failures?

ANSWER: Initially allocate new test cases for a release to new operations, using the procedure described in Sec. 4.2.1.3. This approach ensures that you will allocate new test cases to new operations in proportion to the use of those operations, with each new operation getting at least one test case. Then use your knowledge and experience in selecting test cases within each operation, substituting whatever method you use for the uniform random selection of levels of direct input variables we describe. Remember that experience is not foolproof; hence you may still want to use random selection of levels of input variables for some of the test cases.

27 If we randomly select test cases, how can we automatically check whether a run associated with a test case executes without failure? With random selection, how can we determine in advance what the results of the run should be?

ANSWER: Perhaps you have misunderstood what we mean by random selection. For each operation, we do randomly select combinations of direct input variables to define the test cases we will prepare. We do this prior to test, not in real time during test. Hence we can determine what the results of executing the test should be well in advance of test and provide this information to an output checker. When we execute load test, we will invoke the test cases at random times and in random sequences, resulting in executing the test cases under many different combinations of indirect input variables. All the different runs associated with a test case should yield the same results. However, some may execute successfully and some may fail, due to the different combinations of indirect input variables.

28 Why do you estimate the number of new test cases for a release based on time and budget available? Why don't you base the estimate on the failure intensity objective?

ANSWER: Unfortunately, dependable algorithms relating number of test cases you need to reach a given failure intensity objective do not exist at present. Certainly we need them, and perhaps that will motivate you to work on them. In the meantime, the most viable approach is to determine what can be done with the time and budget available. You then check the number you estimate against previous experience. If the number is grossly inadequate, go argue for more time and/or budget based on test information.

29 We believe that we need a large number of test cases to adequately test our product, but the cost of test case preparation seems too high for us. What can we do?

ANSWER: Because the test cases within an operation are similar except for differences in levels of the direct input variables, develop the test cases for each operation together. You can save a lot of time, effort, and cost by doing this.

4.4 Background

We will discuss the general concept of test efficiency here and the potential for increasing test efficiency by using run categories.

4.4.1 Test efficiency

Because testing is an activity that has a major impact on product quality attributes, there is strong motivation to pursue research that will improve testing. The key question is, What do we mean by "improve"? In order to define a test efficiency metric, we look to the two product quality attributes that appear to predominate with most users, reliability and rapid delivery of new capabilities. Of course, failures have varying impact depending on their severities, but we are taking a macroscopic view here, and overall impact on the average is proportional to failure intensity. Sometimes development cost is more important to users than rapid delivery, but both rapid delivery and development cost affect testing in the same way: Testing must be short.

Consequently, we define test efficiency in terms of failure intensity and time. We interpret *time* as *execution time* (or natural units where appropriate) to remove the confounding variable of test hours planned per day. Test efficiency η is the relative rate of reduction of failure intensity with respect to execution time, specifically defined by

$$\eta = \frac{1}{\lambda} \frac{d\lambda}{d\tau} \qquad (4.1)$$

where λ is the failure intensity, τ is execution time, and $d/d\tau$ is the derivative with respect to execution time. Note that test efficiency is an instantaneous quality that is itself a function of execution time. It is a normalized quantity, expressing relative or percentage change in failure intensity rather than absolute change. Thus we have a metric that depends primarily on test strategy. In comparing test strategies, note that higher test efficiency is more desirable. We will apply the test strategy over a period of time. Hence we will measure test efficiency as an average over that time period.

4.4.2 Increasing test efficiency by using run categories

The *homogeneity* of a set of runs is the proportion that share the same failure behavior. It is always less than or equal to 1.

There is considerable promise for improving test efficiency if we can define sets of runs with homogeneity close to 1. This area is a topic of current research. We will call such sets of runs *run categories*. Because runs can occur across noncontiguous time segments and different machines, run categories can also. The failure behavior of each run category differs from that of other run categories.

If one run in the run category executes successfully, there is a high probability that all will. Similarly, if one run in the run category experiences a failure, there is a high probability that all runs will experience the same failure. This means that any run in the run category can with high probability represent all runs. This implies a theoretical improvement in test efficiency by a factor equal to the number of runs in the run category. You would still select runs with equal probability within the operation but would not in theory allow more than one per run category. Alternatively, you could look on this as sampling run categories without replacement and then selecting a run within the run category.

When we define run categories, test case selection becomes a three-step procedure. You select operation, then run category, then run. Although this concept is not currently in wide use, its application is expected to increase as we learn how to define run categories. The greatest difficulty in assessing homogeneity will probably come in determining what indirect input variables exist and how much influence they are having.

All the runs in a run category have the same input variables (including environmental variables) and the same levels for the input variables, although their values may differ. However, runs having the same levels for all their direct inputs are not necessarily in the same run category. Different values of the indirect input variables can cause substantially different processing and hence failure behavior. The runs in a run category execute the same code paths. On the other hand, many runs in an operation will have some differences among execution paths. The runs in different operations will have considerable differences in execution paths.

For this partitioning into run categories to be worthwhile, it must be inexpensive and you must be able to identify which run categories have failure probability close to 1. Only then does test efficiency improve sufficiently over uniform random selection throughout the operation to justify the cost of partitioning. In order to identify run categories with failure probability close to 1, you need knowledge of implementation difficulty, development process weaknesses (often suggested by project history), and programmer experience with respect to the code paths associated with the run categories.

Run categories should be defined so that they have approximately equal occurrence probabilities because testers will be selecting uniformly from among them (or executing all of them). However, we don't actually determine these probabilities because of the cost. We probably will find that there is tradeoff among size and other characteristics of the run category, test efficiency, and level of reliability assurance.

The requirements that run categories should be approximately homogeneous and that all of them should have equal occurrence probabilities can conflict. When they do, emphasize equal occurrence probability. Because you can achieve only near-homogeneity, the possible testing waste resulting from dividing a homogeneous region into multiple test cases is not important. Dividing run categories to equalize occurrence probabilities (avoid grouping them) often reduces the risk of nonhomogeneity because smaller run categories tend to be more homogeneous.

In theory, only one run is required per run category, greatly increasing test efficiency. In practice, you may employ n (perhaps two or several) runs to reduce the risk of missing a failure because of the fact that the homogeneity of run categories we attempt to determine is generally less than 1. In either case, it is best to select the runs randomly from the run category. Guidelines as to what is "enough" knowledge to make partitioning advantageous and the number of runs to sample per run category are topics of current research.

If you are using run categories and failures repeat for runs in the same run category, you can reasonably conclude that you are seeing the same failure behavior; hence you don't count the repeats during reliability growth test. However, if the runs are in different run categories, you can't assume that you are seeing the same failure behavior. Hence you must always count them.

Although in theory exhaustive testing is impractical even for very small components due to the very large number of possible input states, the fact that sets of these input states may be homogeneous or nearly homogeneous may make exhaustive testing practical for components of small size.

Another possibility for improving test efficiency is to use experimental designs such as orthogonal arrays to select run categories, given the situation where the input variables that define the run categories are limited in their degree of interaction.

4.4.3   A graphical view of test selection

The following background may help to clarify how we select test runs when we apply software reliability engineering. The run space shown in Fig. 4.1 represents all the runs that will occur during the life of the system we are testing and over all copies of the system that will be installed in the field. Because all the input variables for two runs will virtually never be identical, each run will be a separate entity, which you can view as a point in the run space.

We position each run in the space in accordance with the values of its input variables. Because there are many input variables, the space has many dimensions. However, for simplicity, we can consider the case of two input variables and hence two dimensions, one of them being time. We can view the distance between the points representing the runs as an indicator of the degree to which processing for the runs is similar.

Because operations consist of sets of runs that share similar input variable values and similar processing, they will be regions in run space. Similarly, operational modes share certain input variable values (for example, times when running) and cover even larger regions of run space. In fact, the run space for a system will consist of its operational mode regions. Because an operation can occur in several operational modes, it will have multiple regions. In any given operational mode, an operation will occupy a fraction of space equal to its occurrence probability in the operational mode operational profile. In the system, an operation will occupy a fraction of space equal to its occurrence probability in the system operational profile.

Each run will either succeed or fail (a run fails when it has one or more failures). Runs that fail tend to share similar input variable values and similar processing, so we typically have failure regions in the run space. A failure region is generally associated with a fault. Resolution of a failure or removal of the fault that is causing it usually prevents many other failures from occurring. Thus the proportion of run space at any given point in time that is associated with failure regions decreases as a function of time. Hence failure intensity also decreases as a function of time. The failure regions in run space will appear as strips parallel to the time coordinate, with the strips decreasing in width or disappearing as you resolve failures.

The issue in selecting test runs is how to select such runs to achieve the greatest reduction in failure impact per test run, the impact involving human life, cost, or capability. In order to simplify the issue, we deal with critical or high-impact operations separately, planning many more tests for them than would normally occur. This approach lets us regard all the other operations and their runs as having equal impact. The issue then simply becomes how to achieve the greatest reduction in the proportion of failing run space for each test run. To do this, we need to choose each test run so that it falls in the largest failing region possible.

Our knowledge of which operations have the greatest use and hence occupy the largest proportion of run space is generally much better than our knowledge of which regions are likely to be failing ones. Hence we base test selection primarily on use. We only modify this approach if we have high confidence that certain regions are failure prone.

Because the run space already incorporates use, we can view the best initial test selection strategy as uniform sampling across the run space. You achieve this by selecting operations in accordance with the operational profile and the runs within the operations by uniform sampling.

It is possible that with time the likelihood of failure for the high occurrence probability operations may decrease more rapidly than for the low occurrence probability operations, because we tend to discover and resolve failures of the former first. Whether that is the case would depend on whether the number of failure regions or faults for an operation increases less or more rapidly than linearly with occurrence probability. If this is the case, and we do not know whether it is at present, it might be possible to increase the efficiency of test in its later phases by adjusting the test operation selection probabilities. A very simplistic approach would be to select operations without replacement (no operation would be selected more than once). A somewhat more sophisticated approach would be limited replacement (select an operation no more than n times). Because we don't know whether limited replacement has value at present, we apply operational profile selection with unlimited replacement in current software reliability engineering practice.

4.5 Problems

4.1 Our project development budget is $5 million. We have high reliability requirements; hence we can spend 10 percent of this budget on preparing test cases. Each test case costs $250 to prepare. We have 25 forty-hour weeks for test, and a staff of 10 available for preparing test cases. Each test case, on the average, requires 3-h preparation time. How many test cases can we prepare?

4.2 How many possible test cases can be developed for the Process Fax operation in Fone Follower? Refer to Table 4.5.

4.3 Suppose you had only allocated one test case to the critical Recover from hardware failure operation for Fone Follower. What would the adjustment factor be? The acceleration factor?

5

Executing Test

In executing test, we will use the test cases and test procedures developed in the preparing for test activity in such a way that we realize the goal of efficient test that we desire. Executing test involves three main activities: allocating test time, invoking the tests, and identifying failures that occur.

5.1 Allocating Test Time

We measure test time in hours. If you have multiple test configurations, test time can easily be greater than real time. Allocation of test time for a release proceeds in three steps:

1. Among the systems to be tested
2. Among feature, regression, and load test for each system that is in reliability growth test (whether or not certification test follows)
3. Among operational modes for each system that is in load test

We allocate the test times for systems in certification test entirely to load test.

In allocating among systems for the current release, we first allocate test time to and among supersystems based on estimated risk. For the other systems and the remaining time, the basic principle we will apply is to divide test time in the same proportions as we have divided new test cases. This makes sense because we have already evaluated these systems relative to each other with respect to their importance and newness (untestedness) by allocating test case resources.

Let us consider Fone Follower, which had a planned test period of 320 h. Based on estimated risk, we allocated 40 h to test of its one supersystem. Recall that the division of new test cases among the other systems to be tested was in the proportions product 0.714 and operating system 0.286. Consequently, the allocation of test time to these systems was product 200 h and operating system 80 h.

For each associated system, continue the allocation as follows. If you are doing reliability growth test (with or without certification test to follow) for that system, you first allow enough time in feature test to execute all the new test cases for the release, plus the regression test for the previous release. Because every critical new operation is allocated at least one test case, and every critical reused operation will be included in the regression test, you will test each critical operation at least once. Also allow enough time for regression test. Then allocate the remaining time to load test. If you are doing certification test only, allocate the total time to load test. For Fone Follower, the 40 h devoted to supersystem test and the 80 h devoted to operating system test will be completely allocated to load test because both of these systems will be only in certification test. For the 200 h devoted to product test, feature test requires 10 h and we estimated 10 regression tests of 1 h each. Thus we allocated 180 h for load test.

You then divide load test among the operational modes in the same proportions as the expected proportions of nonfiller field use (natural or time units) those operational modes will experience in the field. By *nonfiller* you will recall that we mean "required as a minimum for proper system operation."

For Fone Follower, we allocated the load test periods among the operational modes in the same proportions as the expected proportions of calls or equivalent units in the field. The expected proportions of calls for Fone Follower are shown in Table 5.1. The allocation of test time hours is given in Table 5.2.

5.2 Invoking Test

Software reliability engineering test starts after the units of the system being tested have been tested or otherwise verified and integrated so that the operations of the system can execute completely. If this condition isn't at least approximately met, it will be difficult to drive tests with the operational profile and create a reasonable representation of

TABLE 5.1 **Proportions of Calls in Field by Operational Mode for Fone Follower**

Operational mode	Proportion of calls
Peak hours	0.1
Prime hours	0.7
Off hours	0.2

TABLE 5.2   Allocation of Test Time Hours for Operational Modes of Fone Follower

	Test time (h)		
Operational mode	Supersystem	Product	Operating system
Peak hours	4	18	8
Prime hours	28	126	56
Off hours	8	36	16

field conditions. For example, you may experience failures that prevent you from executing certain paths and hence certain operations or certain runs within operations.

You should generally test the systems in the sequence

1. Acquired components

2. Product and variations

3. Supersystems

The reason for this sequence is that it is also the sequence in which you will need information about the results of testing in order to make development decisions. However, there is nothing in software reliability engineering theory that would prevent you from changing this sequence or even testing different systems in parallel.

In the case of the product and its variations in reliability growth test, perform feature test first and then load test. Following that, conduct regression test after each build that has a significant change. In feature test you select in random order from the set of all new test cases plus the regression test cases of the previous release. Note that this set will include the test cases for the rarely occurring critical operations of all releases. In load test, invoke each operational mode each day for its allotted proportion of time, using the appropriate test procedure. The number of test cases invoked will be determined automatically based on the time the operational mode runs and its occurrence rate. As noted before, the invocation of test cases should occur at random times. In regression test, invoke all or a randomly selected subset of test cases from feature test (including all critical operations), choosing them in random order.

Note that you will be dividing test execution among operations essentially on the basis of the operational mode operational profiles. This is both realistic and rational because there ordinarily will be no basis for having more faults in one operation than another (assuming the same amount of code is involved) nor is one operation likely to have greater homogeneity (runs with the same failure behavior) than another.

Testing driven by an operational profile is very efficient because it identifies failures (and hence the faults causing them), on average, in order of how often they occur. This approach rapidly reduces failure intensity as test proceeds because the failures that occur most frequently are caused by the faulty operations used most frequently. Users will also detect failures on average in order of their frequency, if they have not already been found in test.

Selection should always be with replacement for operations. After test, replace the element in the population, allowing reselection. If you performed selection without replacement at the operation level, you could only choose an operation once. This is unwise because operations can be associated with multiple faults. There is a high risk that different runs within an operation may show different behavior.

Selection should be with replacement for test cases in the case of load test but not in the case of feature or regression test. In load test, the resulting runs will almost certainly be different, and their failure behavior will often also differ. The number of runs is so large that the probability of wasting test resources by repeating many runs is infinitesimal. But in feature or regression test, the runs are much less likely to be different because indirect input variables are tightly controlled.

In invoking test cases, you should repeat a *run* (remember, this is not the same as a test case) only in certain special circumstances:

1. To collect more data to improve failure identification, either in the sense of more failures or better describing known failures

2. To verify failure resolution (fault removal)

Repetitions are inefficient. They yield no new information, the input state being exactly the same. Repeating a test case is not necessarily inefficient because the indirect variables can still vary, causing you to explore the failure behavior of different runs. In load test, the fact that test cases are invoked at different times is probably sufficient to ensure differences in indirect input variables and hence in runs. In fact, in load test, it may be difficult to repeat a run when you want to.

You need to record each test case executed, its time of invocation, the operational mode under test, and any pertinent environmental conditions so that you can repeat a run as closely as possible when necessary.

Selection of one run per operation will very rarely be adequate. Usually more than one fault will be associated with an operation; you will require some number n of runs per operation to achieve reasonable confidence that the operation is failure-free. The number n cannot be chosen in general; it depends on the nature of the operation and the code that implements it. If the occurrence probability of the operation is very small and the operation is noncritical, you can often accept the risk of remaining fault(s). If occurrence probability is very small and the operation is critical, the number of runs for that operation must be increased. If the occurrence probability is not very small, you may need to increase the total amount of testing planned.

TABLE 5.3   Sample Operational
Profile

Operation	Occurrence probability
A	0.7
B	0.3

Implement the same data cleanup procedure that is used in the field
to make the degree of data degradation versus time experienced in test
representative of the pattern of data degradation experienced in the
field. You can accomplish data cleanup through continuous audit and
correction or by reinitializations. Reinitializations or reboots can occur
at start-up, at recovery after a failure, or periodically.

Note that the occurrence probabilities with which we select operations for execution should be *stationary,* or unchanging with time.
Nonstationary probabilities generally occur because the tester reorders
the selection of operations from what would occur naturally.

To illustrate the concept of stationary selection probability for operations, consider the operational profile of Table 5.3. A set of runs (Set 1)
could reasonably be assigned an order of operations

ABAABAAABA

However, the set (Set 2) with order of operations

AAAAAAABBB

is highly likely to represent nonstationary selection probability and is
therefore unacceptable. You can see this in Table 5.4 by computing
selection probabilities "to date" for each operation after each run and

TABLE 5.4   Stationary and Nonstationary
Selection Probabilities

Order of operations	Selection probability of A	
	Set 1	Set 2
1	1	1
2	0.5	1
3	0.67	1
4	0.75	1
5	0.6	1
6	0.67	1
7	0.71	1
8	0.75	0.88
9	0.67	0.78
10	0.7	0.7

after the starting transient and noting the deviations from the desired occurrence probabilities.

However, if the field probability of selection of operations is time-varying, the probability of selection in test should follow the same pattern rather than be stationary.

5.3   Identifying System Failures

To identify failures,

1. Analyze the test output for deviations

2. Determine which deviations are failures

3. Establish when the failures occurred

4. Assign failure severity classes, which you will use in prioritizing failure resolution

We will cover each of the first three tasks in considerably more detail.

5.3.1   Analyzing test output for deviations

A *deviation* is any departure of system behavior in execution from expected behavior. There are many standard types of deviations that you can detect with generic tools: interprocess communication failures, illegal memory references, deviant return code values, deadlocks, resource threshold overruns, process crashes or hangs, etc. It may also be possible to detect easily recognized behaviors of the application by automatic means. For example, in telecommunications systems you can detect incomplete calls or undelivered messages automatically. In addition, you can manually insert assertions in the code to set flags that permit programmer-defined deviations to be detected by generic tools. If you do insert assertions, it is important that you document the deviations they detect because this information is frequently lost. Finally, you can examine the output automatically with built-in audit code or an external checker. Of course, it may require considerable labor to specify what output variables you will check and their correct values. When using an output checker, you can save preparation time by specifying ranges of output variables that are acceptable instead of computing precise values.

However, some degree of manual inspection of test results may be necessary. There may be failure-related deviations that are difficult to specify in advance and hence are not amenable to automatic detection. Deviations are sometimes missed in load test because they cannot be detected automatically and not enough effort is devoted to detecting them manually. This is most likely to happen when unit test and feature test are inadequate.

We usually do not count departures of program behavior with respect to performance requirements (throughput, time response). Thus, we don't allow these departures to affect failure intensity estimates. The departures are generally dependent on hardware and software capacity as well as correct execution of hardware and software. Therefore it is usually easier to study and analyze them separately. However, you can consider the departures as deviations and study them together with deviations from required function if you desire. The result will be failure intensity estimates that include departures from function and performance.

Cascaded deviations (additional deviations that result directly from an initial deviation) are not counted. "Directly" implies proximate cause in relation to cascaded deviations. We don't consider deviations cascaded if they occur because an intermediate fault-tolerant feature fails. Deviations generally "cascade" from the same run. However, they can cascade from a previous run when the failure in that run degrades the system to such an extent that proper execution of any run is at substantial risk. You may observe a series of deviations and not recognize that they are really cascaded deviations. For example, you may not realize that the first deviation degraded the system and caused the deviations that followed. You may hence identify them as independent deviations. If you later discover that they were cascaded, you should correct for this and not count the following deviations.

5.3.2 Determining which deviations are failures

Manual analysis of deviations is often necessary to determine whether they violate user requirements and hence represent failures. However, it is quite likely that you can detect failures of higher severity directly (without analyzing deviations) and automatically because they involve easily observable effects that would unquestionably violate user requirements. These effects may be either generic (for example, process crashes) or project-specific (for example, incomplete transactions).

Note that deviations in fault-tolerant systems are often not failures. But intolerance of deviations by a fault-tolerant system that is supposed to be tolerant of them may be a failure. Incident, trouble, modification, and change reports do not necessarily indicate failures. An event or incident reported by a user may not necessarily be a software failure; investigation and interpretation may be required. It may represent a failure of the human component of a system (possibly due to insufficient training), a desire for a new feature, a documentation problem (such as lack of clarity), etc. If the user's concept of "failure" is changing, this can probably best be handled by "averaging" the concept and fixing it for one release. Then change it for the next release.

Sometimes there is a question about whether a failure exists if system behavior doesn't violate any written requirement. Insisting that a written requirement be violated for a failure to exist is a self-defeating proposition, except in the case where extremely serious consequences are likely in admitting to a failure, such as loss of a vital legal action. In almost all cases it is best in the long run to interpret general dissatisfaction with behavior by the user community as a failure. We refer to "user community" rather than "user" dissatisfaction to imply that there is a considered consensus of expectations of users and their managers who are funding the product and not simply desires of a very small number of unreasonable users.

A deliberately unresolved failure or nonfix is really a requirements change, at least for the software version in question. This is true because the user has explicitly or implicitly noted that allowing the failure to continue to occur is acceptable (its nonoccurrence is no longer a requirement). We may not fix some faults because the failures associated with them occur infrequently or they may not be severe. The cost of failure of a particular fault may thus be small with respect to the cost of removing it or of delaying delivery to allow it to be removed.

If you experience multiple failures associated with the same fault, count them in certification test or field reliability measurement because you want to know the failure intensity actually being experienced. Do not count them in reliability growth test because the first occurrence sets in motion a process that will with high probability resolve (remove the fault that is causing the failure) them. Hence you are more interested in estimating the "repaired" failure intensity that will exist after the discovered faults are removed because this is a better indicator of the progress in reliability growth test. This is the estimate you will obtain by not counting repeated failures associated with the same fault. We can also estimate an "unrepaired" failure intensity that indicates the current but temporary state of the software. Some projects during system test track both unique failures and all (including repeated) failures. Failure intensity of all failures indicates what the customer would experience with the software in its current state, where some failures remain unresolved. Failure intensity of unique failures indicates what the customer *will* experience when all failures are resolved. The size of the gap between these failure intensities indicates the amount of work the debugging team has yet to do.

Occasionally failures are resolved as they occur in field operation. This generally occurs only when there is one or at most a few field sites and immediate reliability improvement is a priority. In this case, we don't count repeated failures from the same fault.

Our focusing on failures of software does not mean that other failures such as hardware or personnel failures should be ignored and not recorded.

5.3.3 Establishing when failures occurred

In establishing when a failure occurred, you should use the same measure, natural or time units, that you used in setting the failure intensity objective for the system whose failure intensity you are tracking, with one exception. If you are measuring the failure intensity for software and using time to describe your failure intensity objective, and the average (taken over a failure interval) computer utilization is not constant, you should use execution time as your unit of measure. Recall that computer utilization is the ratio of execution time to clock time; it represents the proportion of time that a processor is executing. Before using the execution time data, convert it to clock time by dividing by the average (over the life of the system) computer utilization. The foregoing manipulation may seem a little strange to you, but in reality it is not. If computer utilization is changing rapidly, a minute of time between 9:01 and 9:02 a.m. may have much more processing occurring than the previous minute of 9:00 to 9:01 a.m. We want to characterize the amount of processing occurring because this will indicate the failure-inducing stress placed on the software. We must measure the actual execution time in order to do this. But then we convert back to ordinary or clock time so that failure intensity is given in the same units as the failure intensity objective. Because the computer utilization we use in converting back is an average over the life of the system, we measure an effective time that is proportional to the actual processing that occurred.

To better understand the conversion of execution time to clock time, consider the following illustration, presented in Table 5.5. The measured execution times of the three failures are as shown. We obtain the adjusted times by dividing the execution times by the average computer utilization 0.4.

In certification test, you measure units at the point at which the failure occurred. For example, in Fone Follower, a failure might occur at 7135 calls.

In reliability growth test, you should measure units at the point at which the failure occurred if possible, because you then retain the most information. However, you can also measure the number of failures

TABLE 5.5   **Illustration of Conversion of Failure Times from Execution Time to Time**

Failure	Execution time (h)	Average computer utilization	Adjusted time (h)
1	0.2	0.4	0.5
2	0.6	0.4	1.5
3	1.2	0.4	3

that occur in an interval, such as three failures in 1000 calls. The latter format is usually referred to as "grouped failure data."

You accumulate units of measure, in the sequence they occur, from all representatively invoked test of the system including feature and regression test and load test over all operational modes. By "representatively invoked" we mean selected in accordance with Sec. 5.2.

Be sure that you take a measurement at the actual occurrence of the failure and not at the time when you prepare the failure report. The foregoing is a common error. Also note that you do not count natural or time units used in repeating a run to collect more data about a failure or in verifying that a failure has been resolved.

If it is difficult to measure execution time, you may be able to measure and weight clock time. You multiply short segments of time by computer utilization or some approximation to computer utilization. Then add the products. One example would be a system where it is easy to get data on the number of users. You could approximate execution time by the product of time and adjusted fraction of maximum possible users. For example, suppose that a system has a maximum feasible load of 40 users. This maximum feasible load occurs for the particular system when computer utilization is 0.8. Above this number, response time on this system becomes intolerable, although more users are physically possible. We sample the number of users at a randomly chosen instant within a 5-min period. The 12 periods occurring in an hour are averaged to give users for that hour (see Table 5.6). The fraction of maximum feasible users, multiplied by 0.8, yields an approximation to computer utilization.

If a failure occurs at 10 a.m. and another at 2 p.m., we may determine the execution time interval by summing the execution time in the intervening hours. This approach yields an interval of 2.64 execution hours.

When making failure time measurements in execution time, you will sometimes have to resolve questions of interpretation. The most basic principle is that you measure execution time on the processor(s) on which the program is running. This would mean, for example, that you don't count the time required to perform input-output functions on peripheral processors or controllers. Of course, if we are measuring the reliability of the peripheral processor software, its execution time *is* the quantity to measure. Care must be taken so that we only measure the execution of those functions that would be included in the deliverable product and normally operated by the customer. For example, you should not include the execution time of utility programs that analyze or display data recorded from the output of the program for the purpose of failure identification or for measuring the failure intervals.

If operations and runs are executing across a distributed system, it will be easiest to use natural units. But if you cannot find a common

TABLE 5.6   Execution Time Determined by Weighting
Elapsed Time by Adjusted Fraction of Maximum Possible

Hour	Number of users	Approximation of utilization
8–9 a.m.	16	0.32
9–10 a.m.	36	0.72
10–11 a.m.	40	0.8
11–12 a.m.	36	0.72
12–1 p.m.	20	0.4
1–2 p.m.	36	0.72
2–3 p.m.	40	0.8
3–4 p.m.	40	0.8
4–5 p.m.	36	0.72
5–6 p.m.	24	0.48

natural unit for the system and must use time, and hence execution time if computer utilization is not constant, you should choose a key processor for measuring execution time. This should ordinarily be the processor that executes the largest proportion of instructions.

Testers sometimes record multiple failures that occurred close together as happening at the same time, resulting in multiple zero failure intervals. This may result in a discontinuous jump in estimated present failure intensity, perhaps to infinity. You must determine the true situation. These may be cascaded failures that you should report as only one failure, or there may actually be short intervals between the failures that you should precisely determine and report.

You will want to record the severity class of failures wherever possible. You will need it to determine the relative priority you should give in responding to various failures. Also, you may need to use it to verify the proportions of occurrence of the different failure severity classes that you have assumed, if you set your total failure intensity objective from requirements based on one severity class. However, failure severity class is not generally used in failure intensity estimation.

Keep records in such a fashion that information is not lost when project personnel are transferred. They should be readily interpretable so that the information is available for use on similar projects in the future. Our convenient way of recording failure times is to note them on the trouble or failure reports that many projects use for all formal testing and often also in the field during operation.

Observation of failures may occur at the time of program operation or when analyzing program output afterward. Therefore, many find it best to allow 1 or 2 days to elapse after a test run before using the failure interval data. Then you can weed out false failures and analyze the results thoroughly to minimize missed failures. Experience indicates that after analysis one is more likely to miss failures than to report false ones. Don't count as failures faults found by a programmer without test (by code reading or other means) during the test period. They are not "failures" by definition. When the development environment is such that extensive code reading accompanies test, the value of the fault reduction factor may be affected.

5.4   Special Situations

Some special situations can occur in practice in executing tests using software reliability engineering. They relate to testing on multiple configurations, dealing with uncertainties in measuring time, or with managing multiple versions of the system. They are covered in this section.

5.4.1   Establishing when failures occurred for tests on multiple configurations

In this situation, you are running tests on multiple configurations. These may involve software that executes only on one machine, in which case we have multiple machines. However, if the software executes on a distributed system, we can have multiple distributed systems, each with its own key machine for measuring execution time. Hence the term *configurations*.

The basic principle is to interleave the failures, using either natural or time units (we will use time in the following discussion to mean either). In the sequence of failures in Table 5.7, times are given in minutes. The failure times are the total of the cumulative times on all configurations. Note that it does not matter in which configuration the failure occurs; the cumulative time over all configurations will be the same.

When multiple configurations are running the same program, you should interleave the failures from the different configurations in the order in which they occurred. Then add the concurrently running times. We use this procedure because all you are really doing is expos-

TABLE 5.7   Measuring Time on Multiple Configurations

		Cumulative time		
Time	Event	Configuration A	Configuration B	Failure times
8:00	Start A	0		
8:30	Start B	30	0	
9:00	Failure 1	60	30	90
9:20	Failure 2	80	50	130

ing the same program to more testing. When we find a failure on one configuration, we normally correct all copies of the program on the other configurations sooner or later. You might argue that we should consider times separately for each program copy and compute failure intervals for that program copy as a separate entity. Such an approach would indeed apply to hardware where wear is occurring and the different accumulated operation times for each system are significant. It *does not* apply to software. Remember that the program is only the logic and not the physical configuration it is running on. The nature of that configuration or its condition is *immaterial.* If you present the software copies with the same operational profile, the runs for these copies may be different but the probability of a given run for any copy is identical. Hence whether you experience time on one copy or many *does not matter,* and you may group time periods together.

In fact, there is another significant difference from the hardware situation. When a failure occurs and you remove the fault that causes it, you generally remove that fault for *all* copies at the same time. In actuality, there may be variations in repair time, but simultaneous repair is a good approximation. Thus the nature of the software changes with time, and it is necessary to keep failure data synchronized between different copies with respect to time. Hence we use the interleaving approach.

Now suppose that the two configurations have different instruction execution rates. The basic principle is that you pick one configuration as the reference configuration, adjust times to the reference configuration, and then interleave failures as before. For example, in the previous illustration, suppose that machine B has twice the average instruction execution rate that machine A has. Let's choose machine A as the reference. Determination of adjusted time is shown in Table 5.8.

5.4.2 Uncertainties in establishing when failures occurred

The number of natural or time units at a failure or start or end of a period of execution may be uncertain due to either limitations in data recording or in record keeping and reporting. To handle this situation, first determine the window during which the event must have occurred. Then choose natural or time units corresponding to the event randomly (assuming a uniform distribution) within that window. The foregoing procedure will yield more accurate results than ignoring the failures and test periods that are not accurately recorded. You can determine the effect of the uncertainty by making estimates using the extreme values of the possible range of failure intervals.

A common application of the procedure is to situations where we only know the number of failures per day and the number of natural or time

TABLE 5.8   Measuring Time on Multiple Configurations with Different Instruction
Execution Rates

		Cumulative time (min)		Adjusted time,	Failure
Time	Event	Configuration A	Configuration B	configuration B (min)	times (min)
8:00	Start A	0			0
8:30	Start B	30	0	0	30
9:00	Failure 1	60	30	60	120
9:20	Failure 2	80	50	100	180

units accumulated for each day. You should assign the failures randomly within the window of the number of natural or time units for the
day. We can readily generalize this approach to the situation where m_W
failures occur in a specified window of uncertainty t_W. Assign all the
failures randomly within this window. An alternative method is to
divide the window into $m_W + 1$ segments of length $t_L = t_W/(m_W + 1)$ and
assign the failures at t_L, $2t_L$, $3t_L$, and so on. However, this latter
approach yields inferior results when you estimate model parameters,
as we will see later in this section. If you don't record the number of
natural or time units accumulated, you can use an estimate of the average number, but this estimate will cause a deterioration in accuracy
and ability to predict. Note that failures-per-interval data that are
mixed with data of the number of natural or time units at failures type
can be handled with the preceding procedure.

Consider the log of a day of testing, recorded in time units, shown in
Table 5.9. Average computer utilization, taken over the period of a failure interval, is constant. We convert the times of the events to minutes
of time for convenience. We then select numbers from a random number table. We multiply these numbers by whatever constant is necessary to adjust their range of variation to the range of uncertainty of
times. You thus establish the failure times and calculate the intervals.
The procedure is illustrated in Table 5.10.

TABLE 5.9   Log for Day of Testing

Event	Time
Start test	8 a.m.
Failure 1	8:30 a.m.
Failure 2	9:30–10:20 a.m.
Failure 3	11:00 a.m.
Stop test for lunch	12 noon
Start test	1:00 p.m.
Failures 4, 5	1:00–4:20 p.m.
Stop test	5:00 p.m.

TABLE 5.10 **Resolution of Failure Time Uncertainties**

Event	Time (min)	Random number	Adjustment factor	Assigned time (min)	Time interval since last failure (min)
Start test	0			0	
Failure 1	30			30	30
Failure 2	90–140	67,557	0.0005	63.8	33.8
Failure 3	180			180	116.2
Stop test	240			240	
Start test	240			240	
Failure 4	240–440	26,446	0.002	292.9	112.9
Failure 5	240–440	97,159	0.002	434.3	141.4
Stop test	480			480	

Sometimes (although this is undesirable) the "when" testers report for a failure comes from the moment of identification rather than the moment of occurrence. This adds to inaccuracy, but it may not be too serious if the mean lag in natural or time units between failure occurrence and identification is relatively constant.

You must beware of the natural tendency of people to "save time" by logging closely occurring failures as happening at the same point in natural or time units. Doing this would result in an excessive number of zero failure intervals, which would yield an overly pessimistic estimate of potential failures in the system. If you have already logged data in this fashion, it is probably best to correct them as follows. Assume there are k identical points between the unequal points t_i and t_{i+k+1}. Pick k random points (for example, from a random number table) in the range $[t_i, t_{i+k+1}]$ and order them as $t_{i+1}, t_{i+2}, \ldots, t_{i+k}$. The *intervals* $t'_{i+1}, t'_{i+2}, \ldots$ that will replace the zero intervals will be found as

$$t'_{i+1} = t_{i+1} - t_i$$

$$t'_{i+2} = t_{i+2} - t_{i+1} \tag{5.1}$$

$$\cdots$$

$$\cdots$$

$$\cdots$$

$$t'_{i+k} = t_{i+k} - t_{i+k-1}$$

and t'_{i+k+1} must be changed to $t_{i+k+1} - t_{i+k}$.

5.4.3 Multiple versions in the field

Large systems that are installed in many locations may have several versions or releases of the program in the field at one time. This can be the result of the need to spread the installation of a new release over a period of time. Other possibilities are differing needs of different locations as to the issue of new features versus reliability or perhaps economic factors. Later releases usually have fixes for at least some of the failures experienced in the earlier releases, but they also typically have new features and performance improvements that introduce new faults. Sometimes, you may want to establish the failure intensity for each version. However, variation in failure intensity from release to release is often not great because the economic, marketing, customer need, and competition factors that cause the first version to be released at a certain reliability level may still be operative for the later versions. We are usually most interested in determining the status of the latest release. You can do this by using any of the techniques for evolving programs, as described in Sec. 6.3.1. However, if the differences between versions are not great, it may be satisfactory and much simpler to pool all the data. This can be done immediately, or you can estimate the failure intensities for the separate versions and then take an average.

Consider an electronic switching system installed in 1000 central offices around the country. There are currently three different releases of software involved, as shown in Table 5.11. All failures are included in the failure intensity data, although only a very small proportion have a sufficiently severe impact to cause service interruption. You can find the overall failure intensity by taking an average of the separate versions, weighted by the proportion of installations of each, which equals 1.95 failures per thousand execution hours.

5.5 Frequently Asked Questions

We will first examine questions that deal with the test process. Then we will consider questions on the topics of counting failures and measuring processing done.

TABLE 5.11 Software with Multiple Releases

Release	Number of installations	Failure intensity (per thousand execution hours)
5	300	2.0
6	500	1.5
7	200	3.0

5.5.1 Test process

1 One can statistically show that proving the reliability level of an ultrareliable system requires an impractically long test period. For example, an aircraft control system might require a failure intensity objective of 10^{-8} failures per hour. Statistical theory would show that a test period at least several times 10^8 h would be required. Doesn't this make software reliability engineering useless for the systems where reliability assumes the greatest importance?

ANSWER: No. The statistical approach ignores many practical software engineering realities, most of which arise from the differing natures of software and hardware reliability. Although an average airline flight might last 2 h, the critical functions requiring ultrareliability occur in less than 1 percent of that period (takeoff and landing). The execution time devoted to aircraft control might be 1 percent of the corresponding time duration. Thus in execution time the failure intensity objective might need to be only 10^{-4} failures per execution hour. Several times 10^4 execution hours of test should be adequate. If you execute test on 100 parallel processors, which is quite practical, you can accomplish this in several hundred hours of operation.

2 Software used on spacecraft flights must have a high reliability over a long mission, yet the time available for testing it is much shorter. How is it possible to adequately test such software so that we have confidence in it?

ANSWER: It would initially seem that you have an impossible task. However, usually only the software that controls the flight trajectory, vehicle attitude, and perhaps a few other functions is really critical to mission success. Occasional failures in other functions (for example, telemetry) can be tolerated. The actual execution time for the critical software during the mission is relatively short, perhaps hours for a mission lasting years. It is readily shown from Musa, Iannino, and Okumoto (1987), Fig. 7.7 and App. E, Sec. E.1, that you need a failure-free period of execution of greater than $-2\tau_C/\ln R$ to demonstrate that the software meets its reliability objective with high confidence. The quantity τ_C is the execution time of the critical operation, and R is the required reliability. If $R = 0.99$ for the critical period, the test period must be 200 τ_C in length. Typical test periods of several months are quite satisfactory for this purpose.

3 Is the rate of failure intensity decay during system test indicative of the efficiency of test?

ANSWER: Yes. The most rapid decay achievable is the rate that occurs when you test without replacement, selecting runs in the order of probability of occurrence. Test efficiency would be measured by taking the ratio of lowest achievable failure intensity to actual failure intensity achieved.

4 How can you tell when the test process has changed such that interpretation of the results of software reliability engineering may be affected?

ANSWER: Of course, you can often observe directly that test strategies have changed. But an otherwise unexplained sudden increase in failure intensity or long period of constant failure intensity can also be a clue.

5 How should we handle regression test when doing software reliability estimation?

ANSWER: We may include regression tests with the rest of the tests we are running. We can merge regression test failure data with the rest of the failure data as long as we select operations randomly in accordance with the operational profile.

6 Our test strategy tends to uncover many failures early. Will that give us a pessimistic estimate of reliability?

ANSWER: No. Reliability models place more emphasis on detecting the *trend* in failure intensity than on the average current value. If you are uncovering a large proportion of failures early and removing their associated faults, the trend in failure intensity will be sharply downward. The model will show that your strategy has given a lower current failure intensity than you would have otherwise obtained.

7 Does the reliability of test drivers have an impact on a software reliability model?

ANSWER: Not directly, because we don't consider test driver failures to be failures of the system being tested. Occasionally, test driver failures are so substantial that they result in a distortion of the operational profile being executed. Then the reliability measured for the system being tested may be in error.

8 How do you test automatic failure detection software?

ANSWER: The same way you test other software. You first need to clearly understand the requirements for this software: It is not practical for automatic failure detection software to detect all possible failures but only some defined subset (which still may be most failures). Determining the expected frequencies of failures by type will help you develop the operational profile for the software. You then test in accordance with the operational profile. The details of test selection are no different from that for other software.

9 Is there a way to estimate how long a certification test will take, in the sense of reaching either acceptance or rejection?

ANSWER: Not really, because you can't predict when failures will occur. However, you can determine a minimum time, as shown in Sec. 5.6.1.

10 Can we test a component using software reliability engineering when we do not know its operational profile but we do know the operational profile of a system of which it is a part?

ANSWER: Yes. Integrate the component with the rest of the system and test with the system operational profile. Set up a separate execution time clock to record execution time just for the component. Record the failures of the component separately from the other failures in the system. It will usually be most convenient to do this testing at the start of test for the larger system.

11 When you experience a failure in test, can you continue testing or must you restart from scratch? If the former, how do you account for the fact that degraded data may cause another failure?

ANSWER: You can continue testing or restart. It doesn't matter. If degraded data cause another failure, the second event is really part of the first failure and shouldn't be counted again. However, if you require the system to recover from the first failure by cleaning up the data, you count the second failure because it represents a failure of the *recovery mechanism*.

12 Field personnel tend not to report multiple failures, because they assume that the first report will result in an appropriate fix. They do not want to incur the paperwork involved in subsequent reports. How can we deal with this problem so that we obtain the data we need?

ANSWER: First, there may not really be a problem if the failure isn't occurring at a high frequency so that it repeats at the same site. Field personnel at different sites *do* tend to report the same problem because they don't usually communicate problems with each other. However, if the problem is recurring at the same site, there are two general ways of handling it (you can probably simplify matters by only worrying about the frequently recurring problems). Automatic recording of high-frequency failures is the first. If manual recording is necessary, however, educate the field force as to the importance of the data, motivate them, and solicit their participation in planning how the collection will be done. Make it as easy as possible for them. If some sort of concrete reward is possible for reports they submit, consider this.

13 You note that a test case becomes a run when it executes in the context of an operational mode so that all the indirect input variables are also specified. In feature test we do not test with operational modes. Does this mean that the test cases we execute here are not really runs?

ANSWER: In the strict sense, Yes. A feature test is not really a complete test in the sense that it would actually occur in the field. You invoke a feature test in a special environment in which you restrict interactions because you are trying to determine if the feature works by itself, without the complication of worrying about interactions.

14 We have allocated 10 h to testing one of our operational modes but one of our operations requires 12 h to execute. What should we do?

ANSWER: You have not properly defined your operations. An operation should take only a very small portion of your total test time to execute. In a typical test effort, you execute *at least* thousands of operations, and you can easily execute millions. Long operations typically duplicate each other to a substantial extent and hence are not conducive to efficient test. For example, if in testing an aircraft control system you choose entire flight trajectories of several hours as operations, you will not be able to test many trajectories and there will be much duplication in your test. Instead, you might consider maneuvers lasting a few seconds as operations, such as climb, dive, left turn, right turn, etc.

5.5.2 Counting failures

1 We are testing at multiple sites. Because of time lags in communicating and fixing problems, failures encountered at one site are often repeated at another. Does this cause any problem?

ANSWER: No. Ignore the second and following occurrences of the same failure, just as you would for faults not yet fixed in single-site testing.

2 We are testing at two different sites, the development site and a field site. There is a time lag in releasing new versions of the program to the field site. Consequently, the field site is always testing an earlier release than the one we are testing at the development site. The later version does not have many new features, but it does have fault corrections not included in the previous release. How can we handle this?

ANSWER: Eliminate from consideration failures that reoccur at the field site but have already been detected at the development site. You can then merge the data as you do for multiple sites with the same release. If you introduced design changes in the later release, the situation is similar to that of design changes being introduced at a single site. However, the effects are somewhat moderated for the period during which you are merging the failure data from the different releases. For example, a sharp increase in estimated total failures due to new faults introduced with the design changes will be "softened" and occur more gradually due to the overlap. Because this problem assumes few new features, you can neglect their effect.

3 When we do system test, at least for certain operational modes, identification of a failure is no guarantee that the fault causing it can be tracked down and fixed. Because finding these faults with the diagnostic information available to us is so difficult, we try to match patterns of failures with areas of the program that might be malfunctioning. We then redesign and redevelop those areas. With this situation, how should we count repeated failures?

ANSWER: Count all repetitions of the failure. You cannot eliminate the repetitions because there is no assurance that the fault causing the failure is being removed.

4 Several testers are executing a component that is part of several products. Which product should we assign a failure to?

ANSWER: Assign the failure to the product that is being tested. This should be obvious. The reason it may not is if you have confused "failure" with "fault." A failure is associated with execution, whereas a fault is associated with the code.

If you were thinking about a fault in common code, there might be a question about which product it belongs to.

5 Do some operating systems provide ways in which automated recording of failures can be simplified?

ANSWER: Some operating systems and message protocols used as platforms for building applications incorporate facilities for detecting application failures of various types and for communicating and recording these failures. You can interface software reliability estimation programs with such facilities. Thus automated failure recording software can be built that is relatively generic and requires only moderate change from application to application, provided all applications use the common operating system and message protocols.

6 What is a cascaded deviation and how do you treat it? Does it differ from a repeated deviation?

ANSWER: Cascaded deviations are a sequence of departures from required operation occurring on one run, where an initial departure results in data degradation that causes the following departures. You count the entire sequence as one deviation occurring at the time of the first departure. A cascaded deviation differs from a repeated deviation. A repeated deviation occurs on a different run than the original deviation. You generally count it at each occurrence in the field but only once in system test.

7 What factors affect the proportion of failures that are reported?

ANSWER: We can summarize the factors as perceived benefit to cost ratio of making the failure report. For example, if users perceive that there is no response to failure reports, the proportion reported will decrease, except perhaps for severe failures (the benefit of getting these resolved is so large that the user will go to considerable trouble and expense to do so).

8 Are there situations during system test where you don't have to worry about identifying and not counting repeated failures?

ANSWER: Yes. If the average time between failures is considerably larger than the average time required for a failure resolution, there will be very few occurrences of repeated failures. In this situation, it isn't necessary to worry about identifying such failures.

9 How do you handle multiple failures resulting from the same fault on a single run during test?

ANSWER: In general, don't count them in test but do in the operational phase.

10 How do you handle failures found by unit test that continue in parallel with system test?

ANSWER: Don't count these failures or execution time spent in unit test. Unit test involves testing only a small part of the software. Here you would have a retrogression because a substantial part of the system would already have been in test. Suppose that the ratio of faults corrected in unit test to failures experienced in system test is relatively constant. Then you could adjust for the extra faults being corrected from unit test by increasing the fault reduction factor B.

11   Do we have different failures when the same software is run on two different machines and fails in the same way on the same runs?

ANSWER: No. We have repeated failures, just as if we had executed the software on the same machine for the same input states. Whether we should count the repetitions depends on the circumstances and the objectives you have in collecting your data.

12   We are working with a compiler that is not fully debugged. Consequently, we often find that a failure is the result of incorrect compilation rather than erroneous programming. Should we account for this in any way?

ANSWER: If you expect that the compiler will be reliable by the time you finally recompile the program before delivery to the customer, do not count failures due to bad compilation when making estimates of program failure intensity or reliability. If it will probably still be unreliable, you may wish to make your estimates twice, with the compiler-caused failures *included* in one estimate and *excluded* in the other. You will then have a range of failure intensities or reliabilities with the extreme values representing a reliable compiler and an unreliable one.

13   Sometimes it is very easy to automatically record certain types of failures because they result in easily recognizable output states. Examples are system crashes and error code states. The recognition of other failures may require considerable manual observation and analysis. Can we apply software reliability engineering to just the failures that are easily recorded?

ANSWER: Yes, but you must recognize that you are measuring the reliability with respect only to a limited class of failures. If the number of failures in this class is proportional to the total number of failures, adjustment by division by this proportion will give the overall number of failures and failure intensity.

14   You noted that we can handle delays in removing faults by simply not counting failures that recur from the same fault. Isn't there some error that occurs from doing this because the discovery of new faults that would be spawned is delayed?

ANSWER: Yes, but the effect is minor. The number of spawned faults is typically relatively small, of the order of 5 percent.

15   How do we measure execution time for distributed systems?

ANSWER: First try to find a natural unit for the system; then you won't have to measure execution time. If you can't find a natural unit, use ordinary time. If the average (over a period comparable to the times between failures) computer utilizations of the processors that execute the majority of the instructions are approximately constant, you can use time directly to measure the intervals between failures, without adjustment. Thus, you will not have to measure execution time. If the computer utilizations are not constant, you must measure execution time and compute an adjusted ordinary time. In that case, choose one of the processors as the key processor and measure execution time on it. Usually this should be the processor that on the average executes the largest proportion of instructions. Over the long haul, the proportions of instructions for the various machines usually stay relatively stable. Hence the execution time for the key machine will generally be a stable fraction of total execution time for the distributed system. Consequently, you can convert back to time by dividing the key machine execution time by its average long-term computer utilization.

16 For distributed systems, if you measure execution time as the processing time expended on the processor that does the largest fraction of processing, you are leaving out the processing done on other processors. Doesn't this cause problems?

ANSWER: In general, No. For periods of time of the order of intervals between failures, the ratios of execution times on the different processors stay relatively stable. Thus the measured execution time is a relatively constant fraction of the total execution time for the system. You should base the failure intensity objective on execution time measured on the same key processor. Then the ratio of failure intensity to failure intensity objective with respect to execution time measured on the key processor will be approximately the same as the ratio measured with respect to total execution time. The only potential problem that might occur is if you were calculating absolute failure intensity for some reason.

17 We are testing a system where most of the failures are not obvious. We must examine the output of each test in some detail to determine if a failure occurred. Because failure identification is expensive, the number of tests we can run is limited. What can we do about this situation?

ANSWER: One answer is to reduce the cost of failure identification by automating it as much as possible. It may actually be more practical to automate deviation rather than failure identification because the latter often requires judgment of what affects users—this judgment may be difficult to automate.

Another possibility is to reduce the cost of failure identification by randomly choosing from among the large number of variables in the output state those that you will examine. This will probably result in identifying only a portion of the failures that occur. However, you may be able to determine what that fraction is from total examination of a small number of output states. You could then adjust the number of failures detected by the fraction as long as there are no conditions operating that would make the fraction highly variable.

If the cost of failure identification still remains sufficiently high such that you must limit the number of tests executed, it will be important for the selection process to be random, with operation selection based on the operational profile and selection of runs within operation, uniform.

18 Suppose a display has an incorrect type face, color, or format. Is that a failure?

ANSWER: Yes, because calling up the display involves a function for which the behavior is incorrect, even though the departure is relatively minor.

5.5.3 Measuring when failures occurred

1 How should we measure regression test time and failures encountered during regression test? For example, suppose development is incremental and suppose that each new system test load contains some new feature and some fixes for failures reported in previous loads. Suppose further that with each load, system test follows the following steps:

  a. Rerun the test cases that caused the failures that have been worked on
  b. Rerun a regression test suite that grows to reflect functions that have been successfully tested
  c. Select test cases at random for the functions that are in the current load, in proportion to the operational profile

Do we treat the execution time and any failures observed in steps a and b the same way we treat failures and execution time in step c?

ANSWER: We don't count execution time and failures observed in step a; we consider this step part of the failure resolution process. You may count execution time and failures from step b if the total effect of steps b and c is representative of operational use, as described by the operational profile. If it is difficult to satisfy this condition, you may prefer not to count data from step b. The effect is to widen the size of the confidence intervals associated with quantities being estimated.

2 What should I do when I do not have easily accessible tools for measuring execution time, such as when I am working on a personal computer?

ANSWER: Work with natural units if possible. If it is important to simplify data collection, especially when failure intensity is high, record the number of failures that occur over some interval of natural units. For example, record number of failures occurring during each thousand transactions.

3 Why don't you see "instructions executed" as the basic software reliability metric? It would seem to be more fundamental because it would be independent of the particular computer used and its throughput.

ANSWER: It is true that instructions executed would be computer-independent, but it is usually not as easy to measure as natural units, ordinary time, or execution time. Also, it is not compatible with hardware reliability metrics.

4 Why don't you use percentage of program segments covered rather than execution time to characterize the failure stress placed on software?

ANSWER: We don't use percentage of program segments covered because

a. Program segments vary greatly in size.

b. Program segments are not a user-oriented measure.

c. Failure also depends on the machine state that exists when a segment is traversed.

d. The coverage measure does not take account of the relative frequencies of execution of the different segments.

5 When we run system tests, we interrupt them frequently to enter commands from the terminal. We do not have the system instrumented to provide execution time. Can we use clock time in spite of the interruptions?

ANSWER: Yes, if the average (over the period between failures) computer utilization is approximately constant.

6 Can we use number of runs as an approximation to execution time?

ANSWER: Yes, provided that average run length does not vary appreciably from failure interval to failure interval. Note that because you generally invoke runs with some sort of system controller, they are very easy to count in practice. Execution time is often more difficult to instrument. Runs are often more closely related to measures that are more meaningful to users, such as those defined as natural units (for example, pages of output, transactions, or telephone calls). In fact, runs and natural units often relate one to one.

7 We are trying to determine the interval between failures for an interactive system with a varying number of users in which measuring execution time is difficult. Is there a better way of doing this than measuring clock time?

ANSWER: Yes. Weight clock time by an estimate of computer utilization. A good approximation of the computer utilization in any time period is given by the ratio of current users to maximum feasible users, multiplied by the computer utilization that corresponds to this maximum.

8 Is there some way we can determine a failure interval in the situation where we only know that the failure occurred during a period of uncertain length?

ANSWER: Yes, use a double randomization procedure. First choose the length of the period by picking a random number (uniformly distributed) from the range of possible period lengths. Then pick another random number that represents the location of the failure within the period. The following example may be illustrative.

Tester A runs tests for 3 h following the previous failure with no new failures. Tester B, who keeps poor records, follows with more tests and experiences a failure but does not record the time for the failure occurrence or the length of test. It is known, however, that the period ran somewhere between 1 and 9 h.

First, select a random number in the range 1 to 9 to establish the length of the period; assume that 3.7179 is selected. We now have the failure occurring sometime between 3 and 6.7179 h since the last failure. Select another random number to fix the failure location. Assume that it is 6.3036. We have a failure interval of 6.3036 and 0.4143 h of failure-free testing that follows it. Ordinarily you may use this information directly in a software reliability estimation program.

The foregoing procedure will yield more accurate results than ignoring the failures and test periods that you didn't accurately record. You can obtain an estimate of the inaccuracy in any derived quantity by computing the quantity using the extreme values of the possible ranges of the unknown failure intervals.

Note that the first step of the procedure will prove useful in establishing the length of a failure-free test period that is uncertain.

9   Suppose a known number of failures occur in a time window at unknown times. When you assign the failure times randomly within the window, why not assume a trend to the failure intervals?

ANSWER: You shouldn't assume a trend because you do not know what the trend is (form) or what its parameters are.

10   It is difficult for us to measure execution time associated with a tester running a particular test. Several tests are usually running simultaneously and they may all be serviced by some common processes. We *can* measure elapsed time and pinpoint the occurrence of failures with respect to it. We can also measure total execution time for the system at various elapsed times (for example, hourly). How can we convert elapsed time between failures into execution time? The number of users on the system varies, so computer utilization is not constant.

ANSWER: The approach is best illustrated by an example. Assume two testers with the test and failure patterns indicated in Table 5.12 for a particular day. Total execution time accumulated is measured as noted in Table 5.13. The utilizations for each hour are readily found from Table 5.13 to be the amounts given in Table 5.14. Because both testers are running on the same system we compute:

TABLE 5.12   Failure Patterns of Two Testers

Tester 1	Tester 2
8:00 a.m. start test	
8:36 a.m. failure A	
	9:00 a.m. start test
	9:15 a.m. failure B
9:40 a.m. failure C	
10:00 a.m. end test	
	10:24 a.m. failure D
	11:00 a.m. end test

TABLE 5.13   Accumulated
Execution Time for Two Testers

Time	Execution time (min)
8:00 a.m.	0
9:00 a.m.	15
10:00 a.m.	45
11:00 a.m.	60

TABLE 5.14   Computer Utilizations
for Each Hour

Time	Utilization
8–9 a.m.	0.25
9–10 a.m.	0.5
10–11 a.m.	0.25

$$\text{Execution time to failure A} = 36(0.25) = 9 \text{ min}$$

$$\text{Execution time between failures A and B} = 24(0.25) + 15(0.5) = 13.5 \text{ min}$$

$$\text{Execution time between failures B and C} = 25(0.5) = 12.5 \text{ min}$$

$$\text{Execution time between failures C and D} = 20(0.5) + 24(0.25) = 16 \text{ min}$$

$$\text{Execution time from failure D to end of test} = 36(0.25) = 9 \text{ min}$$

The execution time intervals between failures are given in Table 5.15.

If the two testers were testing different components and we wanted to keep the failure data separate (to get component reliability estimates), we could proceed as follows. Note that execution time measured between 9 and 10 a.m. is for both components. Thus it must be allocated. The utilizations for each component for each hour are given in Table 5.16. We would compute for component X:

$$\text{Execution time to failure A} = 36(0.25) = 9 \text{ min}$$

$$\text{Execution time between failures A and C} = 64(0.25) = 16 \text{ min}$$

$$\text{Execution time from failure C to end of test} = 20(0.25) = 5 \text{ min}$$

For component Y we would calculate

$$\text{Execution time to failure B} = 12(0.25) = 3 \text{ min}$$

$$\text{Execution time between failures B and D} = 72(0.25) = 18 \text{ min}$$

$$\text{Execution time from failure D to end of test} = 36(0.25) = 9 \text{ min}$$

The execution time intervals between failures on each component are given in Table 5.17.

TABLE 5.15   Execution Time Intervals between Failures

Failure	Execution time interval from previous failure (min)
A	9
B	13.5
C	12.5
D	16
End of test	9

TABLE 5.16   Computer Utilizations for Each
Component for Each Hour

Time	Utilization	
	Component X	Component Y
8–9 a.m.	0.25	
9–10 a.m.	0.25	0.25
10–11 a.m.		0.25

11   What precision is required in measuring execution time?

ANSWER: Estimate the largest failure intensity you expect to encounter (usually the initial failure intensity). Take its reciprocal. A precision in measurement of 1 percent of its value will generally be reasonable because of the presence of other possible sources of error.

12   What is the significance of the "zero interval" of time between failures that is sometimes seen in software failure data?

ANSWER: Two failures don't actually take place at exactly the same time; the behavior occurring would be interpreted as one failure. The zero interval simply reflects the fact that a small interval has been rounded, with the closest value being zero.

13   Why must we interleave the natural or time units of failures experienced on systems running in parallel on multiple configurations? Why not just determine failure times on one computer, followed by failure times on the next?

ANSWER: You must do this during reliability growth test because you only count the first instance of repeated failures originating from the same fault, assuming that this fault will be removed. This means that the chronological order of occurrence is significant; consequently, interleaving of the natural or time units accumulated on the various machines is essential. Also, at each point in time you want to be able to determine failure intensity status. Hence you want to know execution time experienced across all computers at each point in time. Also, a failure of the software on one computer sets in motion a process to find the fault causing it and remove that fault in *all* copies of the software. Interleaving is not essential during certification test; however, we do it so that the procedure that is explained to practitioners is simpler.

TABLE 5.17   Execution Time Intervals between Failures on Each Component

Component X		Component Y	
Failure	Execution time interval from previous failure (min)	Failure	Execution time interval from previous failure (min)
A	9	B	3
C	16	D	18
End of test	5	End of test	9

14 Do you really count *all* testing during system test in determining total execution time that has occurred?

ANSWER: No. Count only the time the failure identification (test) team uses for general system test that is devoted to initial failure identification. We don't count additional selective testing undertaken to verify the existence of the failure or collect data on it. We do not count time required to diagnose the fault causing the failure. Neither do we count time needed to show that we have resolved the failure.

15 During test we record much data on tape and then examine these data interactively on a display afterward. Do we count the examination time as execution time?

ANSWER: No.

16 Nonoperating time can affect hardware failures because aging can occur even without operation. Can this happen for software?

ANSWER: No.

17 We log our failures in real time against a "clock" that keeps track of cumulative execution time. Because determining that a failure really occurred involves a delay, all the failures are logged at a time later than they actually occurred. Does this cause a problem in estimation during system test?

ANSWER: It could, especially if you are tracking failure intensity frequently or if there are multiple test configurations. It is best to subtract the delay from all the failure times before processing them.

18 We have automatic failure identification, recording, and reporting programs built into our application program. Do we count their execution time?

ANSWER: If you are determining failure intensity just for the application program proper, no. If you are determining failure intensity for the complete set of application program and failure identification, recording, and reporting programs, yes.

19 How can you estimate and project software failure intensity for systems in which you collect the failure data with respect to number of runs (for example, transactions) executed?

ANSWER: If the runs can be related to natural units (as in the case of transactions), convert numbers of runs at failures to natural units at failures. If not, use average run duration in execution time to convert numbers of runs at failures to average execution times at failures. Then estimate failure intensity using either natural units or execution times. Convert failure intensity in execution time to failure intensity in time by multiplying by long-term average computer utilization.

5.6   Background

This section will present material on allocating test time, invoking tests, and counting failures.

5.6.1   Allocating test time

We do not currently have guidelines for determining the total amount of feature and load test time required in reliability growth test. The amount of time should be a function of the failure intensity objective for the developed software, the degree of fault tolerance implemented, the intensity of reviews, and other product and process variables. We know many of the principal variables and relationships that affect the amount of test needed (Musa, Iannino, and Okumoto, 1987), but we don't know the exact values of the constants in the relationships at present. Collection of project data is likely to lead to determination of these constants, making a method for determining the test periods required feasible. At present, we choose the amounts of time as a result of past experience with similar projects.

We can estimate the minimum amount of certification test required to achieve the desired level of confidence in a level of failure intensity as

$$t = \frac{T_N}{\lambda_F} \tag{5.2}$$

where t is the amount of test in natural or clock time units, T_N is the normalized measure (number of MTTF's), and λ_F is the failure intensity objective in natural or clock time units. We determine the normalized measure T_N from

$$T_N = \frac{\ln (\text{ß}/(1 - \alpha))}{1 - \gamma)} \tag{5.3}$$

where α is the producer risk, ß is the consumer risk, and γ is the discrimination ratio.

The optimum allocation of test time between feature test and load test is not currently known. It may be that the percentage of time allocated to feature test should decrease as the failure intensity objective decreases (stringent failure intensity objectives require more load test).

5.6.2   Invoking tests

You should exclude data cleanup operations from the process of random selection of operations if they are selected at fixed intervals. Note that some *are* selected at random times.

If your regression test suite consists of only some of your feature test cases, it is desirable to rotate them, preferably by selecting them randomly. Then you are not only checking the operation of previously working code, but you may also be flushing out new failures.

Note that random selection of test cases doesn't imply lack of control or lack of a strategy. Bias usually relates to time. Data corruption increases with the length of time between reinitializations, for example, so that if you always execute one operation early and another late, your tests may miss significant failure behavior. You might counter data corruption bias by reinitializing at random times.

Random selection is feasible for test cases with input variables that are not difficult to change. However, some input variables can be very difficult and expensive to change, such as those that represent characteristics of a hardware configuration. In this case, you must select some input variables deterministically because changing variables during system test must be scheduled. Carefully consider the bias that might result from those you select deterministically and try to counter it.

If there appears to be an unusual number of failures for an *operation,* this *may* indicate that it has even more potential failures. If other information (for example, project history of poor design, many changes, complexity, an inexperienced designer, poorly defined requirements, poor project communication, etc., related to the operation) confirms this hypothesis, you may wish to increase the test occurrence probability for the operation. Be careful that you have solid information before you do this.

5.6.3   Counting failures

Sometimes you must carefully consider whether and how to count certain failures and the rationale for the guidelines you apply.

First, you may deliberately decide not to repair the fault causing a failure. The failure impact may not be severe. The cost of distributing the fix may be high. There can be schedule pressures. A *deliberate* decision not to fix a fault is really a redefinition of the system requirements. You are now saying that the associated failure(s) can be accepted. Hence, you should not count them. There is one exception to this rule. If the failures will still be counted in the field, obviously you are *not* redefining the system requirements.

Second, people often ask how to handle multiple failures associated with the same fault. These can occur at the same site or at different sites. They occur because you have not removed the fault underlying the failure. Do not count them in test because the failure resolution

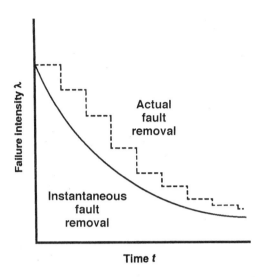

Figure 5.1 Actual failure intensity compared to instant repair failure intensity.

process has been set in motion, and reduction in failure intensity of some sort has been assured. The multiple failures would not occur if you removed the fault instantaneously.

Figure 5.1 illustrates the effect of delay in removing faults. Such a delay can be the result of the normal process involved in identifying and removing the fault. Alternatively, it may result from a deliberate policy of holding the installation of changes for a later software release. Instantaneous fault removal yields the failure intensity curve shown by the solid line. The dashed line indicates the actual failure intensity plot that results from delaying the removal of faults. The offset of the plot to the right is due to the delay between failure identification and the associated fault removal. The discontinuous, stepped effect results from the grouping of fault corrections into builds. The horizontal length of the steps varies with the delay time for installation of the changes. The vertical height of the steps varies with the number of fault removals being delayed and their effect on failure intensity.

When we do not count multiple failures associated with the same fault, we obtain a failure intensity estimate based on unknown remaining faults rather than all remaining faults. This is a better indicator of progress and status if fault removal action is going on. Thus, if you are in the test phase, it is probably best *not* to count the recurrences. Because testing is in practice a fairly centralized and controlled activity, it is generally not difficult to recognize failures associated with the same fault.

On the other hand, in the operational phase, it probably is best to count *all* failures. You generally make repairs at the test site, batch them, and deliver them in a new release. A release may remain in operation for a period of a few weeks to 2 or 3 years. It makes sense to measure what users actually experience over the life of the release. It is generally not practical to try to identify and "eliminate" failures associated with the same fault anyway. Operational personnel generally have less system knowledge than testers and may not recognize the associated failures. Furthermore, we usually install the system at multiple sites. Communication between sites is usually not good enough for most of the associated failures to be jointly identified. Finally, documentation of the failures is usually not thorough enough for the "elimination" to be done at the central site with high confidence.

Suppose you want to obtain data during test on the effect of different operational profiles on failure intensity. Then the counting of repeated failures during test will be significant. You must partition the testing, and the selection of runs for each partition must be representative of the corresponding operational profile. Alternatively, the test and operational profiles could differ, if enough information were available to permit adjustment of the results.

Third, some failures may result from defects in the *tools* used to design and develop a system. This is not a common occurrence. It can occur when you develop tools in parallel with or only slightly ahead of the systems you will use them on. Examples are compilers (for software) or computer-aided design/computer-aided manufacturing (CAD/CAM) systems (for hardware). Consider the final use of the tool for the product before delivery. If the tool is expected to be reliable, do not count these failures when making estimates of failure intensity or reliability. If it will probably still be unreliable, you may wish to make your estimates twice. Include the tool-caused failures in one and exclude them in the other. You will then have a range of failure intensities or reliabilities. The extreme values will represent a reliable tool and an unreliable one.

Fourth, there may be some question of what a failure is in fault-tolerant systems. Fault-tolerant systems include design features (either hardware or software, but frequently software) that counter the effects of hardware or software faults. We can view fault-tolerant software as software that we design to respond specially to deviations from expected behavior of the system.

Software is called *hardware-fault-tolerant* or *software-fault-tolerant* in accordance with the faults that cause the deviations it defends against. Note that a malfunction of a fault-tolerant feature, which is a requirement that a system defend against certain faults, is a failure. Two common fault-tolerant techniques applied to software are audits

and recovery blocks.* The extra code needed for fault tolerance introduced additional faults into the system that you must find and remove,
increasing the development time and costs. Fault tolerance also adds
operational overhead.

Data in a system can degrade with time as they are affected by deviations. Once a deviation occurs, the deviations it causes on the same
run are not counted as additional deviations, but they may degrade the
data. The effect is that later runs are made with input states that are
different from what they otherwise would have been. One frequent
attribute of software-fault-tolerant systems is that they constrain what
the outputs resulting from all or some of such "degraded" input states
can be. Thus, such systems are, in effect, more tightly and broadly specified than are systems without such tolerance.

5.7 Problems

5.1 We have decided that during feature test we will invoke our test cases in
precisely the same order that we have created and stored them so that we do
not miss any of them. We have them ordered so that all the test cases for the
most frequently occurring operation are first, second most frequently occurring, second, etc. Will this work well? If not, why not?

5.2 In the armored amphibious vehicle system we discussed in Problem 3.4, we
expect that 20 percent of the use will be by trainees and 80 percent by veterans.
The vehicles will be used on land 90 percent of the time, in the water, 10 percent. We expect to have 200 h for system load test. How should this be divided?

5.3 We started our system at 1 p.m. and recorded failures occurring at 2, 3,
and 4 p.m. The computer utilizations during these 3 h of operation were respectively, 0.3, 0.5, and 0.7. What are the adjusted failure times?

---

*For a thorough survey of this topic, see Anderson and Lee (1981). A method of relia-
bility modeling of recovery blocks is given in Laprie (1984).

6

Applying Failure Data to Guide Decisions

You will apply the failure data collected for each system separately. There are several decisions it can help you make, listed here in the approximate chronological order they occur during development:

1. Accepting or rejecting an acquired component

2. Guiding your software development process for the product and its variations

3. Accepting or rejecting a supersystem

4. Releasing a product

Decision 1 and 3 are made by the use of certification test, so we will discuss them in the context of that activity, as described in Sec. 6.1.

Decision 2 is actually a type of decision that is usually made a number of times. You will apply Decision 2 to software you are developing; if you are just integrating components to develop the product, this decision is not relevant. Decision 2 includes two subdecisions:

1. Guiding process changes

2. Prioritizing failures for resolution

To guide process changes, you will use the estimate of present total (based on all severity classes) failure intensity and its trend that is made during reliability growth test, as discussed in Sec. 6.2. You prioritize failures for resolution based on their impact, which depends on their severity class and their frequency. To do this, assign a metric with different values corresponding to each failure severity class and multiply the metric by the frequency of occurrence of the failure. For example, if cost impact is your criterion for defining failure severity classes, use the average per failure cost for each failure severity class as your metric.

We will discuss Decision 4 as part of reliability growth test in Sec. 6.2.

6.1 Certification Test

Certification test uses a reliability demonstration chart (Musa, Iannino, and Okumoto, 1987), illustrated in Fig. 6.1. It is based on sequential sampling theory, which is particularly efficient in the sense of giving a result at the earliest possible time (smallest possible sample). Certification test requires that you have units measured at the

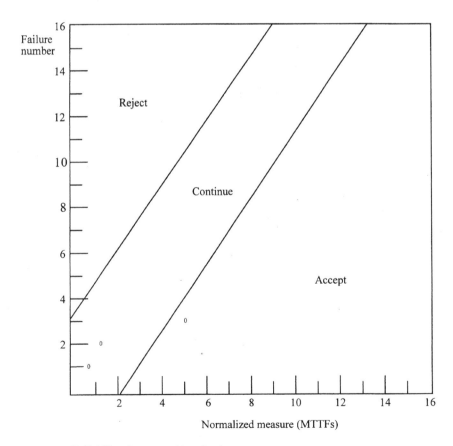

Figure 6.1 Reliability demonstration chart.

point at which failures occurred; number of failures in an interval of units (grouped data) will not work. Normalize the failure data by multiplying by the failure intensity objective in the same units. This in effect expresses the measure in terms of number of mean times to failure (MTTFs).

Plot each failure on the chart as it occurs. Depending on the region in which it falls, you may accept or reject the software being tested or continue testing. The particular chart you use will depend on

1. The *discrimination ratio,* or the factor of error in estimating failure intensity you are willing to accept (2 for Fig. 6.1)

2. The *consumer risk* level, or the probability you are willing to accept of falsely saying the failure intensity objective is met when it is not (0.1 for Fig. 6.1)

3. The *supplier risk* level, or the probability you are willing to accept of falsely saying the failure intensity objective is not met when it is (0.1 for Fig. 6.1)

When risk levels and/or the discrimination ratio decrease, the continue region becomes larger. In that case, it requires more testing before you can reach either the accept or reject region. Charts for other risk levels and discrimination ratios are provided in Sec. 6.3.3, as are formulas for constructing charts for any discrimination ratio, consumer risk level, and supplier risk level.

Taken together, the discrimination ratio and risk levels may be interpreted as follows (for the case of Fig. 6.1, for example):

1. There is a 10 percent risk of wrongly accepting the software when its failure intensity is actually equal to or greater than twice the failure intensity objective.

2. There is a 10 percent risk of wrongly rejecting the software when its failure intensity is equal to or less than half the failure intensity objective.

Consider the case of Fone Follower. We have decided to conduct certification test on the operating system, which has a failure intensity objective of four failures per million calls. The first three failures occur as shown in Table 6.1. They are plotted in Fig. 6.1. The first two occur in the continue region and the third in the accept region. Thus we can accept the operating system at the third failure.

One might ask if, in certification test, there can be a case where you never leave the continue region on the reliability demonstration chart. This is of course possible, but it is unlikely because it would require the

TABLE 6.1   Failures in Certification Test of
Operating System for Fone Follower

Failure number	Measure (million calls)	Normalized measure (MTTFs)
1	0.1875	0.75
2	0.3125	1.25
3	1.25	5

failure intensity to continually increase. Consider the case of a constant actual failure intensity that is equal to the failure intensity objective λ_F. Failures would occur at $1/\lambda_F$, $2/\lambda_F$, ... The normalized failure times would be 1, 2, ... Note that these times will eventually leave the continue region. The plot of these lines has a somewhat lesser slope than the lower boundary of the continue region. For example, the tenth failure, which occurs at a normalized time of 10, lies in the accept region.

Note that you can actually accept or reject the software as soon as you cross the accept or reject boundary and need not wait until another failure occurs. Thus, in the case of Fig. 6.1, you could accept at the intersection of the failure 2 line and the accept boundary (a normalized measure of 3.7), even though the third failure has not yet occurred. Similarly, if the software ran from the start without failure for a normalized failure time of 2, you could accept it.

If you reach the end of your certification test period without leaving the continue region, you should compute a demonstrable failure intensity to failure intensity objective (FI/FIO) ratio as a guide to what to do. The demonstrable FI/FIO ratio indicates the normalized failure intensity that has been demonstrated at the levels of discrimination ratio, consumer risk, and supplier risk that were selected for the reliability demonstration chart. The demonstrable FI/FIO ratio $\tilde{\lambda}_D$ is given by

$$\tilde{\lambda}_D = \frac{T_N(n)}{t_t \lambda_F} \tag{6.1}$$

where $T_N(n)$ is the normalized measure for the continue-accept boundary at the number of failures that have been experienced, t_t is the number of natural or time units at the end of test, and λ_F is the failure intensity objective. Note that $T_N(n)$ is given by Eq. (6.4).

If the certification test is for components, continue test only if no failures have occurred and if the demonstrable FI/FIO ratio is large (perhaps greater than 5). Continuing the certification test is only worthwhile if there is a good chance of proving the acceptability of an unknown component that might otherwise hold considerable risk for the project. If the demonstrable FI/FIO ratio is large and failures have occurred, consider rejecting the component. If the demonstrable FI/FIO ratio is not large, accept the component.

If the certification test is for the product or product variations, if failures have occurred, and if the demonstrable FI/FIO ratio is large, the chances of the software being accepted with further certification test are not good. Hence you should return to reliability growth test, if it was previously used (it may not have been if the product is constructed by integrating acquired components). You then remove the faults that are causing the failures you identify until you reach an FI/FIO ratio of 0.5. Otherwise continue certification test.

If the certification test is for supersystems, if you have accepted the product, and if the demonstrable FI/FIO is reasonable (perhaps not more than 2 or 3), end the test. Otherwise, continue.

There are no known practical limits to the size of components or systems tested in certification test, either minimum or maximum.

If certification test fails and a software component is rejected, you should retest it if it is later resubmitted. You may want to review what has been done to improve the component's reliability before undertaking the effort to retest it.

6.2   Reliability Growth Test

In reliability growth test, we make periodic estimates of the FI/FIO ratio, based on failure data. The periods depend on how frequently you want to assess progress toward the failure intensity objective and take actions based on that assessment. Some approximate guidelines for the frequency for applying failure data are noted in Table 6.2.

We use a reliability estimation program that is based on software reliability models and statistical inference to make the FI/FIO estimates. Two of the generally known, widely distributed programs are SMERFS (Farr and Smith, 1992) and CASRE (Nikora, 1994). CASRE is built on top of SMERFS, adding a convenient graphical user interface with pull-down menus, dialog boxes, etc. You can obtain SMERFS from its developers. CASRE is distributed on CD-ROM as part of the *Handbook of Software Reliability Engineering* (Lyu, 1996).

TABLE 6.2   Guidelines for Frequency for
Executing Software Reliability Engineering
Estimation Program

Length of test remaining	Frequency of application of data
<1 month	Daily
1–3 months	Semiweekly
>3 months	Weekly

SMERFS developers are currently building a graphical interface for SMERFS. CASRE developers are planning a simplified interface for CASRE (the current one was designed for researchers, but practitioners can use it with guidance). The goal of both efforts is to provide a simple interface for practitioner users that will only present options they are expected to use. The more complex capabilities required by researchers will generally be hidden from practitioners to simplify use of the programs. Users have also requested that the normalized failure intensity (FI/FIO ratio) and its 50, 70, 90, and 95 percent confidence intervals be directly computed and displayed. Information on these new programs will be provided on the Software Reliability Engineering web site (Musa, 1997h) when it is available. If they are made available for distribution on the Internet, hypertext links to the sites from which you can download them will be included. Meanwhile, the current version of CASRE is arguably the most convenient readily accessible software reliability estimation program. Hence, simplified instructions for installing and executing it are in App. F; and an overview of its operation is presented here.

CASRE will accept either the number of units accumulated at each point at which a failure occurred or the number of failures in an interval of units since the last failure or since the start of test. You can have either natural or clock time units. You should first normalize the natural or time units by multiplying by the failure intensity objective in the same units. This is easily done by CASRE, as explained in App. F. The units are now expressed in the number of MTTFs. For example, you might have a failure occurring at four MTTFs or you might have three failures occurring in two MTTFs.

When executing CASRE, you run the logarithmic (Musa-Okumoto) and exponential (Musa Basic) models. The models get their names from the shapes of the plots of the mean value functions of the random processes that describe the failure behavior (logarithmic or exponential). The exponential model assumes that you will experience finite failures in infinite time; the logarithmic model assumes infinite failures. The exponential model tends to be optimistic (low) in estimating the FI/FIO ratio, sometimes choosing too small a finite number of failures. The logarithmic model tends to be pessimistic (high). Thus use of one model may be unsatisfactory. On the other hand, the two models tend to bound the extremes of behavior (finite and infinite failures). Hence one of them almost always provides a good fit. In practice you experience sharply diminishing returns with more than two models; the extra effort required to learn and use them simply isn't worth it. In using the two models, you evaluate goodness of fit to the data and choose the model that fits best. One might think of combining the two models in some way, but there is not convincing evidence that this would be worth the added complexity. There is a thorough discussion of models and the reasons for selecting the two applied here in Chap. 8.

Statisticians may object to changing models during the course of testing. Changing really is not unreasonable because with our present lack of much knowledge, the basis for initial choice is not well established. If and when it becomes so, we may want to disallow changes.

The output we will use from CASRE is the Next step prediction (see App. F), which will be in MTTFs when we have normalized the failure data as described above. Invert it to obtain the normalized failure intensity or FI/FIO ratio. Sometimes the Next step prediction is not available. This occurs when neither model detects any reliability growth. In this case, there is an alternative way to obtain the FI/FIO ratio; see App. F for details. Plot the FI/FIO ratio against time so that you can clearly see trends.

Accuracy of estimation of the FI/FIO ratio depends on the number of failures experienced (i.e., the sample size). Good results in estimating failure intensity are generally experienced for programs with 5000 or more developed source lines and satisfactory results are obtained for programs with 1000 or more developed source lines. During the period when only feature or feature and regression test have been performed, the FI/FIO estimates will tend to be on the low side because failures caused by the interactions between operations that occur during load test will not be happening. This error will usually have become minimal by the time the FI/FIO ratio approaches 1.

When the FI/FIO ratio is very large and the trend indicates little chance of achieving the failure intensity objective by the scheduled release date, consider taking one or more of the following actions:

1. Adding test and debugging resources
2. Adjusting the balance among the objectives for failure intensity, development time, and development cost
3. Deferring features

When the FI/FIO ratio is greater than 2, inspect the most recent five values to see if they show a steady, substantial upward trend. If they do, determine the causes. Take action if meeting the product objectives is endangered. One possibility is unexpected program evolution (new developed code is being added), in which case you need better change control. The other most common cause is changing test selection probabilities. The latter can happen when some operations receive all their testing first, then another set is tested, etc. Here you need better control of test execution; otherwise, operations that are tested late may yield unpleasant surprises that threaten schedules.

Consider terminating test for the system when normalized failure intensity drops to 0.5 or less. We use 0.5 rather than 1 as the criterion because the estimate of normalized failure intensity has a range of uncertainty, and we want to compensate for this. A somewhat more precise approach would be to compute the pth percent confidence limit for normalized failure intensity and release the system when that value reached the failure intensity objective. For example, if you computed the 90 percent confidence limit and released the system when that value reached the failure intensity objective, you would have a system that met its failure intensity objective with 90 percent confidence. The present version of CASRE does not compute confidence limits; hence we use an approximate approach that assumes that the 90 percent confidence interval for failure intensity near release is approximately equal to the failure intensity and thus extends from 0.5 to 1.5 times the failure intensity.

Consider releasing the product when you have

1. Terminated test satisfactorily for the product

2. Terminated test satisfactorily for all the product variations or the FI/FIO ratios for these variations don't appreciably exceed 0.5

3. Accepted the product and its variations in any acceptance test rehearsals planned for them

4. Accepted all supersystems

We say "consider" because you must always be alert for factors that cannot be reduced to numbers. For example, if there are any outstanding severe failures that have not yet been resolved (faults causing them found and removed), you would not release a product.

Appendix F presents a "walk-through" example for Fone Follower. Try it with CASRE on your personal computer. As you do so, you will observe several interesting points as you retrace the test history for the project:

1. At 10 failures, we can't detect any reliability growth. Using the alternative method for estimating the FI/FIO ratio, we obtain 15.4. This value is acceptable for early test.

2. At 11 failures, we detect reliability growth and obtain an FI/FIO ratio of 12.0.

3. At 29 failures, the FI/FIO ratio is 1.92. We find at 30, 31, 32, 33, and 34 failures, respectively, FI/FIO ratios of 2.06, 2.20, 2.38, 2.61, and 3.08. Note the significant, steady upward movement. When checking the cause, we found program evolution due to inadequate

change control. New features had been added to the program without the knowledge of the testers, introducing new faults and hence increasing the failure intensity.

4. At 68 failures, the FI/FIO ratio is 1.91. Continue testing.

5. At 92 failures, the FI/FIO ratio is 0.93. We do not assume that the failure intensity objective has been achieved because of the uncertainty in the estimate.

6. At 93 failures, after a long time interval from the previous failure, we find that the FI/FIO ratio is 0.44. We can assume that we have achieved the failure intensity objective with a small amount of risk.

In addition to meeting the failure intensity objective, a common exit criterion for release of a product from system test is that all outstanding severity 1 and 2 failures have been resolved. This generally means that you don't release a system with unresolved failures that affect customers substantially unless the failures have workarounds. Sometimes, it is also required that resolution dates for outstanding severity 3 (and perhaps 4) failures be established.

6.3   Special Situations

Programs may evolve in size as you test them. You may not observe some failures. Finally, you may wish to conduct your certification test at different risk levels and/or discrimination ratios than those we have described. These topics are all discussed in this section.

6.3.1   Evolving programs

Reliability models used in estimating failure intensity during reliability growth test assume that the program being executed is stable (not changing, except for those changes that result from failure correction). This is often not the case in reality. Programs can evolve due to either requirements changes or integration of parts during development. Requirements changes may occur to provide enhancement of the features of the system or to respond to competition, changing customer needs, and other factors. They may be necessary for adaptation of the system to changing hardware and software. Frequently the latter changes occur because of the opportunity to reduce operating costs provided by technological progress. Finally, a project may change requirements to provide necessary or desirable system performance improvement. Such improvement might involve redesign for faster operation or program restructuring to improve maintainability (ease with which program can permit future evolution). Evolution also occurs naturally as part of the development process itself. It is quite common to test a system as it is integrated. Because evolution is essentially independent of the failure correction process, we must deal with it separately.

If programs are evolving slowly and in small size increments (increments of less than 5 percent of total code per week), experience indicates that you can usually ignore the evolution. Estimates of model parameters and FI/FIO ratios will lag the true situation and be somewhat in error, but the range of errors will generally be acceptable.

The continual reestimation of model parameters and FI/FIO ratios, based on the latest data, will reflect the fact that they are changing due to program change. The estimates will be somewhat in error because we are making them by combining data from the execution of slightly different programs. Because you are weighting recent data most heavily, the error will not be substantial unless the program is changing rapidly. The obvious advantage of this approach is that no extra data collection or other effort is required.

As an extreme example of what happens when change is ignored, on one project code changes were introduced in a system amounting to about 21 percent of the total system size. The project personnel applied the basic execution time model to the failure data they collected. The actual total failures parameter (expected failures in infinite time) for the system increased immediately and discontinuously when the new code was added. However, the estimates of the total failures parameter lagged the change at first and then tended to overshoot by about 20 percent before settling down to a stable value. Similarly, the FI/FIO ratio increased sharply, overshot, and then stabilized. Except for the transition period, the behavior was quite robust with respect to even large program changes.

For a sudden and substantial change, you might consider discarding all the data on the old phase of the program. You would base estimates on the new phase only. The disadvantage (a strong one) of this approach is the sometimes substantial period of time that can elapse before a large enough sample of data is again in hand to make estimates of reasonable accuracy. The old data, when combined with the new, often yield a better estimate than no data at all. Whether you should discard old data depends on the size of the design change being made.

The more substantial evolution that you can and must deal with occurs in steps and falls into two general categories:

1. Component by component

2. Operation group by operation group

The approaches for dealing with this stepwise evolution require that the failure intensities of the elements (components or operation groups) be independent of each other. First you estimate the separate failure intensities of the elements that exist at each stage of integration. Then if the program is evolving component by component, and all components must work for the program to work, you add the appropriate component failure intensities separately to obtain the system failure intensity at each stage. For example, suppose you estimate the current failure intensities of independent components A and B as 15 and 20 failures per 1000 h, respectively. The failure intensity of the system would be 35 failures per 1000 h.

If the program is evolving operation group by operation group (i.e., a set of related operations is added, then another, etc.), take the weighted sum of the operation group failure intensities for the operation groups that exist at the stage in question, with the weight for each operation group taken as the sum of the occurrence probabilities of its operations.

For example, assume operation group A has a failure intensity of 5 failures per 1000 h and operation failure group B has a failure intensity of 10 failures per 1000 h. The occurrence probabilities for the operations in A total 0.6 and for B they are 0.4. Then the system failure intensity is given by $0.6(5) + 0.4(10) = 7$ failures per 1000 h.

You can theoretically extend these approaches to any number of elements. However, the increasing complexity of data collection and processing restricts the number in practice. Also, the quality of statistical estimation may suffer at some point if the elements become too small to yield good samples of failures. Hence, the stepwise evolution approaches generally work best when you have a small number of large changes, each resulting from the addition of an independent element. One example of this situation is that of an application program added to an operating system to implement a particular set of features.

The disadvantages of the stepwise evolution approaches are

1. The extra data collection required because of the multiple elements
2. Greater estimation error (or later achievement of a specified degree of accuracy) due to smaller sample sizes

There are two additional situations that are analogous to program evolution and can be handled in the same way:

1. A program is fully integrated, but it is tested in an evolutionary fashion. One component or operation group is turned on, then another, then another, and so on.

2. A program is fully integrated and active, but the observation of the components for failures is handled in an evolutionary fashion. You start with a narrow focus of observation and then widen it component by component or operation group by operation group. This can happen when new failure diagnosis tools (usually diagnostic software) are added at intervals during test.

One clue to the presence of program evolution or an analogous situation is a sharp upward trend in failure intensity that persists for several failures.

A summary of approaches, the situations to which each is best suited, and the advantages and disadvantages of each are given in Table 6.3.

6.3.2 Unreported failures

There are many situations where some failures may not be reported, especially those that occur in the field. This occurs most frequently with less severe failures and particularly with failures that do not stop the execution of the program. Incidentally, note that you can miss reporting failures in hardware just as easily as in software systems. Sometimes you observe failures but don't report them; sometimes you never observe them. You can decrease the proportion of unreported failures through training, efforts to motivate the personnel in question, and devoting more effort to checking program output. However, you probably can't reduce the proportion to zero.

There may be more failures missed in load test than in feature or regression test. The latter tests involve individual test cases run independently, with all of the input variables known. Thus you can determine what the output variables should be. You can check them

TABLE 6.3   Approaches to Handling Evolving Systems

Approach	Best area of application	Advantages	Disadvantages
Component by component	Small number of components, each independent	Failure intensity of each component known, making adjustments to different use easier	Extra data collection, lower estimation accuracy
Operation group by operation group	Operational development	System operational profiles apply directly	Extra data collection, lower estimation accuracy
Ignoring change	Many small changes	Simple, minimum effort	Estimation transients

carefully, either by hand or with output checkers. Hence, with care, you will observe most of the failures. Load tests involve indirect input variables. It is often not practical to determine how these variables will affect the output variables. Thus you may not know exactly what the output state should be. You must rely on applying your knowledge, based on the system requirements, that certain output variables outside certain ranges of values are unacceptable. Thus with care you will observe most of the failures, but you may miss some.

The fact that some failures are not reported means that in general you will underestimate failure intensity. The saving grace is that ordinarily the users miss more failures than the system testers. In other words, underestimation of failure intensity by the system test personnel is less than that by users. Thus, the users will generally think the system is more reliable than the system testers do. This will be the case if the observation and reporting difference is greater than the change of environment in going from test to operation. Occasionally it may happen that things look worse in the field. If so, this may be due to poor system test planning. If system test doesn't represent the conditions that will be encountered in the field, indeed you may see an increase in failure intensity when the program is released. This increase occurs when the effect of the change in environment is greater than the pseudo "improvement" you see because the customers are not observing some of the failures.

If you think it is desirable to adjust for unreported failures, you can. However, it is a bit of a risky endeavor. You need good data on a similar project that indicate the proportion of failures that you miss. To find out how many failures you miss, you have to do a comprehensive analysis of the history of failure observations. You don't know how many you missed until they are ultimately found. So it is best to do this on a project with a long operational history. You would look for "late" failures that "must" have occurred earlier and been missed. You might be able to infer earlier occurrence if you know that the same input states were exercised earlier during the operational history.

Some projects use correction reports as well as trouble or failure reports. Correction reports close out failure reports for which repairs have been made and note the program changes. Other projects have reports of program changes available from automated configuration control systems. One might think that comparison of failure reports with correction reports could yield valuable clues about missing reports of failures. Unfortunately, they do not indicate the total proportion of unreported failures. They only represent failures that have been observed and fixed but not reported for some reason.

You should be careful to ascertain whether unreported failures are significant. The fact that they are not reported *may* be a clue to a misunderstanding between developer and user about what the system requirements really are. A large proportion of unreported failures may indicate that inadequate attention has been given in system design to failure recording functions and procedures. This can particularly be a problem for unattended systems.

Tools may be necessary to help locate failures if the output of a system is voluminous. This requires identification of patterns of output variables that establish failure. However, you must exercise special care for failures identified by automated reporting systems. Because you must program these systems to recognize what behaviors constitute failures, there is a substantial risk that you will miss some failures. Frequently, the unexpected failures are the most significant ones; if they were known, you might have eliminated them in the design.

Let us consider how unreported failures affect failure intensity estimates in reliability growth test. The basic and logarithmic Poisson execution time models will be used to investigate the effects at various times during testing.

We applied the basic execution time model to an actual software project for which we believed that we missed some proportion (increasing with time) of failures. Project personnel indicated that after they tested a function, they paid less attention to looking for failures associated with it, and therefore they may have missed some failures. Also a good portion of the latter data was collected by the end user of the product, who paid less attention to program behavior. Thus a higher proportion of failures probably was missed. The results for this project suggested that the model tended to underpredict the failure intensity.* In the following we present results that emanate from these observations.

Denote the probability that the ith failure goes unnoticed as $P(i)$. Many forms for $P(i)$ are possible, but for simplicity we consider only the linear case (Fig. 6.2), that is,

$$P(i) = p_1 + \frac{i}{a}(p_2 - p_1) \qquad i < a$$

$$= p_2 i \geq a \qquad\qquad (6.2)$$

At the start of system test the probability of not observing any particular failure will be p_1. As testing progresses, this probability changes linearly to its final value of p_2. The rate of change is governed by the constant a. When p_2 is set equal to p_1, the proportion of missed failures is constant throughout the test phase.

---

*This is entirely reasonable because the number of failures observed is less than normal. It appears that fewer failures are occurring in the same amount of time, thus, the lower failure intensity.

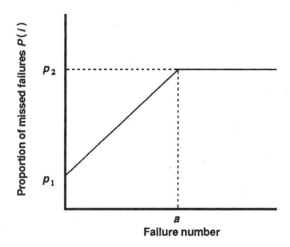

Figure 6.2 Probability that ith failure goes unreported.

6.3.2.1 Basic execution time model. The *expected* failure intensity at execution time τ for the basic execution time model is given by

$$\lambda(\tau) = \nu_0 \phi B \exp\left(-\phi B \tau\right) \tag{6.3}$$

We conducted simulations to see how closely the *estimated* failure intensity at time τ followed the value given by Eq. (6.3) when we missed failures according to Eq. (6.2). The model parameters used in the following simulations were $\nu_0 = 250$ failures, $\phi = 0.005$/s, and $B = 1$. We generated 1000 different failure time sequences for this model. Then, we removed failures with probability given by Eq. (6.2). For each resulting failure time sequence, we determined $\lambda(\tau)$ and the ratio of $\hat{\lambda}(\tau)$ to $\lambda(\tau)$ at various values of τ. Finally, we calculated the average value of this ratio, using the results of all 1000 failure time sequences. Values of this ratio near 1 tell us that our estimation is about what is expected. Values less than 1 indicate an underestimation, and values greater than 1 indicate an overestimation. We repeated this entire process for different values of p_1 and p_2.

Figure 6.3 shows how the ratio varied with τ for some different values of (p_1, p_2). Because we selected the unreported failures randomly, you can observe some noise in the ratio as a function of execution time. The results show that

1. If $P(i)$ is constant ($p_1 = p_2$), estimates for failure intensity are low.*

---

*We would expect the value of the ratio to be about equal to $1-p$, because this is the fraction of failures actually observed. The data do bear this out.

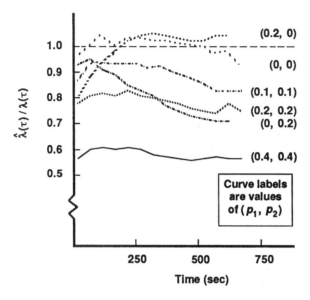

Figure 6.3   Effect of unreported failures: estimated-actual failure intensity ratio for basic execution time model.

2. If $P(i)$ increases with time, the estimate for failure intensity is low and becomes lower still as time passes.

3. If $P(i)$ decreases with time, the estimate for failure intensity is initially low but becomes better as time passes.

In summary, you can apply a simple correction [just divide by $(1-p_1)$] to the estimated failure intensity if the proportion of missed failures does not change over time. When the proportion decreases over time, you can do one of two things. First, you can ignore the problem because the missed early failures do not significantly affect estimates made later. The second option is to divide the estimated failure intensity by the current probability of observing a failure. This option is only feasible if you can estimate the current probability. When the proportion increases over time, care must be exercised. Here the missed failures occur late during testing, and they are the ones having the greatest impact on the estimated failure intensity.*

6.3.2.2   Logarithmic Poisson execution time model.   We conducted the same simulations using a logarithmic Poisson execution time model with $\theta = 0.05$ per failure and $\lambda_0 = 0.005$ failure per second. Figure 6.4

---

*In all this we are assuming that the missed failures do not constitute an implicit redefinition of what a failure really is.

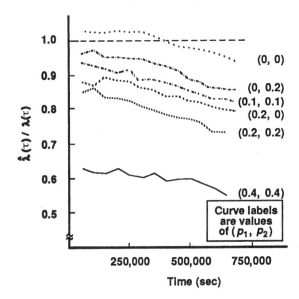

Figure 6.4 Effect of unobserved failures: estimated-actual failure intensity ratio for logarithmic Poisson execution time model.

shows how the ratio of $\hat\lambda(\tau)$ to $\lambda(\tau)$ varied with τ for some different values of (p_1, p_2). Again, you can observe some noise in the ratio as a function of execution time. The results show that the estimated failure intensity is low under a broad range of conditions. For a constant $P(i)$, dividing the estimated failure intensity by $1-p_1$ will result in values not far from those obtained when all failures are observed. The correction here is not as good as that for the basic model.

6.3.3   Certification test at different risk levels and discrimination ratios

All charts have the same general shape but differ in the boundaries between the reject and continue and continue and accept regions. These boundary lines are given by

$$T_N = \frac{A - n \ln \gamma}{1 - \gamma} \tag{6.4}$$

and

$$T_N = \frac{B - n \ln \gamma}{1 - \gamma} \tag{6.5}$$

where T_N is the normalized measure of when failures occur (horizontal coordinate), n is the failure number, γ is the discrimination ratio or the ratio of the maximum acceptable failure intensity to the failure intensity objective, and A and B are given by

$$A = \ln \frac{\text{ß}}{1-\alpha} \qquad (6.6)$$

and

$$B = \ln \frac{1-\text{ß}}{\alpha} \qquad (6.7)$$

Note that α is the supplier risk (probability of falsely saying objective is not met when it is) and ß is the consumer risk (probability of falsely saying objective is met when it is not). For typically occurring values of α and ß, Eq. 6.4 defines the boundary between the accept and continue regions and Eq. 6.5 defines the boundary between the continue and reject regions.

To construct the chart, note that the intercepts of the boundaries with the horizontal line at $n = 0$ are given by

$$T_N(0) = \frac{A}{1 - \gamma} \qquad T_N(0) = \frac{B}{1 - \gamma} \qquad (6.8)$$

and with the horizontal line at $n = 16$ they are given by

$$T_N(16) = \frac{A - 16 \ln \gamma}{1 - \gamma} \qquad T_N(16) = \frac{B - 16 \ln \gamma}{1 - \gamma} \qquad (6.9)$$

The intercepts of the boundaries with the vertical line at $T_N = 0$ are given by

$$n(0) = \frac{A}{\ln \gamma} \qquad n(0) = \frac{B}{\ln \gamma} \qquad (6.10)$$

and with the vertical line at $T_N = 16$ they are given by

$$n(16) = \frac{A - 16(1 - \gamma)}{\ln \gamma} \qquad n(16) = \frac{B - 16(1 - \gamma)}{\ln \gamma} \qquad (6.11)$$

We will construct charts for discrimination ratios $\gamma = 2, 1.5, 1.1$. Equations 6.8 through 6.11 yield the values shown in Table 6.4. The values of A and B for various supplier and consumer risk levels are given in Table 6.5.

When producer and consumer risks are symmetric, note that $\alpha = \text{ß}$ and

$$A = -B = \ln \frac{\alpha}{1 - \alpha} \qquad (6.12)$$

This can be observed in Table 6.5.

Note that A changes rapidly with consumer risk but only very slightly with supplier risk. It determines the intercept of the accept bound-

TABLE 6.4   Values of Intercepts of Boundaries with Various Horizontal and Vertical Lines

	Discrimination ratio γ		
Intercept with	2	1.5	1.1
Horizontal line at $n = 0$	$-A, -B$	$-2A, -2B$	$-10A, -10B$
Horizontal line at $n = 16$	$-A + 11.1, -B + 11.1$	$-2A + 13.0, -2B + 13.0$	$-10A + 15.2, -10B + 15.2$
Vertical line at $T_N = 0$	$1.44\,A, 1.44\,B$	$2.47\,A, 2.47\,B$	$10.5\,A, 10.5\,B$
Vertical line at $T_N = 16$	$\dfrac{A + 16}{0.693}, \dfrac{B + 16}{0.693}$	$\dfrac{A + 8}{0.405}, \dfrac{B + 8}{0.405}$	$\dfrac{A + 1.6}{0.0953}, \dfrac{B + 1.6}{0.0953}$

ary with the horizontal line $n = 0$. Thus the accept boundary changes rapidly with consumer risk but only very slightly with supplier risk.

Similarly, B changes rapidly with supplier risk but only very slightly with consumer risk. It determines the intercept of the reject boundary with the vertical line $T_N = 0$. Thus the reject boundary changes rapidly with supplier risk but only very slightly with consumer risk.

In theory, we should construct reliability demonstration charts based on all combinations of the desired consumer and supplier risks. However, we will take advantage of the "slowly changing" property described above to reduce the number of charts needed. We will construct charts only for symmetric values of consumer and supplier risk and use two charts when the values are asymmetric, which is a satisfactory approximation.

For example, for a given discrimination ratio, if the desired consumer risk level is 0.05, and the desired supplier risk level is 0.1, we will use the chart for consumer risk = 0.05, supplier risk = 0.05 to determine if

TABLE 6.5   Values of A and B for Various Supplier and Consumer Risk Levels

		Consumer risk			
Supplier risk	Parameter	0.1	0.05	0.01	0.001
0.1	A	-2.20	-2.89	-4.50	-6.80
	B	2.20	2.25	2.29	2.30
0.05	A	-2.25	-2.94	-4.55	-6.86
	B	2.89	2.94	2.99	2.99
0.01	A	-2.29	-2.99	-4.60	-6.90
	B	4.50	4.55	4.60	4.60
0.001	A	-2.30	-2.99	-4.60	-6.91
	B	6.80	6.86	6.90	6.91

and when you can accept the system under test (as a practical matter, it is best to choose the chart with the matching consumer risk level). The accept boundary will only be slightly in error, so the effect on acceptance will be minimal. If the plotted failures appear to be moving toward the reject region, switch to the chart for consumer risk = 0.1, supplier risk = 0.1 to determine when the reject boundary is crossed. The reject boundary will also be slightly in error, but the effect will again be minimal.

We have chosen discrimination ratios of 2, 1.5, and 1.2 and symmetric consumer-supplier risk levels of 0.1, 0.05, 0.01, and 0.001 for the charts. We did not construct some charts because one or more boundaries fall off their areas. The charts are provided in Figs. 6.5 through 6.12. Note that the continue region widens as discrimination ratio, consumer risk level, or supplier risk level decrease. Thus it requires more testing, in general, to reach either a reject or accept decision if we want

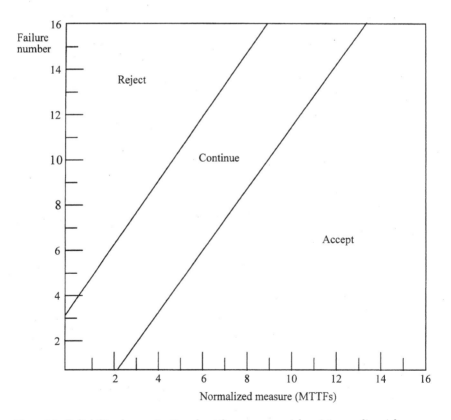

Figure 6.5 Reliability demonstration chart for consumer risk = 0.1, supplier risk = 0.1, discrimination ratio = 2.

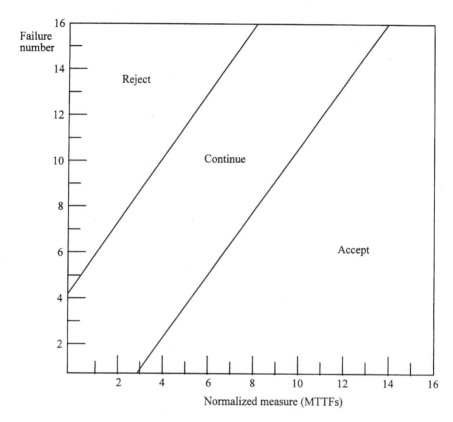

Figure 6.6 Reliability demonstration chart for consumer risk = 0.05, supplier risk = 0.05, discrimination ratio = 2.

to decrease the error we are willing to tolerate in estimating failure intensity or we wish to reduce the risks of making a wrong decision.

6.3.4 Operational profile variation

Suppose that you have estimated the failure intensity of a system undergoing reliability growth test with a particular operational profile. The system is expected to encounter a number of different operational profiles in the field. You wish to determine the effect of these different operational profiles on failure intensity to see if the results are still acceptable with respect to the failure intensity objective.

Posing the problem in mathematical form, you have measured failure intensity λ_D for operational profile p_{Dk}, where p_{Dk} is the occurrence probability for the kth operation. You wish to find the transformation factor Γ that yields the failure intensity λ_M for operational profile p_{Mk} in

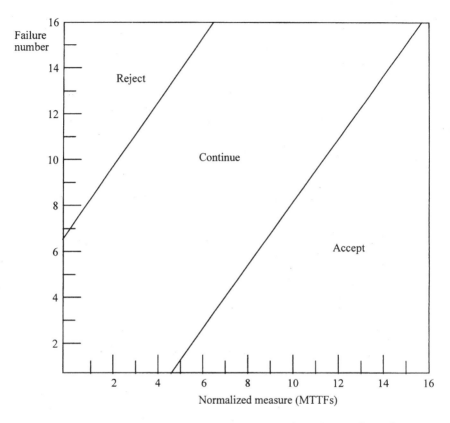

Figure 6.7 Reliability demonstration chart for consumer risk = 0.01, supplier risk = 0.01, discrimination ratio = 2.

$$\lambda_M = \Gamma\lambda_D \qquad (6.13)$$

Note that you do not know the failure intensities of individual operations nor can you measure them with any reasonable degree of accuracy in practice because the number of failures that occur per operation is usually small. Hence you cannot simply adjust the individual operation failure intensities by the ratios of their occurrence probabilities and sum the result. The solution for the problem is given in Musa (1994a):

$$\Gamma = \frac{\displaystyle\sum_{k=1}^{Q_0} p_{Mk}\lambda_k}{\displaystyle\sum_{k=1}^{Q_0} p_{Dk}\lambda_k} \qquad (6.14)$$

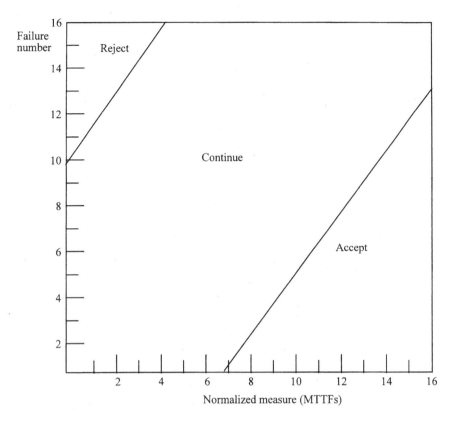

Figure 6.8 Reliability demonstration chart for consumer risk = 0.001, supplier risk = 0.001, discrimination ratio = 2.

where Q_0 is the number of operations, and λ_k depends upon whether the field failure intensity is estimated at the end of test using the exponential or the logarithmic model. The formula assumes that the average run length is independent of operation (if it isn't, there is a correction factor). If estimated with the exponential model

$$\lambda_k = \chi^{-p_{Dk}} \tag{6.15}$$

$$\chi = \exp(\phi\tau_F) \tag{6.16}$$

where ϕ is a parameter of the exponential model, which is estimated in fitting the model to the data, and τ_F is the execution time of test.

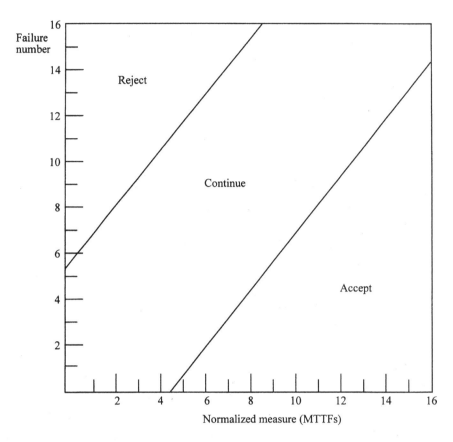

Figure 6.9 Reliability demonstration chart for consumer risk = 0.1, supplier risk = 0.1, discrimination ratio = 1.5.

If estimated with the logarithmic model

$$\lambda_k = \frac{1}{p_{Dk}(\chi - 1) + 1} \tag{6.17}$$

where

$$\chi = \lambda_0 \theta \tau_F + 1 \tag{6.18}$$

and λ_0 and θ are the parameters of the logarithmic model that are estimated when it is fit to the data.

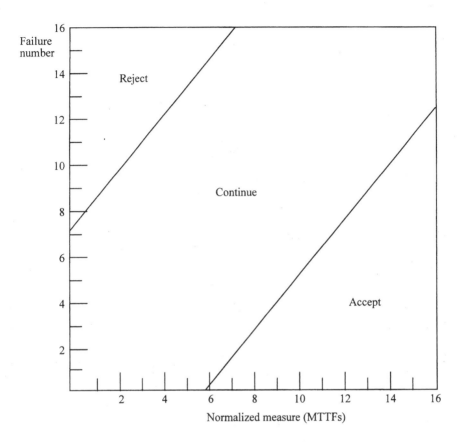

Figure 6.10 Reliability demonstration chart for consumer risk = 0.05, supplier risk = 0.05, discrimination ratio = 1.5.

6.4   Frequently Asked Questions

6.4.1   Theory

1 If a program and its associated data are reloaded, won't this affect the length of the failure interval and hence the accuracy of failure intensity estimates just afterward, because degraded data will be cleaned up by the reload?

ANSWER: Yes, to some extent, *for that particular interval.* Reloads or some other form of data cleanup occur frequently in feature and regression test and much less frequently in load test. Reloads generally occur either just after a failure (to clean up the system) or randomly with respect to failures (routine periodic reloads). For any sample of failures of reasonable size, the effects tend to average out, so the estimation of failure intensities is reasonable, although the averages in feature and regression test may be lower than what you can expect in the field. In any case, we never try to predict *individual* failure intervals. Note

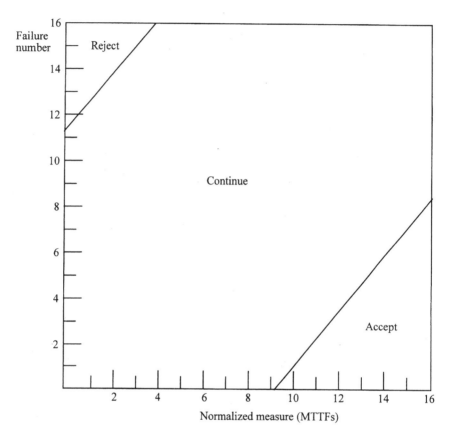

Figure 6.11   Reliability demonstration chart for consumer risk = 0.01, supplier risk = 0.01, discrimination ratio = 1.5.

that if the frequency of reload for load test is substantially different from that expected in the field, this could conceivably result in an estimate of failure intensity that differs substantially from what you will experience in the field.

2   We would like to measure the reliability of our software-based system in operation by simply counting failures per calendar week. Is this valid?

ANSWER: Yes, if the computer utilization is approximately the same from week to week. You will be obtaining the overall system reliability. If you wish just the reliability of the software, you should count only the failures due to software faults. You may find it desirable to measure the computer utilization over the week if you might want to estimate what the failure intensity would be for the same software running under a different computer utilization. Note that the period over which you count failures should not extend past any points at which the software is changed, either by removing faults or adding new features. In such a case, valuable trend information could be lost.

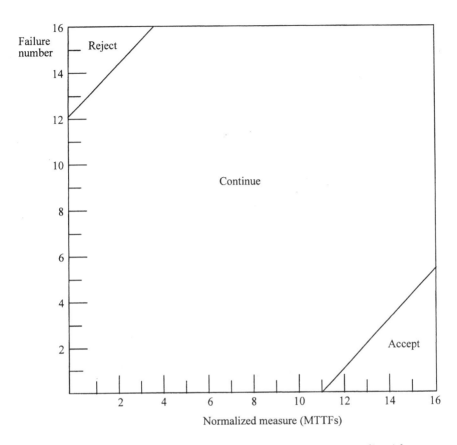

Figure 6.12   Reliability demonstration chart for consumer risk = 0.1, supplier risk = 0.1, discrimination ratio = 1.2.

3   Is there a simple way of modeling the variation in failure intensity that a software product that undergoes many releases experiences in the field?

ANSWER: We illustrate the variation of the failure intensity of a software product through many releases in Fig. 6.13. Note that the failure intensity changes discontinuously at each release but is constant during the life of that release. As long as the faults removed with each release as a result of field trouble reports and added testing exceeds faults introduced by new features, the general trend of failure intensity will be as shown. This entire trend can be fit by one appropriate model. Note that the fit is not as good as when net (removal minus introduction) fault change action is continuous. However, additional factors can make the actual failure intensity curve smoother than is illustrated. For example, suppose that Fig. 6.13 includes data from several sites. The introduction of new releases is often staggered rather than synchronous. At any one time then, the curve is based on data from different releases, so the steps tend to be smoothed out. Some products will show a failure intensity versus release curve

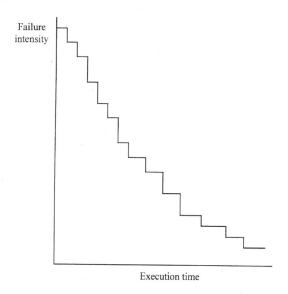

Failure
intensity

Execution time

Figure 6.13 Variation in failure intensity of software
product with multiple releases.

that is more level. This is particularly true when developers take advantage of
any failure intensity improvements that occur to introduce new features.

4 We are load testing some software with a computer utilization of 0.2, and
we are experiencing a failure intensity of 10 failures per 1000 h. If we test it at
a computer utilization of 0.4, what will be the failure intensity?

ANSWER: To a first approximation, the failure intensity will be constant with
respect to execution time. Thus when we double the computer utilization, we
double the execution time per unit time. Hence we double the failure intensity
with respect to time, yielding 20 failures per 1000 h. Note that the execution
environment will be different under the heavier load. In fact, the failure intensity is likely to be somewhat higher because of problems resulting from the
increased load.

5 What is the impact of inefficient programs on failure intensity? Couldn't
an inefficient program give a spuriously low failure intensity?

ANSWER: The inefficient program will give a failure intensity that is realistic
for that program. The system engineer must interpret failure intensity in the
light of all other system characteristics, particularly performance, in establishing the quality of a particular implementation. For example, consider an
airline reservation system that handles 10,000 reservations per hour and has
a failure intensity of one failure per hour. It may be superior in quality to a system that handles 1000 reservations per hour and has a failure intensity of 0.5

failures per hour. In a case such as this it may be useful for comparison purposes to transform time units to natural units. In other words, the systems have 0.1 and 0.5 failures per 1000 reservations, respectively.

6 Why do you use the term *failure intensity* instead of *failure rate?*

ANSWER: The term *failure intensity* was chosen to avoid confusion with the *incorrect* but occasional use of *failure rate* as a synonym for hazard rate.

7 What is the difference between failure intensity and failure density, as used in software reliability models?

ANSWER: Failure intensity is the derivative with respect to time or natural units of expected failures. Failure density is the derivative with respect to time or natural units of the probability that the failure interval is less than or equal to some value.

8 You refer to "estimates" of present failure intensity. If we have data on times of failures, can't we determine the *actual* failure intensities?

ANSWER: Remember that failures occur randomly with respect to time. We only have a *sample* of failures and not data on all failures to use in determining the failure intensity. Hence, we can't determine it exactly but must estimate it. Statistically speaking, we are computing *sample* quantities and using them as estimates of population quantities.

9 Can repairing a fault actually increase the failure intensity?

ANSWER: Yes. This is most likely to happen when the repair spawns a fault in a part of the program that is executed more frequently than the part in which the fault is repaired. It is also possible to spawn more faults than you repair and hence increase failure intensity, but this is less common. In any case, the foregoing may be a good reason for not attempting to correct failures of low frequency that occur in programs that you don't understand. Examples of such programs are old, complex, poorly documented programs whose creators may no longer be available for consultation.

10 The failure intensity of our computer systems increases with workload and it increases at greater than a linear rate close to full utilization. Can we explain this with software reliability theory?

ANSWER: Yes. Increasing utilization results in a corresponding linear increase in execution time and hence failure intensity with respect to time. Utilization close to the limit can fill system control tables, resulting in execution in a different part of the input space that we may not have tested as thoroughly, hence the greater than linear increase in failure intensity.

11 It appears that the accuracy of determining when we will reach a failure intensity objective will get worse for smaller objectives because the slope of failure intensity with respect to time is decreasing. Is this true?

TABLE 6.6   Execution Times of Reaching Various Failure Intensity
Objectives, Basic Model, Project T1

Objective (failures/execution hours)	Execution time to objective (execution hours)	
	Estimate	75% confidence interval
0.05	23.0	18.0–29.5
0.01	36.1	29.5–44.6
0.005	41.7	34.4–51.1
0.001	54.8	45.9–66.3
0.0001	73.5	62.4–88.0
0.00001	92.2	78.8–109.7

SOURCE: Musa, Iannino, and Okumoto, 1987, Table 13.1.

ANSWER: Perhaps in absolute but not in relative terms. The effect mentioned is counteracted by the fact that the accuracy with which you can estimate failure intensity is increasing with time. This results from a larger sample of failure data being available. Software reliability models have at least two parameters, with associated accuracies. Both affect the geometry of the interaction of the failure intensity curve with the failure intensity objective. Therefore, a simple geometric analysis of this situation is not feasible. Instead, let's look at an example from an actual project. Using the basic model, we estimated hours of execution time required to reach various failure intensity objectives, along with the 75 percent confidence intervals. We show the results in Table 6.6. Note that the absolute size of the confidence interval increases as the failure intensity objective decreases, but the relative size *decreases*.

12   Which models is the reliability demonstration chart valid for?

ANSWER: The reliability demonstration chart is used for certification test, not reliability growth test. Models are only applied to reliability growth test, so they do not affect reliability demonstration charts.

13   We have noticed that the logarithmic model often fits failure data better than the exponential model when the system is slowly and continuously evolving. Can you explain why?

ANSWER: Slow evolution of the program will increase the number of failures that can be experienced. The effect is to produce a slow but continual increase in the number of failures that *are* experienced. Such a pattern may be best fit by the logarithmic model.

14   How can you determine the number of total failures and the number of unique failures that will occur in a given period of execution after release?

ANSWER: To find the number of total failures occurring in a given period, multiply the failure intensity at release by the period of execution. To find the number of unique failures, project the failure intensity versus execution time curve from system test into the operational period. The integral of (or area under) the curve for the given period will yield the quantity desired.

15 What form will the failure intensity curve take if you count only the first occurrence of failures?

ANSWER: Assuming that the program is stable (no additional developed code is being added) and that execution is in accord with the operational profile, failure intensity will decrease with execution time. This happens because when you don't count repeated occurrences of failures, you are implicitly assuming that repair action is occurring.

16 What does *reliability assurance* mean?

ANSWER: Reliability assurance is concerned with the level of confidence you have in the reliability you are measuring. For reliability assurance to be high, the variance in measured reliability must be small.

17 Is there any way you can combine the reliability level you want to achieve with the degree of assurance you require?

ANSWER: You express the reliability in terms of a percentile such as 90th or 95th. For example, you may specify that the 95th percentile reliability must be greater than 0.99 for 10 h. That means that the true reliability must be greater than 0.99 with a confidence of 0.95.

18 Is there any logical reason why you might experience an infinite number of different failures in infinite testing time?

ANSWER: Yes. It could happen if the input space continues to grow with time. This might be quite realistic if users keep finding new ways to employ the software.

19 How can we have a finite number of failures in an infinite amount of time? If we have a particular failure intensity, won't the number of failures increase without limit as time passes?

ANSWER: The "finite failures in infinite time" situation occurs only during reliability growth, when the faults that are causing failures are removed after the failures occur. The failure intensity decreases as time passes, making a finite number of failures possible.

6.4.2 Application

1 How rapid must program evolution be before ignoring change is no longer satisfactory?

ANSWER: There is no fixed answer to this question. The key quantity that is related to the deviation of estimates from reality is the ratio of new faults introduced to failures experienced (note that there is no causal connection between these two quantities). Each new fault increases the deviation of the estimates and each additional failure experienced provides data that improves the accuracy of the estimates. The number of new faults we introduce depends on the change in the amount of developed code. The fault-to-failure ratio that we can tolerate depends on the accuracy desired in the estimates, smaller ratios yielding greater accuracy.

2   Should you test for some period of time past the point at which you meet the failure intensity objective to be conservative in making a release decision?

ANSWER: Not for a period of time but to some definite fraction of the failure intensity objective such as 0.5.

3   What are the effects of better testing on the variation of failure intensity with execution time?

ANSWER: The effects of better testing on the variation of failure intensity with time are illustrated in Figs. 6.14 and 6.15. Better test selection will increase the potential rate at which failure intensity decreases with execution time. Such selection will ensure that the most frequently occurring operations are tested first. If faults are associated with these input states, the related failures will occur early. Thus potential failure intensity reduction will be rapid.

Better failure identification and resolution, which depends on appropriate recording of relevant information and careful observation of results, will maximize the number of failures you identify and the value of the fault reduction factor B that you can attain. This will ensure that the rate of decrease of failure intensity with execution time is as close to the potential rate as possible.

4   Can the software reliability estimation programs be used for hardware?

ANSWER: Yes.

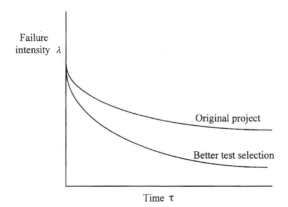

Figure 6.14   Effect of better test selection.

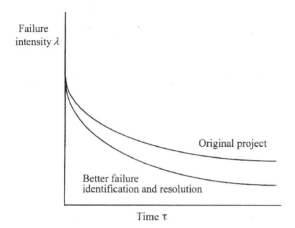

Figure 6.15 Effect of better identification and resolution.

5 I am interested not only in overall failure intensity but also failure intensity of a certain critical operation. How can I determine this?

ANSWER: Compute the acceleration factor for the critical operation, which is the ratio of the test occurrence probability of the operation to its field occurrence probability (the occurrence probability of the operational profile). Divide the failure intensity achieved by the system by the acceleration factor to get an estimate of the failure intensity for the critical operation.

6 How does the quality of software documentation affect failure intensity?

ANSWER: The effect of software documentation on failure intensity depends on whether it is user or program documentation. User documentation affects the human component of a system, where the system may be viewed as having hardware, software, and human components (see Fig. 6.16). All components must function properly for the system to function properly. They may be viewed as an event diagram with an AND configuration.

The reliability of the human component of the system depends on the reliability of the operators and the reliability of the user documentation. In other words, failures may result from operator malfunction or incorrect, ambiguous, or confusing user documentation. User documentation that is correct but sim-

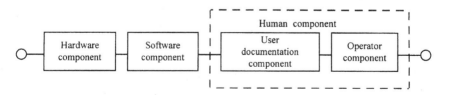

Figure 6.16 Effect of user documentation on system failure intensity.

ply disorganized or poorly written may not affect system reliability as much as it may affect the training time required for system operators.

Program documentation that is incorrect, ambiguous, or confusing will affect the reliability of the software when it is changed. The number of faults introduced per line of developed code resulting from change will increase. When program documentation is correct but poorly organized or poorly written, the effect on work effort necessary to make changes may be greater than the effect on reliability.

7   Is there any way to reduce the failure intensity of a software-based system without removing faults?

ANSWER: Yes. You can restrict the input space to avoid failing input states. Thus you trade functionality for reliability.

8   Suppose a later failure or failures are missed because a run aborts due to a failure. Will this cause you to underestimate the true failure intensity?

ANSWER: Only very, very slightly in most cases, Unless runs are very long, it is relatively rare to have two or more failures in a run, especially at system test or later. Hence the effects on measured failure intensity will ordinarily be very small.

9   If your failure intensity variation follows the exponential model, how can you rapidly (without substantial calculations) make projections of the execution time required to reach various failure intensity objectives?

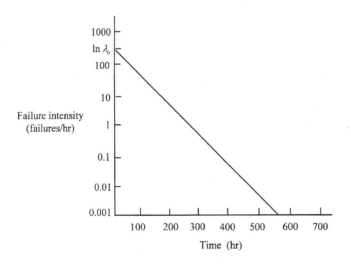

Figure 6.17   Failure intensity for basic model, plotted on logarithmic scale.

ANSWER: Plot the logarithm of the failure intensity function, given by

$$\ln \lambda = \ln \lambda_0 - \frac{\lambda_0}{v_0} t \qquad (6.19)$$

You will note that it is a straight line (Fig. 6.17). Hence it is easy to project the model and read off times corresponding to various failure intensity objectives.

10 It would seem that software reliability projection is directly dependent on factors like individual capabilities, development methodologies, and tools that are highly variable from project to project. Doesn't this make using it difficult?

ANSWER: Most applications involve *estimating* software reliability from actual failure data. Here, it is obtained directly with no need to know the values of the factors that affect it and how they do so.

Although predicting software reliability does require this information, the problem is not as difficult as it may sound. Most projects are sufficiently large that individual skill differences average out considerably. The effects of the multiple tools and methodologies employed also average out somewhat. Further, companies tend to standardize tools and methodologies, and there is a general trend in the software engineering field to adopt the effective ones (which of course narrows the differences).

11 Because the accuracy of software reliability projection can vary between different models, and no one model appears to always be right, why not use a large number of models and take the model with the best projection at any time?

ANSWER: This approach is too complex. Using many models makes it difficult for the practitioner to make the valuable connection between model and physical reality that provides insight.

And there is no need for this complexity. The logarithmic Poisson and basic models appear to bound the range of behaviors you encounter, and at least one of them almost always provides good projection. Note in Musa, Iannino, and Okumoto (1987), Fig. 13.4, that the geometric model group, to which the logarithmic Poisson execution time model belongs, has a median accuracy that is superior to the other models.

The exponential group (basic execution time model) does not perform as well but does show better than 10 percent accuracy for the last 40 percent of system test. This is good enough, and better projection does not add much when other possible sources of error are considered. This model has the advantage of being closely connected to physical characteristics of the software system.

12 How can corrected faults be proportional to identified failures? What you correct depends on what it is profitable to correct or what the customer pays for.

ANSWER: If the user determines that some failures are not to be corrected (either by direct order or by what is paid for), the specification has been effectively changed. The system behavior in question is no longer unacceptable.

Thus the failure has been redefined out of existence. Once you remove this category of failures from consideration, the number of faults that you can correct does relate to the number of failures you identify.

13   What factors affect fault density and hence failure intensity?

ANSWER: The factors that affect fault density are not completely known at present. It appears likely that the significant factors will be those that affect projects as a whole rather than individuals, except for those projects where the number of people involved is sufficiently small to make individual differences important. There is evidence that volatility of requirements, thoroughness of documentation, and programmer skill level do affect fault density. It is likely that certain methodologies such as design reviews also have an impact.

14   What kinds of output from software reliability estimation programs are useful and what do they tell you?

ANSWER: The answer to this question depends on the application. However, present failure intensity, which gives you the current reliability status of the software, is generally the most useful. Graphical representations of this data are helpful for highlighting trends.

15   I can understand why plots of failure intensity against time (for example, Fig. 6.18) might show sudden upward jumps in failure intensity when new developed code is added. But why do downward jumps occur?

ANSWER: Some plots of failure intensity such as Fig. 6.18 are made against days rather than continuous time. There can be a substantial amount of time occurring on one day, which would lie on one vertical line. During this period of time, the failure intensity can drop appreciably. Thus there will be the *appearance* of a sharp drop in failure intensity due to the way in which the graph is plotted.

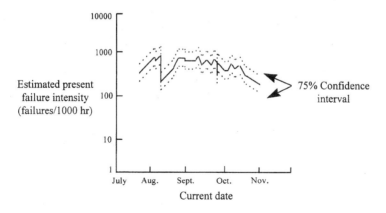

Figure 6.18   History of estimates of present failure intensity.

16 Can we use a software reliability model to help establish the priority with which different components should be tested?

ANSWER: Yes. It can provide information on the present failure intensity of each component. To decide on priorities for test, you will also need information on the relative criticalities of the operations implemented by the component and knowledge of how system failure is related to failures of the individual components.

17 We are using automated test and we are experiencing a higher failure intensity than anticipated. Any ideas as to what might be wrong?

ANSWER: There are at least two possibilities. You may be using automated failure detection that compares the actual output state of a test with a required output state with no allowance for tolerances. Frequently in practice, one does not consider some minor input variables as part of the input state because they have only insignificant and acceptable effects on the output state. However, if you do not allow for the small variations in values of the output state that can occur, the program that analyzes the test results will register "failures" that are not real.

A second possibility is that the test driver is failing to reinitialize variables that are both input and output variables after a run, often because no one recognized the relationship. The program sets an output variable that then becomes the input variable of the next run. The next run no longer has the input state that you think. It may not be one for which you designed the program; hence the program may fail.

18 Is there a limit to the size of components or systems you can test with certification test?

ANSWER: No.

19 If a certification test fails and a software-based system is rejected, what should be done if it is resubmitted for certification test?

ANSWER: Review what actions have been taken to improve the system's reliability before undertaking the effort and expense of retesting.

20 What will be the effect of hourly or daily fluctuations in the operational profile resulting from natural work patterns?

ANSWER: These can cause similar hourly or daily fluctuations in failure intensity, but they will be markedly reduced by the robustness of failure intensity with respect to operational profile variations (Musa, 1994b). Further, you won't observe these fluctuations if the time between failures is greater than the period of fluctuation, which will usually be the case.

21 We find in testing that we tend to locate the most severe failures first and the failures with less impact later. Note that "severity of failure" is not the same thing as "complexity of fault" in that severity relates to impact on the user. Does this affect the application of the theory?

ANSWER: Usually not. But suppose you are estimating failure intensity based on all failures and deriving failure intensities for different failure severity classes from it by use of average proportions of severities. Then you may be temporarily overestimating the severe failure intensity just after the severe failures have been removed. However, the estimate will be correct in the long run. We should remark that your experience is *not* typical. Most projects do not have any correlation between severity and point in the test phase.

22   If you are far from your failure intensity objective and approaching it so slowly that it appears that it will take an inordinate time to get there, what should you do?

ANSWER: Consider terminating testing and reengineering the system. The design and/or implementation may be so faulty that there is limited failure intensity reduction that can be practically and economically achieved.

23   Can you determine reliability growth in some sense from failure data when you won't resolve any of the failures (remove any of the faults) until the next release?

ANSWER: Yes, if you are using only the first occurrence of each failure, the failure intensity you estimate will be the value that will exist when all failures outstanding up to that point have been resolved. Thus it will be a measure of the quality of the testing effort in that it indicates how well this effort is identifying failures that may occur.

24   Can CASRE be used for systems with evolving programs?

ANSWER: No, not directly. If a component by component or operation group by operation group evolution is occurring, you can use CASRE for an individual component or operation group.

25   We have serious reliability problems with a release that we are constrained to ship in the near future. The chance of solving these problems in the time remaining is poor. Is there any way we can trade functionality for reliability?

ANSWER: Yes, if the reliability problems are confined to certain operations and these operations have fairly substantial occurrence probabilities. Determine which of the these operations you can defer to a later release to give you more time to work on them. Assuming that you performed your system testing to date using the operational profile and stationary selection probabilities, you can estimate the failure intensity you can expect for the remaining operations. Remove all data for failures that have occurred for the operations whose release is being deferred. Execute the reliability estimation program for the remaining failure data, and you will obtain a failure intensity estimate for the remaining operations.

26   Can anything be gained by careful analyses of the causes of failures?

ANSWER: Yes, up to the point where the analysis is more costly than the benefits that result. To avoid this problem, rank the failures on the basis of expected failure cost, which is the product of expected number of failures over the lifetime of a release and severity (expressed in monetary terms). You can estimate the expected number of failures from release lifetime and the operational profile. Release lifetime is the sum of lifetimes over all copies of the systems.

Analyze the failures in the order of this ranking until you reach a point of diminishing returns. The analysis will usually suggest process improvements for you to implement.

27   One of the people on my project wants to use a new software reliability model that is different from the ones you recommend because he contends it takes into account more of the factors that affect reliability and hence should yield better projections of reliability behavior.

ANSWER: Watch out. New reliability models are a dime a dozen. This is not to say that a better model may not come along, but there are many pitfalls. If the model accounts for more factors, it is probably more complex. It is inadvisable to employ a new model until it has been tested on many projects, at least more than 10. Accurate projection of reliability is very dependent on the accuracy with which you can determine model parameters, and this is generally more important than which model you use. Because projection for any appreciable length of time is not very accurate at the current state of the art due to the lack of accuracy of parameters, we do not use projection very much currently as a management or engineering tool. Thus employing a new model to obtain better accuracy is not particularly effective or useful.

28   Could failure intensity that increases as test proceeds occur because we are removing a fault that blocks part of the program from being executed and that part contains many faults?

ANSWER: It is possible but unlikely. Software reliability engineering test is done after units have been tested or verified in some fashion. Blocking tends to occur at the unit level. Experience has shown it to occur rarely during software reliability engineering test.

29   Could rising failure intensity occur because we are spawning new faults?

ANSWER: A newly spawned fault could cause a short uptick in failure intensity, but it is unlikely that it would cause failure intensity to increase substantially over any length of time.

30   We find that we have nowhere near enough time in certification test to prove in the level of failure intensity that we want. Is there anything we can do?

ANSWER: Work with deviations instead of failures, if their ratio is approximately constant over the period of test. Generally you can accept a much higher deviation intensity than you can a failure intensity. You should be able to prove this with less testing. For example, if no deviations occur, you can accept the software at about 2.2 normalized units, assuming a discrimination ratio of

2 and consumer and supplier risks of 0.1. Suppose your failure intensity objective were 10 failures per 1000 h. You would need 220 h of test with no failures to prove in this level. Now assume that there are 10 deviations for every failure so that the deviation failure intensity objective is 100 deviations per 1000 h. You could prove this level with 22 h of test with no deviations.

31 We are locked into our supplier and can't really reject their system. What can we do if the certification test indicates "Reject?"

ANSWER: If certification test indicates Reject, this does not mean that you reject the supplier permanently. It only means that you reject the release they have delivered to you in its present form. You can expect that most suppliers will attempt to reduce the failure intensity of the release and redeliver it.

6.4.3 Special situations

1 We are testing a program in such a way that we expose only part of the code to possible execution at any one time, but that fraction increases in stages. Can we apply the theory of evolving programs to the situation?

ANSWER: Yes. You may have completely integrated the code physically, but if you are not actively executing all parts by plan, you are artificially restricting the number of faults that can cause failures. The code might just as well not be there.

2 How should we handle a program that contains artificial intelligence elements and learns with time?

ANSWER: You may view a program that learns as an evolving program and handle it with these techniques. The specific evolutionary path will depend on the history of input states experienced. It is probably best to deal with the average evolutionary path, which will depend on the operational profile. The most important thing you must do is to relate the rate of evolution to the operational profile.

3 Physical constraints may result in the available memory in a system being constrained, although constraints are decreasing with advances in memory technology. One example of constraint has been computerized systems on spacecraft, where memory is limited by weight considerations. When new features are added to such systems, developers may have to remove certain old features or recode them in a smaller amount of memory. How should we handle failure intensity estimation?

ANSWER: The best approach is to view the removed code as one system component, the added code as another, and the reused code as a third. The failure intensity of each is determined. Then the change in the overall program is determined by combining the "before" components and then the "after" components.

4 How should we handle programs ported to another computer?

ANSWER: When you port a program to another computer, you usually must modify some (possibly very small) portions of the code. View the program as an evolving program, and apply the techniques for such programs. Note that if average instruction execution rates differ between the two machines, you should first adjust all execution times to the target machine.

5 How do we combine failure intervals from projects with several different versions of software simultaneously in test?

ANSWER: First determine whether the versions are substantially different. Two versions are different if the code of one contains appreciable additions and modifications with respect to the other. If they are not substantially different, we can merge the failure data from the two directly. If they *are* different, consider the technique of breakdown into components for combining the data. Sometimes it may be possible to directly merge failure data from different components, with acceptable error occurring in the estimates based on the data.

If one version has removed faults that have not been removed in other versions, do not recount the reoccurrence of failures due to these faults.

To a first approximation, the total number of inherent faults for all versions will be proportional to the total number of source lines that you develop (don't count source lines inherited by one version from another).

6 Does it make sense to handle substantial design changes made at one time by separating the pre- and postchange estimation procedures and then later combining the estimates in some way?

ANSWER: Only if we can characterize the changes as the addition of a new component or components so that you can combine it or them with the previous component, using combinatorial rules for reliability. If not, it is best to work with both pre- and postchange data together. The larger sample size generally means that you will reduce perturbations in estimated quantities resulting from changes, and recovery from the perturbations will be faster.

7 How does failure intensity change when software is used with different hardware configurations?

ANSWER: The answer to this question depends on what the difference is. Let's consider four possible differences.

Suppose the software is a component in different systems. The systems are distinguished by different sets of hardware components or different "failure logic" relationships among the same set of hardware components. In this case you determine the failure intensity differences among the systems by applying the appropriate combinatoric rules.

A different situation occurs if you move a software component from a processor with average instruction execution rate r_1 to a processor with average instruction execution r_2. The failure intensity will change by the factor r_2/r_1. For example, a failure intensity of one failure per hour will increase to two failures per hour when you move the software to a machine that is twice as fast.

The third situation occurs when you move a program to a processor that has a different instruction set. Suppose the program is designed to be highly portable and is written in a high-level language. If the program can be interpreted or compiled on both machines with an interpreter/compiler that is highly reliable (doesn't introduce faults), the failure intensity on both machines will be the same, except for adjustment for change in average instruction execution rate. If the program is not portable, we will have to change some code, with a resultant quantity of developed code. We now have an evolving program, which can be handled by all the techniques available for such programs.

The fourth situation occurs when program behavior changes as the result of the different hardware configuration. For example, the nature of the configuration may be an input variable to the program, causing different operations to execute with a different operational profile. Here you may not be able to predict what the change in failure intensity will be until you execute the program in the new environment; you only know that there will definitely be one.

8 We plan to test our program first with a software environment simulator and later in the real environment. Would you expect present failure intensity to increase or decrease in making the transition?

ANSWER: It could be either. It would tend to increase if the simulator didn't adequately represent the environment. Note that the software simulator itself may have failures due to faults, but you shouldn't be including these with the system you are testing. If the simulator itself represents deliverable software (for example, for system exerciser purposes), an estimate of its independent failure intensity may be desirable.

9 Can we apply software reliability engineering to a situation where we release a program to the field with some failures not yet addressed?

ANSWER: Yes. You can predict the failure intensity to be expected by backing up in the test phase by the number of failures outstanding. You estimate parameters and calculate various quantities of interest at this point.

10 We use different diagnostic tools during different phases of test. As a result, some new failures may be found that we missed during an earlier phase. How should we handle this?

ANSWER: Note that you are really estimating *observable* failure intensity and the observability has suddenly changed. You might view this in the same light as a program you are testing in a new environment. This violates the general assumptions of software reliability models to some extent, but the effects are usually not serious. A new crop of failures will occur. Behavior will be analogous to behavior occurring when a substantial number of design changes are made at one time.

11 Can we apply software reliability models to individual programmers who are testing components?

ANSWER: Yes, nothing prevents it in theory. In practice, however, if the components are *too* small, failure sample sizes will be small, and the accuracy of failure intensity estimates may be low for a large part of the test period. Hence they may be of limited value.

12 Can we apply a software reliability model when we run formal system tests at widely spaced intervals during the test period? We record interval data for the formal tests but not otherwise, except that we note number of failures and total execution time per day or week.

ANSWER: Yes. You could rederive the maximum likelihood estimation formulas to account for missing or unknown data and change the supporting computation programs accordingly, but that would not be worthwhile. Picking failure times randomly within the period to which they are limited (for example, day or week) will give better results than assuming that the data are completely missing.

13 How would you determine the effect of built-in tests (audits) on software reliability?

ANSWER: This is really an "evaluation of software engineering technology" problem *except* that the technology in general cannot be evaluated. You can only evaluate the effect of the particular audits for the particular program in question. This must be done by a comparative test of the program with and without audits. The test must be sufficiently extensive that the part of the operational profile covered totals up to a high probability.

14 When we uncover faults during test, we generally add fault-tolerant features to the programs to counter faults of this type. The net effect is a greater improvement in reliability than if we just corrected the fault in question. Do software reliability models handle this effect?

ANSWER: The basic and logarithmic Poisson models handle this effect automatically. They do it in the same fashion that they handle removal of related faults by inspection that is stimulated by a fault found during test. The addition of the fault tolerant code will cause failures to occur less frequently and the model will sense this. Note that accuracy of predictions of future failure intensity depend on the extra percentage of improvement resulting from addition of fault tolerant features to remain relatively constant, an assumption that is reasonably likely to hold.

6.5 Problems

6.1 We are conducting certification test on printer software. The failure intensity objective is one failure per 10,000 pages. We observe failures at 2000, 5000, 7000, 9000, and 12,000 pages. Can we conclude anything about the software? When?

6.2 We have been doing certification test on a system for a brokerage firm. The failure intensity objective is one failure per million transactions. At four failures, we have tested 2 million transactions and reached the end of our test period. What is our demonstrable FI/FIO ratio?

7

Deploying Software Reliability Engineering

We will assume that you have been personally convinced of the value of software reliability engineering and now wish to deploy it in your organization. You may be a manager or simply a member of the organization. Your two principal tasks will be addressed, persuading the organization to deploy software reliability engineering and executing the deployment. Because you may decide to use a consultant, we will also discuss some of the issues you need to consider in that situation.

7.1 Persuasion

We discussed many of the reasons for deploying software reliability engineering in Chap. 1. We say "many" because we're certainly not aware of all the advantages. Therefore, you should determine the advantages specifically for your organization. First, establish the key problems the members of your organization are facing in developing and testing software-based systems. Although it is possible to conduct a poll to do this, a focus group brainstorming meeting is much better because the interaction stimulates recollection and refines and prioritizes the issues. In many cases it will be advantageous to include users of your product in the focus group. The output of this group should be a prioritized software development problem list. You should then review the list in the context of what you have learned about software reliability engineering in Chaps. 1 through 6 and look for ways in which software reliability engineering can help solve these problems.

You will then want to introduce your organization to software reliability engineering. Experience shows that an overview of 1 to $1\frac{1}{2}$ h works best, with particular emphasis on the material in Chap. 1 and additional benefits of software reliability engineering you have developed in your analysis of your organization's needs. You will probably want to add some material from Chaps. 2 through 6 in the broadest outline form, just to give participants a concrete feel for software reliability engineering practice. The overview should encourage questions and interaction and not discourage those who challenge the practice or bring up problems. If you suppress the concerns of these people, they will only resurface later in ways that may endanger the deployment. Hence you should deal with them in a positive and constructive way.

You need to understand that deploying software reliability engineering is a change like any other and that people resist change. Some of this is desirable. It protects the organization against uncritically considered ideas and hasty decisions. It prevents disruption of processes that are functioning well. Some of the resistance is undesirable but natural. Change disturbs people, forcing them to invest extra efforts in learning new knowledge and skills and in adapting. Thus you can expect some hostility, whether or not it is justified.

To overcome the resistance, you need to show people how software reliability engineering will help them *personally* and to minimize any problems it may cause them. "Management by machismo" (i.e., ordering change or asking a manager to order change) does not work. You may obtain the appearance of deployment, but it will occur grudgingly and without much consideration or thought. Consequently, the results will usually be of questionable quality.

Organizations adopt software reliability engineering practice most readily when we are able to show each person in that organization how he or she would benefit by

1. Working more productively on the job
2. Improving his or her competitiveness (and hence job security) in the marketplace

We show each manager how software reliability engineering would improve the productivity and competitiveness of the organization and reflect on his or her competitiveness as a manager. Sometimes you can motivate people by showing the benefit to the organization, especially if the organization is very team-oriented, but this is definitely a secondary motivator. You can motivate a few people by showing them that they are participants in advancing the state of the practice of their profession.

Make sure you understand the existing development process before introducing change. Then you will retain its good features. Also, you are giving the people concerned the implicit message that you respect the competence they have exhibited in the past in developing and evolving their development process and merely want to improve it and their skills.

It is possible that, as a result of this orientation meeting, your organization decides not to deploy software reliability engineering at the present time. However, this is relatively rare because of its very cost-effective advantages. Usually the orientation meeting will end in a decision to deploy. Then you will proceed to the activities described in the next section.

7.2   Executing the Deployment

It is probably best to start by developing a deployment plan, even if it needs to change later. Laner (1985) has pointed out that, "A plan is only a common base for changes. Everyone needs to know the plan so they can change easily."

It is important to involve all the members in your organization in the planning process (or at least to offer involvement to them and to make it easy for them to participate to whatever degree they wish). If you do not do this, the interest and motivation you have stimulated in persuading them to deploy software reliability engineering is likely to languish and turn into resistance. Further, you may make some serious mistakes in deployment if you don't take advantage of the reservoir of experience these people possess. In fact, directly asking the members of the organization to join the planning process because you want to benefit from their experience is a strong motivator.

There are several approaches to organizing the initial planning meeting. Coming in with a totally organized plan and informing people how to carry it out does not seem to work. On the other hand, sitting down and saying We have to prepare a plan, so what are we going to put in it? generally does not work too well either. Some of the people involved may not be willing to devote a large amount of time to something they don't yet view as having a high priority.

The approach that seems to work best is to start with a first draft of a plan that you state is tentative and incomplete and needs their input. You may include issues that you cannot resolve and for which you need their ideas, but it is best to note all of the factors you know of that may bear on the decision. Provide the draft plan to the potential attendees of the meeting in advance so that they may read it. Then call the meeting and present the main features of the plan. Ask the participants to identify problems and to suggest improvements. Generally you will then have a small number of problems to deal with. Elicit the participation of the attendees at the meeting in solving the problems. You are likely to leave the meeting with a set of suggested changes to your plan.

Sometimes you may have some action items that have to be resolved, and perhaps another meeting may be required before things stabilize. Finally, you modify and issue the plan. Generally, we have found that the group in any given meeting should not be larger than 15 or so. It is difficult to have a participative session with a larger group.

Once the plan has been developed, it must be disseminated. You need to give each member of the organization a clear picture of the plan *and the logic behind it.* The latter is important; each person must be able to make intelligent decisions and interpretations when confronted with a problem in applying the plan. An oral presentation is usually best for this purpose; a meeting gives attendees the opportunity to ask questions and to test their understanding of the material presented. The written plan should be provided for reference, however.

We have been involved in or observed six different strategies for transferring the knowledge needed to deploy software reliability engineering:

1. Consultant leads deployment

2. Custom jump start

3. Group jump start

4. Course with workshops (typically 2 days)

5. Course only (typically 1 day)

6. Self-teaching

Let's discuss each of these briefly with it pros and cons. In all cases, only a few members of your organization need to learn these details of applying software reliability engineering, although all should learn something about it, perhaps a 1- to 2-h overview as noted in Sec. 7.1.

Most of our experiences with a consultant leading the deployment have been negative. This approach has the virtue of reducing the time required of the members of an organization, but that is exactly the problem. It is too easy to "leave it to the consultant." Consequently, deployment of software reliability engineering becomes a low-priority activity for members, and they do not really learn how to use it. The deployment is often poorly adapted to the needs of the organization. A consultant cannot hope to absorb the culture, domain background, and procedures of an organization and develop the degree of judgment in these areas that an organization's members have. Thus decisions and interpretations by the consultant carry a high risk of error, leading to poor-quality results that may damage software practitioners' views of the practice. On top of all this, it is the most expensive approach. Consequently, we strongly advise against it.

The two jump start approaches are both feasible ones. *Jump start* means that a consultant helps the organization get started, but the motive power and leadership for the deployment remain with the organization. The consultant acts solely as an adviser. Jump starts usually begin with a course like the 2-day course with workshops for educating several members of the organization who will apply software reliability engineering. The consultant then works with the organization, regularly checking and reviewing the progress of the deployment with the organization members who are implementing it. Both jump starts result in greater commitment to deployment than the consultant leader approach. Both cost less than the consultant leader approach but more than the last three approaches. A custom jump start is tailored for one organization, a group jump start is for several. The custom jump start costs more than the group one. It has the advantage of more focused dedication of the consultant to one organization but the disadvantage of less interplay and cross-fertilization among organizations.

The course with workshops approach is the most cost-effective one for highly motivated organizations. Here the course for educating the members of the organization is combined with workshops for applying what they have learned. It is most desirable to have several brief workshops, each involving practice of a task that has just been learned. The workshops should be structured on project lines so that each group gets to apply software reliability engineering to a simplified representation of its product. It is particularly effective if you bring this course to your location, where you have ready access to project information and staff. This can also be desirable to protect proprietary or classified information. It's also a good idea to make the instructor available after the course as a consultant for some period so that he or she can answer questions (perhaps by telephone) and review documents as needed. With this approach, members are strongly encouraged to do as much on their own as they think prudent, but they can initiate contact with the consultant when needed. Thus the course with workshops approach is considerably less expensive than either of the jump starts. The jump starts have more involvement on the part of the consultant, with the consultant checking on the progress of each project regularly. Thus they may be preferable for moderately motivated organizations or organizations with limited software development experience.

The course without workshops is less expensive than the one with them, but the saving is not that great. Because participants do not get the guided practice with constructive feedback for the software reliability engineering activities that those in the course with workshops do, retention of what has been learned is definitely inferior. Attendees do not learn how to adapt software reliability engineering to their organizations. If you can afford to send some of the members of your organization to a course, send them to one with workshops.

Self-teaching is by far the most economical approach. It involves self-study, preferably using a book such as this one. The big danger with self-teaching is that you have no opportunity to ask questions or to be critiqued by others. Thus there is some risk that you will not apply software reliability engineering correctly. You can counteract this danger by participating in group self-study, where you critique and question each other. Also, there are an increasing number of professional and Internet resources available to help you (see Table 7.1).

Managers play a key role in deployment because they will use software reliability engineering to aid them in functions such as

1. Monitoring the status of projects that include software

2. Allocating resources

3. Deciding when to rebalance the objectives of failure intensity, schedule, and cost

4. Deciding whether to accept delivery of subcontracted software

The managers involved are usually the project managers. They are most frequently at low or middle levels but can be at relatively high levels for large projects. They are most commonly software managers, but large numbers are system or hardware managers. Managers must receive sufficient background in software reliability engineering to make intelligent decisions in these areas *in the context of their projects or organizations.* They must be able to evaluate the information generated for them to aid such decisions. Finally, they must supervise the people performing the other software reliability engineering roles.

TABLE 7.1 Software Reliability Engineering Support Services

Resource	Internet or web address
Web site on software reliability engineering (includes overview, briefing for managers, bibliography of articles by software reliability engineering users, course information, useful references, Question of the Month)	http://members.aol.com/JohnDMusa/
Bulletin board on software reliability engineering	
Subscribe/unsubscribe	vishwa@hac2arpa.hac.com
Post	sw-rel@igate1.hac.com
Technical Committee on Software Reliability Engineering	http://www.tcse.org

Deployment of software reliability engineering will typically involve system testers as the technical leaders. System engineers will play a major role (defining *failure*, setting failure intensity objectives, and developing operational profiles). Depending on organizational structure, system architects and quality assurance engineers may also have major roles.

7.3 Using a Consultant

Consultants frequently play an important role in technology transfer. This includes both professional external consultants and individuals inside an organization, who by virtue of their technical leadership and initiative have a seminal impact throughout the organization. In order for consulting to be effective, consultant and consultee must each understand both roles. Sometimes one person may take on both roles during a project. For example, you might engage a consultant to advise you in applying software reliability engineering to a project. You might then take on the role of consultant yourself in trying to disseminate the consultant's ideas to your project team.

7.3.1 Consultee

Engaging a consultant, of course, involves the expenditure of resources by the consultee. Ordinarily the cost of the associated effort expended by other project personnel outweighs the compensation and expenses of the consultant or the costs charged to your organization from an internal consultant. A substantial investment of effort by project personnel is usually desirable so that they can learn from the consultant and apply this knowledge in the future. The potential benefits from effective consulting generally dwarf the resources expended. For all the foregoing reasons, we will concentrate on maximizing the effectiveness rather than minimizing the costs of the consultant. In fact, the cost-cutting strategy usually backfires because it focuses attention on the wrong objective.

The consultee should place great importance on the process of selecting the consultant. The extra cost of a consultant of superior quality is negligible with respect to the likely greater benefits. It is important for you to realize that you are not just "buying" expertise from the consultant but trying to apply expertise effectively in the solution of project problems. Therefore, you must be open and honest in providing the consultant with information. It is desirable to truly incorporate the consultant as a part of your team. Invest some effort in determining the needs and problems of your project and conveying them to the consultant. Provide any technical background information that may be relevant to the problem, and give the consultant some guidance about which information is likely to be most important. If you provide a set of reports and memoranda, a rank ordering of the value of this material is useful.

One area of vital information that is frequently overlooked is that of organizational power structure and politics. The consultant may develop good ideas, but it is likely that they will wither on the vine without this knowledge. You need to help the consultant help you by identifying the key people on the project with respect to the particular area being addressed. These may be people with power in either the formal structure (for example, managers) or the informal structure (for example, people generally recognized as technical innovators, initiators, or mentors among their peers).

The following may sound strange with respect to someone you may be hiring, but it usually pays to devote some effort to understanding the motivations of the consultant. It is often possible to relate these motivations to the goals of the project, multiplying the consultant's effectiveness. There are many consultants "with a mission," who are more interested in spreading a set of ideas than in their compensation. An organization can profit by helping disseminate them. Positive feedback, when appropriate, to the consultant, to your management and project, and to potential "customers" of the consultant can be especially productive.

Finally, feedback of all kinds is important. The consultant usually has only a short time to learn the needs of the project and the appropriate background, develop appropriate recommendations, and help implement them. Hence, a high level of interaction is essential. It is particularly important for the consultant to be able to report problems that are interfering with the ability to work. A consultant needs to be told when he or she is on the wrong track. Honesty with tact on both sides will usually be most effective.

7.3.2 Consultant

The role of the consultant is demanding because he or she must work rapidly and efficiently to be effective. The first order of business is to define project needs and problems. Next, the consultant must identify information sources and evaluate their relative importance. Third, the consultant develops plans about what should be done.

At this point, it is necessary to gain an understanding of the formal and informal power structures of the organization and the organizational politics. The consultant must identify the key people. It is desirable to concentrate one's efforts on them and to gain an understanding of their attitudes and motivations. The consultant must plan what to do in the light of the reality of the organization. The plans should then be modified into a set of objectives that have a realistic chance of success. Searching for project objectives that are also likely to satisfy the objectives of the individual key players is an approach that often works. The consultant must then seek strategies that will sell them on this synergy. In the case of software reliability engineering, where one must disseminate new concepts, the consultant should look for high-visibility activities that will make as many project personnel aware of the concepts as possible. He or she should also look for "multiplier" activities that enlist other people in the cause and spawn other activities.

Once the consultant develops a plan of action, he or she must sell project members on the plan. Here, the help and ideas of the key people who have been cultivated can be vital. It usually helps if the consultant has developed a thorough understanding of the needs of the project and its environment *and* exhibits this understanding with high visibility. It is desirable to fit new approaches into the existing ones. Use of terminology, concepts, and approaches already familiar to project members and in use on the project is helpful. The consultant should be generous with praise and credit for good aspects of the project and good performance of its members. The praise should be provided directly to the people involved, to their managers, and to people on other projects with whom he or she may come in contact. Positive feedback is important not only as a strategy for getting ideas accepted but also as a way of making sure that the project team understands which things are being done right and should not be changed. The consultant must deal with negative aspects honestly, privately, and with tact but not avoid them. He or she must maintain project confidentiality when dealing with several projects. This can apply even within one company, because the projects may be competing with each other. However, when the consultant has obtained the necessary permission, he or she is in an excellent position to spread good ideas. Ensuring that the idea originators get proper credit will strengthen relationships.

7.4 Frequently Asked Questions

1. How can we best convince other engineers and managers of the benefits of software reliability engineering?

ANSWER: This is a question that could receive a 20-page answer. However, to be brief, the best approach is probably to demonstrate how software reliability engineering can help the engineer or manager perform more effectively on the job and advance his or her career. Select and present those advantages that are most relevant to the particular person. A few possibilities are

    a. Better dialog with your customers and more accurate specification of customer needs

  b. Improved system engineering and project planning, with reliability receiving more precise and equal consideration

  c. Higher productivity, due to more exact and cost-effective satisfaction of customer needs

  d. More efficient testing, due to precise tracking of the current reliability level and better understanding of the factors affecting it

  e. More cost-effective use of your product in operation, through selecting the optimum reliability level and controlling change to maintain that level while introducing product improvements

  f. More effective choice of software engineering technologies, based on quantitative evaluation of their relative impacts on reliability

  g. Better control of reliability of software provided by others

2. We often find that researchers in the field damage our attempt to transfer technology to practitioners by critiquing software reliability engineering incorrectly and causing practitioners to lose confidence in it. What can we do about this?

ANSWER: First, remember that criticism is a natural part of research, a part that is necessary to ensure its validity. Second, be sure that you are indeed correct and your critic is not. Third, you should determine how severe the threat really is in dissuading practitioners from trying the technology. Is the criticism in a research-oriented meeting or journal or a practitioner-oriented medium? It may not be worth the effort to respond if practitioners are not likely to hear of it.

If you do decide to respond, remember that a researcher must criticize existing work to justify his or her own. If you attack the criticism directly, you will have a fight because you are cornering the researcher and threatening him or her with the loss of the justification for the research.

The best strategy for dealing with the criticism is to first determine what corrections are really essential to avoid damage to your technology transfer efforts. Then communicate the corrections to practitioners so that they have a positive opinion of the work of the researcher. Make the corrections as "additions," "amplifications," or "interpretations," not as corrections proper. Leave as many graceful "out's" as possible for the critic such as "semantic differences," "miscommunication," or "new information changes things." If you are skillful and tactful, the critic may note that he or she was criticizing *other* material in the field and certainly not yours and perhaps even note that your interpretations help express what he or she meant more precisely.

3. What is the impact of software reliability engineering on software quality assurance organizations?

ANSWER: Software reliability engineering usually increases the productivity of software quality assurance people. The quantification of reliability enables them to concentrate on the product. In its absence, they are forced to concentrate on the software engineering process, studying and measuring all the divergent ones that exist. They generally meet with more resistance because telling people *how* to do things ("use process X") is much more difficult than giving them objectives to meet, with the "how" left to them.

4. What kinds of people need to be on the team that is introducing software reliability engineering technology in a company?

ANSWER: You need someone who will be a centralized focus within a company to transfer the technology and to coordinate support functions, perhaps one person per 2000 technical employees. Technology transfer involves making professionals throughout the company aware of software reliability engineering and showing how it can benefit them, thus persuading them to use it. Support functions include such activities as arranging training, providing consulting, organizing a user group, and publishing a newsletter. Technology transfer requires an experienced technical professional with some background in software who has marketing and oral and written communication skills. Coordination of support functions requires background in software engineering and consulting skills.

We have found it desirable to have a local consultant in each major division of several hundred people. This person should have some software background and should receive in-depth training in software reliability engineering. The person may be associated with the quality assurance function of the division and may be required to work on software reliability engineering just part time.

There should also be at least one person on each project who is trained in software reliability engineering. That person is usually a software engineer who has this as a part-time assignment (typically 1/16 to 1/4 time).

5. Does it take a statistician to do software reliability engineering?

ANSWER: No.

6. If you get a position with a company that doesn't have a software reliability engineering program, what initial steps would you take to get a software reliability engineering program started?

ANSWER: First you need to raise awareness of software reliability engineering and how it can help your company. One of the best ways is to bring in an outside speaker who has experience in applying software reliability engineering in practice. The broader the speaker's experience, the better, because that will help convince people that this is a stable practice that is in wide use. Also, there is then a good chance that some of the speaker's experience will be relevant to your company. You should follow up this introduction to software reliability engineering rapidly, while interest remains high, by trying to find a project that will pilot the application of software reliability engineering. Do everything you can to make the pilot successful. Then disseminate the news of the success.

7. What are the prerequisites for deploying software reliability engineering? For example, a stable development process, solid requirements, test planning, a well-defined system test phase, a software development process at Capability Maturity Model level 3 or better, or what?

ANSWER: There are no absolute prerequisites for deploying software reliability engineering. All of the factors you mention will help. However, software reliability engineering can work in the context of a "problem" development process. In fact, it can also help improve that process. For example, developing operational profiles can help improve the quality of requirements and can stimulate good test planning.

8.   Our top management has issued an edict that all of our products shall be shipped free of major defects and at worst with only a small number of minor defects (preferably none if this can be achieved economically). We therefore test all our software releases thoroughly to remove all major defects and until our testers observe relatively infrequent occurrence of minor defects that our customers have told us would be tolerable to them. Why do we need more formal software reliability engineering methods?

ANSWER: You may not be testing as efficiently as you could be. You may be satisfying your customers' needs for reliability but neither as rapidly or as economically as you might be. Hence you are vulnerable to a competitor who could use software reliability engineering to beat you out.

9.   Our software releases (versions) come out at regular and frequent intervals. We have only a short, fixed time window for testing. We don't have any time for software reliability engineering techniques, and not much use for them, because a software release has to ship by a certain day no matter what its reliability measure is. Of course, we will fix all major faults detected before shipment. We will fix as many minor faults as time permits. We have ways of taking care of the minor faults that surface after shipment when the customer complains. Why should we worry about software reliability engineering?

ANSWER: It certainly does not seem desirable to have a reactive reliability program that is based on waiting for customers to complain. This is not the kind of image that increases market share and profitability. You may be overemphasizing schedule at the expense of reliability. A software reliability engineering program would push you into talking in specific terms with customers to find out what balance between delivery date and reliability best meets their needs.

10.   A typical comment on software reliability engineering (or any software technique) is that a team doesn't have time to do it. What are the ways to promote the technology to show that the up-front effort will reduce life-cycle effort?

ANSWER: Use of the operational profile, one of the key elements of software reliability engineering, pays quick dividends in reducing effort. It guides you precisely in focusing on the operations that are frequently used (or critical) and ignoring those that aren't. If you start applying software reliability engineering by implementing the operational profile, the project is likely to see benefits fairly early (for example, in guiding the division of effort for requirements reviews), motivating them to continue.

11.   Our processes for software (as well as hardware) are ISO 9000 certified. Therefore they meet the international standards for quality. We obtained ISO certification without having a formal software reliability engineering program. Our top management is committed to rigorously adhering to our present ISO-certified processes. Why should we change them now by introducing a software reliability engineering program?

ANSWER: ISO certification simply verifies that you have implemented the process that you claim to be using. This could be an antiquated, inefficient process that leaves you far from being competitive in your industry. Software reliability engineering is essential if your process is to become competitive, and it is essential if you are to reach the higher levels of the Capability Maturity Model evaluation, which do correlate with the level of quality of your software process.

12.   Our software product has been around for several years and has gone through several releases. We don't use software reliability engineering methods. Nonetheless, we haven't had a major failure of the product in the field or frequent customer complaints. This indicates that our current process is adequate. Why should we bother with software reliability engineering?

ANSWER: You are looking only at reliability, which is just one aspect of quality. The other important aspects are development time and cost. Software reliability engineering focuses on getting the right balance among reliability, development time, and cost in accordance with customer needs. There is a substantial likelihood that you are not meeting customer needs as well as you could be because you don't seem to know what they are in quantitative terms. Hence you are vulnerable to a competitor taking away your customers.

13.   We have been estimating the reliability of each release, using failure data from system test. However, we don't have an operational profile and won't develop one in the near future; it is too expensive and time-consuming to develop an operational profile and then to keep updating it for periodic software releases. We just learned that without an operational profile, our reliability estimates may be inaccurate. We have decided that it's not worth continuing our reliability estimation process. Is this the right decision?

ANSWER: No. Are you following the right approach in developing your operational profile? It usually doesn't require more than 1 to 2 staff months of effort (or perhaps 3 on very large projects) to develop the relevant operational profile(s). This is usually less than 1 percent of total project effort, so you shouldn't find developing an operational profile "too expensive and time consuming." Also, if you are only using the operational profile to improve the accuracy of reliability estimation, you may be missing some of the benefits. For example, the operational profile can be valuable in guiding allocation of development resources to the different operations and thus using them more efficiently.

14.   We have a software reliability engineering program in place. It includes a failure intensity objective for major faults, which is nonzero. Our customers know that our actual failure intensity will not be zero, but they expect us to at least aim for "perfection," which means a failure intensity of zero. How can we explain to them that our failure intensity objective is nonzero?

ANSWER: The best approach is to note that perfection is only attainable with infinite development time and infinite cost. Thus what they really want is "near perfection." The question is how near, and you are asking them to help you set a nonzero failure intensity objective to make your understanding of their needs more precise.

15.   Our company had a good software reliability engineering program before a major reorganization. After the reorganization, the software reliability engineering program deteriorated companywide, in all departments. How can we save it?

ANSWER: Make a list of the people previously involved in the software reliability engineering program who were convinced advocates. Organize a brainstorming meeting of these people to analyze the current situation (strengths, weaknesses, needs, assets) and determine the best strategies for rebuilding the program.

16.   Our company also had a good software reliability engineering program before a major reorganization. Now the program is still good in some departments, but weak or nonexistent in others. What can we do to bring the software reliability engineering program back on track?

ANSWER: Take a very similar approach to that described in the answer to Question 15, except that you should focus first on strengthening the good departments and second on spreading software reliability engineering to those departments where it is weak or nonexistent.

17.   There is a change of management in our organization. We have a software reliability engineering program. We also have a new boss who is a cost-cutter. She is proposing to reduce the budgets for all projects and programs across the board, by approximately the same percentage. What should we do to save the program?

ANSWER: Determine which projects are making the best use of software reliability engineering and where the strongest advocates of software reliability engineering are. Use your limited resources to support these projects and people. See if you can wean the projects that are making full use of software reliability engineering from support; it should be paying for itself, so they should be willing to support it as part of their normal development process.

18.   We also have a new cost-cutting boss. He wants to eliminate what he considers to be "nonessentials" (software reliability engineering is included) and leave the funding for "essentials" intact. How can we save the program?

ANSWER: Clearly you have to take the bull by the horns here and try to persuade your boss that software reliability engineering is essential. Because costs are important to him, muster all the financial evidence you can that shows that the financial benefits coming from software reliability engineering to his organization exceed the costs.

19.   One of the key people in our software reliability engineering program has just left the organization. She must be replaced as soon as possible in order to continue the program at an adequate level. Unfortunately, there is a temporary freeze on hiring, including replacements. What steps can we take to prevent the software reliability engineering program from being adversely affected?

ANSWER: Determine who are the best, most experienced advocates of software reliability engineering in the organization. Transfer one of these people into the key position.

20.   Many organizations have one or two technology zealots. These people can often bring in an approach and make it work out of sheer force of personality and skill. Once they leave, the technique often dies. What can be done to lower the risk of "donor rejection" such as this?

ANSWER: Try to institutionalize the practice so that it doesn't depend on one or two zealots. Introduce the practice originally in a group setting, with a group of practitioners brainstorming on how to best introduce it. Thus several people get to own the practice.

21.   Our software products are not very large in terms of lines of code. In our functional testing as well as system testing, most of the faults we find are minor. The number of major faults we find is usually too small for applying any of the statistical reliability estimation models or tools. We don't think it's worthwhile to apply the software reliability engineering tools to minor faults or to the combined count of major and minor faults, in which minor fault counts dominate. Therefore, we doubt that software reliability engineering is useful to us. Are we right?

ANSWER: You are viewing software reliability engineering in a very narrow sense: reliability growth models. Let us assume that you decide not to track reliability growth. You still can benefit greatly from applying operational profiles and certification test. Remember that certification test can work with zero failures occurring. If you don't do reliability growth test, you should definitely do certification test so that you know whether customers' needs are met prior to delivery.

22.   We have an existing product that is updated periodically. Each major release introduces new, additional features. We have an operational profile for the product, but it has to be updated for each major release to accommodate the new features. We have no real use data for the new features and must rely on engineering and marketing judgment. Some of our managers question the updated operational profile accuracy and think the use of software reliability engineering technology is not sufficiently accurate for us.

ANSWER: Fortunately, errors in the operational profile do not have serious effects. A 10 percent error in the occurrence probability for an operation will result in a 10 percent overallocation or underallocation of personnel to that operation. Present methods for allocating personnel certainly do no better and probably much worse than this. Measures of failure intensity are robust with respect to errors in the operational profile; a 10 percent error in an occurrence probability used in driving testing might cause the resulting failure intensity at the end of test to depart by 1 to 2 percent from what it otherwise would be.

23. Our test program tries to maximize test coverage (e.g., code and/or path coverage). We believe this is more effective for assuring software quality than the use of software reliability engineering techniques.

ANSWER: Test coverage is correlated with reliability. However, maximizing test coverage is not as efficient as applying software reliability engineering. You may test a lot of code or many paths that are seldom used. Thus test is likely to be more time consuming and more costly than would otherwise be the case.

24. We are developing a brand new product. We have no field data for a "similar product" and no experience with the use of the product. As a result, we have no real data on which to base the development of a realistic operational profile or a reliability objective. Although we could collect the opinions and judgments of our system engineers and marketing folks, we have doubts about whether such input data is sufficiently accurate for the use of software reliability engineering techniques. We therefore have doubts about the usefulness of software reliability engineering techniques at the present time.

ANSWER: Experience indicates that obtaining use data is much easier than you would think. Your product may be brand new, but it probably provides functions to users that were provided by a different technology in the past. Therefore, the use information often exists somewhere; you just have to dig it out. We have found many situations in which the use information was not in the technical but in the business side of the house. For example, billing is often based on use, and old billing records may be available. And as noted in Question 22, errors in the operational profile usually don't cause serious problems.

25. How many people does a project need to implement software reliability engineering?

ANSWER: The equivalent of one person part time should be sufficient for all but the largest projects (more than several hundred software developers). As you develop the operational profile for medium-size projects (perhaps 20 or more developers), you may involve several people part time because they have complementary areas of expertise. However, this will be for only a short time. One person working a few hours per week can handle software reliability engineering for the rest of the project. Because of the needs for peak staffing and for backup, you should train several people as a minimum. Training typically requires 2 days. The foregoing numbers relate to the incremental staffing required for software reliability engineering; clearly the effort for preparation of test cases and the execution of tests should not be included because it is required in any case.

26. Suppose you are not given sufficient resources or time to implement software reliability engineering or encounter too much resistance to implement it completely. Can you implement it partially? How?

ANSWER: Yes, you can implement software reliability engineering partially. How depends to some degree on the specifics of your project; you may find a consultant helpful here. However, implementing just the operational profile is often a good bet. Because it helps focus your effort, it often rapidly produces visible benefits, helping you win support.

27. How can I get the attention of busy people who do not read written material I send them on software reliability engineering?

ANSWER: You may be able to persuade some of these people to watch videos, either in a group or individually at home, as it is a pleasant break in their routine. Two possible videos you might lend them are Musa (1994c) and Musa, Keene, and Keller (1996).

8

Software Reliability Models

Recall that this is a background chapter. Hence it focuses more on the theory behind the practice of applying failure data to guide decisions than on the practice itself. In fact, it deals with just part of this theory, reliability growth models and their use in estimating failure intensity during reliability growth test.

To model software reliability one must first consider the principal factors that affect it: fault introduction, fault removal, and use. Fault introduction depends primarily on the characteristics of the product and the development process. Fault removal depends on time, the operational profile used in test, and the quality of the removal activity. Use is characterized by the operational profile. Because some of the foregoing factors are probabilistic in nature and operate over time, we usually formulate software reliability models in terms of random processes. We distinguish the models from each other in general terms by the probability distribution of failure times or the number of failures experienced and by the nature of the variation of the random process with time.

A software reliability model specifies the general form of the dependence of the failure process on the factors mentioned. We have assumed that it is, by definition, time-based. Although natural units are used extensively in practice in place of time, the two are proportional if computer utilization is constant. Hence we commonly develop models in terms of time, with the understanding that natural units can be substituted. We will follow this practice. The possibilities for different mathematical forms to describe the failure process are almost limitless. We have restricted ourselves to considering well-developed models that practitioners have applied fairly broadly with real data, experiencing reasonable results. You can determine the specific form from the general form by establishing the values of the parameters of the model through either (Hecht, 1977):

1. *Estimation.* Applying statistical inference procedures to system failure data

2. *Prediction.* Determining the values from properties of the software product and the development process (this can be done before any execution of the program)

There is always some uncertainty in the determination of the specific form.

Once you establish the specific form, you can determine many different characteristics of the failure process. For many models there are analytic expressions for the

1. Average number of failures experienced at any point in time

2. Average number of failures in a time interval

3. Failure intensity at any point in time

4. Probability distribution of failure intervals

A good software reliability model has several important characteristics. It

1. Gives good projections of future failure behavior

2. Computes useful quantities

3. Is simple

4. Is widely applicable

5. Is based on sound assumptions

Projection of future failure behavior assumes that the values of model parameters will not change for the period of projection. If the net effect of the opposing influences of fault introduction and fault removal should change substantially, we must either compensate for the change or wait until enough new failures have occurred so that we can reestimate the model parameters. Incorporating such changes into the models themselves is theoretically possible but has generally been impractical due to the added complexity. In any event, the complexity is not worthwhile, considering the accuracy with which we generally know parameters.

Most software reliability models are based on (although this is often not stated explicitly) using a stable program in a stable way. This means that neither the code nor the operational profile is changing. If the program and environment do change, they often do so and are usually handled in a piecewise fashion. Thus, the models focus mainly on fault removal. Most models can account for the effects of slow fault introduction, however. Some assume that the average net long-term effect of all factors must be a decrease in failure intensity. If neither fault introduction, fault removal, or operational profile changes are occurring, the failure intensity will be constant, and the model should simplify to accommodate this fact. We assume that we compare the behavior of the program with the requirements with enough thoroughness that we detect all failures. However, if we miss some, it is possible to compensate for them as discussed in Sec. 6.3.2.

For a program that has been released and is operational, it is common to defer installation of both new features and repairs to the next release. Assuming a constant operational profile, the program will exhibit a constant failure intensity.

In general terms, a good model enhances communication on a project and provides a common framework of understanding for the software development process. It also enhances visibility to management and other interested parties. These advantages are valuable even if the projections made with the model in a specific case are not as accurate as one might like.

Developing a software reliability model that is useful in practice involves substantial theoretical work, tool building, and the accumulation of a body of lore from practical experience. This effort generally requires several person years. In contrast, the application of a model that is well established in practice requires a very small fraction of project resources. Consequently, we will consider this factor as one of the criteria for selection.

Some have suggested applying a range of models to each project. The ones that perform best (or some weighted combination of them) would be used. This approach may be suitable for research investigations. However, the use of more than one or two models is conceptually and economically impractical for real projects. It is necessary that project members understand what the parameters of the models mean in physical terms related to the software so that they can make intelligent judgments. They cannot readily understand and use many models simultaneously. Also, the time and costs involved escalate rapidly as you increase the number of models you apply.

8.1 General Characteristics

A *software reliability model,* as previously noted, usually has the form of a random process that describes the behavior of failures with respect to time. Specification of the model generally includes specification of a function of time such as the mean value function (expected number of failures) or failure intensity. The parameters of the function are primarily dependent on fault removal activity and properties of the software product and the development process (recall that we generally handle a substantial addition of features by starting a new "piece" of the time function; we can handle a small continuous addition of features by adjusting parameter values). Properties of the product include size, complexity, and structure. The most significant product characteristic is the size of the developed (created or modified for this application) code. Properties of the development process include, among others, software engineering technologies, tools used, and level of experience of personnel. The "time" involved in the characterization of the models is a cumulative time. The origin may be arbitrarily set. It is frequently the start of system test.

Software reliability models almost always assume that failures are independent of each other. They may do this through assuming that failure times are independent of each other or by making the Poisson process assumption of independent increments. This condition would appear to be met for most situations. Failures are the result of two processes: the introduction of faults and their activation through selection of the input states. Because both of these processes are random, the chance of influence on one failure by another is small. Influence would require two conditions. One fault would have to affect the introduction of another during development. Further, an input state that results in failure for the first fault would have to cause the selection of an input state that results in failure for the second fault. It is very unlikely that both conditions would occur together.

Theoreticians sometimes dispute the independence assumption because they do not recognize the "two-process" situation. For example, they may argue that programmers tend to have patterns of errors (that is, one error may influence the next one). The possibility that this might create related faults does not by itself imply the existence of related failures.

Similarly, they sometimes state that one failure can prevent another failure from occurring because the failure prevents access to or "hides" certain code. Prevention of access to code may occur occasionally in unit test, but it is much less common in practice in the later project phases where practitioners commonly apply software reliability models. The failures that mask other failures tend to have been eliminated by this point.

In any case, an investigation of 15 projects (1 in subsystem test, 8 in system test, 6 in operational phase) in Musa (1979d) strongly supports the independence conclusion, in that no significant correlation was found.

It is possible to develop both macromodels and micromodels of software reliability. We have concentrated on macromodels. They generally have the greatest usefulness per unit effort required to apply them. They deal with the major factors and effects that are the principal concerns of software engineers and managers. Data collection for such models is usually easy. Micromodels may be more accurate in certain circumstances because they may deal with particular factors that are important in those circumstances. However, they usually attain the accuracy through added complexity and a limited sphere of applicability. They may sometimes have the potential of providing theoretical insight into underlying processes. For example, Shooman (1983) presents a path decomposition model that is related to program structure. Unfortunately, the theory is usually very difficult to verify because of the complex data collection and analysis involved.

One example of microbehavior that has been observed in certain circumstances is clustering of failures (Crow and Singpurwalla, 1984). In many cases, these may be cascaded failures, and one should not define the second and following failures as failures at all. The other most likely cause of clustering is localization of input state selection to an area of the input space associated with a high fault density. Localization typically occurs when successive input states are related to one another. This frequently happens in cyclic systems like feedback control systems. An example would be an aircraft control system. A common reason for entering a region of input space associated with high fault density is the effect of data corruption. Data corruption can drive you into an area of input space for which the system was not designed. Thus clustering might occur for a cyclic system in which the data had been corrupted beyond the point at which the system could handle them properly.

8.1.1 Random process

Both the human error process that introduces defects into code and the run selection process that determines which code is being executed at any time are dependent on an enormous number of time-varying variables. The use of a random process model is appropriate for such a situation. There are two equivalent ways of describing the failure random process: the times of failures or the number of failures in a given period.

We denote T_i and T_i' the random variables representing times to the ith failure and between the $(i-1)$th and the ith failures, respectively. The realizations (specific instances) of T_i and T_i' will be denoted by t_i and t_i', respectively. Let $M(t)$ be a random process representing the number of failures experienced by time t. The realization of this random process will be denoted $m(t)$. The mean value function $\mu(t)$ is defined as

$$\mu(t) = E(M(t)) \tag{8.1}$$

which represents the expected number of failures at time t. We will assume that the function $\mu(t)$ is a nondecreasing, continuous, and differentiable function of time t. The failure intensity function of the $M(t)$ process is the instantaneous rate of change of the expected number of failures with respect to time. We define it by

$$\lambda(t) = \frac{d\mu(t)}{dt} \tag{8.2}$$

It is possible that one could plan or manipulate the selection of runs during test. The tester has at least partial control of the environment, and this could make random selection of input states a poor model. However, a random process is still a reasonable model of failure behavior. The introduction of faults into code and the relationship between input state and code executed are usually both sufficiently complex processes to make deterministic prediction of failure impractical. In other words, you cannot predict which input states are more likely to yield failures. Consequently, a deterministic selection of input states will not have a deterministic effect on reliability. Of course, if the relative frequencies of selection have changed, the operational profile has changed and that will affect the reliability.

There is one case in which manipulation of the characteristics of the random process can occur. It requires that

1. The program segments executed for different input states are disjoint with respect to each other.

2. There are clear differences in fault density between different program segments.

Disjoint means that each input state maps to a different set of program segments executed, and there are no program segments executed in common by different input states. The clear differences in fault density may occur when some segments may be reused code from previous programs and some may be newly written. In this situation, it is possible to manipulate reliability figures to somewhat higher or lower figures by biasing the selection of input states. You select input states that exercise code that has either high or low fault density. Note that the essential character of failures as a random process is unchanged. You cannot predict when the next failure will occur, even if you can manipulate average behavior. One example of manipulation would be to select input states deterministically in such a way that no code segments are reexecuted. If fault density is the same for all segments, the observed failure intensity would tend to be constant. Fault repair would show no effect on failure intensity. In reality, failure intensity based on random selection of input states would be decreasing.

8.1.2 With and without fault removal

Software reliability models must cover two situations, programs in which faults are being removed when failures occur and programs in which they are not. The situation of "no removal" occurs during certification test and operation in the field. The situation of "no fault removal" is simple; we will cover it in this section. The situation of "with fault removal" occurs in reliability growth test. When we say "no fault removal," we really mean "deferred fault removal." Testers identify the failures, but debuggers do not remove the underlying faults from the program until the next release.

With no fault removal, the failure intensity is constant for the duration of the release. Hence, we can conveniently model the failure process by a homogeneous Poisson process. This implies that the failure intervals are exponentially distributed and that the number of failures in a given time period follows a Poisson distribution. If the failure intensity is λ and the period of execution of the program is t, the number of failures during this period is distributed Poisson with parameter λt.

As mentioned previously, a principal factor that causes reliability to vary with time is the removal of faults that have caused failures. In general, the time of removal does not coincide with the time of original failure. This could lead to substantial complication in characterizing the failure process. However, you can handle it by assuming instantaneous removal and not counting the reoccurrence of the same failure. You would recount it, however, if the recurrence were due to inability to locate and remove the fault. Although the result is not precisely equivalent, it is a very good approximation. All the leading models take this approach.

8.1.3 Particularization

The model specifies the general form of the dependence of the failure process on the variables mentioned. We can determine the specific form from the general form, at least in theory, through determination of parameters. This can occur in one of two ways:

1. *Prediction.*   We use properties of the software product and the development process to particularize the model by determination of its parameters (this can be done prior to any execution of the program).

2. *Estimation.*   We apply inference (for example, parameter estimation) procedures to failure data.

A model and an inference procedure are commonly associated. Together, they provide projection through time. Without a model, you could not make inferences about reliability outside the time period for which failure data have been taken. In fact, you could not make inferences at all because the size of the failure sample would be 1. The model provides the structure that relates behavior at different points in time. It thus, in effect, provides for a sample of reasonable size to be taken.

Inference also generally includes the determination of the range of uncertainty. We either establish confidence intervals for the parameters or determine posterior probability distributions for significant quantities in the case of bayesian inference. A confidence interval represents a range of values within which we expect a parameter to lie with a certain statistical degree of confidence. For example, the 0.75 confidence interval of total failures that we will experience in infinite time may be 150 to 175. We generally extend the determination of ranges of uncertainty to quantities that are derived from the models as well.

8.2   Classification

Musa and Okumoto (1983) developed a classification scheme for software reliability models. The scheme permits you to derive relationships for groups of models. It highlights relationships among the models and suggests new models where gaps occur in the classification scheme. It reduces the task of model comparison.

The scheme classifies models in terms of five different attributes:

1. *Time domain.*   Calendar or execution (CPU or processor) time.

2. *Category.*   The number of failures that you can experience in infinite time is *finite* or *infinite.*

3. *Type.*   The distribution of the number of failures experienced by the time specified.

4. *Class* (finite failures category only).   Functional form of the failure intensity in terms of time.

5. *Family* (infinite failures category only).   Functional form of the failure intensity in terms of the expected number of failures experienced.

Finite failures models seem to have a natural affinity, from a credibility viewpoint, with situations in which there is a vigorous fault removal program. On the other hand, it would appear that infinite failures models might have an affinity for the weak fault-removal situation. Note that infinite failures does not necessarily imply infinite faults. A situation of infinite faults appears improbable because the amount of code is finite. The case of infinite failures is credible for a program executed for infinite time.

Musa and Okumoto chose the classification approach to be different for the two different categories because of greater analytical simplicity and physical meaning. For finite failures models of Poisson and binomial types, the class represents both the functional form of the failure intensity in terms of time and the failure time distribution of an individual fault. The classes take their names from these distributions. The distribution of the intervals between failures depends on both type and class. The families of the infinite failures models take their names from the functional form of the failure intensity in terms of expected failures.

Table 8.1 illustrates the classification scheme with respect to the last four attributes. It is identical for both kinds of time. We illustrate the scheme by showing where many of the published models fit within it. Poisson is currently the most important type, followed by binomial. The references indicated in the table provide detailed descriptions of the models.

Only the Musa basic (exponential) and Musa-Okumoto logarithmic Poisson (logarithmic) execution time models have been explicitly defined as being in the execution time domain. The other models are either calendar time models, or their time domain is not explicitly stated. Many special distributions can occur that do not have common names. We denote them with letter-number codes (for example, T1, T2, T3, where T stands for type). Similarly, there is a class without a commonly named per-fault failure distribution; it is denoted C1. The Littlewood-Verrall general model can fall in different classifications depending on the form of the reliability change function $\xi(i)$ for the ith failure. For the infinite failures category, a specified family may lead to a particular type of model. "Holes" in the table do not imply that models can always be developed to fill them. Some combinations of family and type or class and type may be impossible.

8.3   Comparison

There are many published models in the literature. This proliferation of models has been useful to the extent that many different approaches have been explored. However, very few of them have been applied practically to a substantial extent.

Some early researchers (for example, Schick and Wolverton, 1978; Sukert, 1979) attempted to compare some of the different models.

TABLE 8.1   Software Reliability Model Classification scheme

	Finite failures category models		
	Type*		
Class†	Poisson	Binomial	Other types
Exponential	Musa (1975) Moranda (1975) Schneidewind (1975) Goel-Okumoto (1979)	Jelinski-Moranda (1972) Shooman (1972)	Goel-Okumoto (1978) Musa (1979a) Keiller et al. (1983)
Weibull		Schick-Wolverton (1973) Wagoner (1973)	
C1		Schick-Wolverton (1978)	
Pareto		Littlewood (1981)	
Gamma	Yamada-Ohba-Osaki (1983)		

	Infinite failures category models			
	Type*			
Family‡	T1	T2	T3	Poisson
Geometric	Moranda (1975)			Musa-Okumoto (1984b)
Inverse linear		Littlewood-Verrall (1973)		
Inverse polynomial (2nd degree)			Littlewood-Verrall (1973)	
Power				Crow (1974)

*Type: Distribution of number of failures experienced.
†Class: Functional form of failure intensity (in terms of time).
‡Family: Functional form of failure intensity (in terms of expected number of failures).

Unfortunately, these efforts were handicapped by insufficient data of high quality and an absence of standards about the comparison or evaluation criteria to be employed. Somewhat later, more good-quality failure data on a variety of software systems became available (for example, Musa, 1979b). Several researchers jointly proposed comparison criteria, incorporating comments from many reviewers in the field (Iannino, Musa, Okumoto, and Littlewood, 1984). To provide a sound and efficient basis for comparison, Musa and Okumoto (1983) classified the various models. They explored and examined the assumptions underlying software reliability theory. Musa, Iannino, and Okumoto (1987) conducted a number of studies that compared substantial groups of models.

We will first describe the studies that relate to time domains. Then we will present the comparisons of groups of models based on other classifications.

8.3.1 Time domains

A great deal of evidence demonstrates the superiority of execution time over calendar (ordinary) time for modeling (Hecht, 1981; Musa and Okumoto, 1984a; and Trachtenberg, 1985). This fact is generally accepted in the field. Execution time is preferable because it best characterizes the failure-inducing stress placed on software. Consider two different facilities associated with an operating system, an editor and a matrix manipulation package. Each is activated by input states that occur randomly in accordance with their operational profiles. The editor, perhaps executing 2 to 3 execution hours daily, is certainly more stressed than the matrix package, which might execute for only a few execution minutes. In practice we tend to work with natural units or ordinary time because of ease of use and familiarity to customers. However, execution time provides the real theoretical base. Hence, unless ordinary time is proportional to execution time, we must in reality work with execution time. We do then convert execution time to ordinary time for the benefit of customers.

You might argue that "instructions executed" is even more fundamental. Hence you might speak of failure intensity in terms of failures per trillion (10^{12}) instructions executed. Note that a machine executing 300 million instructions per second executes this number in less than an hour. The "more fundamental" contention is probably valid. It takes account of the fact that software can execute on machines of different instruction rates. No compensation is necessary for different machines. However, there are serious problems with the foregoing approach. Most engineers have a better physical grasp of time. But more important, hardware reliability is defined in terms of time. It is essential that we be able to combine hardware and software reliabilities to get system reliability. Consequently, we use execution time rather than instructions executed and make adjustments where necessary.

We will demonstrate the superiority of execution time with some actual data. We use a flexible generic failure intensity function that can represent most published models and fit it to observed failure intensities expressed in each of the time domains. We then compare the fits and examine how well trends are shown as a function of time domain. Consult Musa and Okumoto (1984a) for a detailed discussion.

8.3.1.1 Defining observed failure intensity.

We will define observed failure intensity (expected failures per unit time) based on groups of failures. Suppose that we have observed m_e failures during $(0, t_e]$. Let the observation interval $(0, t_e]$ be partitioned at every kth failure occurrence time so that there are p disjoint subintervals. (Note that p is the smallest integer greater than or equal to m_e/k.) The observed intensity r_l for the lth subinterval $(t_{k \times (l-1)}, t_{k \times l}]$ is given by

$$r_l = \begin{cases} \dfrac{k}{t_{k \times l} - t_{k \times (l-1)}} & l = 1, \ldots, p - 1 \\[3ex] \dfrac{m_e - k(p - 1)}{t_e - t_{k \times (l-1)}} & l = p \end{cases} \tag{8.3}$$

where the subscript notation denotes the product of the two indices. For example, for $k = 5$ we can obtain the observed failure intensity for the second ($l = 2$) subinterval (t_5, t_{10}] as $5/(t_{10} - t_5)$.

Note that the observed failure intensities as such are *independent* of each other because each subinterval is chosen to be disjoint with respect to the others. This independence of the data makes it possible to apply the least squares method. The ordinary least squares method cannot be applied if the relationship of the cumulative number of failures with time is used because cumulative failures are dependent on the previous data.

The observed failure intensity is associated with time

$$t_l = \frac{t_{k \times (l-1)} + t_{k \times l}}{2} \tag{8.4}$$

Note that the r_ls are assumed to be independent of each other because the subintervals are disjoint.

The failure data described in Table 8.2 are available as successive failure intervals in seconds for execution time and days for calendar time, respectively. The observation interval is partitioned at every kth failure occurrence time, so there are at least k failures in each subinterval. Grouping a small number of failures (a small value of k) will result in large variations in the estimated failure intensity, whereas grouping a large number of failures (a large value of k) will result in too much smoothing. We have selected a group of five failures ($k = 5$) as a reasonable compromise in the following analysis. We investigated the use of different values of k; there was little effect on the results of the comparison. Although we may lose some information because of grouping failures, an advantage of the failure intensity approach is that we do not assume any specific model or distribution. This approach is useful, especially in analyzing a general trend or functional relationship of the failure intensity with respect to time.

We obtained the observed failure intensity using Eq. 8.3, based on execution and calendar time for each of 15 data sets. Figures 8.1 and 8.2 show plots of the observed failure intensity (marked points connected by a dashed line) for the data set T1 based on execution and calendar time, respectively. They are useful for studying a general trend. For instance, for the system T1 there is a decreasing trend as a whole in the execution time data (see Fig. 8.1). On the other hand, there are

TABLE 8.2 Characteristics of Software Systems Studied

System designator	System designator—reference source	Reference source	Delivered object instructions	Programmers	Execution time (h)	Calendar time (days)	Size of failure sample	Nature of system
					Total test time			
T1	1	Musa (1979b)	21,700	9	24.6	92	136	Real time command and control
T2	2	Musa (1979b)	27,700	5	30.2	72	54	Real time command and control
T3	3	Musa (1979b)	23,400	6	18.7	55	38	Real time command and control
T4	4	Musa (1979b)	33,500	7	14.6	71	53	Real time command and control
T5	5	Musa (1979b)	2,445,000	275	1785	173	831	Real time commercial
T6	6	Musa (1979b)	5,700	8	1.4	58	73	Commercial (subsystem)
T16	27	Musa (1979b)	126,100	8	1197.9	79	41	Military
T17	40	Musa (1979b)	180,000	8	5436.7	347	101	Military
T18		Musa (1979b)	?	?	9935.2	897	163	Military
T19	17	Musa (1979b)	61,900	8	64.9	56	38	Military
T20		Sukert (1976)	115,346	?	615.3	162	2191	Military command and control
T21		Musa (1979b)	25,000	?	32.3	89	75	Military
T22	ISEE-C	Miller (1980)	75,000*	4	8.2	42	118	Space
T23	AEM	Miller (1980)	50,000*	4	16.2	58	180	Space
T25	SMM	Miller (1980)	85,000*	7	21.6	216	213	Space

*High-level source statements, including comments.

271

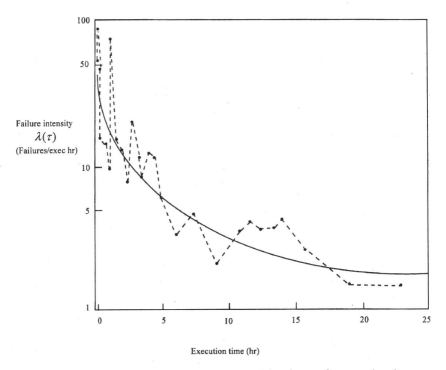

Figure 8.1 Failure intensity for system T1: data and fitted curve for execution time data.

large variations in the calendar time data (see Fig. 8.2) and hence, a trend is not so evident as for the execution time data. It appears likely that the daily use of the program is both increasing rapidly and exhibiting substantial variability and that this is confounding the failure intensity picture. The failure intensity in calendar time is consequently generally increasing and highly variable.

In the following section we will discuss the procedure we used for fitting a generic function to the observed failure intensity.

8.3.1.2 Fitting the observed failure intensity. Let $\lambda(t)$ be a theoretical failure intensity function of generic time t. In searching the data for possible trends we used the generic function

$$\lambda(t) = \alpha t^{\gamma - 1} \exp(-\beta t^{\gamma}) \tag{8.5}$$

where α, β, and γ are real-valued parameters. Note that the assumed function Eq. 8.5 is flexible. Depending on the values of the parameters, it can describe such cases for the failure intensity as a monotonically increasing or decreasing function or a unimodal function of time. The

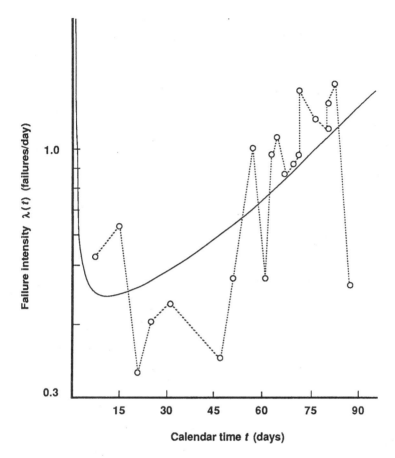

Figure 8.2 Failure intensity for system T1: data and fitted curve for calendar time data.

function represents the exponential and Weibull classes, and it is also a good approximation of the Pareto class and the geometric and inverse linear families. Therefore, the function can represent most published models.

Figures 8.3 and 8.4 show the flexibility of the function. In Fig. 8.3, where $\beta > 0$, the function is monotonically decreasing for $\gamma \leq 1$ or unimodal (first increasing and then decreasing) for $\mu > 1$. On the other hand, in Fig. 8.4, where $\beta < 0$, the function is monotonically increasing for $\gamma \geq 1$ or monotonically decreasing for $0 < \gamma < 1$. Finally, you can easily see from Eq. 8.5 that the function will be time-invariant (that is, constant) when $\beta = 0$ and $\gamma = 1$.

We have shown the flexibility of the function given in Eq. 8.5. It is also simple to work with. We therefore used this function to analyze trends in the observed failure intensity γ_l at times t_l, $l = 1, ..., p$.

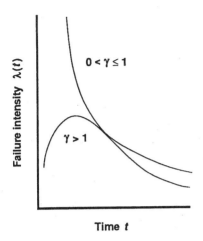

Figure 8.3 Shapes of the function for $\lambda(t) = \alpha t^{\gamma-1} \exp(\mu \beta t^\gamma)$ for $\beta > 0$.

We also developed a method that finds the estimates of the unknown parameters α, β, and γ using the least squares method. Note that in tracking and predicting reliability status, software managers or engineers usually need a constant *relative* (rather than absolute) accuracy for MTTF and hence failure intensity. Therefore, we will minimize the sum of squares of the logarithms of the ratio of $\lambda(t_l)$ to r_l to estimate the unknown parameters. This approach also yields analytical simplicity.

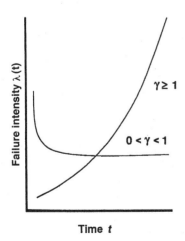

Figure 8.4 Shapes of the function $\lambda(t) = \alpha t^{\gamma-1} \exp(-\mu \beta t^\gamma)$ for $\beta < 0$.

Let ε_l represent the logarithm of the relative error of the lth data point. Thus, we have

$$\ln r_l = \ln \lambda(t_l) + \varepsilon_l$$
$$= \ln \alpha + (\gamma - 1) \ln t_l - \beta t_l^\gamma + \varepsilon_l \tag{8.6}$$

where we obtained the last equality by substituting Eq. 8.5 into the first. We can then find the estimates $\hat{\alpha}$, $\hat{\beta}$, and $\hat{\gamma}$ by minimizing

$$S(\alpha, \beta, \gamma) = \sum_{l=1}^{p} \varepsilon_l^2$$
$$= \sum_{l=1}^{p} [\ln r_l - \ln \alpha - (\gamma - 1)\ln t_l + \beta t_l^\gamma]^2 \tag{8.7}$$

Equation 8.7 represents a nonlinear regression or a nonlinear minimization problem. Hence, we can find the estimates only through numerical procedures. There are several algorithms available that find the minimum of a nonlinear function. We used the procedure described in App. D of Musa, Iannino, and Okumoto (1987) to find $\hat{\alpha}$, $\hat{\beta}$, and $\hat{\gamma}$ for 15 data sets based on execution and calendar time.

Table 8.3 summarizes the results for both execution and calendar time. For illustration, consider the data set T1. The fitted curve, shown as a solid line in Fig. 8.1, is a decreasing function of execution time (because $\hat{\beta} > 0$, $\hat{\gamma} < 1$). Similarly, we plotted a fitted curve for the data

TABLE 8.3   A Summary of Regression Analysis of Log-Failure Intensity

System	Execution time			Calendar time		
	$\hat{\beta}$	$\hat{\gamma}$	R^2	$\hat{\beta}$	$\hat{\gamma}$	R^2
T1	0.2672×10^{-2}	0.5185	0.939*	-0.9190×10^{-1}	0.7181	0.465*
T2	0.4849×10^{-2}	0.3786	0.965*	0.1139×10^{-2}	1.726	0.442
T3	0.2948×10^{-1}	0.3142	0.992*	-0.7863	0.1022	0.849†
T4	0.9029×10^{-3}	0.7644	0.961*	0.4757×10^{-1}	0.7561	0.724†
T5	-0.4682×10^{-6}	0.7465	0.203*	-0.3453×10^{-1}	0.6070	0.063*
T6	-0.1010	0.3260	0.658*	-0.6879	0.2459	0.658*
T16	0.3072×10^{-3}	0.5654	0.906*	-0.7367	0.1310	0.862*
T17	0.9669×10^{-3}	0.4544	0.882*	0.1558×10^{-2}	1.250	0.564*
T18	0.2085×10^{-3}	0.5331	0.917*	0.5935×10^{-2}	0.7838	0.624*
T19	0.9476×10^{-4}	0.7921	0.996*	0.8499×10^{-2}	1.377	0.740
T20	0.8861×10^{-5}	0.7907	0.378*	0.1833×10^{-2}	1.388	0.262*
T21	-0.9702×10^{-1}	0.2326	0.835*	-0.5925	0.3038	0.334
T22	0.3606×10^{-3}	0.7185	0.627*	-0.6846	0.3048	0.383*
T23	-0.2210×10^{-2}	0.5373	0.397*	-0.4780	0.3791	0.197†
T25	-0.2391×10^{-2}	0.4949	0.619*	0.4983×10^{-2}	0.8576	0.364*

*Highly significant (99 percent).

†Significant (95 percent).

set T1 based on calendar time in Fig. 8.2. Because $\hat{\beta}<0$, $\hat{\gamma}<1$, the fitted curve (as shown in Fig. 8.2) is decreasing and then increasing. Using the results obtained in this section, we investigated the appropriate time metric (execution time versus calendar time) for software reliability models, described in the following section.

8.3.1.3 Comparing execution time and calendar time.
We compared the use of execution time with that of calendar time for software reliability models based on the regression analysis for 15 sets of failure data. We considered the following two criteria: estimated variance of regression errors and coefficient of multiple determination.

Estimated variance of regression errors. To compare the fit for the two time domains, we assumed that the ε_is were independently and identically distributed with a variance of σ^2. Because we estimated three parameters from p data points, the degrees of freedom were reduced to $p-3$. We then estimated the variance as

$$\hat{\sigma}^2 = \frac{S(\hat{\alpha}, \hat{\beta}, \hat{\gamma})}{p-3} \tag{8.8}$$

which represents variation of the data points around the fitted curve. The smaller value of $\hat{\sigma}^2$ suggests the better fit.

Note that the estimated intensities have different units, that is, failures per second for execution time and failures per day for calendar time. Therefore, if the sum of the *absolute* errors were minimized for estimating the parameters, it would not make sense to compare the estimated variances for execution time with those for calendar time. In the regression analysis described in Eq. 8.7, however, we minimize the sum of the *relative* errors. Hence, we can compare the values of the estimated variance $\hat{\sigma}^2$ to decide which time metric yields the better fit.

Let $\hat{\sigma}_{ET}$ and $\hat{\sigma}_{CT}$ be the estimated standard deviations for execution and calendar time, respectively. Figure 8.5 shows plots of $\hat{\sigma}_{CT}$ versus $\hat{\sigma}_{ET}$ for the 15 data sets. A point associated with any data set will fall in the upper-left area of the triangle if execution time models fit better than calendar time models, that is, $\hat{\sigma}_{ET}<\hat{\sigma}_{CT}$. It will fall in the lower-right area if calendar time models fit better $(\hat{\sigma}_{ET}>\hat{\sigma}_{CT})$. If both are almost equal, the point will be close to the dashed line, that is, $\hat{\sigma}_{ET} = \hat{\sigma}_{CT}$. Only three points (T17, T20, and T25) out of the 15 points show superiority of calendar to execution time. For the rest of the data sets execution time is shown to be either equivalent (T6) or superior (T1, T2, T3, T4, T5, T16, T18, T19, T21, T22, and T23)

It is of further interest to statistically determine, based on the results, whether there is a difference between paired values of the estimated standard deviation. The sign test is an extremely simple test that can be used for this case. It is useful for many such engineering cases when the underlying distributions are not known or are too diffi-

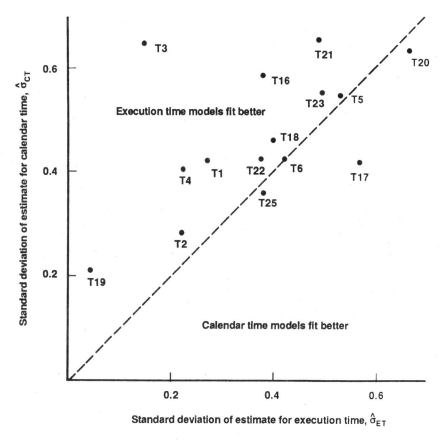

Figure 8.5 Standard deviations of regression error for calendar time and execution time.

cult to determine. Because we don't use the magnitude of the difference between two values, this test is less powerful than a parametric test. This disadvantage is offset by the advantage of being quick and simple. We therefore use the sign test in the analysis.

The sign test is based on the binomial distribution, which involves analyzing pairs of data points based on the sign of the differences (that is, $\sigma_{ET} - \sigma_{CT}$). With a null hypothesis H_0: $\sigma_{ET} = \sigma_{CT}$, you would expect that the probability of a positive or negative difference is 1/2. Therefore, if H_0 is true, there should be nearly an equal number of positive and negative signs. If one sign appears a significantly small or large number of times for the size of the sample, we reject H_0 because there is a significant difference between them. Note that we can apply the sign test only where there are no ties in the data. When there is a tie, the practice is to discard that piece of data and reduce the sample size by 1.

In comparing the paired values of $\hat{\sigma}_{ET}$ and $\hat{\sigma}_{CT}$ for each data set, there is only one tie and hence the sample size is $15 - 1 = 14$. The critical value for rejecting H_0 at the 90 percent confidence level is 3 (Lipson and Sheth, 1973). Because the three points (T17, T20, and T25) were shown as $\hat{\sigma}_{ET} > \hat{\sigma}_{CT}$, we could conclude from the sign test at the 90 percent confidence level that execution time data can be fit significantly better than the corresponding calendar time data. Therefore, we can consider execution time as the appropriate metric for software reliability models.

Coefficient of multiple determination. We now investigate whether a significant trend exists in the observed failure intensity using a coefficient of multiple determination R^2. We define this coefficient as the ratio of the sum of squares resulting from the trend model to that from a constant model subtracted from 1, that is,

$$R^2 = 1 - \frac{S(\hat{\alpha}, \hat{\beta}, \hat{\gamma})}{S(\hat{\hat{\alpha}}, 0, 1)} \tag{8.9}$$

Note that $\hat{\hat{\alpha}}$ represents the least squares estimate of α for the model with only a constant term, that is, $\beta = 0$ and $\gamma = 1$ in Eq. 8.6. It is given by

$$\ln \hat{\hat{\alpha}} = \frac{1}{p} \sum_{l=1}^{p} \ln r_l \tag{8.10}$$

Recall that r_l is given by Eq. 8.3. Therefore, R^2 measures the percentage of the total variation about the mean accounted for by the fitted curve. In other words, it is a measure of usefulness of the terms, other than the constant, in the models. The larger it is, the better the fitted equation explains the variation in the data.

For 15 data sets we compute the R^2 values from Eq. 8.9 for the execution and calendar time data and summarize the results in Table 8.3. Note that fitting curves to the model-free failure intensity estimates accounts for a greater percentage of variability about the mean when using execution time than when using calendar time.

To investigate whether a significant trend exists in the estimated intensity, we will test the null hypothesis and $H_0 : \beta = 0$ and $\gamma = 1$ against $H_0 : \beta \neq 0$ or $\gamma \neq 1$ using the F-test (Litzau, 1986). Because the degrees of freedom associated with $S(\hat{\hat{\alpha}}, 0, 1) - S(\hat{\alpha}, \hat{\beta}, \hat{\gamma})$ and $S(\hat{\alpha}, \hat{\beta}, \hat{\gamma})$ are 2 and $p - 3$, respectively, the quantities $[S(\hat{\hat{\alpha}}, 0, 1) - S(\hat{\alpha}, \hat{\beta}, \hat{\gamma})]/2$ and $S(\hat{\alpha}, \hat{\beta}, \hat{\gamma})/(p - 3)$ yield the estimated variances due to the two parameters β and γ and for the trend model of Eq. 8.5, respectively. Then the ratio

$$F = \frac{[S(\hat{\hat{\alpha}}, 0, 1) - S(\hat{\alpha}, \hat{\beta}, \hat{\gamma})]/2}{S(\hat{\alpha}, \hat{\beta}, \hat{\gamma})/(p - 3)} \tag{8.11}$$

should follow the F distribution with degrees of freedom 2 and $p-3$ under the normality assumption of ε_ls. If the calculated value F from

Eq. 8.11 is greater than $F_{2,p-3;\alpha}$, which is the α percentile of the F distribution with degrees of freedom 2 and $p - 3$, we can be $(1 - \alpha)$ 100 percent confident that we should reject H_0 (that is, there is a significant trend). The results will be said to be significant if H_0 is rejected at the significance level $\alpha = 0.05$ and highly significant if at $\alpha = 0.01$.

Table 8.3 summarizes the results from this significance test for 15 data sets. We observe that the fitted models are all highly significant for execution time. Also note from the estimates that the fitted curves show decreasing trends because in most cases $\beta > 0$ and $0 \beta \gamma = 1$. Even for T5, T6, T21, T23, and T25, the curves are decreasing most of the time.

On the other hand, results for calendar time indicate that H_0 should be accepted half of the time (that is, $\beta > 0$ and $\gamma = 1$). The trend model is not any better than the constant model in explaining the data. This means either

1. We don't have the right model.
2. Calendar time is a poor metric or independent variable for software reliability models.

Note that we have picked a flexible generic function as given in Eq. 8.5, which should represent many models of interest to us. We do not want more complex models (that is, more parameters). Therefore, the second statement appears to be the case. There is no structure or pattern to the failure intensity when expressed in calendar time.

The superiority of execution time has also been demonstrated by, among others, Hecht (1981) and Trachtenberg (1985).

8.3.2 Model groups

We will now discuss the comparison of model groups in the execution time domain based on category, type, and class or family. These groups include the models that have been most widely applied in practice. We first discuss the evaluation criteria employed in making the comparisons and then the failure data used. We will then evaluate the important model attributes.

8.3.2.1 Criteria. Iannino, Musa, Okumoto, and Littlewood (1984) proposed the criteria discussed in this section. Note that the criteria are "intrinsic." Attributes such as the documentation quality and the human interface quality of supporting tools are very important, but they depend on the implementation. They are not characteristic of the model per se. It should be pointed out that functional validity and "insight gained" are valuable characteristics of models, even though not mentioned by Iannino, Musa, Okumoto, and Littlewood (1984).

We can use these criteria for assessment (determining the absolute worth of a model) as well as comparison. Comparison should be done with relation to a variety of software systems. We must, of course, collect the data with care. It would not be reasonable to compare models with poor quality data or, worse, data of unequal quality. However, tolerance to or capability to compensate for certain types of poor data is a desirable quality in a model.

We expect that comparisons will cause some models to be rejected because they meet few of the criteria discussed here. On the other hand, there may or may not be a clear choice between the more acceptable models. The relative weight to be placed on the different criteria may depend on the context in which we are applying the model. When comparing two models, we should consider all criteria simultaneously. We should not eliminate models by one criterion before considering other criteria, except if projective validity is grossly unsatisfactory. It is not expected that a model must satisfy *all* criteria to be useful.

The proposed criteria included projective validity, quality of assumptions, applicability, and simplicity. We will discuss each of the criteria in more detail in the following sections. We will then describe the model comparisons that have been made using the criteria.

Projective validity. Projective validity is the capability of the model to project future failure behavior from present and past failure behavior (that is, data). This capability is significant only when failure behavior is changing. Hence, it is usually considered for a test phase, but it can be applied to the field when repairs are being regularly made.

Software reliability engineering in current practice estimates just current failure intensity, which is effectively a projection of zero execution time. In comparing models here, we use a more stringent criterion of nonzero projection time so that we select models with the potential to handle more demanding practice needs in the future. This means, however, that we cannot use projective validity as a basis for choosing between multiple models that we might recommend for use in applying data in reliability growth test (both would have zero projection error because of zero projection time). Hence we use goodness of fit of the model to the existing failure data as the criterion for choice for that case.

We use a simple number of failures approach here, because it is easy to understand and apply. From this point on in this chapter, we will characterize time as execution time τ, due to its superiority for failure models. We describe the failure random process by $(M(\tau), \tau \geq 0)$, representing failures experienced by time τ. Such a counting process is characterized by specifying the distribution of $M(\tau)$, including the mean value function $\mu(\tau)$.

Assume that we have observed q failures by the end of test time τ_q. We use the failure data up to time $\tau_e (\leq \tau_q)$ to estimate the parameters of

$\mu(\tau)$. Substituting the estimates of the parameters in the mean value function yields the estimate of the number of failures $\hat{\mu}(\tau_q)$ by τ_q. We compare the estimate with the actually observed number q. This procedure is repeated for various values of τ_e.

We can visually check the projective validity by plotting the relative error $(\hat{\mu}(\tau_q) - q)/q$ against the normalized test time τ_e/τ_q. The error will approach 0 as τ_e approaches τ_q. If the points are positive (negative), the model tends to overestimate (underestimate). Numbers closer to 0 imply more accurate projection and hence a better model.

The use of normalization enables one to overlay relative error curves obtained from different failure data sets. For an overall conclusion about the relative projective validity of models, we may compare plots of the medians (taken with respect to the various data sets). We will consider a model to be superior if it yields the curve closest to 0.

Although most models have been developed in association with a particular inference procedure (for example, maximum likelihood method or least squares method), we should consider other inference procedures if projection is poor. We can examine the quality of inference by generating simulated failure intervals based on the model with assumed parameter values and using them in the projection scheme (combination of model and inference procedure). This method removes any effects of the model. Any consistent differences between the projected distribution and the actual distribution represent the effects of inference above. Alternatively, we may compare the distributions of the parameter estimates with the observed values to evaluate inference quality. However, it appears unlikely that different estimation methods will have a substantial effect on projective validity.

Any capability of a model for projection of software reliability in the system design and early development phases is extremely valuable because of the resultant value for system engineering and planning purposes. We must make these projections through measurable characteristics of the software (size, complexity, structure, etc.), the software development environment, and the operational environment.

Quality of assumptions. The following considerations of quality were applied to each assumption in turn. If it is possible to test an assumption, the degree to which it is supported by data is an important consideration. This is especially true of assumptions that may be common to an entire group of models. If it is not possible to test the assumption, we should evaluate its *plausibility* from the viewpoint of logical consistency and software engineering experience. For example, does it relate rationally to other information about software and software development? Finally, we should judge the clarity and explicitness of an assumption. These characteristics are often necessary to determine whether a model applies to particular software system or project circumstances.

Applicability. Another important characteristic of a model is its applicability. We judged models on their degree of applicability across software projects that vary in size, structure, and function. It is also desirable that a model be usable in different development environments, different operational environments, and different life-cycle phases. However, if a particular model gave outstanding results for just a narrow range of products or development environments, we did not necessarily eliminate the model.

There are at least three special situations that are encountered commonly in practice. A model should either be capable of dealing with them directly or should be compatible with procedures that can deal with them. These are

1. Program evolution

2. Ability to handle incomplete failure data or data with measurement uncertainties (although not without loss of projective validity)

3. Operation of the same program on computers of different speeds

Finally, it is desirable that a model be robust with respect to departures from its assumptions, errors in the data or parameters it employs, and unusual conditions.

Simplicity. A model should be simple in three respects. The most important consideration is that it must be simple and inexpensive to collect the data required to particularize the model; otherwise we will not use the model. Second, the model should be simple in concept. Software engineers without extensive mathematical background should be able to understand the model and its assumptions. They can then determine when it is applicable and the extent to which the model may diverge from reality in an application. Parameters should have readily understood interpretations. This property makes it more feasible for software engineers to estimate the values of the parameters when data are not available. The number of parameters in the model is also an important consideration for simplicity.

Finally, a model must be readily implementable as a program that is a practical management and engineering tool. This means that the program must run rapidly and inexpensively with no manual intervention *required* (does not rule out *possibility* of intervention) other than the initial input.

It would seem that simplicity is just common sense. However, it is easy for all of us to get carried away with intellectual elegance and power. We must consciously resist this appeal in modeling, whose purpose, after all, is pragmatic.

8.3.2.2 Failure data. The failure time data used for the evaluations in this chapter are composed of 15 sets of data and come from three sources (Miller, 1980; Musa, 1979b; Sukert, 1976). Table 8.2 shows the data source and system characteristics for each set of failure data. Note that in this chapter we have chosen the total time of testing to be the last failure time. The data represent a wide variety of applications (such as real-time command and control, real-time commercial, military, and space systems) and system sizes ranging from small (5.7 thousand object instructions) to large (2.4 million object instructions).

The failure data sets T1, T2, T3, T4, T5, T6, T16, T17, T18, T19, and T21 from Musa (1979b) are generally of the best quality. They were collected under Musa's supervision and carefully controlled to ensure their accuracy. All data represent execution time or clock time with constant computer utilization. In the latter case, the data are proportional to execution time. Several data sets in Musa 1979b (specifically, data set 14C and those data sets with an SS prefix) were excluded from the study because the data is in clock time, and we are not sure that the computer utilization was constant.

The failure data sets T20 from Sukert (1976) and T22, T23, and T25 from Miller (1980) were developed from information on failures and clock time per day. We established the failure times randomly within the clock time window each day. A uniform distribution was assumed because this is a "model-free" assumption that is a good approximation for the short windows involved. Thus these data represent an approximation to execution time failure data, with a somewhat higher degree of noise.

These data sets were all taken during system test (except for T6, which was taken during subsystem test). The data represent complete test phases, except for T18. Data sets T1, T3, T4, and T18 are known to have had some data taken before the respective systems were completely integrated (only two failure intervals for T3). Data set T2 is known to include only data taken after it was completely integrated. The remaining data sets probably involve systems that were completely integrated for all the data that were taken, but we do not know for certain.

8.3.2.3 Comparison of projective validity. We made comparisons of projective validity using the following seven model groups based on classes or families, which include many of the published models:

1. Exponential class
2. Weibull class

3. Pareto class

4. Geometric family

5. Inverse linear family

6. Inverse polynomial (second degree only) family

7. Power family

Note that these groups cover both categories of models. We did not differentiate between binomial- and Poisson-type models because the mean value function is independent of type. It is this function that is the primary determinant of the model projective validity.

Because execution time proved to be a better time domain than calendar time, we used execution time data in this comparison study. We employed maximum likelihood inference. Using maximum likelihood estimation yields an exact comparison for most models. It provides an approximate comparison for the Littlewood-Verrall model, which uses bayesian inference.

To illustrate the comparison method, we will consider the projective validity of the geometric family (logarithmic Poisson execution time model) for the data set T1. The logarithmic Poisson execution time model has its mean value function given in Eq. 8.57 and its intensity function given in Eq. 8.58. We must first obtain estimates of the model parameters λ_0 and θ. We have found the estimates $\hat{\lambda}_0$ and $\hat{\theta}$ based on the failure data up to execution time values of τ_e. These values of τ_e range from 20 to 100 percent, in increments of 5 percent, of the total execution time $\tau_q = 24.6$ execution hours. Table 8.4 summarizes the results. For example, for the failure data up to 60 percent of the total execution time (that is, $\tau_e = 14.8$ execution hours), we have $\hat{\lambda}_0 = 40$ failures per execution hour and $\hat{\theta} = 0.0238$ per failure. We can then obtain the fitted mean value function by substituting these estimates into the mean value function as

$$\hat{\mu}(\tau) = \frac{1}{\hat{\theta}} \ln (\hat{\lambda}_0 \, \hat{\theta} \, \tau + 1)$$

$$= \frac{1}{0.0238} \ln [(40)(0.0238)\tau + 1]$$

Figure 8.6 shows the cumulative failures and the fitted curve plotted against the normalized execution time.

We can project failures that will be experienced by the end of testing τ_q by evaluating the fitted mean value function at $\tau = \tau_q$. We obtain $\hat{\mu}(\tau_q) = 134$. Note that there were 136 failures experienced at the end of testing. Therefore, we compute the relative error in projection (to three places) as

TABLE 8.4   Maximum Likelihood Estimates, Predicted Number of Failures, and Relative Errors for System T1 Based on the Logarithmic Poisson Execution Time Model

τ_e/τ_q (%)	$\hat{\lambda}_0$ (failures per execution hour)	$\hat{\theta}$	$\hat{\mu}(\tau_q)$ (failures)	$\hat{\mu}(\tau_q)-q/q$ (%)
20	39.7	0.0231	137	0.7
25	39.9	0.0232	137	0.7
30	44.0	0.0267	127	−6.6
35	43.1	0.0260	129	−5.1
40	45.6	0.0281	124	−8.8
45	44.7	0.0273	126	−7.4
50	42.6	0.0257	130	−4.4
55	42.1	0.0254	130	−4.4
60	40.0	0.0238	134	−1.5
65	36.4	0.0213	141	3.7
70	38.8	0.0229	137	0.7
75	36.8	0.0214	141	3.7
80	38.6	0.0227	137	0.7
85	38.8	0.0229	137	0.7
90	39.0	0.0230	136	0.0
95	39.3	0.0232	136	0.0
100	39.2	0.0232	136	0.0

$$\frac{\hat{\mu}(\tau_q) - 136}{136} = \frac{134 - 136}{136} = -0.015$$

In other words, for the 60 percent of the total failure data, the logarithmic Poisson execution time model, using the maximum likelihood estimation method, underestimates by 1.5 percent.

Table 8.4 also shows the projected values and relative errors for execution time values of τ_e that are from 20 to 100 percent of τ_q in increments of 5 percent. Figure 8.7 shows the relative errors plotted against the normalized execution time (that is τ_e/τ_q). Note that the error will approach zero as τ_e approaches τ_q. Positive values of error indicate overestimation; negative values indicate underestimation. Numbers closer to zero imply more accurate projection. Figure 8.7 shows that the model projects the future behavior well for this data set. The error curve is usually within ±5 percent.

The use of normalization enables us to overlay relative error curves obtained from different failure data sets. We overlay the relative error curves for the 15 failure data sets and summarize the results in Fig. 8.8. The model again seems to project the future behavior well because the error curves are, in general, within ±10 percent when projection is

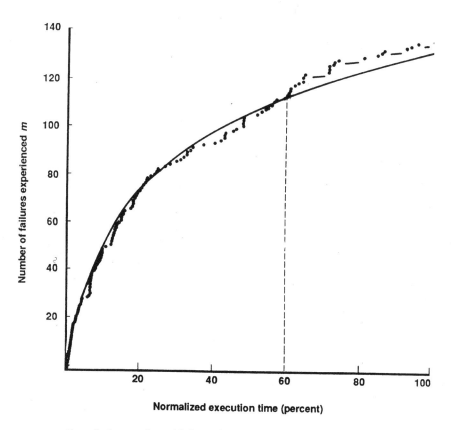

Figure 8.6 Cumulative number of failures for system T1: data and the fitted curve for logarithmic Poisson execution time model based on 60 percent of the total execution time.

made after 50 percent of the total execution time. Furthermore, there is no specific pattern such as overestimation or underestimation. This can be better seen in the median plot shown in Fig. 8.9. Note that some of the dispersion in the projection in Fig. 8.8 may be because of different sizes of data sets. Because projection accuracy is related to the size of the sample of failures, we will achieve greater accuracy at the same normalized time for larger data sets.

Plots of the medians (taken with respect to the various data sets) are useful tools for drawing overall conclusions about the relative projective validity of models. Figure 8.9 shows the median error curves for the model groups. Exponential, Pareto, and Weibull classes tend to underestimate, whereas inverse linear and power families tend to overestimate. The geometric and inverse polynomial families on the whole yield the best projection. However, the inverse polynomial family tends

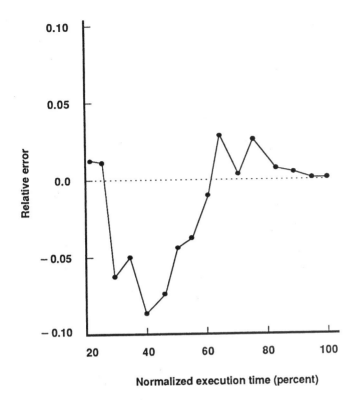

Figure 8.7 Relative error curve for logarithmic Poisson execution time model based on system T1 data set.

to be biased to the overestimation side, especially when projection is made after 60 percent of τ_q. We can also confirm this pattern for the inverse polynomial family by examining its upper and lower quartile curves. We conclude that the geometric family is superior to the other software reliability model groups in projective validity. Note that after 60 percent of the execution period, all model groups yield better than 10 percent accuracy. Hence after this point, criteria other than projective validity may be more important.

Note that most of the models fit the data sets when goodness of fit tests were applied. The projection bias, therefore, is probably because of parameter estimation bias. Maximum likelihood estimates generally tend to be biased. It is possible to obtain unbiased or less biased estimates for some models (see Crow, 1974, for the power family model and Joe and Reid, 1985, for the exponential class), but for others this may be difficult. If projection bias for a model can be removed by parameter estimation correction or improved parameter estimation, the average

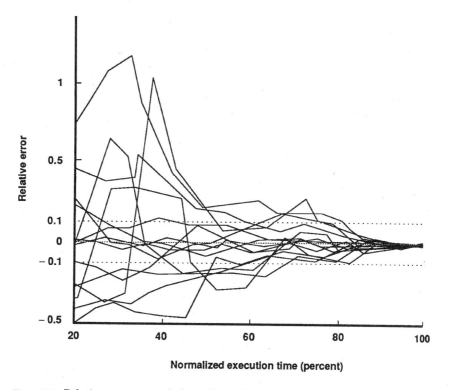

Figure 8.8 Relative error curves for logarithmic Poisson execution time model based on 15 failure data sets.

relative error in projection would tend to be near zero. Adaptive projection (Musa, Iannino, and Okumoto, 1987) may reduce projection bias substantially, but it adds complexity. With adaptive projection, comparison criteria other than projective validity may become more important. In our comparison study, the projection bias was not removed, so the comparison is on the degree of projection bias with unadjusted parameter estimates.

8.3.2.4 Evaluation of other criteria. There has not been a general evaluation of all the assumptions on which the published models are based. In general, the published models seem to be widely applicable to most types or sizes of software products under various conditions. It appears that you can apply these models to any type or size of system with the following exception. Very small projects (less than about 5000 lines of code) may not experience sufficient failures to permit accurate estimation of the parameters and the various derived quantities. You can usually make some kind of estimate, however, yielding a result of the form "present failure intensity is at least X failures per execution hour." If

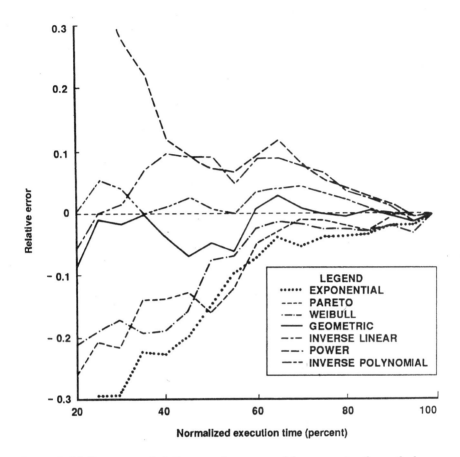

Figure 8.9 Median curves of relative error for seven model groups using the method of maximum likelihood.

the operational profile is highly nonuniform, the decrement in failure intensity per failure experienced will tend to be nonuniform. In this case models of class or family other than exponential (for example, geometric) may tend to fit better and yield better projective validity.

The basic and logarithmic Poisson execution time models are the ones that have been most widely applied to projects. Hence, much information and lore is available about their use, and convenient programs have been developed and refined to do the calculations.

Both the basic and logarithmic Poisson execution time models are simple in concept. Both have only two parameters. You can readily interpret these parameters as physical quantities, especially for the basic model. On the other hand, the Weibull and Pareto types have three parameters, and their physical significance is not as readily apparent. The Littlewood-Verrall general model uses bayesian inference. Most software engineers and managers find this a difficult approach to comprehend. The analysis is frequently complex. The computer programs that implement the Littlewood-Verrall model are substantially more difficult to develop and debug, and the run times are sometimes several orders of magnitude greater than those of the two execution time models with maximum likelihood estimation.

8.4   Recommended Models

Practitioners have found that it is necessary to strictly limit the number of models they work with. There is a substantial effort involved in becoming sufficiently familiar and proficient with a model to be able to insightfully relate that model with your software product and development process. You will be collecting and interpreting data for your environment, and the effort in doing this for numerous models is impractical. Ideally, you would use only one model. However, experience to date has shown that there is sufficient diversity of software products and software development projects that no one model has been able to satisfy all needs. Two models seems to be a very good solution, and three appears to take you past the point of diminishing returns.

Based on the evaluation of the previous section, the two models that are particularly recommended are the basic (Musa) and logarithmic Poisson (Musa-Okumoto) execution time models (Musa, 1975; Musa and Donnelly, 1994; and Musa and Okumoto, 1984b). These models are also commonly called the exponential and logarithmic models. Both were developed with special regard for the needs of engineers and managers who would use them. They have been widely applied to actual projects and have been implemented in several different computer programs.

Both employ execution time. These models have calendar time components associated with them (Musa, Iannino, and Okumoto, 1987) that can convert execution time into calendar time if it should be needed. The conversion is based on a model of the calendar to execution time ratio during test. The accuracy of the conversion depends on parameters relating to the human and computer resources needed to identify and resolve failures during test. One can also convert execution time to calendar time by dividing by the average computer utilization over the test period. This gives approximate results for calendar time, because the computer utilization is often not constant.

In evaluating the basic execution time model, Dale (1982) states, "This is arguably the most practical model of all. It is a statistical model, and has been developed to the extent that it takes into account various personnel and resource constraints." Ramamoorthy and Bastani (1982) note that, "[the basic model]...is better developed and is the first model to insist on execution time." Farr (1996) states that, "This [the basic] model has had the widest distribution among the software reliability models..." Farr (1996) also notes that the logarithmic Poisson model has been extensively applied.

Malaiya, Karunanithi, and Verma (1992) independently studied the projective validity of five models using failure data from 18 projects. The models included the basic and logarithmic Poisson models plus the inverse polynomial model (Littlewood and Verrall, 1973), the power model (Crow, 1974), and the delayed S-shaped model (Yamada, Ohba, and Osaki, 1983). The logarithmic Poisson model had the best average projective validity, followed by the inverse polynomial and basic models. The inverse polynomial model performed best for two projects, and the basic model, for one. The power and delayed S-shaped models performed poorly, with the delayed S-shaped model by far the worst. In selecting models for application, we did not select the inverse polynomial model because its projective validity isn't substantially better than the basic model, and it is quite complex to understand and apply.

Jones (1991) compared several models on 11 releases of a large software system. He concluded that "the LPET [Logarithmic Poisson Execution Time] model...performed best overall in forecasting failures *and* faults *and* in characterizing the failure behavior in the testing phases." Jones observed that the Littlewood-Verrall model appears unsuitable for forecasting failures using least squares. He noted that the forecasts of the WP (Weibull Process) model were highly variable and provided the worst results overall.

Derriennic and Le Gall (1995) compared a variety of models on three telecommunication products at France Telecom. They state, "The experiments show that the logarithmic [Poisson] model is the most accurate."

Managers involved in the projects on which these two models have been applied have observed benefits beyond the quantitative measures. They noted that the models provided an intuitively appealing and well-structured conceptual framework that gave a new perspective on the test process. Developers and their customers were stimulated to think more carefully about just what should be considered a failure for the system involved. Also, they gave more careful consideration to what their reliability objective should be.

Before we leave the subject of models, we need to examine why we did *not* choose a number of other models. Many model in calendar time, resulting in severe disadvantages, or the time domain is unspecified. Most models do not provide all the useful quantities that the basic execution time and logarithmic Poisson execution time models do. Concepts from several of the models (Goel and Okumoto, 1979; Jelinski and Moranda, 1972; and Shooman, 1972) have been incorporated in the basic execution time model. Consequently, you can enjoy most of their advantages and those of the basic model itself when you use it. Some models such as the Littlewood-Verrall general model (Littlewood and Verrall, 1973) are very complex. They are difficult to understand and visualize physically and are relatively difficult and costly to implement on a computer for practical and economical use. Finally, none of the other models match the two models in the extent of the practical experience that has been gained with them.

8.4.1 Description

Both models assume that failures occur as a random process, to be specific, a nonhomogeneous Poisson process. Don't be frightened by the term *nonhomogeneous Poisson process. Poisson* simply refers to the probability distribution of the value of the process at each point in time. The term *nonhomogeneous* indicates that the characteristics of the probability distributions that make up the random process vary with time. This is exhibited in a variation of failure intensity with time. You would expect that, because faults are both being introduced and removed as time passes.

8.4.1.1 Failure intensity versus failures experienced. The two models have failure intensity functions that differ as functions of execution time. However, the difference between them is best described in terms of the change per failure experienced (Fig. 8.10). The change in the fail-

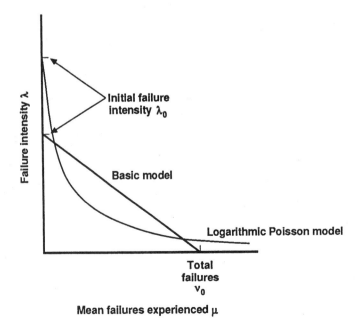

Figure 8.10 Failure intensity functions.

ure intensity function per failure experienced remains constant for the basic execution time model whether it is the first failure that is being fixed or the last. By contrast, for the logarithmic Poisson execution time model, the change per failure experienced becomes smaller with failures experienced. In fact, it decreases exponentially. The first failure initiates a repair process that yields a substantial change in failure intensity, whereas later failures result in much smaller changes.

The failure intensity λ for the basic model as a function of failures experienced is

$$\lambda(\mu) = \lambda_0 \left(1 - \frac{\mu}{v_0}\right) \tag{8.12}$$

The quantity λ_0 is the initial failure intensity at the start of execution. Note that μ is the average or expected number of failures experienced at a given point in time. The quantity v_0 is the total number of failures that would occur in infinite time.

Assume that a program will experience 100 failures in infinite time and that the initial failure intensity was 10 failures per execution hour. It has now experienced 50 failures. The current failure intensity is then

$$\lambda(\mu) = \lambda_0 \left(1 - \frac{\mu}{v_0}\right)$$

$$= 10 \left(1 - \frac{50}{100}\right)$$

$$= 5 \text{ failures per execution hour}$$

The slope of failure intensity, $d\lambda/d\mu$, is given by

$$\frac{d\lambda}{d\mu} = -\frac{\lambda_0}{v_0} \tag{8.13}$$

for the basic model. The slope of the failure intensity for the specific example is

$$\frac{d\lambda}{d\mu} = -\frac{\lambda_0}{v_0}$$

$$= -\frac{10}{100}$$

$$= -0.1 \text{ per execution hour}$$

The failure intensity for the logarithmic Poisson model as a function of the failures experienced is

$$\lambda(\mu) = \lambda_0 \exp(-\theta\mu) \tag{8.14}$$

The quantity θ is called the failure intensity decay parameter. Suppose we plot the natural logarithm of failure intensity against mean failures experienced. Then we can see by transforming Eq. 8.14 that the failure intensity decay parameter θ is the magnitude of the slope of the line we have plotted. It represents the relative change of failure intensity per failure experienced.

Assume that the initial failure intensity is again 10 failures per execution hour and that the failure intensity decay parameter is 0.02 per failure. We will assume that we have experienced 50 failures. The current failure intensity is

$$\lambda(\mu) = \lambda_0 \exp(-\theta\mu)$$

$$= 10 \exp[-(0.02)(50)]$$

$$= 10 - \exp(-1)$$

$$= 3.68 \text{ failures per execution hour}$$

The slope of the failure intensity is

$$\frac{d\lambda}{d\mu} = -\lambda_0\theta \exp(-\theta\mu) = -\theta\lambda \qquad (8.15)$$

for the logarithmic Poisson model.

The change in failure intensity per failure in the example is given by

$$\frac{d\lambda}{d\mu} = -\lambda_0\theta \exp(-\theta\mu)$$

$$= -10(0.02) \exp(-0.02\mu)$$

$$= -0.2 \exp(-0.02\mu) \text{ per execution hour}$$

When no failures have been experienced, we have a change of -0.2 per execution hour, greater than that for the basic model. After 50 failures have been experienced, the decrement is -0.0736 per execution hour. Note the decrease to an amount smaller than the corresponding amount for the basic model. The *relative* change in failure intensity per failure experienced is constant at 0.02. In other words, the failure intensity at a given number of failures experienced is 0.98 of that at the preceding failure.

The basic model could imply testing with an operational profile that tends toward uniformity, as noted in studies by Downs (1985) and Trachtenberg (1985). They also show that highly nonuniform operational profiles yield failure intensity curves that are convex (of decreasing slope) with respect to number of failures experienced. However, other explanations are also possible. The operational profile could be nonuniform, but the changes in failure intensity per failure experienced could still be uniform. This could happen if the reductions in fail sets resulting from each failure resolution action increase with time due to increasing understanding of the software. This trend might balance the effect of a nonuniform operational profile producing the most frequently occurring failures early in test.

The logarithmic Poisson model may be superior for fitting data from test with highly nonuniform operational profiles, where some functions are executed much more frequently than others. The first occurrences of operations will, on the average, be in the same order as the occurrence probability rank. If a particular input state stimulates a fault and thus results in a failure, that failure will occur on the first instance of that input state being executed. Once the failure has been identified, the fault will in general be removed. Then you won't see the failure recurring on subsequent instances of the particular input state. If the repair happens to be imperfect, the failure could return. In general, however, the failures tend to occur only on the early occurrences of the input states. Thus, the early failures that you tend to experience during a period of execution are associated with the frequently occurring operations. Consequently, when you repair the early failures, you tend to have a greater reduction in failure intensity. With a highly nonuniform operational profile, the early failures result in sharp decreases in failure intensity and the later failures show much smaller ones. Thus a highly nonuniform operational profile yields a failure intensity history that tends to be more suitably modeled by the logarithmic Poisson execution time model. We emphasize the point *highly* nonuniform because the basic execution time model appears to be quite tolerant to a substantial degree of nonuniformity. This fact has been demonstrated by both Downs (1985) and Trachtenberg (1985).

Note that failure intensity eventually decreases very slowly for the logarithmic Poisson model. This results from the very infrequent execution of the input states that still contain faults. Sometimes test planners deliberately transform the operational profile to reduce the system test execution time required to expose the problems of a system. One could adjust for the transformed operational profile. It may be easier, however, to handle the situation indirectly by employing the less pessimistic basic model.

The curve for the logarithmic Poisson model may or may not cross the straight line characterizing the basic model, depending on its parameter values (see Fig. 8.10). Each failure that is experienced will generate some fault removal activity, and the result of this fault removal activity is a decrement in failure intensity. Neither model makes any assumption about the quality of the fault removal process (debugging may be imperfect). They both can allow for possible introduction of new faults during fault removal. Both models assume that the removal of faults following failures is immediate. In actuality, there is always some delay, but the effects of the delay are not serious and can easily be accounted for, as discussed in Sec. 8.1.2.

Sometimes you may wish to determine the present failure intensity of a program that is released to the field with some faults not corrected. This, of course, depends on the particular faults that are not corrected. However, you can obtain a first approximation of the present failure intensity by running the software reliability estimation program with a number of the latest failure intervals removed. This number should correspond to the faults outstanding.

8.4.1.2 Failures experienced. The expected number of failures experienced as a function of execution time is illustrated for both models in Fig. 8.11. Whether the curve for the logarithmic Poisson model crosses that for the basic model depends on its parameter values. Note that the expected number of failures for the logarithmic Poisson model is always infinite at infinite time. This number can be and usually is finite for the basic model during test, although it is usually infinite during the operational phase. The curve for the former model is logarithmic, hence the name. The curve for the latter is "negative" exponential, approaching a limit. Infinite failures can occur for the logarithmic Poisson model, even though the number of faults may be finite, because the model assumes decreasing effectiveness of the fault removal action, as explained in Musa, Iannino, and Okumoto (1987), Chap. 11.

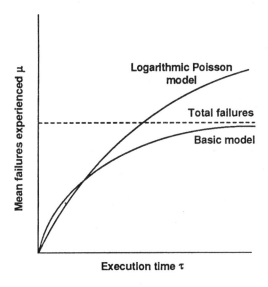

Figure 8.11 Mean failures experienced versus execution time.

Let execution time be denoted by τ. We can write, for the basic model

$$\mu(\tau) = \nu_0 \left[1 - \exp\left(-\frac{\lambda_0}{\nu_0} \tau \right) \right] \tag{8.16}$$

Let's again consider a program with an initial failure intensity of 10 failures per execution hour and 100 total failures. We will look at the failures experienced after 10 and 100 execution hours of execution. We have, for 10 execution hours,

$$\mu(\tau) = \nu_0 \left[1 - \exp\left(-\frac{\lambda_0}{\nu_0} \tau \right) \right]$$

$$= 100 \left\{ 1 - \exp\left[-\frac{10}{100}(10) \right] \right\}$$

$$= 100[1 - \exp(-1)]$$

$$= 100(1 - 0.368)$$

$$= 100(0.632)$$

$$= 63 \text{ failures}$$

For 100 execution hours, we have

$$\mu(\tau) = 100 \left\{ 1 - \exp\left[-\frac{10}{100}(100) \right] \right\}$$

$$= 100[1 - \exp(-10)]$$

$$= 100(1 - 0.0000454)$$

$$= 100 \text{ failures (almost)}$$

For the logarithmic Poisson model, we have

$$\mu(\tau) = \frac{1}{\theta} \ln(\lambda_0 \, \theta \, \tau + 1) \tag{8.17}$$

Let's find the number of failures experienced for the logarithmic Poisson model at 10 and 100 hours of execution. The initial failure intensity is again 10 failures per execution hour and the failure intensity decay parameter is 0.02 per failure. We have at 10 execution hours

$$\mu(\tau) = \frac{1}{\theta} \ln(\lambda_0 \, \theta \, \tau + 1)$$

$$= \frac{1}{0.02} \ln[(10)(0.02)(10) + 1]$$

$$= 50 \ln(2 + 1)$$

$$= 50 \ln 3$$

$$= 50(1.099)$$

$$= 55 \text{ failures}$$

This is smaller than the number of failures experienced by the basic model at 10 execution hours. At 100 execution hours we have

$$\mu(\tau) = \frac{1}{0.02} \ln [(10)(0.02)(100) + 1]$$

$$= 50 \ln(20 + 1)$$

$$= 50 \ln 21$$

$$= 50(3.045)$$

$$= 152 \text{ failures}$$

Note that we now have more failures than the basic model. In fact, the number exceeds the total failures that the basic model can experience.

8.4.1.3   Failure intensity versus execution time.   The failure intensity as a function of execution time for both models is shown in Fig. 8.12. Again, the curves for the two models may or may not cross, depending on the parameter values. This relationship is useful for determining the present failure intensity at any given value of execution time.

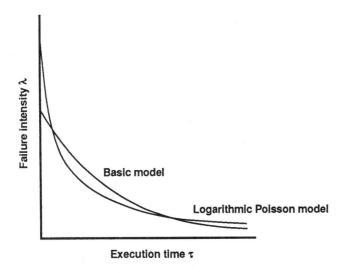

Figure 8.12   Failure intensity versus execution time.

Compare Fig. 8.12 with Fig. 8.10. Because intervals between failures increase as failures are experienced, the curves of Fig. 8.10 are stretched out to the right when plotted against execution time. For the same set of data, the failure intensity of the logarithmic Poisson model drops more rapidly than that of the basic model at first. Later, it drops more slowly. At large values of execution time, the logarithmic Poisson model will always eventually have larger values of failure intensity than the basic model.

We have, for the basic model,

$$\lambda(\tau) = \lambda_0 \exp\left(-\frac{\lambda_0}{v_0}\right)\tau \tag{8.18}$$

We will look at the failure intensities at 10 and 100 execution hours. The initial failure intensity is 10 failures per execution hour and the total failures experienced in infinite time is 100. We have, at 10 execution hours,

$$\lambda(\tau) = \lambda_0 \exp\left(-\frac{\lambda_0}{v_0}\right)\tau$$

$$= 10 \exp\left[-\frac{10}{100}(10)\right]$$

$$= 10 \exp(-1)$$

$$= 10(0.368)$$

$$= 3.68 \text{ failures per execution hour}$$

At 100 execution hours we have

$$\lambda(\tau) = 10 \exp\left[-\frac{10}{100}(100)\right]$$

$$= 10 \exp(-10)$$

$$= 10(0.0000454)$$

$$= 0.000454 \text{ failure per execution hour}$$

We can write, for the logarithmic Poisson model,

$$\lambda(\tau) = \frac{\lambda_0}{\lambda_0 \theta \tau + 1} \tag{8.19}$$

Consider the failure intensities for the logarithmic Poisson model at 10 and 100 execution hours. The initial failure intensity is 10 failures per execution hour and the failure intensity decay parameter is 0.02 per failure. We have for 10 execution hours

$$\lambda(\tau) = \frac{\lambda_0}{\lambda_0 \theta \tau + 1}$$

$$= \frac{10}{10(0.02)(10) + 1}$$

$$= \frac{10}{2 + 1}$$

$$= \frac{10}{3}$$

$$= 3.33 \text{ failures per execution hour}$$

This is slightly lower than the corresponding failure intensity for the basic model. At 100 execution hours we have

$$\lambda(\tau) = \frac{10}{10(0.02)(100) + 1}$$

$$= \frac{10}{20 + 1}$$

$$= \frac{10}{21}$$

$$= 0.476 \text{ failure per execution hours}$$

The failure intensity at the higher execution time is larger for the logarithmic Poisson model.

8.4.1.4 Parameters. As we have seen, the execution time components of both models are characterized by two parameters. They are listed in Table 8.5. The significance of changes in their values is shown in Figs. 8.13 to 8.16 with respect to mean failures experienced. Both models have initial failure intensity as one parameter. It affects the "scale" (overall vertical positioning) of the failure intensity curve with respect to mean failures experienced. The basic model has total failures (failures expected in infinite time) as the second parameter and the loga-

TABLE 8.5   Parameters

	Model	
Parameter	Basic	Logarithmic Poisson
Initial failure intensity	λ_0	λ_0
Failure intensity change		
Total failures	ν_0	
Failure intensity decay parameter		θ

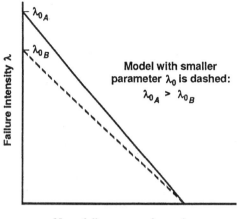

Figure 8.13 Variation of failure intensity versus mean failures experienced with initial failure intensity parameter—basic execution time model.

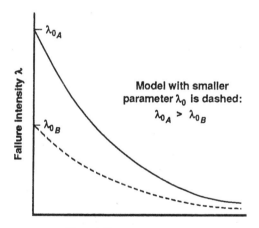

Figure 8.14 Variation of failure intensity versus mean failures experienced with initial failure intensity parameter—logarithmic Poisson execution time model.

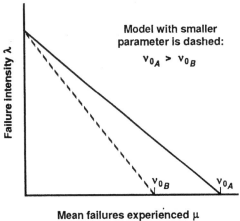

Figure 8.15 Variation of failure intensity versus mean failures experienced with total failures parameter—basic execution time model.

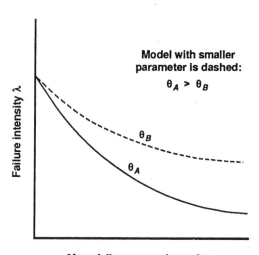

Figure 8.16 Variation of failure intensity versus mean failures experienced with failure intensity decay parameter—logarithmic Poisson execution time model.

rithmic model as the failure intensity decay parameter. Both of these parameters relate to how fast the failure intensity changes. If initial failure intensity is held constant, a large value for total failures means that failure intensity becomes smaller less rapidly with the number of failures experienced. A larger value for the failure intensity decay parameter means that failure intensity and the failure intensity decrements become smaller more rapidly with the number of failures experienced.

The significance of changes in parameter values for relationships between failure intensity and execution time is shown in Figs. 8.17 through 8.20. They are a little more complicated than you might think at first look. The initial failure intensity affects the shape (nature of variation) of each curve as well as the scale. The shape depends on the quantity λ_0/ν_0 for the basic model and $\lambda_0\theta$ for the logarithmic model. Recall that λ_0 is initial failure intensity, ν_0 is total failures, and θ is the failure intensity decay parameter. If the shape quantities are held constant while λ_0 is varied, the λ_0 variations affect only the scale of the curves.

For the two models just described, the values of two parameters must be determined. We need the value of initial failure intensity λ_0 in both cases, total failures experienced ν_0 for the basic execution time model (Musa and Iannino, 1991a), and failure intensity decay parameter θ for the logarithmic Poisson model. Initially, we can *predict* (determine

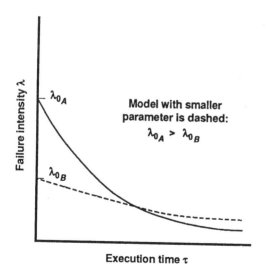

Figure 8.17 Variation of failure intensity versus execution time with initial failure intensity parameter—basic execution time model.

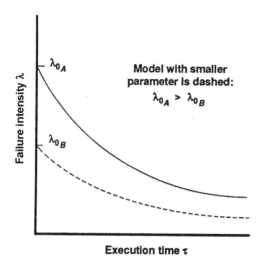

Figure 8.18 Variation of failure intensity versus execution time with initial failure intensity parameter—logarithmic Poisson execution time model.

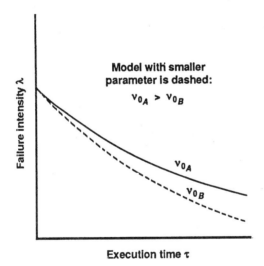

Figure 8.19 Variation of failure intensity versus execution time with total failures parameter— basic execution time model.

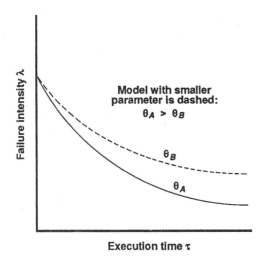

Figure 8.20 Variation of failure intensity versus execution time with failure intensity decay parameter—logarithmic Poisson execution time model.

before program execution) the parameter values for the basic model from characteristics of the program itself. There will be some degree of uncertainty associated with these predictions. Once a program has executed long enough so that failure data are available, we can *estimate* these parameters. Maximum likelihood estimation or other methods may be used. Maximum likelihood estimation yields that set of parameters that make it most likely that the observed data could have occurred. The accuracy with which they are known generally increases with the size of the sample of failures for small and moderate size samples. The accuracy may be characterized by estimating confidence intervals. The confidence intervals represent that range of parameters that could possibly "explain" the data experienced, at some level of confidence (for example, 75 percent).

Prediction of parameters is needed whenever system engineering studies are required in project phases before failure data are available. Procedures for predicting the values of parameters are currently developed for the basic execution time model. They have not yet been developed for the logarithmic Poisson model. They are established from the size and fault density of the program and the average instruction execution rate of the computer on which the program is running. At present, the accuracy of prediction is limited because little work has been done in this area and only a small amount of data has been collected.

However, because system engineering studies can be very significant in realizing substantial cost savings for a project, further work in this area is vital. Limited accuracy is not a handicap for studies in which only the *relative* values of quantities are important. Even where absolute quantities are needed, limited accuracy is usually preferable to making no study at all.

You can perform estimation in subsystem test, system test, or in the operational phase. It is usually more accurate than prediction. Estimation is a statistical method that is based on either the failure times or the number of failures per time interval (for example, failures per hour). The two formulations of the method are essentially equivalent theoretically. The use of failure times is usually more accurate. It is easy to convert failures per time interval into failure times and hence handle a mix of both kinds of data. To do this, you randomly assign the failures in the interval in which they are experienced. For example, if you have three failures in an hour, you would assign those three failures randomly within that time interval.

Estimation and the computation of derived quantities is straightforward; however, the calculations required are tedious. Consequently, it makes sense to develop computer programs to do the dirty work.

8.4.1.5 Other quantities. Assume that you have chosen a failure intensity objective for the software product being developed. Suppose you are removing some portion of the failures through correction of their associated faults. Then you can use the objective and the present value of failure intensity to determine the additional expected number of failures that must be experienced to reach that objective. The process is illustrated graphically in Fig. 8.21.

You can derive equations describing the relationships in closed form for both models (Musa, Iannino, and Okumoto 1987, Chap. 11). Then you can perform manual calculations. The equations are

$$\Delta\mu = \frac{\nu_0}{\lambda_0}(\lambda_P - \lambda_F) \tag{8.20}$$

for the basic model and

$$\Delta\mu = \frac{1}{\theta}\ln\frac{\lambda_P}{\lambda_F} \tag{8.21}$$

for the logarithmic Poisson model. The quantity $\Delta\mu$ is the expected number of failures to reach the failure intensity objective, λ_P is the present failure intensity, and λ_F is the failure intensity objective.

To obtain an estimate of total remaining failures rather than failures to reach the failure intensity objective, set the failure intensity objec-

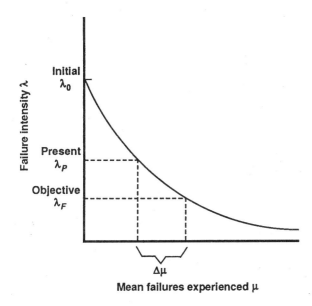

Figure 8.21 Additional failures to failure intensity objective.

tive to zero. For the basic model, we will determine the expected number of failures that will be experienced between a present failure intensity of 3.68 failures per execution hour and an objective of 0.000454 failure per execution hour. The initial failure intensity is 10 and the total failures experienced in infinite time is 100. Thus,

$$\Delta\mu = \frac{\nu_0}{\lambda_0}(\lambda_P - \lambda_F)$$

$$= \frac{100}{10}(3.68 - 0.000454)$$

$$= 10\,(3.68)$$

$$= 37 \text{ failures}$$

We will find, for the logarithmic Poisson model, the expected number of failures experienced between a present failure intensity of 3.33 failures per execution hour and an objective of 0.476 failure per execution hour. The failure intensity decay parameter is 0.02 per failure. We have

$$\Delta\mu = \frac{1}{\theta}\ln\frac{\lambda_P}{\lambda_F}$$

$$= \frac{1}{0.02}\ln\frac{3.33}{0.476}$$

$$= 50\ln 6.996$$

$$= 50\,(1.945)$$

$$= 97 \text{ failures}$$

Similarly, you can determine the additional execution time $\Delta\tau$ required to reach the failure intensity objective for either model. This is

$$\Delta\tau = \frac{\nu_0}{\lambda_0}\ln\frac{\lambda_P}{\lambda_F} \tag{8.22}$$

for the basic model and

$$\Delta\tau = \frac{1}{\theta}\left(\frac{1}{\lambda_F} - \frac{1}{\lambda_P}\right) \tag{8.23}$$

for the logarithmic Poisson model and is illustrated in Fig. 8.22. For the basic model, we will determine the execution time between a present failure intensity of 3.68 failures per execution hour and an objective of

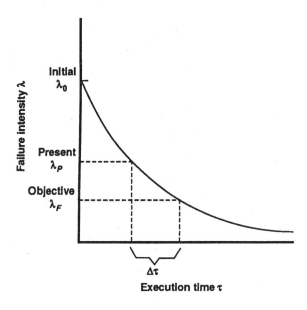

Figure 8.22   Additional execution time to failure intensity objective.

0.000454 failure per execution hour. The initial failure intensity is 10 failures per execution hour and the total failures experienced in infinite time is 100. We have

$$\Delta\tau = \frac{\nu_0}{\lambda_0} \ln \frac{\lambda_P}{\lambda_F}$$

$$= \frac{100}{10} \ln \frac{3.68}{0.000454}$$

$$= 10 \ln 8106$$

$$= 10(9)$$

$$= 90 \text{ execution hours}$$

For the logarithmic Poisson model, we will find the execution time between a present failure intensity of 3.33 failures per execution hour and an objective of 0.476 failure per execution hour. The failure intensity decay parameter is 0.02 per failure. We have

$$\Delta\tau = \frac{1}{\theta}\left(\frac{1}{\lambda_F} - \frac{1}{\lambda_P}\right)$$

$$= \frac{1}{0.02}\left(\frac{1}{0.476} - \frac{1}{3.33}\right)$$

$$= 50(2.10 - 0.30)$$

$$= 50(1.80)$$

$$= 90 \text{ execution hours}$$

The additional expected number of failures required to reach the failure intensity objective gives some idea of the failure resolution workload. The additional execution time indicates the remaining amount of test required.

If we use the failure data for system T1 (in Musa, Iannino, and Okumoto, 1987, Table 12.1) and estimate parameters for both the basic and logarithmic Poisson models, we obtain the results given in Table 8.6.

By using Eqs. 2.7 and 2.8 we can determine the length of the system test period for various failure intensity improvement factors, as shown in Table 8.7.

TABLE 8.6 Parameters for System T1

Basic	Logarithmic Poisson
$\lambda_0 = 17.8$ failures per execution hour	$\lambda_0 = 39.9$ failures per execution hour
$\nu_0 = 142$ failures	$\theta = 0.0236$ per failure

TABLE 8.7   Length of System Test Period for System T1 for Different Failure Intensity Improvement Factors

Improvement factor	Execution time (execution hours)	
	Basic	Logarithmic Poisson
10	18.4	9.56
100	36.7	106.1
1000	55.1	1060.9
10,000	73.5	10,619

In most situations for the logarithmic Poisson model, an alternative formulation is also possible. The MTTF exists for this model in most circumstances (it does not for the basic model). We can set an MTTF objective instead of a failure intensity objective. You can determine the additional expected number of failures that must be experienced and the additional execution time required to reach that objective in terms of the present and objective MTTFs.

We can never determine the values of the parameters precisely. We will always have some range of uncertainty, often expressed through confidence intervals. This uncertainty results in corresponding uncertainty in the derived quantities described above. One can visualize the effects of confidence intervals for the parameters on confidence intervals for the derived quantities by thinking of the model curves being expanded to bands in Figs. 8.21 and 8.22.

8.4.1.6 Field failure intensity.   If a program has been released to the field, and no features are added or faults removed between releases, the failure intensity will be constant. Then both models, as nonhomogeneous Poisson processes, reduce to homogeneous Poisson processes with the failure intensity as a parameter. The number of failures in a given time period follows a Poisson distribution. The failure intervals follow an exponential distribution. The reliability R and failure intensity are related by

$$R(\tau) = \exp\left(-\lambda\tau\right) \tag{8.24}$$

Note that the reliability is dependent not only on the failure intensity but also on the period of execution time. The reliability (probability of no failures in a period of execution time τ) is lower for longer time periods as is illustrated in Fig. 8.23.

The operational phase of many programs consists of a series of releases. The reliability and failure intensity will then be step functions, with the level of the quantities changing at each release. If the releases are

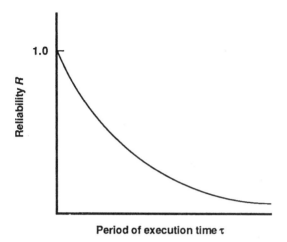

Figure 8.23 Reliability versus period of execution time.

frequent and the trend of failure intensity is decreasing, one can often approximate the step functions with one of the software reliability models we have presented. Alternatively, one may apply the software reliability models directly to reported unique failures (not counting repetitions). Note that the model now represents the failure intensity that will occur when the failures have been resolved. This approach is analogous to the one commonly taking place during system test of ignoring the failure resolution delay, except that the delay is much longer here. Of course, if the failures are actually resolved in the field, the operational phase should be handled just like the system test phase.

8.4.2 Interpretation of parameters of logarithmic Poisson execution time model

As mentioned previously, we wish to relate the execution time component parameters of the logarithmic Poisson execution time model to characteristics of the software product, the development process, and the execution environment. We would also like to understand how an infinite quantity of failures can arise from a finite quantity of faults ω_0. The following derivation is not a proof but an attempt to provide a heuristic interpretation.

We will start by considering the run profile of the program being executed. The run profile is the set of probabilities of execution for the (finite) set of possible runs of the program. The runs may be arranged in order of decreasing probability without loss of generality. We now have the situation of Fig. 8.24, where the runs are plotted sufficiently

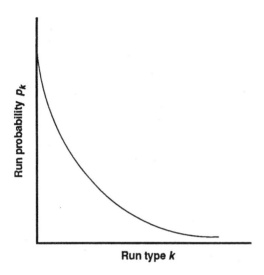

Figure 8.24 Nonuniform operational profile.

close together on the horizontal axis that the run profile appears as a continuous curve.

Some of the runs will have faults associated with them, and these will lead to failures. When you execute these runs, the potential for reducing the failure intensity through fault removal will depend on the sum of the frequencies of occurrence of the runs of the fault's fail set. On the average, these potential reductions will form a decreasing function with respect to the number of faults removed (or increasing with respect to the number of faults remaining ω). The latter relationship is illustrated in Fig. 8.25. We will assume the very general function where

$$\frac{d\lambda}{d\omega} = \beta_1 \omega^{\beta_2} \tag{8.25}$$

where $\beta_2 \geq 0$. This should be capable of expressing a very wide range of possible forms of increasing functions.

Consider a generalization of the fault reduction factor B defined for the basic execution time model. Let

$$B(\tau) = \frac{d\eta(\tau)}{d\mu(\tau)} \tag{8.26}$$

when η is faults removed and μ is failures experienced. For the logarithmic Poisson model, assume that $B(\tau)$ has the form

$$B(\tau) = B_0 \exp\left(-\beta_3 \mu(\tau)\right) \tag{8.27}$$

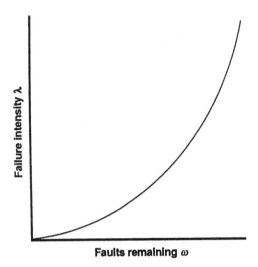

Figure 8.25 Behavior of change in failure intensity with respect to faults remaining.

where B_0 is the initial fault reduction factor, and β_3 is the fault reduction factor decay parameter.

This assumption expresses the concept that fault removal effectiveness can drop as failures experienced increases. This can occur because of the following:

1. It becomes more and more difficult to find the faults that are causing the failures. The hardest ones to find tend to remain in the program.

2. Often, for a given failure, the associated fault has only part of its fail set removed. The fraction removed could become smaller with time, the later failures usually affecting a smaller part of the fail set.

3. Results of executing the program tend to be more poorly recorded as the program approaches the operational phase and in the operational phase itself. There are probably two reasons for this. First, the amount of recording per failure becomes more and more onerous as failures become less frequent. Second, the average level of experience and motivation of the personnel executing the program may drop, as we will note.

4. The average level of experience and motivation of failure resolution personnel may drop, both in terms of overall experience and experience with the particular program. This can result from experienced personnel moving on to other projects during system test and being

replaced by less experienced people. These people may feel less of a sense of "ownership" of the code because they didn't create it. This factor reduces net fault removal effectiveness both through faults not corrected and a higher rate of new faults spawned during the resolution process.

5. When fewer faults remain, the fault correction personnel may be less likely to recognize relationships among them. Hence the discovery of one fault would be less likely to lead to the discovery of others.

Note that the assumption implies that $B \to 0$ as $\tau \to \infty$. If $\beta_3 = 0$, we would have had the case of the basic execution time model (constant B).

We shall now find the form of the failure intensity function. First find the relationship between ω and μ. Note that we can write Eq. 8.27 as

$$\frac{d\eta(\tau)}{d\mu(\tau)} = B_0 \exp\left(-\beta_3 \mu(\tau)\right) \qquad (8.28)$$

Integrating, and noting that $\eta(0) = 0$ and $\mu(0) = 0$, we obtain

$$\eta(\tau) = \frac{B_0}{\beta_3} \left[1 - \exp(-\beta_3 \mu(\tau))\right] \qquad (8.29)$$

At $\tau = \infty$, $\mu(\tau) = \infty$ and $\eta(\tau) = \omega_0$. Thus,

$$\omega_0 = \frac{B_0}{\beta_3} \qquad (8.30)$$

Note that

$$\omega = \omega_0 - \eta \qquad (8.31)$$

Now using Eqs. 8.30 and 8.31, we have

$$\omega(\tau) = \omega_0 \exp\left(-\beta_3 \mu(\tau)\right) \qquad (8.32)$$

Note that we must have $\beta_3 > 0$ to have both infinite expected failures and finite expected faults.

Now consider the relationship between λ and ω. Substituting Eq. 8.32 into Eq. 8.25, we obtain

$$\frac{d\lambda}{d\omega} = \beta_1 \omega_0^{\beta_2} \exp\left(-\beta_2 \beta_3 \mu(\tau)\right) \qquad (8.33)$$

Now, using Eqs. 8.32 and 8.33 we can show that

$$\frac{d\lambda}{d\mu} = -\beta_1 \beta_3 \omega_0^{\beta_2+1} \exp\left[-(\beta_2 + 1)\beta_3 \mu(\tau)\right] \qquad (8.34)$$

Integrating and noting that $\mu(\infty) = \infty$ and $\lambda(\infty) = 0$, we obtain

$$\lambda(\tau) = \frac{\beta_1 \omega_0^{\beta_2 + 1}}{\beta_2 + 1} \exp[-(\beta_2 + 1)\beta_3 \mu(\tau)] \qquad (8.35)$$

Now Eq. 8.35 has the form of the Musa-Okumoto logarithmic model with

$$\lambda_0 = \frac{\beta_1 \omega_0^{\beta_2 = 1}}{\beta_2 + 1} \qquad (8.36)$$

and

$$\theta = (\beta_2 + 1)\beta_3 \qquad (8.37)$$

Consider the failure intensity decay parameter θ. From Eqs. 8.30 and 8.37 we obtain

$$\theta = \frac{(\beta_2 + 1)B_0}{\omega_0} \qquad (8.38)$$

Note that β_2 describes the shape of the failure intensity against faults remaining, curve B_0 is the initial (at $\tau = 0$) fault reduction factor, and ω_0 is the number of inherent faults. It is probably often the case that β_0 is 1 or close to it.

Note from Eq. 8.36 that λ_0 is related to ω_0 through the shape parameter β_2 and the scale parameter β_1 of the failure intensity against the faults remaining curve. It is likely that β_1 is related to the linear execution frequency and perhaps a proportionality constant that may not vary between projects. If you can determine β_2 (it may be project independent), you open the possibility for projections of reliability in the system engineering phase for the logarithmic Poisson execution time model. Note that if $\beta_2 = 0$, the initial failure intensity reduces to that for the basic model:

$$\lambda_0 = \beta_1 \omega_0 \qquad (8.39)$$

8.4.3   Derivation of models

We present here simplified derivations of the Musa basic and Musa-Okumoto logarithmic Poisson models. For very general and extensive derivations for model groups, see Musa, Iannino, and Okumoto (1987). The model group derivations start with markovian models and derive most model groups as special cases. There is also an extensive treatment of parameter estimation. These presentations show many connections between models and may stimulate a number of insights, so they may be particularly valuable for researchers. The discussions here are focused on giving practitioners a limited amount of theory, sufficient for appreciating the two models presented.

8.4.3.1 Musa basic model. The basic execution time model of Musa (1975) is best characterized as a Poisson-type model of the exponential class, although it was not originally described as such. Goel and Okumoto (1979) later specifically addressed this kind of model and described it in terms of a nonhomogeneous Poisson process.

These models assume that time to failure of an individual fault has an exponential distribution, that is, $f_a(\tau) = \phi \exp(-\phi\mu\ \tau)$. The per-fault hazard rate is constant at ϕ, that is $z_a(\tau) = \phi$. Musa described ϕ, using additional elements, as

$$\phi = fK \tag{8.40}$$

where f is the linear execution frequency of the program or the ratio of average instruction rate to program size in object instructions. Note that K is the fault exposure ratio. It accounts for the effects of program dynamic structure and data dependency on the hazard rate (Musa, 1991a).

For a given fault reduction factor B, the expected number of failures experienced by τ for the basic execution time model is

$$\mu(\tau) = \nu_0[1 - \exp(-\phi B\tau)] \tag{8.41}$$

This relationship is illustrated in Fig. 8.11. Also, we can find the failure intensity by differentiating Eq. 8.41 to yield

$$\lambda(\tau) = \nu_0\phi B \exp(-\phi B\tau) \tag{8.42}$$

This is an exponentially decaying function of τ with the initial failure intensity $\lambda_0 = \nu_0\phi B$. The relationship is illustrated in Fig. 8.12.

Alternatively, we may derive these models from the postulate that the failure intensity function has a constant slope with respect to average failures experienced. We write

$$\lambda(\mu) = \phi B(\nu_0 - \mu) \tag{8.43}$$

or

$$\lambda(\tau) = \phi B(\nu_0 - \mu(\tau)) \tag{8.44}$$

Because $\lambda(\tau)$ is the derivative of $\mu(\tau)$, we have

$$\frac{d\mu(\tau)}{d\tau} + \phi B\mu(\tau) = \phi B\nu_0 \tag{8.45}$$

This differential equation has the solution given by Eq. 8.41.

You can find expressions for various useful quantities by substituting Eqs. 8.41 and 8.42 into appropriate equations derived in Musa,

Iannino, and Okumoto (1987). Specifically, substituting Eq. 8.41 into Eq. 10.13 of Musa, Iannino, and Okumoto (1987) gives the cumulative probability distribution of time to the ith failure

$$P[T_i \leq \tau] = \exp\{-\nu_0[1 - \exp(-\phi B\tau)]\} \sum_{j=i}^{\infty} \frac{\nu_0^j[1-\exp(-\phi B\tau)]^j}{j!} \quad (8.46)$$

Substituting Eq. 8.41 into Eq. 10.16 of Musa, Iannino, and Okumoto (1987) yields the program reliability after the $(i-1)$th failure

$$R(\tau_i' \,|\, \tau_{i-1}) = \exp\{-[\nu_0 \exp(-\phi B\tau_{i-1})][1-\exp(-\phi B\tau_i')]\} \quad (8.47)$$

and substitution of Eq. 8.42 into Eq. 10.18 of Musa, Iannino, and Okumoto (1987) yields the program hazard rate

$$z(\tau_i' \,|\, \tau_{i-1}) = \nu_0 \phi \exp(-\phi B\tau_{i-1})\exp(-\phi B\tau_i') \quad (8.48)$$

If failure intensity objective λ_F has been set for the program, you can derive an expression for the additional number of failures that must be experienced to meet this objective from Eq. 8.43 as

$$\Delta\mu = \frac{\nu_0}{\lambda_0}(-\mu\,\lambda_F) \quad (8.49)$$

Similarly, using Eq. 8.42, the additional execution time is

$$\Delta\tau = \frac{\nu_0}{\lambda_0} \ln\left(\frac{\lambda}{\lambda_F}\right) \quad (8.50)$$

8.4.3.2 Musa-Okumoto logarithmic Poisson model. The logarithmic Poisson execution time model (Musa and Okumoto, 1984b) has a failure intensity function that decreases exponentially with expected failures experienced:

$$\lambda(\tau) = \lambda_0 \exp(-\theta\mu(\tau)) \quad (8.51)$$

Note that λ_0 denotes the initial failure intensity, and θ denotes the failure intensity decay parameter, where $\theta > 0$. The quantity μ represents the expected number of failures. Again, the quantity τ represents execution time.

Expressions for $\lambda(\tau)$ and $\mu(\tau)$ can be derived as follows. Because $\lambda(\tau)$ is the derivative of $\mu(\tau)$, we get the differential equation

$$\frac{d\mu(\tau)}{d\tau} = \lambda_0 \exp(-\theta\mu(\tau)) \quad (8.52)$$

or

$$\frac{d\mu(\tau)}{d\tau} \exp(\theta\mu(\tau)) = \lambda_0 \qquad (8.53)$$

Noting that

$$\frac{d \exp(\theta\mu(\tau))}{d\tau} = \theta \frac{d\mu(\tau)}{d\tau} \exp(\theta\mu(\tau)) \qquad (8.54)$$

we obtain from Eq. 8.53

$$\frac{d \exp(\theta\mu(\tau))}{d\tau} = \lambda_0 \theta \qquad (8.55)$$

Integrating Eq. 8.55 yields

$$\exp(\theta\mu(\tau)) = \lambda_0 \theta \tau + C \qquad (8.56)$$

where C is the constant of integration. Because $\mu(0) = 0$, we get $C = 1$. Hence, the mean value function is obtained as

$$\mu(\tau) = \frac{1}{\theta} \ln(\lambda_0 \theta \tau + 1) \qquad (8.57)$$

which is a logarithmic function of τ. Furthermore, from the definition of $\lambda(\tau)$ the failure intensity function is given by

$$\lambda(\tau) = \frac{\lambda_0}{\lambda_0 \theta \tau + 1} \qquad (8.58)$$

which is an inverse linear function of τ. This relationship is illustrated in Fig. 8.12.

You can find expressions for various useful quantities by substituting Eqs. 8.57 and 8.58 into appropriate equations derived in Sec. 10.2 of Musa, Iannino, and Okumoto (1987). Specifically, substituting Eq. 8.57 into Eq. 10.13 of Musa, Iannino, and Okumoto (1987) gives the cumulative probability distribution of time to failure

$$P[T_i \leq \tau] = (\lambda_0 \theta \tau + 1)^{-1/\theta} \sum_{j=i}^{\infty} \frac{\ln(\lambda_0 \theta \tau + 1)^j}{\theta^j j!} \qquad (8.59)$$

Substituting Eq. 8.57 into Eq. 10.16 of Musa, Iannino, and Okumoto (1987) yields the program reliability

$$R(\tau_i' | \tau_{i-1}) = \left[\frac{\lambda_0 \theta \tau_{i-1} + 1}{\lambda_0 \theta(\tau_{i-1} + \tau_i') + 1} \right]^{1/\theta} \qquad (8.60)$$

Substitution of Eq. 8.58 into Eq. 10.18 of Musa, Iannino, and Okumoto (1987) yields the program hazard rate

$$z(\tau_i' \mid \tau_{i-1}) = \frac{\lambda_0}{\lambda_0 \phi(\tau_{i-1} + \tau_i') + 1} \qquad (8.61)$$

The MTTF is defined only for $\theta\mu < 1$, but θ generally satisfies this constraint for actual projects. You can determine the MTTF by substituting Eq. 8.60 in Eq. 9.4 of Musa, Iannino, and Okumoto (1987) and integrating. We obtain

$$\Theta(\tau_{i-1}) = \frac{\theta}{1-\theta}(\lambda_0 \, \theta\tau_{i-1} + 1)^{1-1/\theta} \qquad (8.62)$$

If a failure intensity objective λ_F has been set for the program, we can derive $\Delta\mu$ and $\Delta\tau$ required to meet the objective from Eq. 8.58 as

$$\Delta\mu = \frac{1}{\theta} = \ln\left(\frac{\lambda}{\lambda_F}\right) \qquad (8.63)$$

and

$$\Delta\tau = \frac{1}{\theta}\left(\frac{1}{\lambda_F} - \frac{1}{\lambda}\right) \qquad (8.64)$$

The total number of failures for this model is infinite. It is very likely that the number of inherent faults in a program is finite. It would be unlikely for a development team to introduce an infinite number of inherent faults. The model should be able to accommodate simultaneously an infinite number of failures and a finite number of faults. It can do this by assuming a time-varying fault reduction factor of a specific form (see Sec. 8.4.2).

It would be very useful if we could relate the execution time component parameters of the model to characteristics of the software product, the development process, and the execution environment. This would enable prediction of these parameters before execution. Initial failure intensity may be a function of linear execution frequency f, number of inherent faults ω_0, and a "constant" analogous to the fault exposure ratio K for the basic model. The failure intensity decay rate θ could be a function of the initial (at $\tau = 0$) fault reduction factor, the number of inherent faults, and the shape of the failure intensity curve with respect to faults remaining.

The problem of parameter prediction for the logarithmic Poisson model will probably be more difficult than that for the basic model. We cannot accurately assess the degree of difficulty now. It was seen in Sec. 8.4.2 that the prediction of initial failure intensity for the logarithmic Poisson model involves a power of the number of inherent faults. Hence, this prediction is likely to be less accurate. Thus, the basic model is likely to be superior for initial, approximate determination of behavior.

8.4.4 Parameter prediction

You can determine the values of parameters for the basic model by prediction from characteristics of the software and the development process. You can do this before any execution of the software. Once the software is executed and failure data is available, you can estimate the parameters statistically from the data. The basic execution time model has two parameters we must predict, total failures v_0 that would be experienced in infinite time and initial failure intensity λ_0.

8.4.4.1 Total failures.

The net number of faults removed is only a portion of the failures experienced, expressed by the fault reduction factor B. Thus you may estimate the total failures v_0, before test, from the number of inherent faults ω_0 and the fault reduction factor B, because

$$v_0 = \frac{\omega_0}{B} \tag{8.65}$$

Faults. You can theoretically determine the number of inherent faults in coded programs by an empirical method, variously called *fault seeding, error seeding,* or *debugging* (Basin 1973; Gilb, 1977; Mills, 1972; and Rudner 1977). To do so, you introduce artificial faults into the program in some suitable random fashion, unknown to the people who will be trying to find program faults. It is assumed that these seeded faults are equivalent to the inherent faults in the program in terms of difficulty of detection. Inspect the code and count separately the inherent and seeded faults discovered. Compute the proportion of seeded faults found to total seeded faults. You can then predict the number of inherent faults in the program. The reasoning is based on the concept that with equal difficulty of discovery, you will uncover the same proportions of both types of faults at any point in time.

For example, suppose that we seed 100 faults into a program that contains an unknown number of inherent faults. After a period of debugging, we have discovered 20 seeded and 10 inherent faults. The seeded faults discovered represent 20 percent of the total number of seeded faults. We assume that we have discovered 20 percent of the inherent faults also. Therefore, the total number of inherent faults must be 50.

Unfortunately, it has proved difficult to implement seeding in practice. It is not easy to introduce artificial faults that are equivalent to inherent faults in difficulty of discovery. It is generally *much* easier to find the seeded faults. Consequently, you usually underestimate the number of inherent faults with this technique. Hence, we usually determine the number of faults from program characteristics.

The size of a program has the most effect on the number of inherent faults it contains. At least several researchers (Akiyama, 1971; Feuer and Fowlkes, 1979; Motley and Brooks, 1977; and Thayer, 1976) have verified this hypothesis. It appears that for *modules,* there may be a constant inherent fault component unrelated to size (Shen et al., 1985), although its existence is in dispute (Card, Church, and Agresti, 1986). Interface faults are a possible source of this component; they are likely to be size-independent (Basili and Perricone, 1984). In any case, we are interested in estimating the number of inherent faults in *systems,* usually of appreciable size, or in increments to systems. The constant inherent fault component for modules should not be significant in either of these situations.

Inherent fault density. You can collect data on average inherent fault densities (faults per instruction) at the start of various phases of testing. These data will permit you to estimate the number of inherent faults ω_0 by simply multiplying the predicted inherent fault density by program size. Implicit in this approach is the assumption that the number of inherent faults is linearly related to program size or that the inherent fault density is independent of program size. The validity of this assumption is supported by Basili and Hutchens (1983) and strongly backed by Takahashi and Kamayachi (1985). The latter found less than 0.03 correlation between inherent fault density and program size over 30 projects, ranging from 4000 to 130,000 lines of developed (new or modified) code. The Basili and Hutchens study also presented evidence to indicate uniform inherent fault distribution across the code. Metrics based only on specific parts of the code were less effective in predicting the number of inherent faults.

You generally estimate program size by analyzing the requirements and applying data on the size of similar functions that have been implemented in the past. The main source of error in making these estimates is usually incomplete or imperfectly understood requirements or lack of size data for some of the functions.

Some variation can occur due to the different way in which programmers implement the same specification. DeMarco and Lister (1989) conducted an experiment in which 122 programmers implemented the same specification in COBOL. The mean length of the program written was 230 noncommentary source statements (executable and declaratory). Eighty percent of the lengths were within one-third of the mean; 93 percent were within two-thirds. Because larger programs can be viewed as conglomerations of smaller ones, the dispersion in size will be inversely proportional to the square root of the size. Thus at slightly over 5000 statements, about 80 percent of the lengths would be within 6 percent of the mean. At 180,000 statements, 80 percent of the lengths would be within 1 percent of the mean.

Experience has indicated that inherent fault quantities are more closely correlated with source than object instructions. Hence we count *deliverable executable source instructions* developed during the project. Thus, we do not count drivers, support programs, data statements, declarations, or comments. When the project involves program changes rather than program creation, we do not count instructions or statements that are left alone or deleted. The incidence of inherent faults associated with such statements is much less than that associated with those that are created or modified. In studies of mathematically oriented FORTRAN routines for space applications, 98 percent of the modules that were reused without change were fault-free. In practice, the number of *instructions* is highly correlated with the number of *lines* of code. Because the latter is easier to count, it is most often used.

Table 8.8 presents a summary of available data on the density of inherent faults found in different phases of a number of projects. The data vary in quality because of differences in the care in defining the terms and collecting the data. Individual references are presented so that the user of these data may investigate them. Possibly, you might make better predictions than those obtained from averages if you matched the characteristics of your product and development process with those of the recorded projects.

There are three likely sources of error in these data:

1. The data usually represent all faults removed, not just inherent faults. Thus, they include the removal of faults that were themselves spawned in the removal process. This factor results in estimates that are probably about 1 to 7 percent high, as we will discuss shortly.

2. The data generally represent corrections reported rather than faults removed. Some faults will be removed by means of multiple corrections, each correction representing a partial fault removal. This factor results in estimates that are high by some unknown amount.

3. Data collection does not usually continue until all faults are removed. Hence estimates are low, probably by not more than 15 percent and perhaps around 8 percent.

Although we do not know the effects of these error sources at present, there appears to be substantial cancellation between them. Hence we can probably ignore the net error.

Failure data specified for the coding phase include all semantic but no syntactic faults. *Semantic faults* are defects arising from programmer error in communicating the meaning of what is to be done. An example would be specifying the wrong variable for an operation. *Syntactic faults* result from errors in following the rules of the language in which the program is written. For example, one might not

TABLE 8.8   Density of Faults Found During Different Life-Cycle Phases for Various Software Systems

Reference	System identifier	Developed code (1000 source lines)	Faults per thousand source lines	Phases[1]
Basili and Perricone (1984)		90	44.1[2]	C, UT, SS, S
Stover (1977)		4.0	71.3	C, UT, SS, S
Albin and Ferreol (1982)		27.6	21.0[2]	C, UT, SS, S
Boehm (1981)		2	75	C, UT, SS, S
Rubey, Dana, and Biché (1975)	Multiple[3]	9	113	C, UT, SS, S
Ostrand and Weyuker (1982)		10	16.0	UT, SS, S
Akiyama (1971)		17.1	20.3	UT, SS, S
Schafer et al. (1979)	4	115.3	36.2	SS, S
Mendis (1981)		28	4.6	S
Motley and Brooks (1977)	S	181	19.5	S
	T	115	17.4	S
Akiyama (1971)		17.1	3.2	S
Schafer et al. (1979)	1	120	17.0	S
	2	610	12.8	S
	3	96.9	3.78	S
	7	1317	2.69	S
	14	32.2	15.6	S
	15	32.4	13.8	S
	16	123.7	10.8	S
Angus, Bowen, and VanDenBerg (1983)		330	10.6	S
Weiss (1981)	SEL 1	46.5	3.87	S
	SEL 2	31.1	3.83	S
	SEL 3	78.6	3.91	S
	ARF	21.8	6.56	S
Bendick (1976)	1	217	4.8	S
	2	31.5	9.8	S
	4	32	5.2	S
	5	73	5.1	S
	6	36	3.6	S
Endres (1975)	DOS/VS	86	6.0	S
Rubey, Dana, and Biché (1975)	Multiple[4]	18.3	4.5	S
Walston and Felix (1977)	Multiple[5]	20	3.1	S
Inglis et al. (1986)	Multiple[6]		4.20	S
Inglis et al. (1986)	Multiple[7]		1.44	OP
Walston and Felix (1977)	Multiple[8]	103	1.4	OP

TABLE 8.8   Density of Faults Found During Different Life-Cycle Phases for Various Software Systems (Continued)

Reference	System identifier	Developed code (1000 source lines)	Faults per thousand source lines	Phases[1]
Schafer et al. (1979)	5	115.3	3.9	OP
McCall et al. (1987)	Multiple[9]		8.76	S
Bush (1990)	FS A	14.0	10.2	S
	FS D	27.8	9.2	S
	GS A	742.2	0.3	S
	GS B	178.3	6.4	S
	GS C	45.3	3.2	S
	GS D	1278.9	1.8	S
	GS G	1292.7	2.6	S

[1]Phases: C = coding, UT = unit test, SS = subsystem test, S = system test, OP = operation.

[2]Likely to be low because of way data were collected.

[3]Average of 12 systems, with size ranging from 3000 to 16,000 source lines (average 9000) and faults from 13 to 320 faults per thousand source lines.

[4]Average of eight systems, with size ranging from 1500 to 27,000 source lines (average 18,300) and faults from 1.7 to 20 faults per thousand source lines.

[5]Data from 46 systems. Median size is 20,000 source lines and lower and upper quartiles are 10,000 and 59,000 source lines. Median fault density is 3.1 faults per thousand source lines and lower and upper quartiles are 0.8 and 8.0 faults per thousand source lines.

[6]Carefully defined data from 55 systems, with fault density ranging from 0.01 to 80.39 faults per thousand source lines. Sizes extended from 4100 to 564,900 source lines of developed code.

[7]Carefully defined data from 50 systems, with fault density ranging from 0 to 10.95 faults per thousand source lines. Average time in operational phase is 11 months, ranging from 0 to 41 months. Sizes ran from 4100 to 523,800 source lines of developed code.

[8]Data from between 3 to 11 projects (exact number not reported). Median size is 103,000 source lines and lower and upper quartiles are 56 and 474 source lines. Median period of operation is 18 months; lower and upper quartiles are 11 and 31 months. Median code changed is 4 percent. Median fault density is 1.4 faults per thousand source lines and lower and upper quartiles are 0.2 and 2.9 faults per thousand source lines.

[9]Data from 83 projects (projects duplicated elsewhere in table removed), with fault densities ranging from 0.1 to 54 faults per thousand source lines. Sizes extend from 4700 to 1,697,000 source lines.

establish the end of a loop properly. The compiler or assembler generally finds syntactic faults. They usually must be removed before successful compilation or assembly can occur. Semantic faults are hence the faults that are left after successful compilation or assembly. Coding phase inherent faults represent inherent faults found by inspection because inherent faults found in unit test are noted separately. Subsystem test represents that phase in which developers, working individually or as a team, perform tests that involve more than one unit or module but not the entire system. Testing is generally functional

TABLE 8.9   Means and Ranges of Fault Density Data

Phase (or group of phases)*	Number of systems providing data	Faults per thousand source lines	
		Range	Average
C, UT, SS, S	16	13–320	98.0
UT, SS, S	2	16.0–20.3	18.2
SS, S	1	36.2	36.2
S	176	0.01–80.4	5.45
OP	51	0–11.0	1.48

*Phases: C = coding, UT = unit test, SS = subsystem test, S = system test, OP = operation.

rather than structural in system test. It is usually performed by an independent test team. Ordinarily, the code is under configuration control and a formal failure reporting system is in use. Operation is, of course, the phase after release to the customer. The number of inherent faults found in a phase varies with the length of the phase. Of all life-cycle phases, the operational phase exhibits the greatest variation in length. Hence we potentially have the most severe problem in specifying these data. One possibility would be to define a period such as 2 years after release as the duration for which you should collect inherent fault data. We have not defined a standard period for the data presented here. Fortunately, the proportion of inherent faults found during operation is small compared to that of other phases, so the effect of any variation is considerably moderated.

If we average the data presented in Table 8.8, we obtain the results shown in Table 8.9. The data for the subsystem and system test phases combined are probably unreliable. The data for the system test phases are probably good because they represent 131 projects. Although operational phase data come from 51 systems, there is some variation due to the length of the phase. If a standard is established for this, the variation will be reduced. The average value will probably not change by more than 1 fault per thousand lines. In Table 8.10, we have estimated mean inherent fault density remaining at the beginning of several different life-cycle phases. The difference in inherent fault density

TABLE 8.10   Mean Fault Density Remaining at Beginning of Various Phases

Phase	Faults per thousand source lines
Coding (after compilation/assembly)	99.5
Unit test	19.7
System test	6.93
Operation	1.48

between the start of coding and the start of unit test is believed to be due to desk checking and code inspections.

Possibly, measures of program complexity can improve the prediction of number of inherent faults. Complexity measures form an active current research area. However, most of the complexity metrics developed to date show a high correlation with program size. They provide little improvement over just program size alone in predicting inherent faults remaining at the start of system test (Sunohara et al., 1981). The metrics considered were

1. McCabe's cyclomatic number (McCabe, 1976)

2. Halstead's effort (Halstead, 1977)

3. A statement count weighted by data references and branches from each statement

4. A data flow metric

Typical coefficients of determination relating program size and inherent faults range between 0.5 and 0.6, so there is room for predictability improvement. The foregoing conclusions are supported by similar findings by Basili and Hutchens (1983) and Gremillion (1984).

Takahashi and Kamayachi (1985) have studied the effects of other factors on improving inherent fault prediction, based on data taken for 30 projects. After normalizing the inherent fault data by program size (the most important predictive factor) to obtain inherent fault density, they found three significant additional factors:

1. Specification change activity, measured in pages of specification changes per thousand lines of code

2. Average programmer skill, measured in years

3. Thoroughness of design documentation, measured in pages of developed (new plus modified) design documents per thousand lines of code

Greater specification change activity increases the inherent fault density. Greater programmer skill and more thorough design documentation decrease inherent fault density. The effect of all three factors accounts for about 60 percent of the variation in inherent fault density experienced for the projects. Card, McGarry, and Page (1987) found that 63 percent of the variation in fault density among 22 projects, carefully matched to remove environmental variations, were explained by programmer general and application-specific skill level and by data complexity (measured in data items per system). The following three factors increased the attributable variation to 73 percent:

1. Percentage of reviews accomplished (of number possible)

2. Percentage of documentation produced (of amount possible)

3. Percentage of code read

Apparently specification change activity also had a significant effect. Technological factors investigated that did *not* have a significant effect on fault density were use of tools, structured programming, top-down development, and the chief programmer team and percentage of total development time spent in design.

A study by Basili and Hutchens (1983) showed that use of a disciplined development methodology in a team setting reduced inherent fault density. DeMarco and Lister (1985) conducted a productivity study that suggests that high productivity and low fault densities are correlated. They noted that individual productivity variation appears to result mainly from work environment factors. Many of these factors relate to the amount of work interruption that occurs. Hence it seems reasonable to suggest that fault density may be a function, among other factors, of the frequency of interruption in the work environment. Most of the research on inherent fault density has been empirical. At this point, adding insight coming from studies of human problem-solving activity to this empiricism may result in inherent fault density models with greater predictability.

Belady and Lehman (1976) have observed a growing "unstructuredness" in systems that undergo a series of releases. The unstructuredness probably results from several factors such as

1. Different people modifying or repairing the system

2. The tendency of modifications and repairs to be made locally and cheaply, degrading the global conceptual integrity of the system

3. Deficiencies in documenting modifications

It appears likely that the inherent fault density of developed code in multirelease systems will increase from release to release, unless deliberate system restructuring activities are undertaken.

The inherent fault density at the start of system test will probably show the least variation from project to project. Earlier measurements will be subject to uncertainties in determining the size of the program until it is well developed and at least partially tested. Later measurements will reflect the fact that reliability goals of different projects vary; hence there will be considerable variation in remaining inherent fault density at release to the field.

Musa (1997f) suggested a small set of factors that appear to be readily measurable and probably have a substantial influence on inherent fault density:

1. Quality of software development process, perhaps measured by the Software Engineering Institute Capability Maturity Model level

2. Requirements volatility (percentage of change weighted by percentage of project duration elapsed)

3. Average domain (for example, aerospace, banking, telecommunications) skill level of personnel, perhaps measured in years of experience

4. Average software development process skill level (with respect to process used, language, etc.), perhaps measured in years of experience

5. Requirements review thoroughness, measured in sum of occurrence probabilities of operations reviewed

6. Design review thoroughness, measured in sum of occurrence probabilities of operations reviewed

7. Code review thoroughness, measured in sum of occurrence probabilities of operations reviewed

8. Work environment, perhaps characterized by frequency of work interruption

Several researchers (for example, Jones, 1986) have raised the issue of the validity of counting instructions or lines of code. However, this question has arisen in the context of *productivity*. This may well be a valid concern because a software engineer can write a lengthy program and appear more productive, while providing no more function than the more concise designer. The approach of function points was developed to handle this concern. This issue is much less of a problem in the area of reliability because we are only interested in predicting the number of faults introduced. This relates to human error processes and thus appears to be strongly related to the amount of design work done. Hence, a longer program with the same function probably *will* have a larger number of inherent faults. Further, instructions or lines of code comprise, when clearly defined, an objective, readily determinable metric. It is a metric that can be fully automated. Finally, despite much effort, no one has been able to develop another metric that is consistently superior with respect to reliability.

Fault reduction factor. The fault reduction factor B is the ratio of the expected values of *net* reduction in faults to failures experienced. If expected values weren't taken, the result would depend on the particular realization of input states executed rather than use probabilities expressed by the operational profile. The *total* number of faults corrected is frequently larger than the net number. As a simple example, 100 failures may occur for a system. Let us assume that insufficient information is available to permit the faults that caused two of them to be found. However, 98 faults are removed. In the correction process, assume that five new faults are spawned. The *total* number of faults corrected is 98, but the *net* number is 93. The fault reduction factor B would be 0.93.

The factors that you must consider in estimating B are

1. Detectability (the proportion of failures whose faults can be found, which depends on the amount of information recorded about the failure)

2. The degree to which debuggers recognize the total scope of a fault and the size of the fail set

3. The degree to which debuggers discern predictable patterns of faults introduced by programmers

4. The extent to which new faults are spawned during fault correction

The proportion of failures whose faults can be identified depends on the amount of information recorded about the failures. It is close to 1 during test phases, although variable during operation. Because we are ordinarily applying B in the period before operation, the latter situation is generally not significant. The second factor relates to whether fault correction in response to a failure is partial or complete. A partial correction may do as little as just remove the cause of that specific failure. A complete correction prevents all failures associated with a fault from recurring. The second, third, and fourth factors probably will not vary much from project to project. There is evidence (Miyamoto, 1975; Musa, 1975) that the fourth one does not. Thus, there is a good possibility that a project-independent value of B can be found, although the value is not known at present.

Some data are currently available that indicate the values of B that typically result from just new fault spawning alone. This is shown in Table 8.11. The range of values is 0.925 to 0.993 and the average is 0.955.

TABLE 8.11   Values of Fault Reduction Factor B Due to Faults Spawned While Correcting Other Faults

Reference	System	System size (thousand source lines)	B
Basili and Perricone (1984)		90	0.94
Weiss (1981)	SEL 1	50.9	0.98
	SEL 2	75.4	>0.925
	SEL 3	85.4	0.952
	ARF	21.8	0.993
Fries (1977)		120	0.939

8.4.4.2 Initial failure intensity. You may predict the initial failure intensity parameter λ_0 from

$$\lambda_0 = fK\omega_0 \tag{8.66}$$

The quantity f is the linear execution frequency of the program. This is the average instruction execution rate r divided by the number of *object* instructions I in the program,

$$f = \frac{r}{I} \tag{8.67}$$

The linear execution frequency is the number of times the program would be executed per unit time if it had no branches or loops. Then it would simply execute all instructions in a linear sequence. If you measure the size of the program in source instructions I_s, you can make an estimate of the number of object instructions I by multiplying by the average expansion ratio Q_x. For a table of approximate expansion ratios, see Jones (1986), p. 49. The fault exposure ratio K relates failure intensity to "fault velocity." The fault velocity $f\omega_0$ is the average rate at which faults in the program would pass by if the program executed linearly. The concept of fault velocity is illustrated in Fig. 8.26.

The fault exposure ratio K represents the fraction of time that the "passage" results in a failure. It accounts for the following facts:

1. Programs don't generally execute in "straight line" fashion but have many loops and branches.

2. The machine state varies and hence the fault associated with an instruction may or may not be exposed at one particular execution of the instruction.

The effect of machine state in exposing a fault is illustrated in Fig. 8.27. Note that when X has a value larger than 25, the faulty program

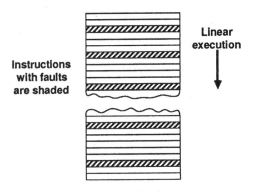

Figure 8.26 Concept of fault velocity.

Correct program   **Faulty program**

IF x > 25   IF x >‥20 ¦--- Fault
   THEN A   THEN A
   ELSE B   ELSE B

Figure 8.27   Effect of machine state in exposing
a fault.

executes correctly by performing A. It also executes correctly by performing B if X is 20 or less. A failure occurs, exposing the fault of the
incorrect conditional statement, only if X is larger than 20 but less than
or equal to 25. Because faults such as this can cover narrow ranges of
data, it is no surprise that K can be small.

At present, you must determine K from a similar program. It may be
possible in the future to relate K to program structure in some way
(Musa, 1991a). Another possibility is that the range of values of K over
different software systems may be small, allowing an average value to
be used without excessive error. This could be due to program dynamic structure averaging out in some fashion for programs of any size. The
small range would require that the average "structuredness" or decision density not vary from one large program to another. This appears
to be the case. It has been shown that cyclomatic complexity, a measure
of the number of decisions in a program, is highly correlated with program size (Basili and Hutchens, 1983). It may be possible to more accurately determine a value for K as a function of some program
characteristic. Values of K for several different systems are given in
Table 8.12. The systems are described in Table 8.2, except for systems
P7, P9, P10, and P15. Systems P7 and P9 are identical copies of an

**TABLE 8.12   Fault Exposure Ratio on
Different Software Systems**

System designator	$K (\times 10^{-7})$
T1	1.87
T2	2.15
T3	4.11
T4	10.6
T5	4.2
T6	3.97
P7	4.43
P9	5.64
P10	1.41
P15	2.09
T16	3.03
T19	4.54
T20	6.5

operating system running in different environments. System P10 is a different operating system, and P15 is a large real-time system. For details, see Musa (1979b), systems SS1A, SS1C, SS4, and 14C, respectively. The average value of K is 4.20×10^{-7} failures per fault cycle and the values cover a total range of 7.5 to 1. It will be seen from the values of K that intervals between failures typically represent cycling through the program a large number of times.

To evaluate K for other projects for which data may be available, we require only four items of information:

1. A set of failure data sufficient to permit $B\phi = \lambda_0/v_0$ to be estimated

2. The fault reduction factor B

3. Program size in object instructions

4. Average instruction execution rate

You must exercise care to ensure that the failure data are true execution time data or that you perform appropriate adjustments to make them so. You can find execution time intervals from clock time intervals by multiplying the clock time intervals by the average computer utilization ρ_C. Adjust data in the form of failures per clock time interval by dividing by the average computer utilization. Estimation of the quantity λ_0/v_0 of the basic execution time model is now done. Compute the linear execution frequency f from the average instruction execution rate and program size. Determine the value of K from Eqs. 8.65 and 8.66 as

$$K = \frac{1}{Bf}\ \frac{\lambda_0}{v_0} \tag{8.68}$$

Consider the case of health insurance claim processing program, involving 50,000 deliverable executable source instructions, that has just been turned over to the system test group. Previous experience in this development environment for similar programs indicates a fault density of 6 faults per 1000 delivered executable source instructions. The fault reduction factor is 1. We have a fault exposure ratio of 2×10^{-7} failure per fault cycle. The code expansion ratio (object instructions per source instruction) is 4. The instruction execution rate of the target machine is 333 million object instructions per execution second. If we apply the basic execution time model, what values of the total failures and initial failure intensity parameters can we expect?

We compute the inherent faults ω_0 from

$$\omega_0 = \omega_I \Delta I \tag{8.69}$$

Note that ΔI is the number of developed source instructions and ω_I is the fault density. Thus

$$\omega_0 = \left(\frac{6 \text{ faults}}{100 \text{ instructions}}\right)(50{,}000 \text{ instructions})$$

$$= 300 \text{ faults}$$

From Eq. 8.65 we have

$$v_0 = \frac{\omega_0}{B}$$

$$= \frac{300}{1}$$

$$= 300 \text{ failures}$$

Now

$$I = I_S Q_X \qquad (8.70)$$

where Q_X is the code expansion ratio. Thus,

$$I = (50{,}000 \text{ instructions}) (4)$$

$$= 200{,}000 \text{ instructions}$$

The linear execution frequency f is

$$f = \frac{r}{I}$$

$$= \frac{333 \times 10^6 \text{ instructions per execution second}}{0.2 \times 10^6 \text{ instructions}}$$

$$= 1670 \text{ cycles per execution second}$$

Using Eq. 8.66, we have

$$\lambda_0 = f K \omega_0$$

$= (1670 \text{ cycles per execution second})(2 \times 10^{-7} \text{ failure per fault}) (300 \text{ faults})$

$= 0.1 \text{ failures per execution second}$

Another example of parameter prediction is a software system for testing telecommunications circuits. We expect it to have 50 faults remaining at the start of system test. The computer has an average instruction rate of 200 million object instructions per execution second. The program has 50,000 object instructions. For the average test, the program executes 1 million instructions. The value of the fault exposure ratio K is 2×10^{-7} failure per fault. We want to express the failure intensity in terms of failures per test.

The linear execution frequency, expressed in terms of cycle per test, is

$$f = \frac{1,000,000}{50,000} = 20 \text{ cycles per test}$$

The failure intensity is then

$$\lambda = fK\omega_0 = (20 \text{ cycles per test})(2 \times 10^{-7} \text{ failure per fault})$$

$$= (20 \text{ cycles per test})(2 \times 10^{-7} \text{ failure per fault})(50 \text{ faults})$$

$$= 2 \times 10^{-4} \text{ failure per test}$$

8.4.5 Parameter estimation

We can use estimation to determine the parameters of either the basic or logarithmic Poisson execution time models as execution progresses. For the basic model, we can use estimation to refine the values established by prediction. We will use maximum likelihood estimation, although other methods are also possible. It is most efficient to use a program to do the calculations. Hence, we will not discuss them in detail but will take a graphical view.

The essential data required for estimation are the failure times or failures per time interval (grouped data) experienced during execution. The process is illustrated schematically for the basic model in Fig. 8.28. We have plotted a set of failure intensities against execution time. They represent the number of failures in a time interval divided by that time interval. The basic execution time model provides the basis for plotting the dashed line of anticipated failure intensity against execution time. Two parameters determine this line, the initial failure intensity λ_0 and the total expected failures ν_0. The first parameter is represented by the vertical axis intercept. Values of the parameters are in effect chosen to maximize the likelihood of occurrence of the set of failure intensities that have been experienced (in the actual statistical derivation, they are chosen to maximize the likelihood of occurrence of the set of failure times or the set of numbers of failures per time interval). In an approximate sense, we are fitting the curve to the data indicated. The plot also illustrates some derived quantities.

The foregoing parameters were selected to describe the basic model because they had the most immediate connection with the characteristics of the product and the development process. We can also define a parameter ϕ, the per-fault hazard rate, given by

$$\phi = \frac{\lambda_0}{\omega_0} \tag{8.71}$$

The quantity ω_0 is the number of faults inherent in the code. Note that the decrement in failure intensity per failure is given by $\lambda_0/\nu_0 = B\phi$, where B is the fault reduction factor, or ratio of net fault reduction to

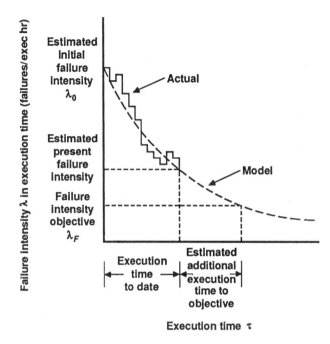

Figure 8.28 Conceptual view of parameter estimation.

failures experienced. We can describe the model in terms of v_0 and $B\phi$. This alternative formulation of the model simplifies parameter estimation. We can readily convert between the different parameters.

Because estimation of the parameters is a statistical process, you will also wish to determine confidence intervals. View the curve as a band. The width increases with the magnitude of the confidence interval. A 90 percent confidence interval requires a wider band than a 75 percent one does. The confidence interval for λ_0 is given by the range of vertical axis intercepts.

The process of estimating the parameters of the logarithmic Poisson model, initial failure intensity λ_0 and failure intensity decay parameter θ, is analogous.

To obtain some idea of the accuracy with which model parameters are being estimated, look at plots of the estimates as functions of execution time. The values should be approximately constant (within statistical variation) if the program is stable except for fault removal. A confidence interval estimated late in the period of execution will be a reasonable approximation of the range of values in which the parameter actually lies. Hence, a confidence interval estimated earlier can be compared with it to check the quality of the estimation.

During the initial use of estimation, accuracy can be low (generally indicated by large confidence intervals) because of the small failure samples available. Note that accuracy is primarily related to the number of failures in the sample. If data are in the form of failures per interval, you can have an adequate sample size even though the number of intervals may be small.

Many projects collect grouped failure data (failures in some time interval) rather than individual failure times or intervals. This is slightly easier to do, involving somewhat less data collection effort, particularly if the time interval is a day. The disadvantage is decreased accuracy in estimating parameters, which we will examine. The following is a summary of a simulation study (Musa, Iannino, and Okumoto 1987, pp. 127–128) of the effect of grouping for fixed time periods. The study included both the basic and logarithmic Poisson execution time models. In each case, we examined estimation of the parameter that affects the rate of failure intensity reduction ($B\phi$ or $\lambda_0\theta$, respectively). The initial failure intensities and all derived quantities depend on the foregoing parameter and its accuracy in the cases of both models. The study was based on a representative rather than an exhaustive set of parameter values. The accuracy depends on the parameter values. Hence, our results convey general effects rather than precise behavior.

We quantified the effect of grouping by comparing the observed information in the grouped data to that in the failure time data. Observed information affects the accuracy of the estimates. More information leads to greater accuracy. Let I_g be the ratio of the observed information in the grouped data to that in the failure time data. Values of I_g that are less than 1 show that our estimates are more variable for grouped data. Values of I_g greater than 1 indicate that the estimates are less variable for grouped data.

Results are presented in Tables 8.13 and 8.14 for the basic and logarithmic Poisson models. Grouped data provides less accurate estimates. However, estimates are only slightly less accurate for the basic model if the number of groups is, say, 10 or more. Quality of estimates from grouped data for the logarithmic Poisson model is markedly inferior.

If we have gathered data in grouped form, there are situations where it may be desirable to convert them to failure times. The most realistic method for doing this is to assign the failure times randomly within the interval in which the data have been collected. We use a uniform distribution, which reflects the fact that we have no knowledge that would favor assignment to any particular part of the collection interval. Let us consider the resulting error introduced into the estimation of the parameter $B\phi$ or $\lambda_0\theta$ under various conditions. We will consider representative cases, illustrated in Tables 8.15 (simulated data) and 8.16 (real project data). In addition to showing the error resulting from ran-

TABLE 8.13   Values of I_g for Equal Time Groups for the Basic Execution Time Model

Number of failures	Number of groups	I_g
100	4	0.899
	8	0.969
	15	0.992
	29	0.995
	48	0.999
	72	0.999
50	5	0.941
	11	0.992
	21	0.997
	42	0.999
25	8	0.987
	16	0.999
	32	1.002

TABLE 8.14   Values of I_g for Equal Time Groups for the Logarithmic Poisson Execution Time Model

Number of groups	I_g
10	0.118
19	0.163
47	0.104
94	0.411
156	0.538
312	1.032

TABLE 8.15   Results of Randomizing Grouped Data for Some Simulated Data Sets

			Maximum likelihood estimate of $B\phi$ or $\lambda_0\theta$ using		
Model group	Number of failures	Number of groups	Original data	Randomly converted data	Uniformly converted data
Exponential	100	4	0.293×10^{-4}	$0.2\,66 \times 10^{-4}$	0.257×10^{-4}
($B\phi = 0.3 \times 10^{-4}$)		15	0.287×10^{-4}	0.284×10^{-4}	0.275×10^{-4}
		50	5	0.347×10^{-4}	0.401×10^{-4}
0.268×10^{-4}					
		11	0.327×10^{-4}	0.326×10^{-4}	0.265×10^{-4}
Geometric	100	10	0.283×10^{-3}	0.253×10^{-3}	0.244×10^{-3}
($\lambda_0\theta = 0.25 \times 10^{-3}$)		20	0.307×10^{-3}	0.301×10^{-3}	0.321×10^{-3}
	50	10	0.246×10^{-3}	0.241×10^{-3}	0.210×10^{-3}
		20	0.249×10^{-3}	0.257×10^{-3}	0.213×10^{-3}

TABLE 8.16   Results of Randomizing Grouped Data for Real Systems

Model group	System	Maximum likelihood estimate of $B\phi$ or $\lambda_0\theta$ using		
		Original data	Randomly converted data	Uniformly converted data
Exponential	T38	0.105×10^{-1}	0.122×10^{-1}	0.089×10^{-1}
	T39	0.664×10^{-6}	0.661×10^{-6}	0.641×10^{-6}
Geometric	T38	0.207×10^{-1}	0.227×10^{-1}	0.170×10^{-1}
	T39	0.377×10^{-5}	0.354×10^{-5}	0.341×10^{-5}

dom assignment, we also show the error resulting from spacing the failures uniformly within the interval (it is greater). Randomization does not cause errors in estimation of $B\phi$ or $\lambda_0\phi$ greater than about 15 percent for either model, even when there are as few as five groups.

8.5   Frequently Asked Questions

1. Why does the occurrence of a number of failures separated by short time intervals (compared to the intervals previously experienced) often lead to a *decrease* in the estimate of initial failure intensity? This seems counterintuitive.

ANSWER: Remember, you are estimating what the initial failure intensity *must have been,* not what the present failure intensity is now. You *will* usually see an increase in present failure intensity. However, the occurrence of a number of short time intervals between failures indicates the proportion of faults that we have removed is not as high as we thought. In other words, the present failure intensity does not represent as much progress from the initial failure intensity as we had believed. This means we must have been overestimating the initial failure intensity. Note that the situation described will happen when a number of design changes are made, introducing new faults. The present failure intensity will rise, but the estimate of initial failure intensity will drop.

2. Your basic model doesn't make sense. Suppose you have a program that runs for 1000 s and has 100 evenly spaced faults in it. After starting test, the first failure will occur at 10 s. If you correct it and resume testing, the next failure will also occur after a 10-s interval. This will continue right up to the last failure, which will also occur after a 10-s interval. Where is the change in failure intensity that is supposed to occur as testing progresses?

ANSWER: You are missing one very important concept. The spacing between faults in "instruction space" is not the same as the spacing between failures in "execution space." The reasons for this are twofold:

Except in very trivial cases, code is not in a straight line but has many loops and branches. Even if code were in a straight line, the state of the machine will most likely not be constant and hence the fault associated with an instruction may or may not be exposed at one particular execution of the instruction.

Experience to date has shown that intervals between failures typically represent cycling through a program a large number of times. The picture you paint depends on all the faults being uncovered in one cycle through the program, which just doesn't happen in practice. With multiple cycles, the fault density is reduced when the first fault is corrected. *On average* the failure intensity will decrease. Thus the failure intensity *does* change as testing progresses.

3. What values will you get for total failures ν_0 and the failure intensity decay parameter θ during the operational phase?

ANSWER: Infinity and 0, respectively.

4. Don't software reliability models sometimes indicate that there are an infinite number of bugs remaining? How can that be?

ANSWER: Remember that software reliability models deal with *failures,* not faults. Certain models imply that there will be an infinite number of failures in an infinite amount of time. This is quite reasonable, for example, when one thinks of a program that has a constant failure intensity.

5. What is the effect on the basic model parameter estimates of a failure that keeps occurring, can't be fixed, and is still counted?

ANSWER: The estimated total failures will be infinite. Note that the fault reduction factor B will be 0, so the actual number of faults can be finite.

6. How can total failures of the basic execution time model be a finite value? If you run a program for an infinite time, won't you get an infinite number of failures?

ANSWER: As long as there is some failure resolution effort (that is, the fault reduction factor B is not 0), we will ultimately eliminate all faults from the program. The interval between failures will approach infinity. Thus it is possible to have a finite number of failures in infinite time.

7. How can we have a finite number of failures in an infinite amount of time? If we have a particular failure intensity, won't the number of failures increase without limit as time passes?

ANSWER: The "finite failures in infinite time" situation occurs only during reliability growth, when the faults that are causing failures are removed after the failures occur. The failure intensity decreases as time passes, making a finite number of failures possible.

8. What factors affect the proportion of failures that we resolve, which is expressed by the fault reduction factor B?

ANSWER: The proportion of failures resolved decreases when the source code is complex or when the correction is lengthy or complex. It increases if the correction undergoes a design review or a code review or is extensively tested.

Sometimes we include the effect of change in the fault reduction factor. If we do, then the fault reduction factor decreases with the amount of requirements or design changes.

9. Why does the estimate of total failures expected in infinite time sometimes keep increasing as we experience additional failures and make the estimates based on larger failure samples?

ANSWER: There are three possible reasons for this. First, the estimate at the smaller sample size may simply have been inaccurate. The more likely possibilities are that you are testing functions that haven't been tested before or that new code is being integrated as test proceeds.

Software Reliability Engineering Process Step by Step

Divider lines represent the steps after which projects new to software reliability engineering can probably gain maximum benefit from review by an expert consultant.

1. Which systems of your product should have separate test?

----

2. Define the failure with severity classes.
3. Choose the natural or time unit you will use.
4. Set the system failure intensity objective for each system to be tested.
5. Determine the developed software failure intensity objective for the product and its variations (unless you integrate components only).
   a. Find the product expected acquired failure intensity.
   b. Compute the product developed software failure intensity objective.
6. Engineer the reliability strategies to meet the failure intensity objective for the developed software of the product and its variations (unless you integrate components only).

----

7. Determine the operational modes of each system to be tested.
8. For each system to be tested, develop the system and operational mode operational profiles.

    a. Identify operation initiators.

    b. Choose between the tabular or graphical representation (the choice should be the same for all operational modes).

    c. Create an operations "list" for each operation initiator.

    d. Determine occurrence rates.

    e. Determine occurrence probabilities.

---

9. Prepare test cases.

    a. Estimate number of new test cases for current release.

    b. Allocate new test cases among systems to be tested.

    c. Allocate each system's new test cases among its new operations.

    d. Specify new test cases.

    e. Add test cases to test cases from previous releases.

10. Prepare test procedures.

---

11. Execute test.

    a. Allocate test time.

    b. Invoke tests.

    c. Identify system failures.

---

12. Apply failure data to guide decisions.

    a. Accept or reject acquired components.

    b. Guide software development process for product and variations (unless you integrate components only).

    c. Accept or reject supersystem.

    d. Release product.

Template for Workshops

Give each participant a copy of the template that follows, which consists of *some* of the major questions a project needs to consider in applying software reliability engineering. The completed template is intended to serve as an aid to a project in starting to apply software reliability engineering. For the complete step-by-step process, see App. A.

Divide attendees as much as possible by projects, with "single" attendees joining a project that is close to their interests. Suggest that those from the core project group lead the discussion, with the single attendees questioning them and providing constructive criticism. Attendees working on projects should be encouraged to bring their requirements and architecture documents to the workshop. Each group may find it useful to choose a "project manager" to lead and someone to record its decisions and action items for distribution to the group and later use.

All of the workshops relate to the chapters of this book. The intent is to apply concepts just after they have been taught. Put particular emphasis on the early steps of the software reliability engineering process, just as you would with the software development process itself. Investing time and care up front will pay off downstream. But note that the software reliability engineering process follows a spiral model; hence many actions will later be corrected as a result.

It is important that you actively question what you are doing as you proceed. Note, as action items for investigation and learning, those activities where you might proceed differently if you repeated them a second time. Because terms may vary from company to company, make sure you understand their meaning here (see App. C).

If you are missing information needed for a decision, make obtaining that information an action item. Make the best estimate or assumption you can for now so that you can proceed. If time does not permit you to fully answer the questions posed here (this is expected for most systems), simplify by considering one part of your project or by making assumptions; record the work not done as action items. When you are dealing with numbers, pick simple ones (even if approximate) that facilitate hand calculations.

This template, when reproduced with space after each question, is designed for you to record your workshop proceedings in a systematic way. You can designate action items by an arrow → in the left margin.

Usually the instructor will visit each group during each workshop. If you encounter a serious roadblock, however, feel free to request an immediate visit. In order to facilitate communication, explain what is different or unusual about your project. Present those things the team has done that you are unsure of and want reviewed.

After each workshop, each group may report briefly to the entire class, with the other groups and the instructor making constructive comments. The focus of the comments should be on noting the things a group did well, that represent good illustrations or adaptations of the concepts, or that constitute interesting new ideas or approaches.

B.1   Defining System Workshop (Chap. 1)

1. What is the software-based product you are developing and what are its principal features? The ideal situation is if you are all members of a project team and have your requirements and architecture documentation with you. If this situation does not exist, try to identify a software-based product that is relevant to the largest portion of the group. "Outsiders" can play a very useful role by forcing "insiders" to explain the product clearly and by challenging ambiguous and missing requirements.

2. Which systems of the product should have separate test? The size of the test effort will increase with the number of systems; hence you should add to this list with care.

B.2   Defining Necessary Reliability Workshop (Chap. 2)

3. How will you define failure for the product (by severity class, as product-specific as possible)? You should be able to give your answer to your test team as a guideline for classifying failures they observe.

4. Choose the natural or time unit you will use for the product.

5. Set the product failure intensity objective.

6. Find the expected product acquired failure intensity, based on the failure intensities of the hardware and acquired software components (if applicable).

7. Determine the product-developed software failure intensity objective (if applicable).

8. How will you balance fault prevention, fault-removal, and fault-tolerance strategies? Consider your specific requirements for reliability, timely delivery, and cost and allocate your resource percentages among the following six activities. You may add other activities to the list if they are significant, but the percentages must total 100.

Fault prevention

Requirements reviews

Design reviews

Fault removal

Code inspection

Unit test

System test

Fault tolerance (design for fault tolerance)

B.3 Developing Operational Profiles Workshop (Chap. 3)

9. What factors are likely to yield different operational modes for your system? Construct a list of possible operational modes. Reduce the list to a set of operational modes that are significantly different from each other and frequently executing. Limiting the number of operational modes is important; otherwise, you may create excessive work for yourself later in the software reliability engineering process.

10. Pick one operational mode of the product of broad scope (usually the one executed the most in the field) for further study. Identify its operation initiators (user types, external systems, own system).

11. Decide between tabular or graphical representation for the operational profile.

12. If you are using the tabular representation, list the operations for the operational mode you have selected (consider the different

initiators to jog your memory). If you are using the graphical representation, draw at least part of the network. Limit the size to not more than 10 operations or attributes.

13. How will you determine occurrence rates and occurrence probabilities for the operational profile of the operational mode you have selected? Estimate them, using simple numbers, so that we can proceed further with the exercise. Be sure to handle filler operations correctly.

B.4   Preparing for Test Workshop (Chap. 4)

14. Estimate the number of test cases you will prepare (if this is not the first release, estimate the number of new test cases for this release).

15. Allocate the number of test cases (new test cases if this is not the first release) among the associated systems to be tested.

16. For simplicity, assume that the system operational profile of your product is identical to the operational profile of the operational mode you selected of the product. Allocate the number of test cases for the product to its operations (new test cases to new operations if not the first release). Make sure you handle critical operations properly.

17. Select an important operation; list its direct input variables and their levels.

18. Specify the test operational profile for the operational mode you selected of the product.

B.5   Executing Test Workshop (Chap. 5)

19. Determine how you will divide hours of test among the associated systems you have defined.

20. Determine the number of hours you will devote to feature, regression, and load test for the product.

21. Allocate the hours of load test among the operational modes.

B.6   Applying Failure Data to Guide
Decisions Workshop (Chap. 6)

22. This involves a demonstration with the possibility of following on your personal computer. If you have a personal computer and the CASRE software available, install CASRE and step through the CASRE exercise (see App. F) as the demonstration proceeds.

acceleration factor Factor by which an operation is more frequently executed in test than it would be in the field because of its criticality.

acquired failure intensity Failure intensity for all hardware and required software components, usually found by adding the failure intensities of the components.

acquired software Software that is contracted for, purchased, or reused.

assertion Code that checks the value of a variable against an anticipated value or range of values and generates a return code or message if the check is not valid.

attribute Characteristic of an operation, represented by a node or set of nodes in a graphical representation of an operational profile.

attribute value Value of a characteristic of an operation, represented by a branch in a graphical representation of an operational profile.

availability Fraction of time during which a system is functioning acceptably.

beta test Test at the first user site.

build Minor version of software that incorporates bug fixes and possible new features; multiple builds occur as a major version is developed.

calendar time Chronological time, including time during which a computer may not be running.

cascaded deviation Deviation directly resulting from an initial deviation.

cascaded failure Failure directly resulting from an initial failure.

certification test Test that is directed solely at accepting or rejecting the software and is not coupled to removal of the faults that are causing the failures.

clock time Elapsed time from start to end of program execution, including periods when processor(s) is/are idle.

common mode failures Failures that are completely dependent on each other and occur together.

component Part of a system, such as a software module, an item of hardware, or a person with a job role.

computer utilization Ratio of execution time to time.

confidence limit One extreme of a range in which a specified percentage of the true values of a variable occur.

configuration profile List of configurations of hardware and software that interfaces with your product, along with their associated probabilities.

consumer risk Risk of falsely saying objective is met when it is not.

criticality Importance of an operation with respect to safety or value added by satisfactory execution or risk to human life, cost, or system capability resulting from failure.

customer Organization or person that is purchasing your product.

customer type Set of customers (purchasers of your product) who have similar businesses and hence tend to have the same user types.

data laundry Checking of data being input to filter out common errors.

demonstrable failure intensity/failure intensity objective (FI/FIO) ratio In certification test, the FI/FIO ratio that has been demonstrated at any point in time for the levels of discrimination ratio, consumer risk, and supplier risk chosen.

design input space Input space program is designed to work in.

developed code New or modified executable delivered instructions.

developed software Software developed by your organization.

deviation Any departure of system behavior in execution from expected behavior.

direct input variable Input variable that controls an operation directly in a known, designed way, such as an argument, menu selection, or entered data item.

discrepancy Difference between the actual value of a variable and the value we expect.

discrimination ratio Factor of error in estimating failure intensity in certification test.

downtime Time a system is not operational.

equivalence partitioning Grouping input states that you expect will have the same failure behavior.

error   Incorrect or missing action by a person or persons that causes a fault in a program.

estimation   Determination of software reliability model parameters and quantities from failure data.

evolving program   Program that is changing for reasons other than correction of failures.

execution time   Time processor(s) is/are executing nonfiller operations, in execution hours.

exponential model   Musa basic software reliability model.

fail set   Set of runs (and hence input states) that will cause a fault to generate a failure.

failure   Departure of system behavior in execution from user requirements.

failure category   Set of failures that have the same *kind* of impact on users such as safety or security. Contrast with failure severity class, where the failures have the same *magnitude* of impact.

failure intensity   Failures per natural or time unit.

failure intensity decay parameter   One of the parameters of the logarithmic (Musa-Okumoto logarithmic Poisson) model.

failure intensity objective   Failure intensity that system is expected to meet before release to the field.

failure severity class   Set of failures with same degree of per-failure impact on users.

failure time   Accumulated elapsed time at which a failure occurs.

fault   Defect in system that causes a failure when executed. A software fault is a defect in the code.

fault density   Faults per line of deliverable executable source code.

fault exposure ratio   Proportionality factor that relates failure intensity with the rate at which faults would be encountered if the program were executed linearly.

fault reduction factor   Ratio of faults removed to failures experienced.

fault tolerance   Capability of a system to counteract deviations and prevent them from becoming failures.

feature test   Test in which runs are executed independently of each other, with interactions and effects of the field environment minimized (sometimes by reinitializing the system).

filler occurrence   Instance of execution of a filler operation above the minimum required for proper system operation (usually for audit and maintenance operations).

filler operation   Operation of low priority that is allowed to execute more frequently than needed when processor capacity is available.

graphical representation   Format for representing operations by paths through a graph.

grouped failure data   Failures per time interval.

homogeneity   Fraction of a set of runs that have the same failure behavior.

homogeneous   Having the same failure behavior.

indirect input variable   Input variable that influences operation even though it doesn't directly control it, such as operational mode, database state, or resource state.

inherent software fault   Fault associated with software product as originally written or modified.

initial failure intensity   Failure intensity at the start of test, usually system test.

input space   Set of all possible input states for a program.

input state   Complete set of input variables for a run and their values.

input variable   Variable that exists external to a run and affects its execution.

level   Value or set of values of an input variable expected to yield the same failure behavior because of processing similarities. Hence a level is an equivalence class.

load test   Test in which runs are executed simultaneously, with full interactions and all the effects of the field environment.

logarithmic model   Musa-Okumoto logarithmic Poisson software reliability model.

machine state   Set of the values of all variables that exist within a machine, whether or not they affect or are set by a particular program.

mean time between failures (MTBF)   Sum of mean time to failure (MTTF) and mean time to repair (MTTR).

mean time to failure (MTTF)   Average time to next failure.

mean time to repair (MTTR)   Average time to restore a system to normal operation. For software, this is the time required to clean up the database and restart, not the time to identify and remove the fault causing the failure.

mean value function   Function that expresses the average value of the number of events experienced by a random process at each point in time.

mission time   Specified interval that relates to the time required to complete the most important function of a product.

module usage table   List of the modules of a program with the probabilities that each is used on any given run of the program.

natural unit   Unit related to output of software-based product, such as pages of output, transactions, or telephone calls.

nonfiller   Within the minimum required for proper system operation and not including execution in excess of it.

occurrence probability   Probability with which an operation or attribute value occurs.

occurrence rate   Frequency at which an operation or attribute value occurs.

operation   Major system logical task of short duration, which returns control to system when complete.

operation group   Set of associated operations.

operation interaction factor   Factor that estimates effect of newly developed operations on reused operations.

operational architecture   Structure of and relations between operations as they are invoked in the field.

operational development   Development that is scheduled operation by operation in such a fashion that the most used and/or critical operations are implemented in the first release and the less used and/or critical are delayed, the net result being faster time to market for the most important capabilities.

operational mode   Distinct pattern of system use; usually tested separately.

operational mode failure intensity   Total failure intensity taken over all failure severity classes for an operational mode.

operational mode failure intensity objective   Total failure intensity objective taken over all severity classes for an operational mode.

operational mode operational profile   Operational profile of a specific operational mode.

operation-module matrix   Matrix that shows which operations use which modules, with 1 indicating that a given operation uses a given module.

operational profile   Set of operations and their probabilities of occurrence.

operations list   Set of possible operations or attributes and attribute values.

output state   Complete set of output variables for a run and their values.

output variable   Variable that exists external to a run and is set by the run.

overall   Pertaining to all operational modes.

prediction   Determination of software reliability model parameters and quantities from characteristics of the software product and development process.

probability   Fraction of occasions on which a specified value or set of values of a quantity occurs, out of all possible values for that quantity.

producer risk   Risk of falsely saying objective is not met when it is.

product System that is sold to customer.

program Set of complete instructions (operators with operands specified) that executes within a single computer and relates to the accomplishment of some major function.

projection Estimation for a point in the future.

random Property of being able to have more than one value at one time, each occurring with some probability.

random process Set of random variables arranged by some other variable, usually time.

reduced operation software (ROS) Software that directly implements only the most used and/or most critical operations; the software analog of RISC for hardware.

regression test Test designed to reveal failures caused by faults introduced by program changes.

reliability Probability of failure-free execution for specified number of natural units or for a specified mission time.

reliability growth test Test that is coupled with attempts to remove the faults causing the failures, which results in a decrease in failure intensity or growth in reliability.

required input space Input space that program is required to work in.

reused operation Operation that has been carried over to a new release from a previous release.

robust Providing an output or change in output that is weaker than the input or change in input.

run Single execution of operation, characterized by input state.

run category Set of runs with the same failure behavior.

safety Aspect of reliability, the probability that no failures occur in a specified period that involve human death or personal injury.

soak time Amount of time since last database reinitialization.

stable program Program in which code is unchanging, with program neither evolving nor having faults removed.

stationary Constant with respect to time.

supersystem System consisting of product and other systems with which it interacts.

supplier risk Risk of falsely saying objective is not met when it is.

system Combination of hardware, software, and/or personnel elements that performs a function for a user or another system.

system failure intensity objective Failure intensity objective taken over all operational modes, each operational mode failure intensity being weighted in accordance with field use.

system operational profile Operational profile based on all operational modes.

tabular representation Format for representing operations by table entry.

test case Partial specification of a run, involving specification of its direct input variables.

test operational profile Operational profile used to drive part or all of test; usually associated with an operational mode.

test procedure Load test controller that sets up environmental conditions and invokes randomly selected test cases at random times. Test case selection is based on the appropriate operational mode test operational profile; invocation times are based on the operational mode run occurrence rate.

total Pertaining to all severity classes.

uniform Having equal probability of occurrence.

unit Part of a software system that is usually developed by one programmer and does not necessarily perform a complete function for a user or another system. In another sense, a measure, such as a time unit.

uptime Time a system is operational.

user Person who directly employs the product.

user type Set of users who tend to employ the product in the same way.

D

Summary of Useful Formulas

Converting failure intensity to reliability

$$R = \exp\left(-\lambda t\right)$$

where R = reliability
λ = failure intensity (per natural or time unit)
t = mission time (in natural or time units)

When $\lambda t < 0.05$,

$$R \approx 1 - \lambda t$$

Converting reliability to failure intensity

$$\lambda = \frac{-\ln R}{t}$$

When $R > 0.95$,

$$\lambda \approx 1 - \frac{R}{t}$$

System reliability for AND combination of components

$$R = \prod_{i=1}^{Q} R_i$$

where R = system reliability
R_i = component reliability
Q = number of components

System failure intensity for AND combination of components

$$\lambda = \sum_{i=1}^{Q} \lambda_1$$

where λ = system failure intensity
λ_i = component failure intensity

System reliability for OR combination of components

$$R = 1 - \prod_{i=1}^{Q} (1 - R_i)$$

Software Reliability Engineering and Testing Functions Aided by Software Tools

The following software reliability engineering and testing functions can be greatly aided by the appropriate software tools. The sixth function requires them.

1. Test case script preparation
   a. Character
   b. Graphical
   c. Task input to application server
2. Test procedure script preparation
3. Test management
4. Operation recording and probability computation
5. Deviation/failure recording with associated natural or time unit recording
6. Reliability estimation and plotting

Using CASRE

CASRE (Computer Aided Software Reliability Estimation) is a software reliability estimation program that runs under Microsoft Windows. *Given guidance,* it is relatively easy to learn and use because it uses menus and dialog boxes. It is widely available as a CD-ROM that is included in the *Handbook of Software Reliability Engineering* (Lyu, 1996).

CASRE was designed primarily for researchers and is hence very comprehensive, with many of its features and models of little interest to practitioners. Hence it is easy for software practitioners to get lost without guidance. The guidance furnished here is more than adequate for the practitioner, but a complete (197-page) user manual is available (Nikora, 1994). This appendix will provide a step-by-step approach to installing CASRE on your computer, creating its failure data file, and executing it. It is restricted to the functions you will need as a software practitioner applying software reliability engineering. Some of the procedures you must follow and data you are asked to supply may seem arbitrary; they are shortcuts that are necessary to make CASRE run properly.

Although CASRE will run under most Microsoft Windows environments, this discussion is focused on Windows 95. It assumes that you have a basic knowledge of Windows 95, including selecting files, editing files, and starting programs. For other versions of Windows, you should translate the Windows 95 instructions given here to their equivalents.

Because CASRE was designed for Windows, most conventions work as they do in Windows (for example, the File, Edit, and Help menus;

Cancel and OK in dialog boxes; and operations on windows such as minimize, maximize, exit, movement, resizing, and scrolling). If your system has the necessary memory and disk space for Windows 95 to operate properly, it will virtually always run CASRE successfully.

We have found it easiest for software practitioners to learn CASRE by using this appendix step by step in conjunction with a personal computer. You can run CASRE directly from your CD-ROM drive, but it is better to install it on your hard drive. After you have installed CASRE, you will find that there are several data sets stored in the folder C:\casre\testdata that you can use for practice in executing CASRE.

F.1 Installation

To install under Windows 95,

1. Insert the CD-ROM in the CD-ROM drive (or floppy disk in disk drive if you have copied the Tool\Casre folder from the CD-ROM to it).
2. Click on Start, then Settings, then Control Panel.
3. When Control Panel window appears, double click on Add/Remove Programs.
4. When Add/Remove Programs Properties window appears, click on Install.
5. When Install Program from Floppy Disk or CD-ROM window appears, click on Next.
6. When Run Installation Program window appears, click on Browse. Navigate to your CD-ROM drive (this may be D:\ or E:\) or disk drive, then Tool\Casre. Double click on Install.bat.
7. Click on Finish.

To install for Windows NT,

1. Using Windows Explorer, copy all of the CASRE files from the CD-ROM or disk to a temporary working folder.
2. Open the install.bat file in the temporary folder with a text editor such as Notepad (instructions on accessing Notepad are in Sec. F.2).
3. Locate the lines

```
copy .\*.hlp c:\windows
copy .\casre.ini c:\windows
```

and change "windows" to the Windows NT root folder (it is often "winnt"). You must also rename casre.ini because it is a read-only file that you will be modifying.

4. "Save as" install.bat to another name; it is a read-only file and cannot be saved with its existing name.

5. Open the casre.ini file in the temporary folder with a text editor such as Notepad.

6. Locate the lines

```
[applications]
Write = c:\windows\write.exe
```

and

```
[HelpDir]
Directory = c:\windows\
```

and change "windows" to the Windows NT root folder.

7. "Save as" casre.ini to the new name you picked for it in step 3.

8. In Windows Explorer, navigate to the renamed Install.bat file in the temporary folder. Double click on it to install CASRE.

For either operating system, we suggest that you place a Casre icon on your desktop for convenience, but this is not mandatory. To do this, click the right mouse button on the desktop, then New, then Shortcut. An icon and a Create Shortcut window will appear. Click on Browse in the window and navigate to C:\casre. Double click on Casre.exe. When the Create Shortcut window is highlighted again, click on Next. The title of the window will change to Select a Title for the Program. Type in "Casre," click on Finish, and the icon will be tagged "Casre." Drag the icon to the desired location on your desktop.

If you decide to run CASRE directly without installation, you must first copy the casre.ini file from the Tool\Casre folder to the appropriate root folder (C:\windows for Windows 95, C:\winnt for Windows NT) on your hard drive. You should also copy the three help files casre.hlp, plot.hlp, and rslttabl.hlp or the help function may not work properly.

F.2   Creating the Failure Data File for CASRE

You will generally find Notepad easiest to use. However, you can use a word processor as long as the file is saved as ASCII text. The procedure for Notepad is as follows:

1. To enter Notepad, click on Start, then Programs, then Accessories, then Notepad. If you are already in the CASRE window, click on

Edit, then External application, then Notepad.

2. A blank Notepad window will appear ready for entering a new file. If you wish to modify an existing file, click on Open. An Open dialog box will appear. Select the file you want and double click on it.

3. Enter or modify the data to conform with either the failure time or failure per interval (grouped) data formats described below. Note that the two formats cannot be mixed in the same file.

4. When finished, save the data by clicking on File, then Save (or Save As if you want to give a modified file a new name). If the file is new or you have chosen Save As, a Save As dialog box will appear. We recommend that you create a folder C:\casre\data for the file so that all failure data files are located in one conventional place and are easily accessible. Enter the file name you desire and click Save.

5. Click on File, then Exit.

Let's look at the format of the failure data file. CASRE nominally uses time units, but you can interpret them as natural units. The first line indicates time units that will be used: It is recommended that "Seconds," "Minutes," or "Hours" be chosen. The following lines differ in format, depending on whether you have number of natural or time units or failures per interval (grouped) data. All fields in the line are separated by blanks. For *number of natural or time units data* follow the format

```
<failure number> <number of natural or time units since previous
failure> <severity class>
```

For *failures per interval data* follow the format

```
<interval number> <failures in interval> <duration of interval
in natural or time units> 0 0 0 <severity class>
```

The failures in an interval can be zero. We will not be tracking failure intensity by severity class, so for simplicity you may set the severity class to 1 (a number must be supplied for the program to work, but you can enter any number between 1 and 9, including the actual severity class). The three zeros placed after the duration of interval field are necessary to void out program features we will not use.

The formats are shown in Tables F.1 and F.2.

F.3   Executing CASRE

CASRE is typically run for two different purposes. During early and mid-test, it is used to guide the test process. Progress is evaluated and

TABLE F.1   Number of Natural or Time Units Data

Seconds		
1	30	1
2	55	1
3	70	1
4	60	1
5	90	1
6	110	1
7	100	1
8	150	1
9	120	1
10	215	1

TABLE F.2   Failures per Interval Data

Hours						
1	5	2.5	0	0	0	1
2	1	1	0	0	0	1
3	4	3	0	0	0	1
4	1	2	0	0	0	1
5	0	1.5	0	0	0	1
6	1	3	0	0	0	1
7	2	4	0	0	0	1
8	1	2.5	0	0	0	1
9	2	3	0	0	0	1
10	2	5	0	0	0	1

modifications are made to the test process as appropriate. Toward the end of test, the emphasis shifts to guiding release because there is no longer sufficient time for changes in the test process to have much effect. The procedure is the same in both cases.

1. Launch CASRE by double clicking on the CASRE application file casre.exe in Windows Explorer. This file will be in C:\ if you have installed CASRE on your hard disk or in D:\ or E:\ if you are executing directly from your CD-ROM drive. Alternatively, you can double click on the icon on your desktop (if you have installed it). A CASRE window will appear.

2. In the CASRE window, click on File, then Open. The Open dialog box will appear with a default folder specified. Navigate to the folder in

which the failure data file you want to use is located. If you don't currently have your own data, use one of the files in C:\casre\testdata. If you would like to simulate the testing history of a real software project and be able to check your results against the correct ones at several points, select file s1.dat and follow Problem F.1 in applying the procedure we are describing here. Double click on [..] if you need to move upward from the default folder before you can reach the target folder. When you have the correct folder, double click on the file you want to use from the list of file names for that folder. The list of failure data will appear in the CASRE window, and a plot window will appear on the right.

3. If you have interval or grouped data (the second column will have the heading Number of Failures), click on Edit, then Change data type. The Change Failure Data Type dialog box will appear with the default Random interfailure times set as the Conversion Method. Click on OK. The data will be converted and failure time data will be displayed in the CASRE window.

4. Normalize the data by multiplying by the failure intensity objective. Click on Filters and then on Scaling and offset. The Transform Failure Data dialog box will appear. Enter the failure intensity objective in the Scaling Factor A box and click OK.

5. Click on Model, then Select data range. The Specify Data Range dialog box will appear. Set the parameter estimation end point to 1 less than the last data point. This quantity determines the minimum number of failures required for estimating failure intensity; setting it at this value maximizes the amount of data used in making the failure intensity estimate. Click on OK.

6. Click on Model, then Select and Run Models. The Select and Execute Models dialog box will appear. Double click on Musa Basic and Musa-Okumoto models. Then click on Run Models and these two models will execute. Note that they are the exponential and logarithmic models, respectively. These models normally execute very rapidly. There have been a few rare occasions where CASRE aborts at this point and disappears from the screen. The situation has always been identical to that of step 7c; take the action described at that point.

7. We will now attempt to select the best model by evaluating goodness of fit. In the plot window click on Results, then Select model results. The Select and Display Model Results dialog box will appear.

   a. If both models appear in the Models executed box, double click on each. Now click on OK. Again in the plot window, click on Display, then Goodness of Fit. The title of the plot window will change to Goodness of Fit. Determine which model has the smallest KS Distance; it has the best fit. Go to step 8.

b. If one model appears in the models executed box, choose it. Go to step 8.

c. If neither model appears in the Models executed box, this means that neither model can detect any reliability growth (the growth may be negative) at this time. Click on Cancel. Click on Results and then click on Model results table. In the Model Partial Results window that appears (it will be the same regardless of which model), divide the Failure no. for the last failure data point (usually the next to last row) by the corresponding Elapsed time T from the test start. This will give you an estimate of the FI/FIO ratio.

8. Still in the plot window, click on Results, then Model Results table. Look at the name of the model in the title of the Model Results window that appears. If it corresponds to the model determined in step 7, proceed to step 9. If not, click on Results and then Next model. Now proceed to step 9.

9. In the Model Results window, take the Next step prediction value at the last failure data point (this is usually the next to last row of the Model Results table) and invert it. You now have the ratio of failure intensity to failure intensity objective (FI/FIO).

F.4   Interpreting CASRE Results

For each execution of CASRE,

1. If the FI/FIO ratio is very large and the trend indicates little chance of achieving the failure intensity objective at the scheduled release date, consider one or more of the following:

a. Adding additional test and debugging resources. (In theory, one could use software reliability models to predict when the failure intensity objective would be reached with existing or modified resources. Unfortunately, the large variation in predictions at the present state of the art makes this impractical at this time.)

b. Adjusting the balance of failure intensity, delivery date, and cost objectives.

c. Deferring features.

2. If FI/FIO > 2, and shows significant upward movement over several data points, determine the cause. Correct if meeting the project objectives is endangered. Possibilities include unexpected system evolution (need better change control) or nonstationary test selection probabilities (need better control of test selection).

3. Otherwise, continue test and consider releasing the system when FI/FIO reaches 0.5. In theory, the system could be released when

the ratio reaches 1. However, because estimation always involves some range of error, a safety margin has been incorporated.

F.5 Problems

F.1 Learn to use CASRE for a realistic set of failure time data. This data comes from an actual project; we are going to alter it for instructional purposes. The result is similar to data experienced for Fone Follower. Access CASRE and open the file C:\casre\testdata\s1.dat. This file will have been installed with the program. To alter the file for our problem, click on Filters and then on Scaling and offset. The Transfers Failure Data dialog box will appear. Enter 12 in the Scaling Factor A box and click OK. This will alter the data as we require.

This problem has multiple parts, each representing a point in time in the history of testing a software system. We will obtain these points in time by selecting subsets of the data in the file we are working with. The failure intensity objective is 95 failures per million calls.

1. Click on Model, then Select data range. The Specify Data Range dialog box will appear. Set the last data point to 10. Then the run you make here will represent a point very early in the project when 10 failures have been experienced. Now follow the standard execution procedure described in this appendix, starting with step 4. Note that neither model appears in the Models executed box. Following step 7c, you will obtain an FI/FIO ratio of 15.4. This is not excessively large for early test.

2. Repeat the process of selecting the data range, this time setting the Last data point to 11. Follow the standard execution procedure as before. Note that the Musa Basic model fits best. The FI/FIO ratio is 12.0.

3. Repeat for the first 29, 30, 31, 32, 33, and 34 failures. Note that the Musa-Okumoto model fits best for 29, 30, 31, and 32 failures, and the Musa basic model fits best for 33 and 34 failures. The FI/FIO ratios are, respectively, 1.92, 2.06, 2.20, 2.38, 2.61, and 3.08. This represents a significant upward movement over several data points. Hence you should investigate to see if any problem with your test process needs correction.

4. Repeat for the first 68 failures. Note that the best-fitting model has changed from the Musa Basic to the Musa-Okumoto model. The FI/FIO ratio is 1.91. There is no particular trend occurring. We simply need to test more to reach our failure intensity objective.

5. Repeat for the first 92 failures. The FI/FIO ratio is 0.93. It appears that we have achieved our objective. However, remember that any statistical estimate has a range of variation. Hence we will not recommend release until FI/FIO drops below 0.5, so we know we have achieved the FIO with substantial confidence.

6. Repeat for the first 93 failures. The best-fitting model has changed back to the Musa Basic again. The FI/FIO ratio is 0.44. We have reached our objective with substantial confidence although there is always some risk that we still haven't achieved it.

1.1 Supersystems that represent all combinations of operating systems and printer systems with the text processing product: 1A, 1B, 1C, 1D, 2A, 2B, 2C, 2D and the product itself. Users in this application will judge this product mostly in terms of how these supersystems work.

1.2 Probably those objects used 20 and 12 times. When you get down to a use of 4 times, the cost effectiveness of separate test becomes dubious.

1.3 No. With the possibility of only 2 weeks remaining before you start system test, little can be done to prevent schedule delay if the database is found to have poor reliability.

2.1 The total failure intensity objective for each product should be 100 failures per 1000 execution hours. The total failure intensity objective for the set of all objects in a product will be 50 percent of the total failure intensity objective of each product, or 50 failures per 1000 execution hours. Each object in the library must therefore have a failure intensity objective of 0.5 failures per 1000 execution hours.

2.2   a. Pages
    b. Calls
    c. Messages
    d. Pages
    e. Transactions
    f. Reservations
    g. Transactions
    h. Travel segments
    i. Inquiries

2.3 To reduce the average failure intensity of the product to 90 failures per hour, we must realize a failure intensity of 80 failures per 1000 hours for the new functionality, assuming that the new and old functions are used equally. The product of the three factors of failure intensity objective, development time, and cost for the old release was 200,000. Hence you can estimate the cost of the new release as 200,000/0.08, or $2.5 million.

2.4   The system failure intensity objective must be 1 failure per 10,000 copies. Note that the hardware failure intensity is 0.4 failure per 10,000 copies. We must set the failure intensity objective for the copier software at 0.6 failures per 10,000 copies or 60 failures per million copies.

3.1   Let C_1 be the current development cost. Then,

$$C_1 = C_0 + C_P P$$

The adjusted variable per-operation component is

$$\frac{p_k}{p_1}(C_P - C_{P0})$$

a.   The development of C_2 using the operational profile to focus effort will be

$$C_2 = C_0 + C_{P0}P + \frac{1}{p_1} \sum_{k=1}^{P} p_k(C_P - C_{P0})$$

$$= C_0 + C_{P0}P + \frac{C_P - C_{P0}}{p_1}$$

$$= C_0 + \frac{C_P}{p_1} + C_{P0}\left(P - \frac{1}{p_1}\right)$$

b.   The saving in development cost ΔC is given by

$$\Delta C = C_1 - C_2 = C_P\left(P - \frac{1}{p_1}\right) - C_{P0}\left(P - \frac{1}{p_1}\right)$$

$$= (C_P - C_{P0})\left(P - \frac{1}{p_1}\right)$$

The percentage saving is

$$\frac{\Delta C}{C_1} = \frac{(C_P - C_{P0})[P - (1/p_1)]}{C_0 + C_P P}$$

Note that the cost saving is greatest when the fixed per-operation cost is low with respect to the total per-operation cost, and the probability of occurrence of the most-used operation is high with respect to the average probability of occurrence. In other words, you can save substantial amounts of money if you have many lightly used operations by allocating less development effort to them.

Interestingly, the cost saving is *independent* of the exact nature of the operational profile, a nice simple result.

c.   When the project base cost C_0 is 10 percent of the initial cost C_1, and there are 45 operations, $C_P = 0.002\ C_1$. Because the per-operation base cost is half the per-operation cost, $C_{P0} = 0.01\ C_1$. Then

$$\frac{\Delta C}{C_1} = 0.01 \left(45 - \frac{1}{p_1} \right) = 0.40$$

The cost saving obtained from using the operational profile to reduce resources is 40 percent.

d. For $p_1 = 0.05$, the saving is 43 percent. If $p_1 = 0.1$, the saving is 35 percent. Note the relative insensitivity of the saving to the probability of occurrence of the most-used operation.

e. For 18 operations we have $C_P = 0.05\ C_1$ and $C_{P0} = 0.025\ C_1$. Then,

$$\frac{\Delta C}{C_1} = 0.025 \left(18 - \frac{1}{p_1} \right)$$

This yields, for $p_1 = 0.2$, a saving of 32.5 percent.

If there are 90 operations, we have $C_P = 0.01\ C_1$ and $C_{P0} = 0.005\ C_1$. Then,

$$\frac{\Delta C}{C_1} = 0.005 \left(90 - \frac{1}{p_1} \right)$$

For $p_1 = 0.02$, we have a saving of 42.5 percent. Again, there is a relative insensitivity to changes in the number of operations.

The main factor seems to be the size of the per-operation variable component of cost with respect to the per-operation base cost. If the former is about half, which seems reasonable and even conservative, savings in the range of 30 to 40 percent of the total project development cost over a wide range of situations can be achieved by applying the operational profile.

3.2 The last five operations are essential for Fone Follower to function properly. We could defer the paging capability to the next release, but then we could not satisfy 39 percent of the expected use of the system. It will probably be best to provide all capabilities except fax forwarding in the first release; you will then satisfy 85 percent of the expected use in the first release and defer 15 percent to the second.

3.3 Assuming that there are no complicating factors, divide the time based on the operational profile. The operations with pager processing represent 39 percent of the use; those without represent 35 percent. This means 2 h 38 min for the paging part of the review and 2 h 22 min for the rest. Of course, you probably wouldn't actually insist on being this precise.

3.4 The factors of environment (land and water) and user experience are likely to be important. Thus you will probably establish four operational modes:

1. Land—trainees
2. Land—veterans
3. Water—trainees
4. Water—veterans

4.1 The test case budget will be $500,000. This will permit us to develop 2000 test cases. The available effort is 10,000 staff hours (10 available people working for 1000 h each). This would allow 3333 test cases. We take the minimum of these two numbers, 2000 test cases.

4.2   224.

4.3   The adjustment factor would be 0.998. The acceleration factor would be 2000.

5.1   It will *not* work. You will not be invoking the test cases with stationary occurrence probabilities. Consequently, you can expect that failure intensity estimates will be considerably in error.

5.2   Recall that there are four operational modes. Table G.1 shows the proportions of use in the field for these operational modes as derived from the problem statement. The system load test time is divided in accordance with these proportions, as shown in the table.

5.3   The average computer utilization is 0.5. Note in Table G.2 that we multiply the intervals between the failure times in the second column by the computer utilizations in the third column to obtain execution time intervals, which are accumulated in the fourth column. We then divide by the average computer utilization 0.5 to obtain the adjusted times of the fifth column.

6.1   Normalize the natural units of the failures by multiplying by the failure intensity objective. You will obtain 0.2, 0.5, 0.7, 0.9, and 1.2. At the fifth failure, we have crossed into the Reject region on the reliability demonstration chart. The software should be returned for reliability improvement.

6.2   The normalized measure at the continue-accept boundary for four failures is 5. Applying the formula for the demonstrable FI/FIO ratio, we obtain 2.5. In other words, the provable failure intensity (for the assumed discrimination ratio and risk levels) is 2.5 times what we wanted to achieve.

TABLE G.1   Allocation of System Load Test Time

Operational mode	Proportion of field use	System load test time (h)
Land—trainees	0.18	36
Land—veterans	0.72	144
Water—trainees	0.02	4
Water—veterans	0.08	16

TABLE G.2   Adjusting Failure Times for Varying Computer Utilization

Failure	Time (h)	Computer utilization	Execution time (execution hours)	Adjusted time (h)
1	1	0.3	0.3	0.6
2	2	0.5	0.8	1.6
3	3	0.7	1.5	3

References to Users of Software Reliability Engineering

Alam, M., W. Chen, W. Ehrlich, M. Engel, D. Kropfl, and P. Verma. 1997. Assessing software reliability performance under highly critical but infrequent event occurrences. *Proceedings, 8th International Symposium on Software Reliability Engineering,* Albuquerque, NM, November 1997, pp. 294–307.

Bennett, J., M. Denoncourt, and J. D. Healy. 1992. Software reliability prediction for telecommunication systems. *Proceedings, 2nd Bellcore/Purdue Symposium on Issues in Software Reliability Estimation,* October 1992, pp. 85–102.

Bentz, R. W., and C. D. Smith. 1996. Experience report for the software reliability program on a military system acquisition and development. *Proceedings, 7th International Symposium on Software Reliability Engineering—Industrial Track,* White Plains, NY, October 30–November 2, 1996, pp. 59–65.

Bergen, L. A. 1989. A practical application of software reliability to a large scale switching system. *IEEE International Workshop: Measurement of Quality During the Life Cycle,* Val David, Quebec, Canada, April 25–27, 1989.

Carman, D. W., A. A. Dolinsky, M. R. Lyu, and J. S. Yu. 1995. Software reliability engineering study of a large-scale telecommunications software system. *Proceedings, 1995 International Symposium on Software Reliability Engineering,* Toulouse, France, October 1995, pp. 350–359.

Carnes, P. 1997. Software reliability in weapon systems. *Proceedings, 8th International Symposium on Software Reliability Engineering: Case Studies,* Albuquerque, NM, November 1997, pp. 95–100.

Christenson, D. A. 1988. Using software reliability models to predict field failure rates in electronic switching systems. *Proceedings, 4th Annual National Joint Conference on Software Quality and Productivity,* Washington, DC.

Chruscielski, K., and J. Tian. 1997. An operational profile for the cartridge support software. *Proceedings, 8th International Symposium on Software Reliability Engineering,* Albuquerque, NM, November 1997, pp. 203–212.

Cramp, R., M. A. Vouk, and W. Jones. 1992. On operational availability of a large software-based telecommunications system. *Proceedings, 3rd International Symposium on Software Reliability Engineering,* Research Triangle Park, NC, October 7–10, 1992, pp. 358–366.

Cusick, J., and M. Fine. 1997. Guiding reengineering with the operational profile. *Proceedings, 8th International Symposium on Software Reliability Engineering: Case Studies,* Albuquerque, NM, November 1997, pp. 15–25.

Derriennic, H., and G. Le Gall. 1995. Use of failure-intensity models in the software-validation phase for telecommunications. *IEEE Transactions on Reliability,* 44(4):658–665.

Dixit, P., M. A. Vouk, D. L. Bitzer, and C. Alix. 1996. Reliability and availability of a wide area network-based education system. *Proceedings, 7th International Symposium on Software Reliability Engineering,* White Plains, NY, October 30–November 2, 1996, pp. 213–218.

Dixit, P., M. A. Vouk, and D. L. Bitzer. 1997. Reliability behavior of a large network based education system. *Proceedings, 8th International Symposium on Software Reliability Engineering: Case Studies,* Albuquerque, NM, November 1997, pp. 43–56.

Donnelly, M., W. W. Everett, J. D. Musa, and G. Wilson. 1996. Best current practice of SRE. In M. R. Lyu (ed.), *Handbook of Software Reliability Engineering,* New York: McGraw-Hill, pp. 219–254.

Drake, H. D., and D. E. Wolting. 1987. Reliability theory applied to software testing. *Hewlett-Packard Journal,* 38(4):35–39.

Ehrlich, W. K., R. Chan, W. J. Donnelly, H. H. Park, M. B. Saltzman, and P Verma. 1996. Validating software architectures for high reliability. *Proceedings, 7th International Symposium on Software Reliability Engineering,* White Plains, NY, October 30–November 2, 1996, pp. 196–206.

Ehrlich, W. K., K. Lee, and R. H. Molisani. 1990. Applying reliability measurement: A case study. *IEEE Software,* 7(2):56–64.

Ehrlich, W. K., B. Prasanna, J. P. Stampfel, and J. R. Wu. 1993. Determining the cost of a stop-test decision. *IEEE Software,* 10(2):33–42.

Ehrlich, W. K., J. P. Stampfel, and J. R. Wu. 1990. Application of software reliability modeling to product quality and test process, *Proceedings, 12th International Conference on Software Engineering,* Nice, France, March 1990, pp. 108–116.

Elentukh, A. 1994. System reliability policy at Motorola Codex. *Proceedings, 5th International Symposium on Software Reliability Engineering,* Monterey, CA, November 6–9, 1994, pp. 289–293.

Everett, W. W., and J. M. Gobat. 1996. DQS's experience with SRE. *Proceedings, 7th International Symposium on Software Reliability Engineering,* White Plains, NY, October 30–November 2, 1996, pp. 219–224.

Hamilton, P. A., and J. D. Musa. 1978. Measuring reliability of computation center software. *Proceedings, 3rd International Conference on Software Engineering,* Atlanta, GA, pp. 29–36.

Hill, S. W., and F. S. Kmetz. 1997. Application of software reliability engineered testing (SRET) to project accounting application (PAA). *Proceedings, 8th International Symposium on Software Reliability Engineering: Case Studies,* Albuquerque, NM, November 1997, pp. 59–68.

Hudepohl, J. P. Measurement of software service quality for large telecommunications systems. *IEEE Journal on Selected Areas in Communications,* 8(2):210–218.

Hudepohl, J. P., W. Snipes, T. Hollack, and W. Jones. 1992. A methodology to improve switching system software service quality and reliability. *Proceedings, IEEE Global Communications Conference,* pp. 1671–1678.

Iannino, A., and J. D. Musa. 1991. Software reliability engineering at AT&T. In G. Apostolakis (ed.), *Probability Safety Assessment and Management,* Vol. 1, New York: Elsevier.

Jensen, B. D. 1995. A software reliability engineering success story: AT&T's Definity® PBX. *Proceedings, 1995 International Symposium on Software Reliability Engineering,* Toulouse, France, October 1995, pp. 338–343.

Jones, W. D. 1991. Reliability models for very large software systems in industry. *Proceedings, 2nd International Symposium on Software Reliability Engineering,* Austin, TX, May 17–18, 1991, pp. 35–42.

Juhlin, B. D. 1992. Applying software reliability engineering to International PBX testing. *Proceedings, 9th International Conference on Testing Computer Software,* Washington, DC, June 16–18, 1992, pp. 165–176.

————. 1992. Implementing operational profiles to measure system reliability. *Proceedings, 3rd International Symposium on Software Reliability Engineering*, Research Triangle Park, NC, October 7–10, 1992, pp. 286–295.

————. 1993. Software reliability engineering in the system test process. *Proceedings 10th International Conference on Testing Computer Software*, Washington, DC, June 14–17, 1993, pp. 97–115.

Kaâniche, M., and K. Kanoun. 1996. Reliability of a commercial telecommunications system. *Proceedings, 7th International Symposium on Software Reliability Engineering*, White Plains, NY, October 30–November 2, 1996, pp. 207–212.

Kanoun, K., M. Bastos Martini, and J. Moreira de Souza,. 1991. A method for software reliability analysis and prediction-application to the TROPICO-R switching system. *IEEE Transactions on Software Engineering*, 17(4):334–344.

Kanoun, K., and T. Sabourin. 1987. Software dependability of a telephone switching system. *Proceedings 17th IEEE International Symposium on Fault-Tolerant Computing*, Pittsburgh, June 1987, pp. 236–241.

Keller, T., and N. Schneidewind. 1997. Successful application of software reliability engineering for the NASA space shuttle. *Proceedings, 8th International Symposium on Software Reliability Engineering: Case Studies*, Albuquerque, NM, November 1997, pp. 71–82.

Kropfl, D., and W. Ehrlich. 1995. Telecommunications network operating systems: Experiences in software reliability engineering. *Proceedings, 1995 International Symposium on Software Reliability Engineering*, Toulouse, France, October 1995, pp. 344–349.

Kruger, G. A. 1988. Project management using software reliability growth models. *Hewlett-Packard Journal*, 39(6):30–35.

Kruger, G. A. 1989. Validation and further application of software reliability growth models. *Hewlett-Packard Journal*, 40(4):75–79.

Lee, I., and R. K. Iyer. 1995. Software dependability in the Tandem GUARDIAN system. *IEEE Transactions on Software Engineering*, 21(5):455–467.

Levendel, Y. 1989. Defects and reliability analysis of large software systems: Field experience. *Proceedings, 19th IEEE International Symposium on Fault-Tolerant Computing*, Chicago, June 1989, pp. 238–244.

————. 1990. Reliability analysis of large software systems: Defect data modeling. *IEEE Transactions on Software Engineering*, SE-16(2):141–152.

————. 1995. The cost effectiveness of telecommunication service dependability. In M. R. Lyu (ed.), *Software Fault Tolerance*, Chichester, U.K.: Wiley, pp. 279–314.

Martini, M. R., K. Kanoun, and J. M. de Souza. 1990. Software reliability evaluation of the TROPICO-R switching system. *IEEE Transactions on Reliability*, 39(3):369–379.

Musa, J. D., G. Fuoco, N. Irving, B. Juhlin, and D. Kropfl. 1996. The operational profile. In M. R. Lyu (ed.), *Handbook of Software Reliability Engineering*, New York: McGraw-Hill, pp. 167–216 (includes three project applications).

Nikora, A. P., and M. R. Lyu. 1996. Software reliability measurement experiences. In M. R. Lyu (ed.), *Handbook of Software Reliability Engineering*, New York: McGraw-Hill, pp. 255–301.

Oshana, R., and F. P. Coyle. 1997. Improving a system regression test with usage models developed using field collected data. *Proceedings, Software Quality Week 1997*.

Pemler, S., and N. Stahl. 1994. An automated environment for software testing and reliability estimation. *Proceedings, 5th International Symposium on Software Reliability Engineering*, Monterey, CA, November 6–9, 1994, pp. 312–317.

Rapp, B. 1990. Application of software reliability models in medical imaging systems. *Proceedings, 1990 International Symposium on Software Reliability Engineering*, Washington, DC, April 1990.

Sandfoss, R. V., and S. A. Meyer. 1997. Input requirements needed to produce an operational profile for a new telecommunications system. *Proceedings, 8th International Symposium on Software Reliability Engineering: Case Studies*, Albuquerque, NM, November 1997, pp. 29–39.

Schneidewind, N. F., and T. W. Keller. 1992. Application of reliability models to the space shuttle. *IEEE Software*, 9(4):28–33.

Teresinski, J. A. 1996. Software reliability: Getting started. *Proceedings, 7th International Symposium on Software Reliability Engineering—Industrial Track,* White Plains, NY, October 30–November 2, 1996, pp. 39–47.

Tian, J., P. Lu, and J. Palma. 1995. Test-execution based reliability measurement and modeling for large commercial software. *IEEE Transactions on Software Engineering,* 21(5):405–414.

Tierney, J. 1996. Putting aspects of software reliability engineering to use. *Proceedings, 7th International Symposium on Software Reliability Engineering—Industrial Track,* White Plains, NY, October 30–November 2, 1996, pp. 89–92.

Weinberg, T. 1996. SoothSayer: A tool for measuring the reliability of Windows NT services. *Proceedings, 7th International Symposium on Software Reliability Engineering—Industrial Track,* White Plains, NY, October 30–November 2, 1996, pp. 49–56.

Bibliography

Abramson, S. R., B. D. Jensen, B. D. Juhlin, and C. L. Spudic. 1992. "Customer satisfaction-based product development," *Proceedings International Switching Symposium*, vol. 2, Yokohama, Japan, Institute of Electronics, Information, and Communication Engineers, pp. 65–69.

AIAA. 1992. *Recommended practice for software reliability*. Washington, DC: AIAA.

Akiyama, F. 1971. "An example of software system debugging," *Information Processing 71*, North-Holland, New York, pp. 353–359.

Albin, J. L., and R. Ferreol. 1982. Collecte et analyse de mesures de logiciel (in French). *Technique et Science Informatique*, 1(4):297–313.

Anderson, T., and P. A. Lee. 1981. *Fault tolerance: Principles and practice*. Englewood Cliffs, NJ: Prentice Hall.

Angus, J. E., J. B. Bowen, and S. J. VanDenBerg. 1983. *Reliability model demonstration study*. Technical Report RADC-TR-83-207. Rome, NY: Rome Air Development Center.

Bardsley, I. 1984. Unpublished communication.

Basili, V. R., and D. H. Hutchens. 1983. An empirical study of a syntactic complexity family. *IEEE Transactions on Software Engineering*, SE-9(6):664–672.

Basili, V. R., and B. T. Perricone. 1984. Software errors and complexity: An empirical investigation. *Communications ACM*, 27(1):42–52.

Basin, S. L. 1973. *Estimation of software error rates via capture-recapture sampling: A critical review*. Palo Alto, CA: Science Applications Report.

Belady, L. A., and M. M. Lehman. 1976. A model of large program development. *IBM Systems Journal*, 15(3):224–252.

Bendick, M. 1976. *Error rate as a management tool*. Computer Sciences Corporation, Report of June 8, 1976.

Boehm, B. W. 1981. *Software engineering economics*. Englewood Cliffs, NJ: Prentice Hall.

Bush, M. 1990. "Getting started on metrics–Jet Propulsion Laboratory productivity and quality." *Proceedings, 12th International Conference on Software Engineering*, Nice, pp. 133–142.

Card, D. N., V. E. Church, and W. W. Agresti. 1986. "An empirical study of software design practices." *IEEE Transactions on Software Engineering*, SE-12(2):264–271.

Card, D. N., F. E. McGarry, and G. T. Page. 1987. "Evaluating software engineering technologies." *IEEE Transactions on Software Engineering*, SE-13(7):845–851.

Cheung, R. C. 1980. A user-oriented software reliability model. *IEEE Transactions on Software Engineering*, SE-6(2):118–125.

Crespo, A. N., P. Matrella, and A. Pasquini. 1996. Sensitivity of reliability growth models to operational profile errors. *Proceedings, 7th International Symposium on Software Reliability Engineering*, White Plains, NY, pp. 35–44.

Crow, L. H. 1974. "Reliability analysis for complex, repairable systems." In F. Proshan and R. J. Serfling (eds.), *Reliability and Biometry*, pp. 379–410. Philadelphia: SIAM.

Crow, L. H., and N. D. Singpurwalla. 1984. "An empirically developed Fourier series model for describing software failures." *IEEE Transactions on Reliability*, R-33(2):176–183.

Dale, C. J. 1982. *Software reliability evaluation methods*. Report ST26750. British Aerospace.

Del Frate, F., P. Garg, A. P. Mathur, and A. Pasquini. 1995. "On the correlation between code coverage and software reliability." *Proceedings, 6th International Symposium on Software Reliability Engineering*, Toulouse, France, pp. 124–132.

DeMarco, T., and T. Lister. 1985. "Programmer performance and the effects of the work-place." *Proceedings, 8th International Conference on Software Engineering,* London, England, pp. 268–272.

———. 1989. "Software development: State of the art vs state of the practice." *Proceedings, 11th International Conference on Software Engineering,* Pittsburgh, pp. 171–275.

Derriennic, H., and G. Le Gall. 1995. "Use of failure-intensity models in the software-validation phase for telecommunications." *IEEE Transactions on Reliability,* 44(4):658–665.

Donnelly, M., W. Everett, J. Musa, and G. Wilson. 1996. In M. Lyu (ed.), *Handbook of Software Reliability Engineering,* pp. 219–254. New York: McGraw-Hill.

Downs, T. 1985. "An approach to the modeling of software testing with some applications." *IEEE Transactions on Software Engineering,* SE-11(4):375–386.

Endres, A. 1975. "An analysis of errors and their causes in system programs." *Proceedings, 1975 International Conference on Reliable Software,* Los Angeles, pp. 328–329. Also *IEEE Transactions on Software Engineering,* SE-1(2):140–149.

Farr, W. 1996. "Software reliability modeling survey." In M. Lyu (ed.), *Handbook of Software Reliability Engineering,* pp. 71–117. New York: McGraw-Hill.

Farr, W., and O. Smith. 1992. "A tool for software reliability modeling." *Proceedings, 1992 International Simulation Technology Conference and Workshop on Neural Nets,* Clear Lake, Texas, November 4–6, 1992, pp. 256–261.

Feuer, A. R., and E. B. Fowlkes. 1979. "Some results from an empirical study of computer software." *Proceedings, 4th International Conference on Software Engineering,* Munich, Germany, pp. 351–355.

Fries, M. J. 1977. *Software error data acquisition.* Technical Report RADC-TR-77-130, Rome, NY: Rome Air Development Center.

Gilb, T. 1977. *Software metrics,* Cambridge: Winthrop, p. 28.

Goel, A. L., and K. Okumoto. 1978. "An analysis of recurrent software errors in real-time control system." *Proceedings, ACM Conference,* pp. 496–501.

———. 1979. "Time-dependent error-detection rate model for software reliability and other performance measures." *IEEE Transactions on Reliability,* R-28(3):206–211.

Gremillion, L. L. 1984. "Determinants of program repair maintenance requirements." *Communications ACM,* 27(8):826–832.

Halstead, M. H. 1977. *Elements of Software Science.* New York: Elsevier.

Hecht, H. 1977. "Measurement, estimation, and prediction of software reliability." In *Software Engineering Technology—Vol. 2,* Infotech International, Maidenhead, Berkshire, England, pp. 209–224.

———. "Allocation of resources for software reliability." *Proceedings, COMPCON Fall 1981,* Washington, DC, pp. 74–82.

Iannino, A., J. D. Musa, K. Okumoto, and B. Littlewood. 1984. "Criteria for software reliability model comparisons." *IEEE Transactions on Software Engineering,* SE-10(6):687–691.

Inglis, J., F. Gray, Jr., D. M. Kane, and M. K. Kaufman. 1986. Unpublished work.

Jelinski, Z., and P. B. Moranda. 1972. "Software reliability research." In W. Freiberger (ed.), *Statistical Computer Performance Evaluation,* pp. 465–484. New York: Academic Press.

Joe, H., and N. Reid. 1985. "Estimating the number of faults in a system." *Journal of the American Statistical Association,* 80(389):222–226.

Jones, C. 1986. *Programming productivity.* New York: McGraw-Hill.

Jones, W. D. 1991. "Reliability models for very large software systems in industry." *Proceedings, 2nd International Symposium on Software Reliability Engineering,* Austin, TX, May 17–18, pp. 35–42.

Juhlin, B. 1992. "Implementing operational profiles to measure system reliability." *Proceedings, 3rd International Symposium on Software Reliability Engineering,* Research Triangle Park, NC, October 7–10, pp. 286–295.

Keiller, P. A., B. Littlewood, D. R. Miller, and A. Sofer. 1983. "On the quality of software reliability prediction." In J. K. Skwirzynski (ed.), *Electronic Systems Effectiveness and Life Cycle Costing,* NATO ASI Series, F3, pp. 441–460. Heidelberg: Springer-Verlag.

Laner, D. 1985. *Commentary on war,* Public Television series.

LaPrie, J. C. 1984. "Dependability evaluation of software systems in operation." *IEEE Transactions on Software Engineering*, SE-10(6):701–714.

Lipson, ₄C., and N. J. Sheth. 1973. *Statistical Design and Analysis of Engineering Experiments*. New York: McGraw-Hill.

Littlewood, B. 1981. "Stochastic reliability-growth: A model for fault removal in computer programs and hardware design." *IEEE Transactions on Reliability*, R-30(4):313–320.

Littlewood, B., and J. L. Verrall. 1973. "A bayesian reliability growth model for computer software." *Journal Royal Statistical Society - Series C*, 22(3):332–346.

Litzau, J. T. 1986. Private communication to J. D. Musa.

Lloyd, D. K., and M. Lipow. 1977. *Reliability: Management, Methods, and Mathematics*, 2d ed. Redondo Beach, CA: published by the authors.

Lyu, M. (ed.) 1996. *Handbook of Software Reliability Engineering*. New York: McGraw-Hill.

Malaiya, Y. K., N. Karunanithi, and P. Verma. 1992. "Predictability of software-reliability models." *IEEE Transactions on Reliability*, R-41(4):539–546.

McCabe, T. J. 1976. "A complexity measure." *IEEE Transactions on Software Engineering*, SE-2(4):308–320.

McCall, J., W. Randall, C. Bowen, N. McKelvey, R. Senn, J. Morris, H. Hecht, S. Fenwick, P. Yates, M. Hecht, and R. Vienneau. 1987. *Methodology for software reliability prediction*. Technical Report RADC-TR-87-171, pp. 4-12 to 4-13. Rome, NY: Rome Air Development Center.

Mendis, K. S. 1981. "Quantifying software quality." *Proceedings, American Institute of Aeronautics and Astronautics*, pp. 300–308.

Miller, A. M. B. 1980. "Study of the Musa reliability model." M.S. thesis, University of Maryland.

Miller, D. R. 1989. "The role of statistical modeling and inference in software quality." In B. de Neumann (ed.), *Software Certification*, pp. 135–152. London: Elsevier.

Mills, H. D. 1972. *On the statistical validation of computer programs*. Report FSC-72-6015. Gaithersburg, MD: IBM Federal Systems Division.

Misra, P. N. 1983. "Software reliability analysis." *IBM Systems Journal*, 22(3):262–270.

Mittermeir, R. T. 1982. "Optimal test effort for software systems." In E. Lauger and J. Moltoft (eds.) *Reliability in Electrical and Electronic Components and Systems*, pp. 650–654. Amsterdam: North-Holland.

Miyamoto, I. 1975. "Software reliability in online real time environment." *Proceedings, 1975 International Conference on Reliable Software*, Los Angeles, pp. 194–203.

Moranda, P. B. 1975. Predictions of software reliability during debugging. *Proceedings, Annual Reliability and Maintainability Symposium*, Washington, DC, pp. 327–332.

Motley, R. W., and W. D. Brooks. 1977. *Statistical prediction of programming errors*. Technical Report RADC-TR-77-175. Rome, NY: Rome Air Development Center.

Musa, J. D. 1975. "A theory of software reliability and its application." *IEEE Transactions on Software Engineering* SE-1(3):312–327.

———. 1979a. Private communication to B. Littlewood.

———. 1979b. *Software reliability data*. Data and Analysis Center for Software Report, Rome, NY: Rome Air Development Center.

———. 1979d. "Validity of execution time theory of software reliability." *IEEE Transactions on Reliability*, R-28(3):181–191.

———. 1988. "Applying software-reliability models in industry: Acceptance is just now happening." *IEEE Software* 3(4):87-88.

———. 1989a. "Faults, failures, and a metrics revolution." *IEEE Software*, 6(2):85–91.

———. 1989b. "Tools for measuring software reliability." *IEEE Spectrum*, 26(2):39–42. Also in Japanese: *IEEE Spectrum Japan*, 2(7):50–56.

———. 1991a. "Rationale for fault exposure ratio K." *Software Engineering Notes*, 16(3):79.

———. 1991b. "Reduced operation software." *Software Engineering Notes*, 16(3):78.

———. 1991c. "The software reliability gap: An opportunity." *Software Engineering Notes*, 16(3):26–27.

———. 1992. "The operational profile in software reliability engineering: An overview." *Proceedings, 3rd International Symposium on Software Reliability Engineering*, Research Triangle Park, NC, pp. 140–154.

———. 1993. "Operational profiles in software-reliability engineering." *IEEE Software,* 10(2):14–32.

———. 1994a. "Adjusting measured field failure intensity for operational profile variation." *Proceedings, 5th International Symposium on Software Reliability Engineering,* Monterey, CA, November 6–9, pp. 330–333.

———. 1994b. "Sensitivity of field failure intensity to operational profile errors." *Proceedings, 5th International Symposium on Software Reliability Engineering,* Monterey, CA, November 6–9, pp. 334–337.

———. 1994c. *Software reliability engineering video.* University Video Communications, 415-813-0506.

———. 1994d. "Ultrareliability." In J. Marciniak (ed.), *Encyclopedia of Software Engineering,* pp. 1379–1380. New York: Wiley.

———. 1995a. "The operational profile." In S. Özekici (ed.), *Reliability and Maintenance of Complex Systems,* pp. 333–344. Berlin: Springer.

———. 1995b. "An overview of software reliability engineering." In S. Özekici (ed.), *Reliability and Maintenance of Complex Systems,* pp. 319–332. Berlin: Springer.

———. 1996a. "Software-reliability-engineered testing." *Computer,* 29(11):61–68.

———. 1996b. "Software-reliability-engineered testing." *Proceedings, 13th International Conference on Testing Computer Software,* Washington, D.C., pp. 131–137.

———. 1996c. "Software reliability engineering for managers." *Proceedings, 1996 EFPDMA Software Managers Conference,* Washington, D.C., pp. 26–30.

———. 1997a. "Applying operational profiles in software-reliability-engineered testing." *Proceedings, Software Quality Week 1997,* San Francisco, CA.

———. 1997b. "Applying operational profiles in testing." *Proceedings, Software Quality Week 1997,* San Francisco, CA.

———. 1997c. "Introduction to software reliability engineering and testing." *Proceedings, 8th International Symposium on Software Reliability Engineering: Case Studies,* Albuquerque, NM, November, pp. 3–12.

———. 1997d. "Le test du logiciel guidé par la fiabilité (in French)." *Genie Logiciel,* March: 36–45.

———. 1997e. "Operational profiles in software-reliability-engineered testing." *Proceedings, Software Testing Analysis and Review Conference, 1997,* San Jose, CA.

———. 1997f. "Reliability prediction: What do we need?" Talk at *Metrics 97,* November 1997, Albuquerque, NM.

———. 1997g. "Software-reliability-engineered testing practice." *Proceedings, 19th International Conference on Software Engineering,* Boston, MA, pp. 628–629.

———. 1997h (updated regularly). *Software reliability engineering.* Web site with URL http://members.aol.com/JohnDMusa/.

Musa, J. D., and A. F. Ackerman. 1989. "Quantifying software validation: When to stop testing"? *IEEE Software,* 6(3):19–27.

———. 1991. "Measuring and managing aerospace software reliability." In C. Anderson and M. Dorfman (eds.), *Aerospace Software Engineering,* pp. 289–317, Washington, D.C.: American Institute of Aeronautics and Astronautics.

Musa, J. D., A. F. Ackerman, and W. W. Everett. 1994. "Software reliability engineering." In John Marciniak (ed.), *Encyclopedia of Software Engineering,* pp. 1223–1236. New York: Wiley.

Musa, J. D., F. Buckley, T. Keller, M. Lyu, and R. Tausworthe. 1995. "Software reliability: To use or not to use?" *Cross-Talk—The Journal of Defense Software Engineering,* 8(2):20–26.

Musa, J. D., and M. Donnelly. 1994. "Logarithmic NHPP model." In J. Marciniak (ed.), *Encyclopedia of Software Engineering,* pp. 614–615. New York: Wiley.

Musa, J. D., and W. K. Ehrlich. 1996. "Advances in software reliability engineering." In M. Zelkowitz (ed.), *Advances in Computers* 42, pp. 78–119. San Diego: Academic Press.

Musa, J. D., and W. W. Everett. 1991. "Software reliability engineering—a technology for the 90's." *IEEE Software,* 7(6):36–43.

———. 1993a. "A software reliability engineering practice." *Computer,* 26(3):77–79.

———. 1993b. "Software reliability and productivity." In J. Keyes (ed.), *Software Engineering Productivity Handbook,* pp. 131–148. New York: McGraw-Hill.

Musa, J. D., E. Fioco, N. Irving, D. Kropfl, and B. Juhlin. 1996. "The operational profile." In M. Lyu (ed.), *Handbook of Software Reliability Engineering*, pp. 167–216. New York: McGraw-Hill.

Musa, J. D., and A. Iannino. 1990. "Software reliability." In Marshall Yovits (ed.), *Advances in Computers* 30, pp. 85–170. San Diego: Academic Press.

———. 1991a. "Estimating the total number of software failures using an exponential model." *Software Engineering Notes* 16(3):80–84.

———. 1991b. "Software reliability engineering at AT&T." *Proceedings, Probabilistic Safety and Risk Management Conference 1991*, pp. 485–491. New York: Elsevier.

Musa, J. D., A. Iannino, and K. Okumoto. 1987. *Software Reliability: Measurement, Prediction, Application*. New York: McGraw Hill.

Musa, J. D., S. Keene, and T. Keller. 1996. *Developing reliable software in the shortest cycle time*. Video. IEEE.

Musa, J. D., and K. Okumoto. 1983. "Software reliability models: concepts, classification, comparisons, and practice." In J. K. Skwirzynski (ed.), *Electronic systems effectiveness and life cycle costing*, NATO ASI Series F3, pp. 395–424. F3. Heidelberg: Springer-Verlag.

———. 1984a. "A comparison of time domains for software reliability models." *Journal of Systems and Software*, 4(4):277–287.

———. 1984b. "A logarithmic Poisson execution time model for software reliability measurement." *Proceedings, 7th International Conference on Software Engineering*, Orlando, pp. 230–238.

———. 1986. "Application of basic and logarithmic Poisson execution time models in software reliability measurement." In J. K. Skwirzynski (ed.), *Software System Design Methods: The Challenge of Advanced Computing Technology*, Berlin: Springer-Verlag, pp. 275–298.

Musa, J. D., and J. Widmaier. 1996. "Software-reliability-engineered testing." *Cross-Talk—The Journal of Defense Software Engineering*, 7(6):27–30.

Nikora, A. P. 1994. *Computer aided software reliability estimation user's guide*, available from the author at mail stop 125–233, Jet Propulsion Laboratory, 4800 Oak Grove Drive, Pasadena, CA 91109-8099.

Ostrand, T. J., and E. J. Weyuker. 1982. *Collecting and categorizing software error data in an industrial environment*. Technical Report 47. New York: New York University.

Ramamoorthy, C. V., and F. B. Bastani. 1982. "Software reliability—status and perspectives." *IEEE Transactions on Software Engineering*, SE-8(4):354–370.

Rubey, R. J., J. A. Dana, and P. W. Biché. 1975. "Quantitative aspects of software validation." *IEEE Transactions on Software Engineering*, SE-1(2):150–155.

Rudner, B. 1977. *Seeding/tagging estimation of software errors: Models and estimates*. Technical Report RADC-TR-77-15. Rome, NY: Rome Air Development Center.

Saunier, P. 1983. "Fiabilité du logiciel: Quelques remarques tirées d'une expérimentation de trois modèles à taux de panne" (in French). *L'Industrie face a la qualité du logiciel*, Belvedere, Toulouse, France, October 20–21, pp. 257–290.

Schafer, R. E., J. F. Alter, J. E. Angus, and S. E. Emoto. 1979. *Validation of software reliability models*. Technical Report RADC-TR-79-147, Rome, NY: Rome Air Development Center.

Schick, G. J., and R. W. Wolverton. 1973. "Assessment of software reliability." *Proceedings, Operations Research*, Physica-Verlag, Wurzburg-Wien, pp. 395–422.

———. 1978. "An analysis of competing software reliability models." *IEEE Transactions on Software Engineering* SE-4(2): 104–120.

Schneidewind, N. F. 1975. "Analysis of error processes in computer software." *Proceedings, 1975 International Conference on Reliable Software*, Los Angeles, pp. 337–346.

Shen, V. Y., T. J. Yu, S. M. Thebaut, and L. R. Paulsen. 1985. "Identifying error-prone software—an empirical study." *IEEE Transactions on Software Engineering*, SE-11(4):317–324.

Shooman, M. L. 1972. "Probabilistic models for software reliability prediction." In W. Freiberger (ed.), *Statistical Computer Performance Evaluation*, pp. 485–502. New York: Academic Press.

———. 1983. *Software Engineering*. New York: McGraw-Hill.

————. 1986. *Probabilistic Reliability: An Engineering Approach.* 1968. New York: McGraw-Hill. Updated and reprinted, Kreger, Malabar, FL, 1986.

Stover, R. E., Jr. 1977. *A statistics collection package for the JOVIAL J3 programming language.* Technical Report RADC-TR-77-293. Rome, NY: Rome Air Development Center.

Sukert, A. N. 1976. *A software reliability modeling study.* Technical Report RADC-TR-76-247. Rome, NY: Rome Air Development Center.

————. 1979. "Empirical validation of three software error prediction models." *IEEE Transactions on Reliability,* R-28(3):199–205.

Sunohara, T., A. Takano, K. Uehara, and T. Ohkawa. 1981. "Program complexity measure for software development management." *Proceedings, 5th International Conference on Software Engineering,* San Diego, pp. 100–106.

Takahashi, N., and Y. Kamayachi. 1985. "An empirical study of a model for program error prediction." *Proceedings, 8th International Conference on Software Engineering,* London, pp. 330–336.

Tierney, J. 1997. *SRE at Microsoft.* Keynote speech at 8th International Symposium on Software Reliability Engineering, November 1997, Albuquerque, NM.

Thayer, T. A. 1976. *Software reliability study.* Technical Report RADC-TR-76-238. Rome, NY: Rome Air Development Center.

Trachtenberg, M. 1985. "The linear software reliability model and uniform testing." *IEEE Transactions Reliability,* R-34(1):8–16.

Wagoner, W. L. 1973. *The final report on a software reliability measurement study.* Report TOR-0074(4112)-1. Aerospace Corporation.

Walston, C. E., and C. P. Felix. 1977. "A method of programming measurement and estimation." *IBM Systems Journal,* 16(1):54–73.

Weiss, D. M. 1981. *Evaluating software development by analysis of change data.* Computer Science Technical Report TR-1120. University of Maryland.

Yamada, S., M. Ohba, and S. Osaki. 1983. "S-shaped reliability growth modeling for software error detection." *IEEE Transactions on Reliability,* R-32(5):475–478.

Index

Acceleration factor, 147, 229
Acquired components, 9–10, 165
Acquired failure intensity, 52
Acquired software, 9–10, 165
Advantages of software reliability
    engineering, 2–5, 11–14, 241–242
Advocate for software reliability
    engineering, 255
Agents, 13
Allocating number of new test cases
    among systems to be tested, 142
Allocating number of new test cases for
    each system among new operations,
    142–145, 153
Applets, 13, 18
Application range, 3, 26
Approximation to execution time, 46, 172,
    187
Artificial intelligence, 236
Assertions, 168
Assigning failure among components, 182
Assumptions, model, 281–282, 292
Attribute value:
    general, 145–146
    specific, 145–146
Audits, 239
Automated test, 149–150, 233
Automatic failure detection software, 180
Availability, 72, 73, 91–92
    definition, 27
    high, reliability strategies required for,
      76
    relationship with failure intensity,
      50–51, 66, 67
    relationship with reliability, 50–51, 66,
      67
Awareness of software reliability
    enigneering, 257

Balance of failure intensities of
    components, 75, 88
Balance of failure intensities of systems,
    75, 88

Baldrige award, 12
Base configuration, 23
Basic execution time model, 202, 338, 339
    derivation, 316–317
    description, 292–310
    parameters, 300–306
    recommendation of, 290–292
Benefits of software reliability
    engineering, 2–5, 11–14, 241–242
Best Current Practice, 3–4
Beta test, 24
Blocked path, 74, 235, 262
Blocking, 79, 235, 262
Boundary values, 150, 151
Bugs (see Faults)
Bulletin board on software reliability
    engineering, 246

Calendar time model, 28
Capability Maturity Model, 13
CASRE, 201–205, 234, 346, 359–366
    execution, 362–365
    failure data file, 361–362
    input file, 361–362
    installation, 360–361
    interpreting results, 365–366
Certification test, 8–9, 198–201, 213–217
    failure data required, 171
    insufficient time, 235
    minimum time required, 192
    reject, 236
    resubmission of rejected system, 233
    time required, 180
Change in deploying software reliability
    engineering, 242
Changes, design, 237
Choosing a common measure for
    associated systems, 46
Classification criteria, 42
Cleanroom, 20
Client server networks, effect on software
    reliability engineering, 18
Client server systems, operations on, 97

Clock time, 187
Code:
    added, 236
    developed, 34
    removed, 236
    reused, 34, 236
Code reading, 74
Collaboratively-developed software,
    23
Combinatoric techniques, 92–94
Common mode failures, 93
Competitive environment, definition of
    failure in, 62
Competitiveness, improved by software
    reliability engineering, 242
Compiler, 153, 184
Complexity, 326
Component testing, 180
Component reliability, 92–94
Computer utilization, 46, 187, 224, 225
    varying, 171
Configuration profile, 23
Consultant, 244, 245, 247–249, 251
Consultee, 247–248
Consumer risk, certification test, 199,
    213–217
Continue region, 198–199
Contractual specification of failure
    intensity objective, 65
Cost of software reliability engineering, 5,
    10, 25, 107
COTS, 14
Course in software reliability
    engineering, 245
Coverage:
    branch, 151, 152
    code, 152, 256
    input state, 154
    instruction, 152, 256
    path, 256
    test, 152
Critical operations:
    adjustment of operational mode
        operational profile for, 146–148
    preassignment of, 143
    regression tests of, 165
Criticality of operations, 64, 75
Critique of software reliability
    engineering, handling, 250
Customer expectations and defining
    failure, 62

Customer satisfaction and defining
    failure, 63
Customer type and operation initiators,
    103
Customer's customer, using information
    on to set failure intensity objective,
    68
Customers, failure intensity objectives set
    by, 22

Data, use, for operational profile, 256
Database cleanup, 80–81, 124, 167
Database cleanup and test invocation,
    192
Database corruption, 80–81, 129, 196
Database degradation, handled by
    database cleanup, 80–81, 124
Data correction, 80–81, 124, 167
Data corruption, 80–81, 129, 196
Data degradation, 80–81, 129, 196
Defects (see Faults)
Defining failure with severity classes,
    45–46, 77–87
Delta configurations, 23
Demonstrable FI/FIO ratio, 200–201
Deployment plan, 243–244
Deployment strategies, 244–246
Design changes, 237
Design process improvement, 12–13
Design reliability, 35
Deterministic selection of input variables,
    193
Developed software failure intensity
    objective, 51–53, 68
Development process characteristics,
    effect on fault introduction, 36
Development process improvement from
    software reliability engineering, 13
Deviations:
    analysis of, 75
    automated detection, 168
    cascaded, 169, 183
    definition, 78
    detection of, 168–169
    relating to failures, 169–170
Diagnostic tools finding new failures, 238
Direct input variables, 154
Discrepancy, 78
Discrimination ratio, certification test,
    199, 213–217

Displays, failure definition for, 186
Distributed systems:
  measuring amount of processing, 46,
    172–173, 184–185
  operations in, 97
Domain engineering, use of operational
  profiles in, 121
Down time:
  effect on severity class, 42
  effective, 66
  relationship to availability, 50

Engineering strategies, 53–56
Environment, effect on fault detection,
  71
Environment changes, as cause of software failures, 69
Environment simulator, effect of use in
  test, 238
Environmental condition, as operation
  initiator, 123
Environmental coverage, 151
Environmental factors, influence on software reliability, 18
Environmental variables, 136
Equation:
  availability, 50–51
  combinatoric, 355–356
  failure density, 35
  failure intensity, 49–51, 355, 356
  failure probability, 34
  hazard rate, 35
  mean time to failure, 35
  reliability, 34, 35, 49–50, 355, 356
  system reliability, 355–356
Equivalence classes, 157–159
Equivalence partitions, 157–159
Errors, 42, 85–86
Estimating number of new test cases for
  release, 140–142
Estimation, 37, 334–338
  maximum likelihood, 305
Evolving programs, 205–208, 234
Example (see Fone Follower)
Execution, partial, 236
Execution time, 16, 68, 171
  approximation to, 46, 172, 187
  compared with calendar time, 276–279
  distributed systems, 184–185
  interpretation, 172

Execution time (Cont.):
  personal computer, measurement on,
    186
  practical measurement, 188–191
  precision, 190
  regression test measurements of, 186
  relationship to natural units, 67
  relationship with runs, 187
  relationship to time, 76, 171
Experimental design, 159
Expert systems, 236
Exponential model (see Basic execution
  time model)
Extremes, 150, 151

Fail safe systems, 75
Fail set, 82
Failure backlog, 69
Failure density, 225
Failure frequency, 67
Failure identification:
  automatic, 155
  effect on failure intensity, 228
Failure impact, 160
Failure inducing stress, 43
Failure intensity:
  critical operation, 229
  decay as indicator of test efficiency, 179
  definition, 31, 225
  delayed failure resolution, 234
  discontinuities, 232
  effect of better testing on, 228
  effect of documentation quality on, 229
  estimates, 225
  factors affecting, 232
  field, 310–311
  graphical projection of variation, 230
  impact of inefficient programs on, 224
  initial, 330–334, 338
  observed, 269–276
  reduction by restricting functionality,
    230
  repaired, 170
  units, 43–44, 76
  unrepaired, 170
  variation with:
    computer utilization, 224
    multiple releases, 223
    repair, 225
    workload, 225

Failure intensity decay parameter, 294, 339
Failure intensity objective:
    allocation to components, 57–59
    contractural specification, 65
    customer's customers, 68
    different failure severity classes, 68
    different operational modes, 67, 68
    different users, 67
    different variations, 68
    far from, 234
    reaching, accuracy of determining, 225
    release decision, 228
    (See also Reliability objective)
Failure intensity versus execution time, 298–300
Failure intensity versus failures experienced, 292–296
Failure Modes and Effects Analysis, 19–20, 69
Failure rate, 225
Failure recording program, 191
Failure region, 160
Failure reporting program, 191
Failure resolution:
    effect of better testing on, 228
    proportions, 339
Failure severity:
    absence of fault tolerance, 73
    assignment by different users, 64
    association with criticality, 64
    association with workaround, 64
    classification criteria, 42, 86–87
    definition, 42–43, 86–87
    order of identification, 233–234
    reduction, 64
    relationship with input space, 152
    relationship with release, 64
    use of, 173
Failure time, errors in, 191
Failures:
    absence of fault tolerance, 73
    automatically-detected, 184
    backlog, 69
    catastrophic, 12, 73
    cause of, 73
    changes in the environment, 69
    cluster, 73
    corrected faults, relationship with, 231
    counting, 193–196, 222
    data, 283
    definition, 41–42, 62, 63, 77–81

Failures (Cont.):
    determination, 73
    different machines, 184
    display, 186
    environment changes, 69
    equal to faults, 69
    experienced, 296–298
    faults equal with, 69
    finite, 227, 339
    first occurrence, 194, 227, 234
    grouping, 56–57
    hardware or software, 73
    identification, 184, 185
    independence, 262–263
    infinite, 227, 339
    interleaving, 190
    multiple, 170, 183, 193–194
    multiple configurations, 190
    number equal to number of faults, 69
    operating systems, 63
    per interval, 172
    proportion resolved, 339
    randomness, 15, 259, 263–265
    recording, 183
    relationship to faults, 10, 70, 71
    remaining, 306,308
    repeated, 170, 182–184
    restart after, 181
    software or hardware, 73
    total, 339, 340
    unique, 226
    unit test, 183
    unreported, 181, 183, 208–213
    unresolved, 170, 193, 238
    unwritten requirement, 170
    zero time interval, 173
Fault density, 232, 321–328
Fault detection, 84
Fault exposure ratio, 330–332
Fault prevention, 53–54
Fault prone, 150–151
Fault reduction factor, 74, 228, 328–329, 339
Fault removal, 34, 36, 54, 71, 83, 225
    with, 265
    without, 265
Fault removal delay, 194
Fault severity, 65
Fault tolerance, 54, 64, 72, 169, 239
    hardware, 72, 195
    software, 72, 195

Faults:
  code reading, found by, 74
  counting, 26–27
  definition, 41–42, 77–78, 81–85
  detection time, 74
  found by customer, 70
  found by programmer without test, 74
  infinite, 339
  introduction of, 36
  number, 69–72
  path unblocking, 74
  prediction of number, 320–321
  relationship to failures, 10, 70, 71
  relationship to operational profile, 71
  relationship to requirements, 71
  remaining, 74
  removal, 36
  removed, 231
  spawning, 235
  time of detection, 74
  undetected, 71
  unrepaired, 193
  virulence, 71–72
Feature test, 8, 137, 152, 154, 163–165, 192
Field data, 125
Field measurements, 73
Filler occurrences, 113
Filler operations, 113
Firmware reliability (see Software reliability)
FMEA, 19–20, 69
Fone Follower:
  allocation of new test cases by associated systems, 142
  allocation of new test cases to operations, 144
  allocation of test time, 163–164
  associated systems, 11
  certification test, 199–200
  description, 7
  developed software failure intensity objective, 48
  direct input variables, 137
  expected acquired failure intensity, 48
  failure severity classes, 45
  filler operations, 76, 113
  indirect input variables, 137
  number of new test cases, 141
  occurrence probabilities, 116
  occurrence rates, 112
  operation initiators, 104

Fone Follower (Cont.):
  operational modes, 102–103
  operational mode operational profile, 147
  operations list, 106–107
  product failure intensity objective, 48
  reliability growth test, 204–205
  specifying test cases, 145
  tabular representation, 104–105
  test cases, number of new, 141
  test cases, specifying, 145
  test operational profile, 148–149
  test procedure specification, 138, 146–149
  test time, allocation of, 163–164
Fone Follower Fast, 58–59
Formula (see Equation)
Function point analysis, 20
Functionality, 19, 122, 234

Graphical method, 230
Graphical representation, 99–100, 104–105, 108, 112, 113, 117, 123, 124, 138–139, 145–146

Hardware configurations, 237
  changing, 193
Hardware fault tolerance, 72–73, 195
Hardware reliability, 228
Hardware reliability, relationship to software reliability, 12, 15, 17, 35–36, 152
Homogeneity, 157–159
Human reliability, 229

Identifying system failures, 168–174
Implementation, partial, of software reliability engineering, 256–257
Indirect input variables, 136, 138, 181
Infrequent operations, preassignment of test cases, 143
Initiation of software reliability engineering program, 251
Initiators of operations, restricted, 127
Input space, 122, 136
  design, 110
  relationship with failure severity, 152
  required, 110
  specified, 110–111
  uncovered, 111

Input state, 130–131, 136
Input variables, 131–132, 136, 159
    control of, 155
    direct, 136–137
    indirect, 136–137
Installation mode, 75
Institutionalization of practice, 255
Instructions executed, as measure of
    processing, 186
Integrator of software components, 14
Interface test, 24
Interfacing hardware, 22–23
Interfacing software, 22–23
Interrupts as input variables, 131–132
Invoking test, 164–168, 192–193
ISO 9000, 252

Java, 18
Jump start, 244–245

Layered architecture, 24
Legacy products, 3, 24
Level, 145–146
Life critical software, 16
Load test, 8, 138, 152, 154, 163–166,
    192
Logarithmic model (see Logarithmic
    Poisson execution time model)
Logarithmic Poisson execution time
    model:
    CASRE, 202
    derivation, 317–319
    description, 292–310
    goodness of fit, 226
    parameters, 300–306, 311–315
    recommendation of, 290–292
Low production volume systems, 14

Machine state, 130
Maintainability, 27, 73
Management, new, effect on development,
    254
Manager, role in deployment, 246
Maximum likelihood estimation, 305
Mean time to repair, 27, 72
Mean value function, 31
Memory, limited, 236
Microbehavior, 263
Micromodels, 263

Misconceptions about software reliability
    engineering, 16–17
Mistakes in applying software reliability
    engineering, 21, 173, 177
Models:
    characteristics for evaluating, 37, 260
    classification, 266–267
    derivation, 315–319
    groups, 279–290
    multiple, 231, 261
    overview, 36–38
    parameters, 300–306
    particularization, 265–266
    recommended, 290–292
Module usage table, 118–119
MTTR, 27, 72
Multimodel approach, 231
Musa model (see Basic execution time
    model)
Musa-Okumoto model (see Logarithmic
    Poisson execution time model)

N version development, 93
Natural units:
    definition, 44
    measurement, 171–173, 186, 191
    multiple, 46
    reason for using, 68
    relationship to operations, 98
Necessary reliability, procedure for defin-
    ing, 44–45
Needs for software reliabiilty engineer-
    ing, 252, 253
Network computing, 18
New features, occurrence probabilities
    for, 122, 205
Noncritical operations, 144
Nonhomogeneous random process, 32
Nonrandom test, 151

Object libraries, 10
Object-oriented development, 10, 21
Object-oriented system, 98
Occurrence probabilities, determining,
    115–116
    stationary, 154, 167
Occurrence rates:
    determining, 112–115
    units, 126
Off the shelf components, 14

One shot systems, 13, 21
Operating systems, failures in, 63
Operation initiators, identifying, 103–104
Operational architecture, evolution of, 108
Operational development for faster time to market, 101
Operational mode operational profile, 100, 159, 165
Operational mode run occurrence rate, 138
Operational modes:
  combining, 127
  definition, 100
  determining, 102–103, 129–130
  different users, 67
  effect on test case, 181
  failure intensity objectives, separate, 67
  input space view, 138, 159
  overlap, 75
  users, different, 67
Operational profiles:
  applications of, 120
  benefits, 253
  concepts, 98–101
  cost, 120, 253
  economizing work in developing, 125
  erroneous command entries, 125
  errors, 120–121
  fault removal, 71
  fluctuations, 233
  hardware, 120
  hierarchies, 127–128
  occurrence rates, 256
  operational mode, 100, 159, 165
  practicality, 123
  procedure for developing, 101–102
  relationship of productivity gain and nonuniformity, 120
  regression test, usefulness in, 120, 124
  robustness, 115
  system, 100
  time-varying, 124
  uncovered by test, 124–125
  usefulness in regression test, 120
  variation, 217–220
Operation-module matrix, 119
Operations:
  critical, 111
  definition, 97–98, 137–138, 159–160
  developed, 153

Operations (Cont.):
  differentiation, 109–110
  differing durations, 125
  evolution, 108, 117–118
  existing, 128–129
  granularity, 109
  grouping, 109–110
  grouping runs into, 122, 124
  infrequent, 111, 143, 155
  infrequent noncritical, 111, 155
  initiators of, 123
  interactions, 129
  long duration, 181–182
  new, 128–129, 148, 153
  number, 107–108
  occurrence rates, 126
  old, 128–129, 148, 153
  rare, 111, 143, 155
  rare noncritical, 111, 155
  recording occurrences, 114
  reused, 128–129, 148, 153
  segments of work, 126
  sequences of work, 126, 128
Operations list, 105–111
Ordinary time, 68, 76
Orthogonal array, 159
Output variable, 131
Overloads, 151
Overview, role in software reliability engineering deployment, 241

Packaged software, 10, 22, 126
Parameters:
  description, 300–306, 311–315
  estimation, 37, 305, 306, 334–338
  prediction, 37, 303, 305, 320–334
Pathological conditions, 150
Perfection, 16, 150, 253–254
Performance, 169
Performance deficiency as failure, 63
Performance test, 136
Personal computer, measuring execution time on, 186
Personnel roles, 80, 251, 254–256
Persuasion in deploying software reliability engineering, 249, 252, 254
Phases of test, failure intensity at different, 16
Planning meeting in deploying software reliability engineering, 243
Practically complete operations list, 110

Prediction, parameter, 37, 303, 305, 320–334
Prerequisites for deploying software reliability engineering, 251–252
Probability distribution of failures, 30
Probability of failure on demand, 66–67
Problems aided with software reliability engineering, 1
Process, software reliability engineering: overview, 5–7
step by step, 341–342
Process improvement, software development, 56
Product, allocation of test time hours to, 165
Product definition, aided by operational profile, 121
Product release, 204
Product variations, 68, 127
Products, multiple, 182
Professional organization for software reliability engineering, 5
Program documentation, effect on failure intensity, 230
Program evolution, 205–208, 226, 227, 234
Program segments, 187
Programmers, individual, 238–239
Programs:
evolving, 205–208, 226, 227, 234
inefficient, 224
ported, 236–237
small, software reliabiilty engineering deployment for, 255
Projection of failure intensity, 37
Projective validity, 280–281, 283–288
Prototype as source for operations list, 105, 106
Psychological effects of reliability on users, 20

Quality, definition of, 2, 17

Random:
failure behavior, 15, 28–30, 253–265
test invocation, 165, 193
Random process to model failure behavior, 30, 263–265, 292
Random selection of test cases, 165, 193
Randomness, failure, 15, 28–30, 253–265

Randomness, in use of software, 15
Range of application, of software reliability engineering in test, 26
Rare operations, preassignment of test cases, 143
Reboot, 81, 221–222
Record and playback, 121
Recording, 166
Recording failures, 183
Reduced Operation Software, 101, 115, 120
Regression test:
definition, 8, 135, 154
indirect input variables, 137
invocation, 165
measuring when failures occurred, 186
reliability estimation during, 180
selection of test cases, 193
using operational profile, 124
Reinitialization, 81, 221–222
Release criteria, 204
Releases, multiple, 223
Reliability:
cost, 72
mission, 122
run-oriented, 17–18
system, from components, 44
time-oriented, 17–18
Reliability assurance, 227
Reliability combinatorics, 92–94
Reliability demonstration chart:
constructing, 213–217
using, 198–201
validity, 226
Reliability estimation program, 201–205
Reliability evaluation, 17
Reliability growth, 17, 234
Reliability growth test, 20, 171, 201–205
Reliability objective, 18, 23, 227
(See also Failure intensity objective)
Reliability strategies, 64
Reliability strategies required for high availability, 76
Reload, effect on failure intensity, 221
Reorganization, effect on deployment of software reliability engineering, 254
Repair, fault, 34, 54, 71, 83, 225
Repeated failures, 170, 182–184
Repeating runs, 152
Replacement, selection with, 166
Representatively-invoked test, 172

Requirements:
  enumerated, effect on operational
    profile, 123
  errors, 71
  inconsistent, 63
  incorrect, 63
  missing, 121
  misunderstanding, 63
  nonfunctional, 64, 123
  relationship to failures, 79–80
  unwritten, effect on failure definition,
    170
Requirements based nature of software
  reliability engineering, 16
Requirements changes, 205
Research and software reliability
  engineering practice, 14
Researchers and software reliability
  engineering deployment, 250
Reuse, effect on reliabiity, 21
Risk assessment, relationship to software
  reliability engineering, 19
Risk levels, 213–217
  acceptable, 16
Risks of software development, 1
Robustness for unexpected input states,
  80
Root cause analysis, 12, 234–235
ROS, 101, 115, 120
Run categories, 157–159
Run category, distributed system, 153
Run profile, 123
Run selection, 159–160
Run space, 139, 159
Runs, 130–132, 136–139, 159, 181
  duplicate, 149, 166
  number, as approximation to execution
    time, 187, 191
  repetition, 149, 166

Safety, 19, 59–62
Sample of failures, small, 255
Self-teaching for software reliability
  engineering deployment, 246
Sequential sampling, 198
Setting system failure intensity
  objectives, 46–51, 87–91
Setup procedure for test, 153
Severity (see Failure severity)
Severity classification criteria, 42
Simplicity in modeling, 282–83

Sites, multiple, 182
Size of system, certification test, 233
SMERFS, 201, 202
Soak time, 129, 136
Software:
  acquired, 9–10, 165
  life critical, 16
  packaged, 10, 22, 126
  reused, 10
  subcontracted, 10
Software development problems
  aided with software reliability
  engineering, 1
Software development process changes
  to deploy software reliability
  engineering, 21
Software documentation, 229
Software fault tolerance, 72, 195
Software quality, 11, 17
Software quality assurance organizations,
  250
Software reliability:
  credibility, 15
  effectiveness, 11
  importance, 11
  manipulation, 15
  projection, 231
  relationship to hardware reliability, 12,
    15, 17, 35–36, 152
  relationship to software quality, 11, 17
Software reliability estimation programs,
  232
Software reliability model (see Models)
Software safety, 19, 59–62
Speeding development, 14
Stable operational profile, 261
Stable program, 261
Standard, 4
Stationary occurrence probabilities, 154,
  167
Statistician, 251
Stopping rule for test, 204
Strategies, 53–56
Substantially different processing, 97,
  105
Success logic expression, 92
Supersystems, 9, 22–23, 165
Supplier risk, certification test, 199,
  213–217
Supplier, collaborating, 20
Support services for software reliability
  engineering, 246

Survivability, 19
System engineers, role, 80
System failure intensity objectives:
  acquired component, 46
  by classes, 49
  guidelines, 47–48
  product:
    standalone, 46–48
    supersystems, 46
  supersystem, 46–48
System operational profile, 100
System reliability, 36, 92
System testers:
  evaluating performance, 150
  role, 80
Systems:
  client-server, operations on, 97
  distributed (see Distributed systems)
  low production volume, 14
  ultrareliable, 14, 179
Systems to test, 9–11

Tabular representation, 98–99, 104–105,
    111, 123–124
Template, 343–346
Test:
  certification (see Certification test)
  feature, 8, 137, 152, 154, 163–165, 192
  load, 8, 138, 152, 154, 163–166, 192
  regression (see Regression test)
  reliability growth, 20, 171, 201–205
  types, 8–9
  view of, 2
Test automation, 149–150, 233
Test cases:
  allocating among new operations,
    142–145, 153
  allocating among systems to be tested,
    142
  cost, 156
  coverage, 151
  definition, 137–138
  efficient, 155
  estimating number for new release,
    140–142
  executing all test cases, 151
  existing, 146
  new, 156
  preparing, 140
  relationship to runs, 181
  selection, 157

Test cases (Cont.):
  selection within operation, 154–155
  specifying, 145–146
Test drivers, 180, 233
Test efficiency, 156–159
Test efficiency metric, 156–157
Test occurrence probability, 147
Test operational profile, 138, 146–149,
    155
Test priority, 233
Test procedure, 138, 146–150
Test process, 179–182
  improvement, 12–13
Test selection, 228
Test sequence, 165
Test time, allocating, 163–164, 192
Tests, formal, 239
Time:
  common, 46
  development, 13–14
  enough for software reliability
    engineering, 252
  regression test, 186
  types, 43, 171
  uncertain, for failure, 187–188
Time domains, 269
Time units, 171–173
Time window, 187–188
Tool defects, 195
Tools, 357
Top down development, 20
Total failures, prediction, 320–329
Total Quality Management, 12
Traceability, 106
Tradeoff:
  functionality, 234
  life cycle, 88–90
  quality characteristics, 47, 67
Transactions, 191

Ultrareliable systems, 14, 59–62, 179
Unit test, 24
Unreported failures, 208–213
Unsupported software, 23
Up time, 50
Use of software, randomness, 15
Use case, 98
Use-dependent, 152
Use recording, 22, 125
Use sampling, 22, 125
User documentation, 229

User manual, 105
User profile, 64
User programmed systems, 13
User sampling, 22
User type, 103
Users, 14, 51, 65, 105
Users of software reliability engineering, 4–5, 371–374

Variations, 165
Versions, 65–66, 237
   multiple, 178
Videos on software reliability engineering, 257
Virus, 71

Web site on software reliability engineering, 246
When failures occurred, 171–174
   multiple configurations, 174–175
   uncertainties, 175–177
Work process flow diagrams, 105–106
Workload, 225
Workshops template, 343–346
Worm, 71

Zealot, 255
Zero defects, 18, 150, 252
Zero interval, 190